P9-CQB-700

THE THEOLOGY OF THE NEW TESTAMENT

According to Its Major Witnesses

Jesus — Paul — John

WERNER GEORG KÜMMEL

ABINGDON PRESS

Nashville ———— New York

THE THEOLOGY OF THE NEW TESTAMENT
ACCORDING TO ITS MAJOR WITNESSES:
JESUS—PAUL—JOHN

Originally published as *Die Theologie des Neuen Testaments*

Copyright © 1973 by Abingdon Press

Translation from the German language with the approval of the Publishing House Vandenhoeck and Ruprecht, Göttingen. © Vandenhoeck & Ruprecht, Göttingen.

All rights in this book are reserved.
No part of the book may be reproduced in any manner whatsoever without written permission of the publishers except brief quotations embodied in critical articles or reviews. For information address Abingdon Press, Nashville, Tennessee.

Library of Congress Cataloging in Publication Data

Kümmel, Werner Georg, 1905-   The theology of the New Testament.
Translation of Die Theologie des Neuen Testaments nach seinen Hauptzeugen Jesus, Paulus, Johannes.
Bibliography: p.   1. Bible. N.T.—Theology. I. Title.
BS2397.K8313   225.6′6   73-6961

ISBN 0-687-41552-7 (cloth)
ISBN 0-687-41553-5 (paper)

Scripture quotations noted RSV are from the Revised Standard Version of the Bible, copyrighted 1946, 1952, 1971 by the Division of Christian Education, National Council of Churches, and are used by permission.

MANUFACTURED BY THE PARTHENON PRESS AT
NASHVILLE, TENNESSEE, UNITED STATES OF AMERICA

To the Senate
of the
University of Glasgow
as a token of gratitude
for the degree of
Doctor of Theology

PREFACE

This preface affords the translator an opportunity to make public acknowledgment of his debt to those whose assistance might otherwise remain unknown. The Southeastern Seminary Alumni Fund once again has provided generous help in defraying the costs of preparing the work for publication, and Mrs. Marian Farrar has skillfully converted my handwritten copy of the translation into typescript.

I am grateful to Professor Kümmel for his gracious response to my inquiries and his encouragement. Any failure to capture his meaning, of course, is my responsibility. Freshest in my mind is the debt I owe to my family for their support and help in this work. They have not observed it from a distance, but have joined in the pleasures and pains of bringing it to completion.

JOHN E. STEELY

Wake Forest, North Carolina
August, 1972

CONTENTS

INTRODUCTION

1. *The problematic of a theology of the New Testament*

To most Christian Bible readers of today, it probably is self-evident that the Bible consists of two different parts, whose thoughts do not simply coincide, the "Old Testament," which is also recognized by the Jews as "Holy Scripture," and the "New Testament," which for Christians has greater importance. But the same Bible reader, if he has not already been influenced by the insights of modern theology, probably will just as naturally assume that the Old Testament and the New Testament are unitary, each in itself, and that therefore one can with full justification ask about the teachings of *the* Old and *the* New Testaments, and that he can unequivocally answer these questions. Now of course even the insight that the views of the Old and New Testaments do not agree with each other has by no means always been self-evident to Christianity; on the other hand, the assumption that the Old Testament and the New Testament represent, each in itself, a substantive unity became questionable during the same time in which the conviction of the agreement of the Old with the New Testament was called into question. And in fact there is a necessary substantive connection between the question as to the agreement of the two Testaments with each other and the question as to the unity of the Old and the New Testament each within itself. Hence when we pose the question of a theology of the New Testament and not of the Bible as a whole, at the same time we are confronted with the question of the unity of this New Testament and of the possible multiplicity of the voices which come to be sounded in it. This happens as soon as we take a look at the emergence of the question of a theology of the New Testament.

Martin Luther declared before the Reichstag at Worms in 1521 that he believed neither the pope nor the councils alone, but only Holy Scripture and convincing arguments, and the other reformers in similar fashion proclaimed the Bible as the sole authority over against the church's teaching. While in this way the Bible was placed in the center as sole authority in such unprecedented clarity, the rejection of the authority of the churchly tradition in favor of the Bible's solitary authority by the reformation theology yet in essence was directed only against the doctrine and form of the medieval church, and for the reformers as for Protestant orthodoxy down to the middle of the eighteenth century, the conviction stood firm that the teaching of the Bible was in agreement with the out-look of the faith and the confessions of the early church. Luther himself, working on the translation of the New Testament at the Wartburg (1521-22), had made the discovery that within the New Testament there are contradictions between individual writings, above all between James and Hebrews on one side and the epistles of Paul on the other, and thus Luther was confronted with the fact of the variety and conflicting character of the New Testament's faith-witnesses. But these insights which were expressed in the prefaces to his translation of 1522 could not have their full consequences, because precisely the newly gained conviction of the sole authority of Holy Scripture stood in the way of the acceptance of such insights in the Protestant churches. Hence for more than two hundred years after Luther, a presentation of the ideas of the Bible that was completely independent of ecclesiastical tradition and that took account of the particularities of the biblical writings was not possible within Protestant theology, and even though in the seventeenth century people began to write books with the title "Biblical Theology," this was done only in order to assemble for orthodox dogmatics the biblical proof texts, detached from their contexts.

This was changed only when, in the second half of the eighteenth century, in connection with the intellectual movement of the Enlightenment, within Protestant theology the insight began to prevail that the Bible is a book written by men, which, like any product of the human mind, can properly be made understandable only from the times in which it appeared and therefore only with the methods of historical science. That is to say, from this insight there resulted the unavoidable conclusion that even the presentation of the thought content of the Bible, i.e., a "Biblical Theology," could properly occur only with the aid of historical inquiry if the thought content were to be uninfluenced by dogmatics and actually be recognized independently. But as soon as people actually became serious with such historical inquiry with respect to the ideas of the Bible, as first happened around 1800, they found themselves compelled not only completely to separate the presentation of the Old and New Testaments from each other, but also, in the portrayal of the ideas of the New Testament, to let Jesus and the various apostolic authors speak each for himself. One simply could not stop halfway: if the Bible must be historically investigated as the work of human authors in order to understand its actual meaning, then one may not and cannot cling to the assumption that the Old Testament and the New Testament form, each in itself, a conceptual unity, and then one must also heed the differences *within* the two Testaments and also take into consideration a possible development and adulteration of the ideas. Consequently the concern about a theology of the New Testament found itself from the outset confronted with the problem of diversity and unity in the New Testament.

Therefore from the very beginning the concern with the theological content of the New Testament as an independent historical entity stood in tension with every form of dogmatic theology. For the presentation of Christian doctrine as answer to the question about the essence of God's revelation in Jesus Christ, from whatever presuppositions it proceeds and whatever connections are placed upon it, obviously must have the aim of setting forth a *unified* teaching. Therefore dogmatics must fall into difficulties when it seeks to find support in the New Testament as the basis of its utterances and finds that biblical theology is unable to exhibit any unitary teaching in the New Testament to that end. Here the actual problem of a "theology of the New Testament" confronts us.

Of course this problem is only one particular problem within the difficulty which any proper exposition of the New Testament faces. For even if the expositor first of all concerns himself with the meaning of the *individual* writings of the New Testament—and this is naturally the presupposition for an inquiry after a theology of the New Testament—he is faced in principle with an insoluble task. The writings collected in the New Testament are, according to their historical character, documents of ancient religious history, written in a dead language and a set of concepts and a conceptual world no longer immediately comprehensible to us. Therefore they can be made to speak only by way of historical research, and only by this way can an understanding of what was meant by the authors be approximated. Such a concern for scientific explanation by its very nature always can lead only to probable and often only to hypothetical results, and it requires the adventuresome *judgment* whether one will follow an achieved result or will replace it with another attempt at explanation. But now the same writings of the New Testament have been collected by the early church into a canon of sacred scriptures, whose extent was no longer seriously disputed after the end of the fourth century. They have thereby acquired the character of normative writings, foundational for the faith of the Christians, to which the Christian had to respond with believing obedience. But it is easy to see that it is basically impossible to confront the writings of the New Testament as a man making judgments in research and at the same time as one who hears in faith. Hence when attempts understandably have repeatedly been made in various ways to escape this dilemma, all such attempts yet were and are doomed to failure because they do not correspond to the state of things. The scientific concern with the understanding of the New Testament must, precisely when it is pursued in the context of the church and from the presupposition of faith, take account of the fact that we also *can* come to a believing hearing of the message of the New Testament only in *one* way: namely, by seeking to make the utterances of the ancient authors of the New Testament understandable, just as their contemporary readers or hearers could and had to understand them. Hence there is no other access to the understanding of the New Testament writings than the method of historical research, which is valid for *all* writings of antiquity. Of course a great deal depends on whether one pursues such research as one uninvolved and in conscious detachment, or as one inwardly involved and hence as one who hears with ultimate openness.

Thus, while one who inquires after the thought content and the address of a New Testament writing sees himself confronted by the necessity of achieving a personal hearing of it by the involved route of the scientific explanation of the ancient text, this difficulty is shown in increased measure in the concern with the theology of the New Testament. For what Luther observed in individual examples has been irrefutably demonstrated by the scientific work with the conceptual material of the New Testament since the beginning of the nineteenth century, namely, that in the New Testament various voices are speaking which are in part contradictory and which in any case speak in such diverse manner that what they say cannot be heard in harmony from the outset without being tested. Therefore the task of a theology of the New Testament can in no case consist primarily in presenting the views of the New Testament comprehensively as a whole. For in such a procedure one of two things would unavoidably occur: either the view of the individual writings or groups of writings are forcibly fitted together into a median outlook, or divergent ideas are sacrificed to the dominant ones. The task of a theology of the New Testament can only consist in first allowing the individual writings or groups of writings to speak for themselves, and only then to ask about the unity which is shown therein, or else to affirm a diversity which cannot be eliminated. Therefore the proclamation of Jesus Christ by the New Testament witnesses must first be questioned according to its various forms. Only then can it be questioned as to its common content.

Of course this process can by no means establish from the outset in what sequence in time and in what possible dependence on one another the individual writings and groups of writings are related. And because these questions can be answered only in a historical way and thus on the basis of a scientific formation of judgment, various answers to these questions are possible. The definition of the circumstances of emergence of the individual writings is an important presupposition for the chronological arrangement of the individual writings and groups of writings. But the decision about these circumstances of emergence is in many cases likewise altogether uncertain. Thus only the comparison of the contents can make the final decision as to the historical connection and the chronological sequence of the various forms of New Testament proclamation. For example, there is wide divergence of opinion on the question as to what place in the temporal sequence must be assigned to the theology of the Gospel of John and of the Epistles of John, and it is similarly disputed whether it is appropriate and possible to introduce the presentation of the theology of the New Testament with a portrayal of Jesus' proclamation, because indeed we know anything of Jesus' proclamation only through the witness of the later believing community, a witness which has been deposited in the first three gospels. And the arrangement of the shorter writings of the New Testament in the context of New Testament theology is even less clearly to be determined. All these questions can be decided only when the thought content of the individual writings or groups of writings is first brought to understanding independent of other conceptual forms. And this implies that the presentation and arrangement of a "theology of the New Testament" can come about only as a *result* of work with the diverse forms of the New Testament proclamation.

Operating from these methodological insights, I shall attempt to set forth the preaching of Jesus, the theology of Paul against the background of the primitive community, and the message of Christ in the Gospel of John, in their essential features, and, on the basis of this presentation, to inquire about the unity which is exhibited in these forms of proclamation. This limitation could appear arbitrary, and it in no way proceeds from the conviction that the other writings of the New Testament are unimportant or at least of less value. But there can be no doubt that these three forms of New Testament proclamation stand out from the rest of the New Testament not only in scope but also in significance. It is therefore both appropriate and possible on the basis of these forms of proclamation to form for oneself a clear and adequate picture of the central proclamation of the New Testament, to which then the message of the remaining writings can be related. But it is important to avoid subjecting the various forms of the proclamation to the same schema, possibly one that is imposed on them from without. For each of the forms of proclamation in the New Testament has its own inner order and its own aim. Hence it will be necessary in each case to allow the arrangement of the presentation to be shown from the character of this proclamation itself and thus to arrive at a historically suitable understanding of each form of the proclamation.

The following presentation does not intend to replace a textbook. It can neither discuss all the questions that come into consideration nor cite all the documentation for the questions that are treated. Therefore, unless it is explicitly stated, one must not assume from the lists of passages that there are no further examples for a concept or an idea.

The translations of New Testament passages offered in the following text have the sole task of letting the meaning of the passages as I understand them, be recognized as clearly as possible. Therefore they do not shy away from harshness of language. But the reader should, by the use of a modern translation of the New Testament, satisfy himself as to whether a different understanding of the text in question is possible, and he should read there the passages that are not quoted, or are quoted only in part. [For the English reader, the *New English Bible,* the Revised Standard Version, or *Good News for Modern Man* may serve this purpose. Tr.] For the first part of the study, the use of a "synopsis" is recommended, i.e., a parallel printing of the first three gospels [an example is *Gospel Parallels,* edited by Burton H. Throckmorton, Jr. Tr.] Since the parallels to a passage cited from the synoptic gospels are easy to find with the help of a synopsis, in the following as a rule reference is made to the existence of parallel texts only with a "par." placed after the passage cited. However, this reference says only that there *is* a parallel, not that it agrees with the passage that has been cited.

When in the following statements I cite a formulation from a scholarly work with the name of the author, I do not intend thereby to refer to the survey of literature which follows, in which in fact specialized works could not be included. Rather, my intention is only that formulations which in my opinion are especially fitting be clearly attributed to those who originated them.

2. *Literature*

On the entire New Testament

For the general reader:
C. T. Craig, *The Beginnings of Christianity,* 1943
F. C. Grant, *An Introduction to New Testament Thought,* 1950
R. Bultmann, *Das Urchristentum im Rahmen der antiken Religionen,* 1949 (ET, *Primitive Christianity in Its Contemporary Setting,* 1956)
R. Bultmann, *Jesus Christus und die Mythologie. Das Neue Testament im Lichte der Bibelkritik,* 1958 (ET, *Jesus Christ and Mythology,* 1958)
J. Jeremias, *The Central Message of the New Testament,* 1965
L. Goppelt, *Die apostolische und nachapostolische Zeit,* 1962 (ET, *Apostolic and Post-Apostolic Times,* 1970)

More difficult:
C. H. Dodd, *The Apostolic Preaching and Its Developments,* 1936
R. Bultmann, *Theologie des Neuen Testaments,* 1953 (ET, *Theology of the New Testament,* 2 vols., 1951, 1955)
R. H. Fuller, *The Foundations of New Testament Christology,* 1965
F. Hahn, *Christologische Hoheitstitel. Ihre Geschichte im frühen Christentum,* 1963 (ET, *The Titles of Jesus in Christology. Their History in Early Christianity,* 1969)
H. Conzelmann, *Grundriss der Theologie des Neuen Testaments,* 1967 (ET, *An Outline of the Theology of the New Testament,* 1968)

On the history of research:
S. Neill, *The Interpretation of the New Testament, 1861-1961,* 1964
W. G. Kümmel, *Das Neue Testament. Geschichte der Erforschung seiner Probleme,* 2nd ed., 1970 (ET, *The New Testament: The History of the Investigation of Its Problems,* 1972)

On the environment of the New Testament:
R. H. Charles, *The Apocrypha and Pseudepigrapha of the Old Testament,* 2 vols., 1913
C. K. Barrett, *The New Testament Background: Selected Documents,* 1957

T. H. Gaster, *The Dead Sea Scriptures in English Translation,* 2nd ed., 1964

W. Foerster, *Neutestamentliche Zeitgeschichte,* 2nd ed., 1955 (ET, *From the Exile to Christ,* 1964, from Vol. I of the 3rd ed. in German)

On the early Christian writings not accepted into the New Testament:
E. Hennecke, *Neutestamentliche Apokryphen,* 3rd ed., 2 vols., edited by W. Schneemelcher, 1959, 1964 (ET, edited by R. McL. Wilson, *New Testament Apocrypha,* 1963, 1965)

On Jesus

For the general reader:
R. Bultmann, *Jesus,* 1926 (ET, *Jesus and the Word,* 1934)
M. Dibelius, *Jesus,* 1939 (ET, *Jesus,* 1949)
G. Bornkamm, *Jesus von Nazareth,* 1956 (ET, *Jesus of Nazareth,* 1960)
E. W. Saunders, *Jesus in the Gospels,* 1967
O. Betz, *Was wissen wir von Jesus?* 1965 (ET, *What Do We Know About Jesus?* 1968)
J. Reumann, *Jesus in the Church's Gospels,* 1968
H. C. Kee, *Jesus in History. An Approach to the Study of the Gospels,* 1970

More difficult:
A. Schweitzer, *Geschichte der Leben-Jesu-Forschung,* 1906 (ET, *The Quest of the Historical Jesus,* 1910)
W. G. Kümmel, *Verheissung und Erfüllung. Untersuchungen zur eschatologischen Verkündigung Jesu,* 3rd ed., 1956 (ET, *Promise and Fulfilment. The Eschatological Message of Jesus,* 1957)
J. M. Robinson, *A New Quest of the Historical Jesus,* 1959
H. Anderson, *Jesus and Christian Origins,* 1964
N. Perrin, *Rediscovering the Teaching of Jesus,* 1967
J. Jeremias, *Neutestamentliche Theologie. 1. Teil: Die Verkündigung Jesu,* 1971 (ET, *New Testament Theology. I: The Proclamation of Jesus,* 1972)

On the primitive community

More difficult:
W. Marxsen, *Die Auferstehung Jesu als historisches und theologisches Problem,* 7th ed., 1968 (ET, "The Resurrection of Jesus as a Historical and Theological Problem," in: *The Significance of the Message of the Resurrection for Faith in Jesus Christ,* 1968)

On Paul

For the general reader:
A. D. Nock, *St. Paul,* 1938
M. Dibelius-W. G. Kümmel, *Paulus,* 1951 (ET, *Paul,* 1953)
G. Bornkamm, *Paulus,* 1969 (ET, *Paul,* 1971)

More difficult:
C. A. Scott, *Christianity According to St. Paul,* 1927, reprint 1961

H. J. Schoeps, *Paulus. Die Theologie des Apostels im Lichte der jüdischen Religionsgeschichte*, 1959 (ET, *Paul: The Theology of the Apostle in the Light of Jewish Religious History*, 1961)

D. E. H. Whiteley, *The Theology of St. Paul*, 1964

B. Rigaux, *Paulus und seine Briefe. Der Stand der Forschung*, 1964 (ET, *The Letters of St. Paul: Modern Studies*, 1968)

On John

For the general reader:
W. F. Howard, *Christianity According to St. John*, 1943

More difficult:
C. H. Dodd, *The Interpretation of the Fourth Gospel*, 1953

F. Mussner, *Die johanneische Sehweise und die Frage nach dem historischen Jesus*, 1965 (ET, *The Historical Jesus in the Gospel of St. John*, 1967)

E. Käsemann, *Jesu letzter Wille nach Johannes*, 1966 (ET, *The Testament of Jesus: A Study of the Gospel of John in the Light of Chapter 17*, 1968)

J. L. Martyn, *History and Theology in the Fourth Gospel*, 1968

CHAPTER I

THE PROCLAMATION OF JESUS ACCORDING TO THE FIRST THREE GOSPELS

1. *The problem of the historical Jesus*

It appears obvious that one must begin the portrayal of the New Testament thought world in its historical emergence with a presentation of the proclamation of Jesus. For is not the person of Jesus and his message after all the event which first made possible all Christian preaching and any Christian theology? Of course this is true, and thus even when at the beginning of the nineteenth century people began to set forth separately the theology of the New Testament in its various forms, they quite understandably placed the proclamation of Jesus at the beginning. And at first there was no doubt that as sources for the presentation of Jesus' proclamation one had to use our four canonical gospels. Since then, however, these two assumptions for the investigation of New Testament theology have become questionable.

a. THE QUESTION OF THE SOURCES

Every reader of the gospels knows that in the first three gospels Jesus speaks a different language and the person of Jesus is differently portrayed than in the fourth gospel. But since D. F. Strauss in his famous *Leben Jesu* (Life of Jesus; 1835/36) first called attention to the advanced character of the reshaping of the Jesus tradition by the Christian faith in the fourth gospel in comparison with the first three gospels, it has become increasingly clear that the Jesus of the fourth gospel not only shows the influence of the belief in the resurrection of Jesus significantly more strongly than the first three gospels, but also religio-historically stands in another context. From this arose the necessity, widely acknowledged today, of refraining from the use of all four gospels as sources for the presentation of the historical Jesus and, instead, for this presentation in principle to use as sources only the first three gospels, and to adduce the fourth gospel as a source at most in a supplementary way in individual cases, where it would have to be justified. But the first three gospels on their part indubitably stand in a literary relationship with one another. Because one can print these three gospels in large part parallel in a synopsis, that is, a "seeing together," it has become customary to call these gospels "synoptic gospels" or "the Synoptics." Although the opinions about the Synoptics' literary relationship to one another still diverge, the view has generally prevailed that our Gospel of Mark was used as a foundation for their gospels by the authors of Matthew and Luke and that the two longer gospels have expanded the Gospel of Mark by means of a now-lost common source and special material peculiar to each. From this insight the inference has been drawn that the report about the life of Jesus in the Gospel of Mark has a claim to being regarded, as the earliest report, as historically reliable and to be made foundational to the presentation of Jesus' activity, while the common tradition of Matthew's and Luke's gospels (the so-called Sayings source) contains the most reliable material for the presentation of the proclamation of Jesus. The Jesus research of the nineteenth century, so sharply criticized by Albert Schweitzer in his *Geschichte der Leben-Jesu-Forschung* (ET, *The Quest of the Historical Jesus*), was pursued, and to some extent is still being pursued today, from these presuppositions.

This reliance on the historical trustworthiness of Mark's gospel and the Sayings source, however, has been shaken in a twofold way now since the beginning of our century. On the one hand, the more exact examination of the structure of Mark showed that there is no knowledge of the historical sequence of events underlying this earliest presentation of Jesus' activity, but that the writer of Mark's gospel arranged the isolated reports or groups of reports that were transmitted to him according to a basic theological idea and thus created an account that hangs together only loosely. The early traditional material behind Mark's gospel thus consists only of isolated stories and sayings, and this is all the more true of the Sayings source, which apparently arranged the transmitted sayings or groups of sayings of Jesus according to topical perspectives. Hence one cannot draw historical conclusions of any kind from the sequence and arrangement of the individual texts in the context of the gospels. On the other hand, the investigation of the individual stories and sayings has yielded the conclusion that they do not simply afford reminiscences from the life of Jesus that have been handed down unmodified, but that entire oral tradition which lies behind our gospels has experienced its shaping and reshaping in the context of the proclamation and teaching of the Christian community, and that we therefore may not simply calculate that the transmitted stories and sayings correspond to the historical actuality of Jesus' life and teachings. In view of the necessity of critical analysis which results from this state of affairs, therefore, the possibility of giving a historically reliable picture of Jesus' life and teaching is today called into question or limited, in different degrees of intensity.

b. THE THEOLOGICAL PROBLEMATIC

But now since the beginning of this century, alongside this dissolution of the historical certainty of the question of the historical Jesus, theological objections have been raised against the adequacy of the question of the historical Jesus. The Halle theologian *Martin Kähler* recognized the impossibility of grounding belief in God's saving act in Jesus Christ on the uncertain and changeable results of scientific study, and therefore disputed the theological right to inquire behind the reports of the gospels about the pre-Easter Jesus of Nazareth: the real picture of Christ is not the "historical Jesus" of modern research but the proclaimed Christ of the apostolic witnesses. And a generation later *Rudolf Bultmann* took up Kähler's thesis in the conviction that we can know only very little about the historical Jesus and that faith is awakened by the proclamation (the "kerygma") of the New Testament witnesses. He took the position that "One may not go behind the kerygma in order to reconstruct a historical Jesus. It is not the historical Jesus, but Jesus Christ, the one proclaimed, who is the Lord." Therewith, however, the question of the historical Jesus became unimportant if one wished to concern oneself with the understanding of the theology of the New Testament, and Bultmann consistently treated the preaching of Jesus within Judaism in the context of his presentation of *Urchristentum im Rahmen der antiken Religionen* (ET, *Primitive Christianity in Its Contemporary Setting*). If this view were correct, it would be impossible and wrong to begin the portrayal of "the theology of the New Testament according to its major witnesses" with the presentation of the preaching of Jesus.

It is, however, very doubtful, and therefore it has recently been much discussed, whether this theological rejection of the question of the historical Jesus is proper and whether, in case this rejection is wrong, a skeptical attitude toward the possibility of gaining a historical picture of Jesus is necessary. On that point, in our context obviously the decisive question above all is whether in our concern with the theology of the New Testament we are to ask about the historical Jesus at all. Obviously, the historian will not allow this question to be ruled out, because he must know something of Jesus if he wishes to understand the rise of Christianity at all. But the Christian also, who perceives in the testimony of the apostles the message of the resurrected Lord Jesus Christ and believes it, encounters in this message the assertion that the risen Lord is the same as the man Jesus of Nazareth, with whom a part of the witnesses of the resurrection were associated during his earthly activity. Therefore faith, when it tries to give an account of its nature, that is, to reflect theologically, has a burning interest in whether and to what extent there is or is not an agreement between the picture which it has of Jesus Christ on the basis of the apostolic proclamation and the historical actuality of this Jesus to whom faith refers. The person and proclamation of Jesus are indeed the presupposition for the confession of the risen One and for the community's preaching of God's revelation in his Son *Jesus* Christ. Therefore the Christian who inquires after the message of the New Testament *must* also inquire after the Jesus who justifies his faith. Hence there can be no doubt that the question of the historical Jesus belongs at the beginning of the concern with the theology of the New Testament.

But is there also the scientific possibility of answering this question? It is widely acknowledged today that we can give no biography of Jesus and likewise no account of the development of Jesus' proclamation, because we know that in the original oral tradition the context and sequence of Jesus' deeds and words were not preserved, but only the isolated stories and sayings or groups of sayings. Only the passion narrative forms an exception to this rule. Therefore the presentation of Jesus' proclamation in the context of the theology of the New Testament must resolutely and consistently refrain from any attempt to draw from the order of the gospel accounts any conclusions as to the development and the change in Jesus' thinking. But that introduces the real methodological problem. The analysis of the gospels has certainly yielded the conclusion that the individual texts represent the original tradition. But just as indubitably it has also shown that the whole of the traditional material appropriated in the gospels was not formed and repeated out of biographical or historical interest, but in the context and for the support of the Christian community's proclamation and teaching, and this means in the context of the belief in the resurrection and heavenly lordship of Jesus Christ. This is no way means that faith has created the tradition. It does mean that there is no route by which we can penetrate to a stratum of the Jesus tradition which would have been preserved independent of faith and thus handed on. Even the recently proposed assumption that Jesus himself arranged for his disciples to hold precisely to his deeds and words contradicts the changing character of the Jesus tradition. This assumption can no more prove the historical reliability of the Jesus tradition as a whole than the suggestion that the basic layer of the Jesus tradition must go back to eyewitnesses of the life of Jesus who later became witnesses to the resurrection. If instead the entire Jesus tradition employed in the gospels stems from the believing and proclaiming community, then only critical examination of the individual bits of tradition can decide whether and to what extent this tradition goes back into the time before Easter and relates the historical actuality of Jesus and his teaching reliably.

If this is correct, on the other hand it is also wrong to approach this task with the demand, often made in recent times, that the "genuineness" of each individual word of Jesus and the historicality of every individual story must be proved. For there is no reason at all for the opinion that the historical reliability of a piece of tradition obviously can only be an exception. The scholar inquiring into the person and proclamation of Jesus will rather see himself confronted with the task of inquiring within the total stock of tradition for that stratum which can be demonstrated to be the earliest. Indispensable methodological aids in this task are the literary comparison of the parallel accounts of the gospels, the analytical delimitation of the individual piece of tradition, the form-critical distinguishing of various forms of narrative and discourse and their arrangement into the circumstances of emergence corresponding to them, the comparison of the ideas with the contemporary Jewish and Hellenistic thought world, the exposure of special forms of discourse or ideas of Jesus or ways of behavior typical of him, the excision of explicit Jewish or primitive Christian conceptions, and so on. Of course the decisive check on the correctness of such a setting apart of the earliest body of tradition can only be the proof that from the fitting together of the pieces of tradition thus gained a historically comprehensible and unitary picture of Jesus and his proclamation results, which also makes the further development of primitive Christianity understandable. Of course with the ambiguity of many arguments and the danger of the researcher's being bound to ecclesiastical, scientific-historical, or personal prejudices, it remains unavoidable that the opinions will always be divergent on the question of the antiquity of individual pieces of tradition and even of entire groups of traditions. But the uncertainty and need of correction of all such judgments must not allow any doubt to arise as to the necessity and importance of the question of the person and proclamation of Jesus in the context of New Testament theology. For "the Lord's position at the head of his community and his believers can and must also be expressed temporally" (E. Käsemann).

2. *The kingdom of God*

a. JOHN THE BAPTIST

Our gospels are written in order to give testimony to the life, work, dying, and resurrection of Jesus Christ, and yet they all begin their account with John the Baptist. There is undoubtedly good reason for this. Of course John the Baptist had to be mentioned, because Jesus, before the beginning of his public activity, let himself be baptized by the Baptist; but for this purpose it would have sufficed to refer to John's baptizing. But all the gospels also report on the preaching and the behavior of the Baptist, and the Gospel of Mark begins explicitly with the affirmation: "The beginning of the good news of Jesus Christ, the Son of God, [occurred] as it is written in the prophet Isaiah: 'Behold, I am sending my messenger before you, and he shall prepare your way. [There is sounding] a voice of one calling in the desert: Prepare the way of the Lord, make his paths straight.' John the Baptist appeared in the desert with the proclamation of the baptism of repentance for the forgiveness of sins" (Mark 1:1-4). Thus, by reference to words of Old Testament prophets (Mal. 3:1; Isa. 40:3), the Baptist is portrayed as the forerunner for Jesus, and the primitive Christians saw this preparation of the way above all in the demand of baptism of repentance for the forgiveness of sins. But this demand for baptism is inseparably connected with the rest of the Baptist's preaching; therefore in the gospels it was necessary, and therefore in this presentation of Jesus' preaching also it is necessary, by way of introduction to speak of the Baptist.

The imminent judgment

It is of course not easy to gain an objective historical view of John the Baptist, because the accounts in the gospels portray him from the presupposition of faith, that he had been the forerunner of Jesus, while the only still extant non-Christian account, that of the Jewish historian Josephus (Antiquities of the Jews 18. 116-119; Barrett, *Background,* p. 197), attempts to set forth the Baptist as a politically harmless preacher of morality, in which case of course it remains incomprehensible that his sovereign had him executed. Even though various things must therefore remain uncertain, still the main features of the Baptist's preaching are quite recognizable, especially insofar as they are of significance for the connection between the preaching of the Baptist and that of Jesus. Here it is clear first of all that the Baptist proclaims the *immediately imminent judgment of God:* "The axe is already laid at the root of the trees; every tree which does not produce good fruit is cut down and thrown into the fire" (Matt. 3:10 par.). Such preaching of judgment had often sounded in Israel since the time of Amos, and further, the belief that this judgment should effect a final separation and should be effected by a superhuman judge (Matt. 3:12 par.) corresponds to apocalyptic expectation. But John actualizes this traditional preaching of judgment in a twofold fashion. First, he takes away from his hearers any possibility of pushing aside the threat of judgment as far as they themselves are concerned, by saying to them that the judgment has *already* begun: the axe already lies at the root of the trees, and no one is to imagine that he can escape the wrath of God (Matt. 3:10,7 par.). Further, the Baptist destroys the delusive hope that God will judge a Jew less strictly simply because he is a descendant of Father Abraham: "Do not think that you can say among yourselves: 'We have Abraham as our father,' for I say to you that God can have children to Abraham raised from these stones" (Matt. 3:9 par.). Herewith any religious advantage of the Jew with God is denied, and the Jew is declared to be responsible for himself before God, like any other man. Not only is the Baptist's preaching of judgment in this way directed at each individual with the same urgency, but the relationship of man to God in principle is defined solely by his being human, and no longer by his belonging to the Jewish people or to any other human group.

Conversion and baptism

But the Baptist not only preaches judgment, which indeed is evident from his apparel and ascetic manner of life (Mark 1:6 par.); he also shows a way of deliverance. He proclaims the baptism of repentance for the forgiveness of sins: "Bring forth fruit that is

worthy of repentance" (Matt. 3:8 par.). One thing about this ex-
hortation is at once clear: John takes up the prophetic call for
"conversion." For the Aramaic word which is misleadingly translated as "repentance" in actuality denotes the turning around, the
abandoning of the wrong road and the resolute taking of the right
road. The concrete demands which the Baptist poses for various
groups (Luke 3:10-14) and the figure of the tree which must
produce good fruit (Matt. 3:10 par.) show clearly that John regards the resolute turning around to the doing of the divine will
as the way of deliverance from the judgment which is already
beginning; only he who produces such fruit shows thereby that he
is converted.

John connects this prophetic demand for conversion with the
summons to be baptized in the Jordan for the forgiveness of sins.
What has immersion in the Jordan to do with conversion, and how
can such submission to baptism accomplish the forgiveness of sins?
The baptismal immersion is to be done only once, in which John
appears as the active agent; hence his surname "the Baptist." And
since the ones baptized confessed their sins at the *baptism* (Mark
1:5 par.), the forgiveness of sins is obviously the aim of being
baptized. The evangelists do not say clearly how this connection is
conceived in detail, and since we do not know for sure in what
religio-historical context the Baptist's baptism is to be fitted, we can
only conjecturally explain this connection. There is, to be sure, a
widely held assumption that the Baptist has taken over the Jewish
custom of baptism of Gentiles who came over to Judaism, the so-
called proselyte baptism, and applied it to his Jewish countrymen,
who thereby were equated with the heathen. But arguing against
this is the fact that the ritually unclean Jordan was not suited for
such a ritual act and that the proselyte baptism had nothing to
do with the forgiveness of sins or with the last judgment. Likewise,
the conjecture, frequently expressed in recent times, that the Baptist
was personally connected with the special Jewish group which we
have come to know in Qumran and adopted their practice of washings, is extremely unlikely, because neither is it proved that this
Jewish group had a once-for-all washing as a rite of admission,
nor is any connection recognizable between the washings customary
there and the final judgment. Yet the washings practiced in Qumran
may belong in the large context of the baptist groups which were
present at that time on the periphery of Judaism and were located
chiefly in the country east of the Jordan; and we know that there
also a washing was occasionally regarded as preparation for with-

standing the final judgment. Hence if the Baptist probably developed his baptism in dependence upon such a peripheral phenomenon of Judaism, still the particular nature of his baptism appears to be without an actual prototype. In view of this uncertainty in the understanding of the religio-historical context of John's baptism, its exact meaning remains hidden from us; yet it may be said with great probability that the baptism, as a sacrament related to the imminent end-time, served as purification to prepare the man who, firmly committed to conversion, allowed himself to be baptized by John, to withstand the final judgment.

The coming of the "one mightier"

But according to the Baptist's proclamation, this final judgment lies in the hand of a more powerful one: "He who is mightier than I is coming after me; I am not worthy to stoop and untie the thongs of his sandals. I have baptized you with water; he will baptize you with the Holy Spirit. His fan is in his hand, to clean the threshing-floor and to gather the wheat into the granary; but he will burn the chaff with unquenchable fire" (Mark 1:7 par.; Luke 3:17 par.). This saying of the Baptist is handed down in widely diverse forms, and we can hardly expect to secure an exact restoration of its original wording. But still two things are clear: the Baptist is conscious of being the forerunner of the heavenly judge whom God will send after him and who, as a heavenly figure, stands far above him; and the latter's judgment will be final. But now according to Mark's account, the Baptist has also said that the mightier one will baptize with the Holy Spirit, while Matthew and Luke speak of a baptism with the Holy Spirit and fire. The figurative language about an "immersion in fire" can be understood altogether as a reference to the testing by fire in the judgment, but "immersion in the Holy Spirit" is an inconceivable image, and besides, with it only an utterance of having to do with salvation could be meant, which is impossible in the same clause as the threat of judgment. Various attempts by means of altering the wording or a different translation to make the "baptism with the Holy Spirit" a threat of judgment after all or to apportion blessing and woe to different groups of men are totally unconvincing, and thus there remains only the conjecture that the mention of the Holy Spirit first crept into the saying of the Baptist in the Christian tradition because for the Christians, baptism and the gift of the Spirit belonged together (see below, p. 132). If this conjecture is correct, then the Baptist announced only the judgment by fire by the "mightier one" coming

30

after him, but of course such a conjecture remains uncertain. This "mightier one" appears to have borne no name for the Baptist, certainly not that of Jesus, as the Gospel of John interprets it from a Christian perspective (1:29-34; 3:27-30). To be sure, John, while imprisoned by his sovereign, addressed the question to Jesus: "Are you the coming one, or are we to look for another?" (Matt. 11:2-3 par.). But we do not learn whether he became convinced by Jesus' referring to his extraordinary deeds and his joyous message to the poor (Matt. 11:4-6 par.) that in Jesus in truth not the expected judge of the world, but God's messenger of joy of the end-time had come. And therefore we do not know whether it was in disappointment over the tarrying of the world's judge or full of hope about God's intervention in the person of his eschatological messenger of good news that John went to his death, which was inflicted upon him by his ruler shortly after this inquiry of Jesus (Mark 6:16-17 par.).

The baptism of Jesus

Surely the authors of the first three gospels hardly doubted that John not only *was*, but also intended to be, Jesus' forerunner. But if the Baptist were the subject at the beginning of their gospels only for this historically inappropriate reason, there would be no cause for us to speak of the Baptist's activity and proclamation at the beginning of a portrayal of Jesus' proclamation. But the evangelists had still two other facts to relate which prompted them to tell of John, and because of these facts the Baptist is important in our context. In the first place, they report that Jesus was among the numerous Jews who came to the Baptist at the Jordan and let themselves be baptized by him, and that in his baptism Jesus had an experience which was decisive for his activity (Mark 1:9-11 par.). In the second place, they preface this report of Jesus' baptism with their explicit recitation of the preaching of the Baptist and in various ways indicate that Jesus associated himself with this preaching. Both these facts are essential for an understanding of the proclamation of Jesus.

It cannot seriously be doubted that Jesus was baptized by John; for the first Christians were offended by the fact that Jesus like other men let himself be baptized by the Baptist "for the forgiveness of sins," and therefore Matt. 3:14-15 and apocryphal gospels in various ways have Jesus defending his baptism as willed by God. The earliest account of Jesus' baptism (Mark 1:9-11) of course portrays this event only in terms of the significance of the occurrence for Jesus himself, and it is an open question whether and to what extent we may reckon herein with historical knowledge in the tradition (see below, p. 74). But in any case, from the fact that Jesus accepted the baptism of John, there follows the fact that he agreed with the Baptist's proclamation of the imminence of the judgment and of the necessity of conversion. Corresponding to this now is the stress placed by the evangelists upon Jesus' connection with the Baptist's preaching. According to Matt. 3:2 and 4:17, Jesus appeared, precisely as did the Baptist, with the cry, "Be converted, for the kingdom of heaven is at hand." We must be doubtful that this wording is correct for the Baptist, because the announcement of the imminence of the kingdom of heaven or similar does not appear elsewhere on the lips of the Baptist, and it is obviously characteristic precisely of *Jesus* (see below). But if the Baptist therefore probably did not speak of the imminence of the kingdom of heaven, yet he undoubtedly did speak of the immediate imminence of the judgment, and Mark 1:15 par. relates that Jesus likewise appeared with the proclamation that the kingdom of God had come near. If the Baptist bound up with his announcement of the imminence of the judgment of the world the demand for conversion, according to Mark 1:15 par. Jesus also follows him in this. Hence the evangelists deliberately tell at the beginning of their gospels not only of the baptism but also of the Baptist's proclamation. .

b. JESUS

But is it correct that, as the gospels relate, Jesus associated himself in this way with the Baptist's proclamation? The account just mentioned, in Mark 1:14-15 par., that Jesus appeared "preaching the gospel of God and saying: The time is fulfilled and the kingdom of God is at hand. Be converted and believe the gospel," is indeed a summary by the evangelist of Jesus' preaching and not a specific saying of Jesus that has been handed down. Even though, by the appropriation of John's baptism, Jesus certainly followed the Baptist's eschatological repentance movement, he did not necessarily also adopt the Baptist's proclamation of the imminence of divine judgment. Nevertheless we have enough of Jesus' individual sayings which show that he announced God's severe judgment: "On the day of judgment it will be more tolerable for Tyre and Sidon than for you" (Matt. 11:22 par.); "I tell you, on the day of judgment men will have to give account for every idle word which they utter" (Matt. 12:36; cf. Luke 17:34-35 par.). The threat of judgment on "this generation" (Matt. 12:41-42 par.) and the reference to the sudden coming of the Son of Man in judgment (Matt. 24:43-44 par.; Mark 8:38 par.) show unmistakably that Jesus also announced the *early* coming of the judgment day. Yet we do not find in Jesus any such threatening reference to the immediate imminence of the judgment as the Baptist's image of the axe which already lies at the root of the trees. The evangelists correspondingly did not place the announcement of the imminent judgment at the beginning of their account of Jesus' proclamation, but the message: "The kingdom of God is at hand" (Matt. 1:15 par.). Therewith they undoubtedly appropriated the concept which was most characteristic of Jesus' proclamation. Jesus sent out his disciples with the message, "The kingdom of God is at hand" (Luke 10:9; cf. Matt. 10:7), and he taught his disciples, just as they were used to inferring the nearness of the harvest from the growth of the leaves of the fig tree, so also to judge their present time: "When you see all this happen, know that it is at the very doors" (Mark 13:29 par.; Luke 21:31 expands, substantially correctly: "know that the kingdom of God is at hand"). And Jesus still more specifically promised his hearers: "Truly, I say to you that some of those standing here will not taste death until they see the kingdom of God coming in power" (Mark 9:1 par.).

The imminence of the kingdom of God

This expectation of Jesus, that the kingdom of God would break in before all the men of his generation should die, is confirmed by the predictions: "This generation will not pass away until all this has happened" (Mark 13:30 par.), and, "Truly, I say to you, you will not be finished with the cities of Israel before the Son of Man comes" (Matt. 10:23 par.). Hence one cannot deny, without doing violence to the texts, that Jesus anticipated a temporally very *near approach of the kingdom of God,* yet it is only a few of the extant words of Jesus which speak of this temporally limited closeness. Along with this, Jesus explicitly emphasized that no one knows the exact date of this coming: "Be ready: for in an hour when you do not expect it, the Son of Man will come" (Matt. 24:44 par.); "Of that day or hour no one knows anything, not even the angels in heaven, nor the Son, but only the Father" (Mark 13:32 par.; of course the wording of this saying on the lips of Jesus is difficult; see below, p. 75). Though Jesus announces the limited imminence of the coming of the kingdom of God, still the date of this event obviously is not therefore in itself important to him—in

Luke 17:20-21, in fact, the question about the date is directly rejected—but only the fact that the kingdom of God will soon come. Therefore Jesus commanded his disciples to pray for the coming of the kingdom of God (Matt. 6:10 par.), and therefore at the last supper he expressed the decision: "I shall drink no more of the fruit of the vine until I drink it new in the kingdom of God" (Mark 14:25 par.), and altogether in harmony with this, Jesus promised those who heeded his words the entrance into the coming kingdom of God or the future inheritance of the kingdom of God (Mark 10: 15, 23 par.; Mark 10:17 par.; Matt. 25:34).

What does Jesus intend to say when he announces the early coming of the kingdom of God? That in the future God may establish his lordship over his people Israel visibly before all peoples was the hope of Israel since the time of the Babylonian exile, and thus in the time of Jesus the pious Jew prayed daily: "Be king over us, thou alone!" Of course the Jew also knew that God is king even now, and hence he could call on God as "our Father, our King," but this kingdom of God is hidden in the present, and hence people hoped for the early manifestation of this lordship. Because the Jew in that time in general sought to avoid making direct utterances about God, he did not speak of God's coming as king, but of the coming or becoming manifest of God's royal rule. Thus Jesus adopts a conception of the Jewish hope for salvation when he speaks of the early coming of the (royal) rule of God. It is highly significant that he chooses precisely this concept. For, in the first place, Jesus' Jewish contemporaries were well acquainted with this conception, but by no means preferred to use it when they wished to speak of the hope of the coming salvation; when Jesus does specifically announce God's rule as coming soon, he does not lay the stress upon the passing away of heaven and earth, although he also expected that (Mark 13:31 par.), but on the fact that God will rule. Hence it is unlikely that Jesus spoke, as Matthew formulates it in the majority of cases (the only exceptions are Matt. 12:28; 21:31, 43), of the "kingdom of heaven," because this is the more common Jewish expression, in which "heaven" is substituted for "God." Still in substance "kingdom of heaven" says nothing different from "kingdom of God," which is consistently found in Mark and Luke. But on the other hand, one recognizes above all from the content which Jesus ascribes to this conception that he deliberately speaks precisely of the kingdom of God. That is to say, with Jesus there is lacking any portrayal of salvation and perdition apart from a few traditional images (Matt. 8:11 par.; Mark 10:40 par.), and Jesus explicitly stresses that in the resurrection things will be altogether different from earthly relationships (Mark 12:25 par.), because one cannot even picture the kingdom of God. Jesus does, however, describe, in part in traditional images, what will happen when the kingdom of God comes: then the resurrection of the dead occurs, the Son of Man comes and pronounces judgment (Matt. 12:41-42 par.; Mark 8:38 par.), then the righteous stream from the east and the west to share in the messianic feast (Matt. 8:11 par.), then Satan and the demons will be robbed of their power (Matt. 12:28 par. speaks in anticipation of this expectation; cf. also Matt. 25:41). But all this is more suggested than described.

We are able to recognize the real meaning of the promise of the coming kingdom of God only when we inquire after the *parallel concepts* with which Jesus describes the blessing of the kingdom of God. Here there appears above all the concept of *"eternal life."* As Jesus speaks of "entering into the kingdom of God," so he speaks of "entering into life" (Mark 9:43, 45, 47 par.); as he speaks of "inheriting the kingdom of God," so also he speaks of "inheriting life" (Matt. 25:34; Mark 10:17 par.), and correspondingly Jesus wishes to show "the way which leads to life" (Matt. 7:14). Further, corresponding to "entering into life" is "entering into joy" (Matt. 25:21, 23), and "sharing in glory" (Mark 10:37) as well as "sharing in the light" (Luke 16:8). All these images portray the same content: anyone who may enter into the soon-to-appear kingdom of God may share in God's life and glory and is admitted to the Father's house (Luke 15:24, 31). When God establishes his rule, then no power will any longer be able to separate the "sons of the kingdom (of God)" (Matt. 8:12) from God. But this promise holds true only for the "little flock" to whom the Father has determined to give the kingdom (Luke 12:32), and in most of the sayings of Jesus just mentioned, alongside the promise of life, etc., is placed the reference to the danger of inheriting death, darkness, hell (Mark 9:43, 45, 47 par.; Matt. 25:41; 7:13; 25:30; 8:12). As much as Jesus promises participation in God's salvation, just so surely this promise of salvation still does not simply apply to everyone, but is bound up with definite conditions, so that Jesus can say: "Narrow is the gate and strait is the way that leads to life, and those who find it are few" (Matt. 7:14). Is Jesus' proclamation of the imminent kingdom of God thus not a preaching of salvation?

The presence of the kingdom of God

The evangelist Mark, to be sure, was of the opposite opinion; for at the beginning of his "gospel" he characterizes Jesus' preaching as proclamation of God's good news, by adding to Jesus' announcement that "the kingdom of God is at hand" the demand of Jesus to "be converted and believe the good news" (Mark 1:14-15). But does this correspond to Jesus' own outlook? The term *"good news"* (= *gospel*) indeed occurs frequently in Jesus' sayings in Mark (8:35; 10:29; 13:10; 14:9), but in all these cases it is questionable whether the wording can be traced back to Jesus. On the other hand, there is found in the Sayings source Jesus' answer to the Baptist's inquiry to Jesus from prison: "Are you the coming One or are we to look for another?" "Go and tell John what you hear and see: the blind see and the lame walk, lepers are cleansed and the deaf hear, and the dead are awakened and the good news is proclaimed to the poor; and blessed is the one who is not offended at me" (Matt. 11:2-5 par.). Since there is no serious reason for doubting the reliability of this account, especially since the Baptist here does not at all appear as a witness for Jesus' mission, this answer of Jesus shows that in his working and preaching Jesus saw fulfilled the promises of the book of Isaiah (Isa. 35:5-6; 61:1): that the good news of God's action of the end-time is being proclaimed to the "poor," i.e., the "little" people who trust in God; and the Baptist is to recognize this as a sign of the fulfillment of the eschatological promise of salvation. Accordingly, Jesus characterizes his preaching as good news of the end-time and, by the reference to his deeds and words as the salvation event of the end-time, gives an affirmative answer to the doubting question of the Baptist as to whether the salvation-bringer of the end-time had perhaps come in the person of Jesus. But this claim of Jesus is also frequently attested elsewhere. Jesus says to his disciples: "Blessed are your eyes, because they see, and your ears, because they hear; for truly I tell you that many prophets and righteous ones have desired to see what you are seeing, and did not see it, and desired to hear what you are hearing, and did not hear it" (Matt. 13:16-17 par.), and with this manner of expression he indicates that his disciples are being permitted to experience what has been promised for the end-time. But Jesus also directly connects this end event in the present with the kingdom of God: "If I by the finger of God drive out demons, then the kingdom of God has come to you" (Luke 11:20 par.). This is undoubtedly a paradoxical

utterance; for the Jew expected that with the coming of the kingdom of God, God's power would come visibly to light, and here it
is only Jesus' power over demons which prompts Jesus to make the
assertion that in his deeds the coming kingdom of God has dawned.
Jesus repeats this claim in a parable, which he uses to defend himself against the charge that he owes his power over the demons to
a treaty with the prince of demons: "No one can go into the house
of the strong man and steal his possessions unless he first has
bound the strong man, and then he will plunder his house" (Mark
3:27 par.). According to Jewish expectations, only the salvation-
bearer of the end-time can bind the prince of demons. Thus with
this expression Jesus indicates that through his doing, eschatological salvation is being accomplished in the present. Jesus' good news
is saying that in his actions and his preaching, God is already now
establishing his rule, and that therefore already now one can gain
a share in this saving activity of God if one adheres in faith to this
message of Jesus.

Because the hearer of Jesus can recognize this presence of the
coming kingdom of God in Jesus' deeds and preaching only if he
acknowledges this claim of Jesus (indeed one can also see the
prince of demons at work in Jesus' deeds and explain his preaching
as blasphemy: Mark 3:22 par.; 2:7 par.!), some scholars have assumed that Jesus saw the kingdom of God as present also in the
circle of his disciples who acknowledged him, especially since according to Matthew's tradition, Jesus promised Peter that he would
build his community upon him as a rock (Matt. 16:18-19). This
assumption has been supported with a reference to Luke 12:32:
"Fear not, little flock, for it is your Father's good pleasure to give
you the kingdom," and with the consideration that, as the one
bringing the kingdom of God, Jesus must also have gathered about
him a circle of members of this kingdom of God. But this line of
argument is hardly tenable. Jesus undoubtedly challenged men to
personal discipleship (Mark 1:17, 20 par.; Luke 9:59 par.), but
he by no means made the promise of participation in the coming
kingdom of God dependent for everyone on entering into personal
discipleship to him (Mark 10:17, 19 par.; 12:34). It is highly
probable that Jesus also gathered around him a narrower circle
of twelve disciples and thereby made visible his claim to be calling
the entire twelve-tribe nation to repentance (Mark 14:10 par.; I
Cor. 15:5; Matt. 19:28 par.; cf. also Mark 3:13 ff. par.; 6:7 ff. par.).
But there is no report that Jesus regarded or labeled this narrower
circle of disciples as an eschatological community of salvation. The

saying about the little flock (Luke 12:32; see above) does indeed contain precisely the promise of participation in the kingdom of God for those who in the time of Jesus have no fear of joining him. *Nowhere* do these contexts indicate in Jesus *the conception of a "community"* gathered around him or even of the presence of the kingdom of God in this community. This is one reason why the famous saying to Peter, which the Roman bishops have claimed for their episcopal throne since the third century, can hardly go back to Jesus ("I say to you that you are Peter, and on this rock I will build my community, and the gates of Hades will have no power over it. I will give you the keys of the kingdom of heaven, and what you bind on earth will be bound in heaven, and what you loose on earth will be loosed in heaven" [Matt. 16:18-19]). Jesus made a claim with respect to the entire Jewish nation; this does not comport with the founding of a separate community through which alone one might gain entrance into the kingdom of God. Moreover, the special position attributed to Peter in this saying, a position which bestows divinely obligatory significance to this man's decisions, contradicts Jesus' view of the relation of the disciples to one another (Mark 10:43-44 par.). Therefore this saying about Peter certainly first arose in the primitive church and cannot prove that Jesus saw the kingdom of God as present in the community of his disciples.

But it also has often been thought that Jesus spoke of the *kingdom of God* as *a reality developing on earth,* and some have been prompted to make this assumption by those parables of Jesus in which the kingdom of God is compared with growing plants (Mark 4:26 ff.; 4:30 ff. par.; Matt. 13:24 ff.) or with the working of yeast (Matt. 13:33 par.). None of these parables clearly state in what respect the kingdom of God is supposed to be illustrated with the reference to the experience of the farmer or of the housewife, and therefore the interpretation of all these parables is much disputed. But if one pays close attention to the features which are stressed in these pictures, one clearly sees that the emphasis does not lie on the growth, but on the fact that the harvest comes surely without the farmer's assistance, that from the minute seed the unexpectedly large plant comes, that the weeds can be removed only at the harvest time, and that a little yeast leavens an immensely large amount of flour (see the commentaries on the passages). All these parables are meant to strengthen the certainty that in spite of the unimpressiveness of Jesus' preaching and activity, the kingdom of God will surely and unexpectedly gloriously come, and in no way is the subject a present growth and self-development of the kingdom of God. Jesus spoke rather of the presence of the kingdom of God only with respect to his working and preaching.

But this unavoidably raises the question why Jesus' proclamation of the coming of the kingdom of God, and its having come, is good news, and in what sense participation in this blessing is tied to apparently insurmountable conditions. In other words, we can actually understand the real meaning of Jesus' proclamation only when we have inquired into the proclamation of God, God's demand, and the significance of the person of Jesus in the preaching of Jesus.

3. *The proclamation about God*

a. THE JUDGE

Since Jesus appeared with the message "The kingdom of God is at hand," one would expect that he also spoke with emphasis of God as king. But this is by no means the case. The occasional identification of Jerusalem as the "city of the great king" (Matt. 5:35) and the equally incidental comparison of God with a king (Matt. 18:23 ff.; but the comparison is actually not at all carried through!) rather show that Jesus saw God in the figure of a king only in a traditional way; and his similarly occasional use of other Jewish names for God (Lord, Matt. 9:38 par.; 11:25 par.; heaven, Luke 15:18; power, Mark 14:62 par.; God, Matt. 6:24 par.; Mark 10:9, *et passim*) is just as little help in revealing anything about Jesus' conception of God. But we have already seen that Jesus connects the expectation of the judgment with the expectation of the future kingdom of God, and correspondingly, he also speaks of God's *future judging:* "Judge not, so that you may not be judged. . . . It will be measured to you with whatever measure you measure" (Matt. 7:1-2 par.; the passive is the Jewish way of speaking of God's action) ; "For every idle word which men shall utter they will give account on the day of judgment. For on the basis of your words you will be acquitted, and on the basis of your words you will be condemned" (Matt. 12:36-37; cf. also Matt. 11:22, 24 par.) . Correspondingly, in a parable God is compared to a master who holds a reckoning with his servants (Matt. 25:14 ff. par.) , and warning is given of God's power as judge: "Fear him who can destroy soul and body in hell" (Matt. 10:28 par.) . Hence it cannot be doubted that Jesus, as did Judaism, expected God as future judge whose sovereign will would allow him (according to the parable) to call away the rich farmer before he can enjoy his accumulated treasures (Luke 12:16-20). But the certainty that Jesus shared this expectation is matched by the rarity with which it occurs in the sayings of Jesus that are handed down, and by the slight extent to which it is characteristic of, and essential for, Jesus' conception of God.

b. THE FATHER WHO WILL ACT IN THE FUTURE

On the other hand, it is striking and unusual that Jesus identified God primarily as "Father." It is true that Palestinian Judaism of Jesus' time is acquainted with the designation of God as "Father" or "heavenly Father," though of course this is not common; in addition, there is found the address in prayer of "our Father," or of "our Father, our king," but never, on the other hand, "my Father." However, a critical examination of the use of language displayed in the gospels shows that Jesus not only spoke of the "heavenly Father" (Matt. 7:11 par.), but also talked to the disciples of "your Father" (Luke 6:36; 12:30 par.; 32) or of "your heavenly Father" (Mark 11:25 par.; Matt. 23:9), but in particular himself called on God in prayer as "Father" (Mark 14:36 par.; Matt. 11:25 par.) and taught the disciples to pray likewise (Luke 11:2 par.). This is quite extraordinary, and therefore one can best recognize Jesus' conception of God when one observes *how* Jesus spoke of God the Father. Here, first of all, even the language itself with which Jesus speaks of the Father and addresses God is striking. The evangelist Mark, as well as the liturgical usage of the Pauline congregations, preserved the wording of this address to God: abba (Mark 14:36; Rom. 8:16; Gal. 4:6), and the form of the model prayer handed down by Luke (Luke 11:2) displays the simple address, "Father," which must go back to the same Aramaic word. But this Aramaic word abba was never used in Judaism as an address or a designation of God; Jesus rather made a word of children's language, which had become the familiar form of address for a father generally, into the designation of God, and thereby made it clear even in the form of his language that he did not want to speak of God with a traditional designation, but wanted to preach with specific urgency that God seeks to encounter man with fatherly love. And just as Jesus spoke of God's future appearance as king and judge, so also now he speaks of God's future actions as Father.

Like a father God will *care* for his children. If God cares even for all his creatures (Matt. 6:26-31 par.), then he cares all the more for men; hence anxiety about food and clothing is unnecessary, "your Father knows what you have need of" (Luke 12:30 par.; cf. Matt. 6:8), and even more than an earthly father, "your heavenly Father will give good things to those who ask him" (Matt. 7:11 par.). Thus even though the father knows what his children need, they are to ask him, and thus Jesus also taught his disciples what they should request from the Father. The form of the "Lord's Prayer" preserved in Luke, which is the shorter and probably also the more original (Luke 11:2-4), however, by no means is oriented primarily to the needs of the present, but in the main to the Father's eschatological activity: the two petitions for the hallowing of the divine name and the coming of the kingdom and the two petitions for the forgiveness of our sins and for preservation from temptation bracket the only petition which concerns the present: "Give us this day the necessary bread." It is true that the meaning of the Greek word translated here as "necessary" (King James Version "daily") still cannot be determined with certainty; some scholars, following the Jewish-Christian translation of the word (reported by Jerome) as "for tomorrow," interpret the petition for "bread for tomorrow" as a petition for the bread of the end-time. But this is questionable on linguistic as well as on substantive grounds, and the assumption that the prayer for bread has in view God's providential care for indispensable human needs of the present is more probable. But for the rest, the first two petitions have as their aim that the Father might bring in the end-time in which he alone is reverenced and there is no longer any danger that his children will be lost, in which rather the promise will become reality: "Fear not, little flock, for it is your Father's good pleasure to give you the kingdom [of God]" (Luke 12:32), and the promise is fulfilled: "Blessed are the peacemakers, for they shall be called God's sons" (Matt. 5:9; cf. also Matt. 5:45). Of course man can attain the kingdom of God only if God accepts and preserves him, and therefore the prayer concludes with the petition for forgiveness at the judgment and for preservation from apostasy in the trials of the last time. Thus Jesus teaches his disciples to pray to the Father for God's coming in his kingdom and for our sharing in this kingdom, and Jesus promises them that if they pray in secret, without wishing to be seen, "your Father who sees in secret will reward you" (Matt. 6:6), that is, God will receive into his kingdom the praying one who sets his hope entirely in God.

But according to Jesus' preaching, God reveals himself as the Father who acts in the future most of all in his promise of *forgive-*

ness to men: "When you stand and pray, forgive, if you have any-thing against any man, so that your heavenly Father may also for-give you your trespasses" (Mark 11:25). With all of Judaism, Jesus knows that man is obligated to unconditional service to God (Luke 17:7-10) and must give account of his service (Matt. 24:45 ff. par.). But because man is evil (Matt. 7:11 par.; 12:34) and cannot in his own power free himself from his guilt and there-fore cannot stand before God (Luke 18:13), man's profoundest need in view of the coming of God's kingdom is guilt, and there-fore also Jesus taught his disciples to ask for the forgiveness of sins (Luke 11:4 par.), as corresponded to the Jewish custom in prayer. However, Jesus does not simply instruct his disciples to hope in God's forgiveness, but he shows God to be the very one who rejoices in the sinner's repentance. He pictures in parables the joy of the shepherd who has found the *one* lost sheep, and the joy of the woman who has found the lost drachma, and from these he draws the conclusion: "I tell you that in the same way, there will be more joy in heaven [i.e., with God] over *one* sinner who repents than over ninety-nine just persons who have no need to repent" (Luke 15:7, 10). And in the parable of the two sons (Luke 15:11 ff.), he makes vivid the joy of the father over the son who returns home, who appeared lost and now is received by the father with open arms, for which he could not have held the remotest hope; he is received thus simply because the father loves the son, although there is nothing lovable left in him. Though here God appears in the image of an earthly father as the one who is rightly stirred to wrath over sinful man, who yet meets the penitent sinner with forgiveness, Jesus of course is concerned to make it clear that such forgiving love of God is unexpected and unaccountable. The parable of the vineyard owner (Matt. 20:1 ff.) shows a man who at different times in the same day secures la-borers to work in his vineyard, at the end has them all paid the same usual day's wages, and explains to the murmuring workers, who in spite of their working the entire day receive the same wages: "Friend, I am doing you no harm; did you not agree with me for a denarius? Take what is yours and be gone! But I intend to give to this last one [the same] as I gave you. May I not do as I will with my possessions? Or are you envious because I am gener-ous?" The legally unassailable conduct of this employer, against which the human sense of justice rebels, lets us see a God who gives out of pure goodness, where according to human judgment a gift is not appropriate. Certainly according to Jesus' utterances

God can mercilessly punish, if man is not ready to repent (Luke 13:1-9); but Jesus ventures to proclaim that God takes pleasure, not in the righteous man who boasts before God of his being righteous, but in the sinner who is conscious of his lost condition (Luke 18:9-14). And therein Jesus fundamentally distinguishes himself from contemporary Judaism, which strongly emphasizes God's readiness to forgive and man's being directed to God's forgiveness, it is true, but always added: "If this is granted to those who transgress his will, how much more to those who do his will." (Bab. Talmud, Makkoth 24b).

C. THE DEMAND FOR CONVERSION

Of course this promise of Jesus of forgiveness, as in contemporary Judaism, would be only a promise which did not alter the present if Jesus had spoken only of God's future activity. But this is not the case, and only when we recognize to what extent Jesus pointed to God's present activity can the question actually be answered whether Jesus' preaching of the kingdom of God was a proclamation of *salvation*, a gospel. We have seen that Jesus announces God's future judgment, and this future judgment casts its shadows forward into the present time of Jesus' hearers by means of the demand which is bound up with the announcement of the early coming of the kingdom of God: "Turn around!" (Mark 1:15). That man must *"turn around"* if he wishes to stand before God is one of the basic views of Judaism in Jesus' time, and thus Jesus also explicitly named conversion as a condition for entrance into the kingdom of God (Matt. 11:21-22 par.; 12:41 par.; Luke 16:29-30). Anyone who, upon hearing of blows of misfortune, judges that those affected by them are particularly grievous sinners has not yet comprehended that he himself must turn around if it is not to go the same way with him (Luke 13:1-5). Thus all men are in need of conversion, and the disciples therefore are sent out with the commission to preach that people should turn around (Mark 6:12).

The special urgency of Jesus' call to conversion is not, however, due merely to his connecting it with the announcement of the imminent kingdom of God. Indeed, the same holds true for the preaching of John the Baptist. Jesus rather with this call at the same time confronts his hearers with the ultimate will of God, as *he* can proclaim it in contrast to the previous understanding of the "old" (Matt. 5:21 ff.). Thus with Jesus the decision to turn around is demanded in view of a man who *now* has the commission to proclaim God's will in perfect fashion and therefore calls to immediate conversion: "Anyone who puts his hand to the plow and looks back is not fit for the kingdom of God" (Luke 9:62). The future judge now confronts man in Jesus' proclamation of God's will, and through God's demand proclaimed by Jesus, the present is connected in a unique way with the imminent future of the kingdom of God. And we shall have to inquire as to the nature of this divine demand proclaimed by Jesus, in order to understand the more precise meaning of this present activity of God.

d. THE FATHER WHO ACTS IN THE PRESENT

As we have seen, however, Jesus spoke of God's actions in the future primarily as a fatherly activity. Does this fatherly activity also extend back into the present? Jesus talked of the Father's concern for men which is extended to the present no less than to the future, and he called doubt about this concern "little faith" (Matt. 6:28-30 par.). But can one actually speak of God's present care for men if God does not actually yet exercise his rule in the present, if instead the demons range through the world to gain power over men (Matt. 12:43-45 par.) and Satan, as a unitary power, intends to let nothing be torn from his grasp (Mark 3:23-26 par.)? Jesus further heightened the Jewish view of the present power of the demons, in that he saw the realm of the demons as a unitary entity, which one can escape only if one is able to overcome Satan himself. But when Jesus now proclaims, "I saw Satan fall as lightning from heaven" (Luke 10:18), he is making the claim that Satan's power is already broken (regardless of whether we have to do here with a vision or with a figure of speech), and indeed we also have seen that in his expulsion of demons he saw God's eschatological kingdom beginning (see above, p. 37). Thus Jesus did not deny that the demons, under their leader Satan, are still at work, and yet in his mighty activity he saw God's eschatological rule and therewith *God's conquest of Satan's empire* realized in the present. Through Jesus' working, God the Father, whose will it is to give the kingdom of God to his own, is making the present time already the time of salvation.

Jesus proclaimed God's fatherly saving activity in the future primarily as forgiveness of sins. However, he not only promised this forgiveness, but also caused it to be a present reality. His opponents described Jesus as *"friend of tax-gatherers and sinners"* (Matt. 11:19 par.), and this description is entirely appropriate for characterizing Jesus' conduct: he had fellowship at table with tax-gatherers and sinners, that is, members of professions which were regarded as especially susceptible to the transgression of God's law (Mark 2:15-16 par.), he made a tax-gatherer his disciple (Mark 2:14 par.), and was guest of a tax-gatherer (Luke 19:1 ff.); indeed, he even allowed his feet to be anointed by "a woman who is a sinner" (Luke 7:36 ff.). He explicitly defended such behavior, intolerable for the pious Jew, with the words: "It is not the healthy who need a physician, but the sick; I have not come to call the righteous, but sinners" (Mark 2:17 par.), and accordingly declared to his adversaries: "Truly, I tell you, the tax-gatherers and the harlots will enter the kingdom of God before you" (Matt. 21:31). Thus in his conduct Jesus took seriously the divine intention which he proclaimed, to accept the sinner and to forgive him, and even by this means caused God's forgiving intention to become present reality.

But he went still further. When a lame man, who could not be brought to him in the ordinary way, was lowered into the house to him through the dismantled roof, "and Jesus saw their faith, he said to the lame man, 'Son, your sins are forgiven.' " When scribes who were present label such dispensing of God's forgiveness as blasphemy, Jesus poses the question: "Which is easier, to say to the lame man, 'your sins are forgiven,' or to say, 'Rise, take your bed, and go to your house'?" The account continues: "But so that you may know that the Son of Man has power on earth to forgive sins—he says to the lame man, 'I say to you, rise, take up your bed, and go to your house,' " whereupon the lame man goes away healed (Mark 2:1 ff. par.). Thus in this narrative, the unity of which often is unjustly doubted, Jesus claims the right to pronounce God's forgiveness of sins, and for this he appeals to the power of the "Son of Man" to forgive sins on earth (on the problem of this title, cf. below, pp. 76 ff.). Thus here, quite concretely and with an authority which the adversaries could only label blasphemous, Jesus actualizes the divine pronouncement of forgiveness and thereby causes his present time to become the time of salvation. Entirely in harmony with this is Jesus' dealing with a sinful woman who at a meal in the house of a Pharisee bathed his feet with her tears, dried them with her hair, and then anointed them. Because Jesus condoned this conduct of a sinful woman, the host concluded that Jesus could not be a prophet; but with a parable of two debtors, Jesus illustrated the truth that the remission of a greater debt also brings with it greater gratitude, and then with respect to the act of the sinful woman explained: "Her many sins are forgiven, because she loved greatly; but the one to whom little is forgiven

[also] loves little." To this woman also Jesus declared: "Your sins are forgiven," and with this claim stirred up objections (Luke 7:36 ff.). Thus in this case also Jesus brings God's forgiveness and causes the forgiving intention on the part of the Father who seeks the sinner to become an experienced reality.

Thus Jesus' message of the imminent coming and the presence of God's kingdom is the context for the proclamation of God's actions as judge and Father, and in Jesus' person, in what he taught and what he did, this activity of God reaches into the present and becomes concrete reality for the believer. Although God's rule remains in the future and man still expectantly moves toward the divine decision and God's salvation, the person who in Jesus' teaching and actions sees God's saving action becoming a reality even now, in the person of Jesus, encounters the God who wills to give us his eschatological gifts of salvation. We must first understand God's demand which addresses us in Jesus' preaching and the claim which confronts us in Jesus; only then can the significance and the abiding meaning of this eschatological saving activity of God which has become a reality through Jesus become entirely transparent to us.

4. God's demand

Jesus connected the demand for conversion with the announcement of the imminent coming of the kingdom of God (see above, pp. 43-44). However, he did not limit himself to this general demand, but very clearly related admission into the kingdom of God to the fulfillment of definite conditions: "If your righteousness does not go beyond that of the scribes and Pharisees, you shall not enter the kingdom of heaven" (Matt. 5:20). Even if the formulation of this saying should stem from Matthew, which however is by no means a necessary assumption, still it correctly summarizes Jesus' outlook. For in sayings which undoubtedly go back to Jesus, cutting off the hand and plucking out the eye are demanded if they hinder the entrance into the kingdom of God (Mark 9:43 ff. par.), and the admonition is given not to make any claims before God: "Truly, I tell you, whoever does not accept the kingdom of God as a child shall not enter in" (Mark 10:15 par.). In the parables of the treasure hidden in the field and of the pearl of great price (Matt. 13:44-46) Jesus therefore makes evident the necessity of staking everything on gaining the kingdom of God, and the demand of Jesus which is characterized as solely essential reads accordingly:

"But seek his kingdom, and this [i.e., God's help in satisfying earthly needs] will be added to you" (Luke 12:31 par.). But conversely, it is said: "No one who puts his hand to the plow and looks back is fit for the kingdom of God" (Luke 9:62). Thus Jesus proclaims God's demand with a view to the coming kingdom of God, and this is the source of the urgency of this demand.

Correspondingly, Jesus promises reward to those who are ready for self-denial and fearless confession of Jesus, but to self-seekers and those who deny Jesus, punishment ("Whoever would save his life shall lose it; but whoever would lose his life for my sake . . . shall save it," Mark 8:35 par.; "Whoever confesses me before men, him will the Son of Man confess before the angels of God; but whoever denies me before men will be denied before the angels of God," Luke 12:8-9 par.). Jesus also says the same thing in parabolic form: the faithful servant will receive a position of trust at his master's coming, but the unfaithful servant will be destroyed (Matt. 24:45-51 par.). And Jesus also speaks thus of the *reward* which God gives to those who do his will: "If you love those who love you, what reward have you?" (Matt. 5:46 par.); those who give alms, pray, or fast in order to be seen by others "have already received their reward" (Matt. 6:2, 5, 16); but whoever is hated or maligned for Jesus' sake is to rejoice: "For behold, your reward in heaven is abundant" (Luke 6:23 par.; cf. also Mark 9:41 par.). Such a reward in heaven is described as "treasure in heaven" which one is to acquire (Matt. 6:20 par.), and to a rich man who clings to his possessions Jesus says: "You lack one thing; go, sell what you have and give it to the poor; then you will have a treasure in heaven; and come and follow me" (Mark 10:21 par.).

In view of this broad tradition it cannot be doubted that Jesus connected the proclamation of God's future and present activity with the demand for obedience to God's will in a twofold way. (1). Jesus was a Jew and in his preaching addressed himself to Jews. But for a Jew it was a self-evident idea that God confronts man with commandments which are to be fulfilled by man and whose fulfillment or nonfulfillment is decisive for man's ultimate destiny before God. Hence it was equally self-evident that with the proclamation of the imminent kingdom of God Jesus connected the reference to the will of *the* God whose kingdom was soon to be actualized and was already being actualized in Jesus. But it was precisely through its connection with the announcement of the imminent coming of God's kingdom that this proclamation by

Jesus of God's will acquired its inescapable urgency, and it must be asked in what way Jesus' demand gained its *particular character* through this connection. (2). Again in agreement with Judaism, Jesus connected the promise of participation in the kingdom of God with man's deeds, by means of the idea of reward and punishment. But this gives rise to the difficulty that participation in the kingdom of God now appears to be not entirely and solely *God's* gift, but something which man can secure for himself by his own achievement, so that once again, now from another side, the question emerges whether Jesus actually could have described the announcement of the coming kingdom of God as good news. We must examine these two problems more closely.

a. THE KINGDOM OF GOD AND THE FULFILLMENT OF THE DIVINE WILL

When Jesus connects the demand for fulfillment of the divine will with the announcement of the imminent coming of the kingdom of God, he is not therein following the Jewish view: "If the Israelites repent, they are redeemed; but if not, they are not redeemed" (Bab. Talmud, Sanhedrin 97*b*). The belief that by their fulfillment of the law the Jews could hasten the coming of the kingdom of God undoubtedly conflicted with Jesus' conviction that the time of the coming of God's kingdom depends entirely on God's will and that the kingdom of God comes without any human contributing factor (Matt. 24:44, 50 par.; Mark 13:32 par.; 4:26 ff.). Of course Luke 16:16 has been repeatedly cited in favor of the assumption that Jesus also spoke of a seizing of the kingdom of God: "The law and the prophets [were in force] until John; from that time on, the good news of the kingdom of God is proclaimed, and everyone presses into it." But it can hardly be doubted that Luke has changed the original wording of the saying, from his point of view of the situation of the church; but the more original wording in Matt. 11:12 ("From the days of John the Baptist until now, the kingdom of heaven suffers violence, and men of violence plunder it") cannot be interpreted to mean a praiseworthy concern on man's part for the kingdom of God. In Jesus' opinion, human effort in fact can neither hasten nor delay the coming of the kingdom of God.

An interim ethic?

The announcement of the *imminent* coming of the kingdom of God, however, is not connected in such a way with God's demand as Jesus proclaims it that awareness of the imminence of the judgment and of the kingdom of God has caused the radical and unconditional character of this demand, so that the divine will proclaimed by Jesus could have validity only for this brief time before the coming of the kingdom of God. *A. Schweitzer* interpreted Jesus' demand in this way and therefore spoke of the "interim ethic." This view is incorrect because Jesus could not support the demand for doing God's will only with a reference to the imminent coming of the kingdom of God. He points rather also to God's behavior: "Love your enemies and pray for those who persecute you, that you may become sons of your Father in heaven; for he causes his sun to rise on evil and good and rain to fall on just and unjust" (Matt. 5:44-45), and issues a challenge to the imitation of God: "Be merciful as your Father is merciful" (Luke 6:36). Matthew, in his reproduction of this saying in the Sermon on the Mount, presumably put the predicate "perfect" in place of "merciful" (Matt. 5:48). By this, however, he does not mean the moral perfection which is to be achieved by progress, but unblemished wholeness like that of a sacrificial animal, and he intends the description to mean nothing different in essence from a way of acting in harmony with God's dealing with man. Alongside the love of God, which is the example for man's conduct, Jesus places the honor of God, which man is to enhance: "Let your light so shine before men that they may see your good deeds and glorify your Father in heaven" (Matt. 5:16). And occasionally Jesus also pointed to his own conduct: "Who is greater, the one who reclines at the table or the one who serves? Is it not the one who reclines at the table? But I am in your midst as the one serving" (Luke 22:27).

These exhortations show that Jesus does not base the particularity of his proclamation of God's will on the short time remaining before the coming of God's kingdom; yet it is also true that in Jesus' preaching in general only isolated cases indicate that there is but a short time in which one can fulfill God's will (Luke 13:6-9; Matt. 25:1 ff.). Furthermore, Jesus not only proclaimed the imminence of the kingdom of God, but also the inbreaking of this kingdom in his working and preaching; hence with Jesus God's demand cannot at all be determined solely by the awareness of the imminence of God's kingdom; instead, it receives its character just as much through the salvation event of the present, which is being achieved in Jesus. But in this salvation event the coming ruler intervenes in the present as the loving Father, and thus the reference to the brief span of time ultimately serves, as does the allusion to the advance working of the final consummation in the present, to set man inescapably before God himself. "Behind Jesus' demand—even though it may accidentally be eschatologically grounded—a 'preknowing' becomes evident: the knowledge of God's absolute holiness, which summons to ultimate theocentricity. . . . In the last analysis, in all the ethical demands Jesus is radically concerned about God: that God's great holiness may not be injured!—Here is where the radical character of many of Jesus' demands has its origin" (H. Schürmann). Thus in spite of Jesus' announcement of the imminent kingdom of God, his ethic is not meant in the sense of an "interim ethic." Jesus' ethic is more fittingly described as "ethics of the time of salvation or new-covenant ethics" (A. Wilder). Hence the validity and obligatory force of Jesus' demand is not even bound to the unique situation of Jesus' generation, but rather to the believing acknowledgment of God's saving action which is begun in the person of Jesus and awaits its consummation.

Jesus' demand and the Jewish tradition

When Jesus proclaims God's will from this point of departure, he obviously must enter into discussion with the fact that the Jewish teachers of his time also proclaimed God's will. In doing so, they by no means appealed simply to the "Holy Scripture" of the Jews, i.e., to the collection of books later named "the Old Testament" by the Christians, although the Scripture, particularly the "Teaching" (Torah, i.e., the Pentateuch), was recognized as unconditional authority: "Wisdom is the book of the commandments of God and the law which exists for eternity; all those who keep them come to life, but those who forsake them will die" (Greek Baruch 4.1). But according to Jewish conviction, God gave his commandments to his people, that they might govern the whole life of the people of God: "Our lawgiver . . . did not leave anything, not even of the smallest matters, to the freewill decision of those for whom his law was designed . . . , so that we should live under it [i.e., the law] as under a father and lord and might sin neither by intention nor from ignorance" (Josephus, Against Apion II, § 173-74). But difficulties arose in the application of this basic principle, because the written law did not give directions for all life situations or for every detail. However, the dominant view in Jesus' time, which was held by the Pharisees, never limited the law to the written "Holy Scripture," but always regarded the scripture only as a part of the tradition. As much as the "scribes" always were concerned with justifying from Holy Scripture the more exact interpretation of a commandment—a commandment or the interpretation of a commandment was shown to be equally unassailable as an expression of God's will if the evidence could be produced to show that this commandment could be traced back to Moses or in any case very far back in the chain of tradition. The affirmation, "These are the words which were spoken to Moses at Sinai" (Tosefta Peah 3.2) declares the words in question without further proof to be a divine and therefore a binding ordinance. Hence the norm for the establishing of the divine will is, for Judaism led by the Pharisees in Jesus' time, the entire tradition preserved by the scribes, and the commandments of God preserved in the Scripture are only a part of this tradition and may be understood only in terms of the tradition which was largely passed along orally.

Jesus grew up in this belief in tradition and held to the usual religious customs, even so far as they were taught only in the oral tradition (for example, he wears the tassels on his robe as prescribed in Num. 15:38 [Matt. 9:20-21], but also, in harmony with the oral tradition, attends the synagogue on the sabbath [Mark 1: 21]). Correspondingly, in his answer to a question about the most important commandment, Jesus refers to the commandments about love of God and neighbor in the books of Moses (Mark 12:28-31 par.), but similarly also to the demand in the tradition that on the sabbath one may lift a beast out of the well (Matt. 12:11 par.). But now the striking thing is that the same Jesus, as numerous examples in the gospel tradition show, did not hesitate to set aside the written law as well as the rules of the scribes. As we have seen (above, p. 45), Jesus not only deliberately disregarded the Pharisaic demands for separation from the "lawless"; he also allowed his disciples on the sabbath to pluck grain by hand to appease their hunger (Mark 2:23 ff. par.), and he himself healed the withered hand of a man on the sabbath; both of these meant a violation of the sabbath commandment as the Pharisees understood it. Jesus' question in Mark 3:4 par., "It it lawful on the sabbath to do good or to do evil, to rescue a person or to kill?" shows altogether plainly that he understands the omission of this healing, demanded by the traditional understanding of the sabbath commandment—what was involved indeed was not a case of a danger to life!—as doing evil, as killing, but that he regards the obligation to heal, that is, to do good, and to rescue the man, as God's will. Thus, as the examples show, Jesus claims to have a more correct knowledge of God's commandment than have the Pharisaic teachers, and, going beyond this, he sets himself unequivocally against certain demands of the written law itself. The sentence, "Nothing that goes into a man from without can make him unclean, but what goes forth from a man makes him unclean" (Mark 7:15 par.), explains the distinction between clean and unclean foods, contrary to the written commandment, as not according to God's will, though Jesus does not give any justification for this assertion from Scripture or tradition; and to the question whether a man might divorce his wife, Jesus affirms, referring to God's ordinance of creation: "What God has joined man must not separate" (Mark 10:2-9 par.), whereby the divorce legislation (Deut. 24) and the tradition connected with it likewise are declared to be not in keeping with God's will. Accordingly Jesus places his knowledge and *his interpretation* of the will of God *against* the understanding of this will as *the Pharisaic tradition* represented in connection with Holy Scripture, and, in doing so, more than once contradicts the wording of Scripture itself.

This attitude of Jesus, which with all its fundamental acknowledgment of the authority of law and tradition so sharply contradicts the contemporary Jewish understanding of the law, most clearly exhibits its meaning and import in the so-called *"Antitheses"* of the Sermon on the Mount (Matt. 5:21-48 par.). Presumably, as it appears from a comparison with Luke, only three of these six pairs of opposites were originally formulated antithetically, namely the instructions about killing, adultery, and taking an oath (Matt. 5:21-22, 27-28, 33-37), while it was Matthew who first transferred this formulation to the three remaining instructions (divorce, revenge, love of enemies; Matt. 5:31-32, 38-39, 43-44 par.). But the three original antitheses may with great likelihood be traced back to Jesus, and here Jesus sets against an Old Testament commandment, introduced with "You have heard that it was said to those of old" or "You have heard that it is said," *his own* interpretation of God's will, introduced with "But I say to you." Now the formulation of these pairs of opposites clearly shows that the Old Testament prohibition is seen as a component part of the tradition and therewith also in the sense of this tradition, but that for *his* understanding of God's will Jesus appeals neither to other words of Scripture nor to any tradition, but with an emphatic "I" authoritatively sets his commands in opposition to the traditional understanding of the will of God. But, as we have seen, Jesus just as authoritatively declared the distinction between clean and unclean foods and the

right to divorce a wife to be in conflict with the will of God, and
the antitheses show us that with such authoritative proclamation of
the will of God, Jesus expressly rejects the unlimited validity of the
previous interpretation of the divine commandment and puts *his*
explanation in its place as normative. "The law and the prophets
[go] until John" (Luke 16:16*a*) ; when Jesus says this, it is clear
that he is claiming that, with *his* proclamation of the will of God,
a new, final time of the revelation of God's will has come. Accordingly, Jesus also described it as his task to give the revelation that
has been handed down its true meaning: "Do not think that I have
come to declare the law and the prophets invalid; I have not come
to declare invalid but to bring [law and prophets] to fulfillment
[through my interpretation]" (Matt. 5:17). And these utterances
of Jesus fit in with his declaration that in his preaching an eschatological event comes to pass (Matt. 11:5 par.; see above, p. 36).
Because in Jesus, his teaching, and his activity, God causes his
eschatological saving activity to become a reality now, to heed
Jesus' proclamation of God's will is of decisive importance for
people who want to enter into the kingdom of God. Therefore to
those Jews who, believing, saw in Jesus the soon-to-come kingdom
of God as having already dawned, *Jesus'* demand appeared as an
"ethic of the time of salvation," in which God's will was finally
and authoritatively proclaimed. Anyone who in listening to the
preaching of Jesus gained the conviction that Jesus "taught as one
having authority, and not as the scribes" (thus Mark 1:22 par.)
was bound to see in Jesus' demand a part of God's eschatological
saving activity which is begun in Jesus.

God's unconditional will

Thus Jesus' demand was not bound up with his proclamation
of the imminence of the kingdom of God in such a way that the
expectation of a brief interim until the arrival of God's kingdom
caused the divine demand to become a short-lived and exceptional
bit of legislation; instead, Jesus' proclamation of the will of God
rather acquired its radical and unconditionally binding character
through the authority of Jesus, through whom God had his will
definitively proclaimed and through whom God caused his coming
kingdom to become a reality already, in the present.

It cannot be the task of this presentation of the main features
of Jesus' preaching to set forth his proclamation of God's will in
detail. Yet the question as to the overall character of this demand
cannot be passed over. In this connection it is helpful to come back

once again to the antitheses of the Sermon on the Mount. In the original antitheses Jesus sets his interpretation of the will of God in opposition to the commandment of Holy Scripture interpreted by tradition, and his authoritatively proclaimed interpretation in a given case goes beyond the traditional commandment: it is not only murder that incurs divine punishment, but even slander of one's neighbor falls under divine judgment; not only actual adultery is against God's will, but the lustful look at another woman already amounts to adultery; not only is frivolous swearing to one's own utterances contrary to God's will, but God rather expects of us a way of speaking in which any oath is unnecessary. In all these cases Jesus heightens the divine demand, and in doing so, agrees with many utterances of Jewish teachers; however, he does not do this by extending the law's validity to additional cases, as would correspond to rabbinical thinking, but by proclaiming God's will without any restriction as a claim laid upon the whole man. This state of things becomes still clearer when we focus our attention on the other three antitheses of the Sermon on the Mount, to which presumably Matthew first gave the antithetical form (Matt. 5:31-32; 38-39; 43-44 par.). Here in each case the Old Testament commandment is not intensified, but taken away, and God's unconditional will is put in its place: the issuing of a letter of divorce is not allowed, and the divorcing of a wife is rather forbidden altogether; no revenge of any kind is permitted, but the acceptance of further injury is commanded; no sort of hate is commanded, but love toward the very people who seek to injure us. In these cases what is involved cannot at all be the question of the correct limitation of an Old Testament commandment; instead, here Jesus is proclaiming on his own authority *God's absolute will* and thus is not binding man to a written or formulated norm, but to the will of the Father, which he is commissioned to proclaim: "Be merciful, as your Father is merciful" (Luke 6:36 par.) .

The encounter with the love of God

However, Jesus did not only talk of this Father, but by means of his conduct he caused the love of this Father to become reality. God's demand, as Jesus proclaims it, is therefore addressed to people who have encountered God in Jesus as the one who forgives and seeks out the sinner, and Jesus does not appeal to the good will or the moral responsibility of man, but points him to the God who confronts him. The parable of the unmerciful servant (Matt. 18:23 ff.) portrays a king who forgives a slave an improbably large debt, whereupon the slave goes out and drags a fellow slave to prison because of a small debt. When the master hears of this conduct, he is enraged and hands the ungrateful servant over to the jailers "until he has paid all he owes. Thus also will my heavenly Father do to you if you do not sincerely forgive your brother." In this parable, God, who forgives man a debt that could never be paid, clearly stands behind the king, and with this picture Jesus means to show that we must pass on to our fellowmen our thanks for the gift of forgiveness which we have received, if we actually have understood what God has given us through Jesus, and that God will not accept the scorning of his gift. Here the *experience of God's love* in the encounter with Jesus is quite clearly *the precondition and the enabling of obedience* to the demand of God proclaimed by Jesus. And entirely in keeping with this, Jesus' interpretation of his anointing by a sinful woman—"Her sins are forgiven, because she has loved much. But whoever has been forgiven little loves little" (Luke 7:47) —presupposes that this sinful woman could show such love only because through Jesus she had experienced divine love. Here also the capacity for love is the result of the divine love which has been received. Because Jesus thus lets God's demand be grounded in the reality of God's eschatological loving action which man encounters, he can sum up all God's demand in the commandment of love for God and for one's neighbor (Mark 12:28 ff. par.). A scribe asks Jesus about the first of all commandments, and by this he means the ordering principle from which all other commandments can be derived, without thereby reducing the obligation to obey. Jesus names not only *one* commandment, but alongside the confession, to be recited by every Jew daily, of the *one* God of Israel, whom one should love with the whole heart (Deut. 6:4-5), he places the commandment, "Thou shalt love thy neighbor as thyself" (Lev. 19:18), and concludes with the affirmation, "There is no other commandment greater than these." In the Jewish tradition there occurs occasionally a juxtaposition of the love of God and love of neighbor, but the coordinating of the two scriptural commandments on principle which Jesus undertakes appears nowhere else. But this coordination of them by Jesus unmistakably has the intention of naming all that man has to do in the sight of God: the response to the encounter with God in Jesus and to the promise of the kingdom of God can only be love for God which is actualized in love for one's neighbor. If love for one's neighbor grows out of the encounter with God's love and is inseparable from love for God, then such love for one's neighbor knows no limits: Jesus explicitly abolishes both cultic and national limitations on love (Mark 3:1 ff. par.; Luke 10:29 ff.). The reference to the analogy of self-love ("thou shalt love thy neighbor as thyself"), and above all the reference to God's example ("be merciful, as your Father is merciful"), show the limitlessness of the love which is the response to God's promise and gift of salvation. "Love, as Jesus demands it, knows no measure, because God in his love himself has no 'measure'" (E. Neuhäusler).

b. THE KINGDOM OF GOD AND THE IDEA OF REWARD AND PUNISHMENT

But with this insight we are put in a position of being able to understand why Jesus could connect man's actions with the promise of the kingdom of God by means of the conception of reward and punishment. We have seen that Jesus speaks without hesitation of reward and punishment which are to be meted out to men at the coming of the kingdom of God on the basis of their deeds. But it is important now to see that in so doing, Jesus does not simply adopt the ideas of reward of the Judaism of his time as a whole. Instead, he undertakes decisive deletions from the traditional conceptions.

(1) When Jesus speaks of retribution, he thinks only of the "treasure in heaven," the kingdom of God, eternal life, but absolutely *forbids thinking of earthly reward or punishment*. The tendency to regard earthly misfortune as punishment for special guilt is therefore just as much rejected by Jesus (Luke 13:1-5) as is the striving to gain recognition among men for one's good deeds: anyone who seeks such recognition has already, with it, been paid his reward in full (Matt. 6:2, 5, 16). Hence Jesus also refrains from any depiction of reward and punishment; the disciple must be satisfied with knowing, "Your Father who sees in secret will reward you" (Matt. 6:3, 6, 18). Even the idea of reward only gives expression to the promise that God will bestow his salvation.

(2) Jesus knows *no sort of balancing of guilt and achievement,* of reward and punishment. Man cannot gain special merit for himself by special exertion; he rather resembles the servant who after completing all the work assigned to him has no claim to thanks: "Thus you also should say, after you have done all that was assigned to you to do, 'We are unworthy servants, we have only done what we were obliged to do'" (Luke 17:10). Of the Pharisee who does significantly more than the law demands of him, and

holds this up before God—"God, I thank thee that I am not like other men, robbers, unjust, adulterers, or even like this tax-gatherer. I fast twice a week, and give tithes of all that I have"—Jesus says, "This man did not go home justified" (Luke 18:9-14). God requires that man be converted and take the narrow way (Luke 18: 13; 13:3, 5; Matt. 7:14), and according to Jesus' parable, God's response to such human behavior corresponds to the reaction of the master to his slave who has worked to the best of his ability with the money entrusted to him: 'Well done, good and loyal servant. You were faithful with a little, I will put you in charge of a lot. Enter into the joy of your master" (Matt. 25:21, 23). God certainly demands full obedience and the exclusive striving for God's kingdom, and only to such utter obedience does he promise the gift of sonship to God (Luke 6:32-35; 12:31 par.), but he demands and recognizes no special achievements (cf. Matt. 23:23a; b par.).

(3) This touches the crucial point at which Jesus is distinguished from the ideas of reward held by his Jewish contemporaries. Where one speaks of "reward," one is actually speaking of a claim, as Paul has fittingly formulated it: "Anyone who performs a work, to him the reward is not given according to grace, but on the basis of an obligation" (Rom. 4:4). But Jesus *disputes any claim* on man's part *to God's reward.* This is to be concluded from the just-mentioned parable of the slave (Luke 17:7-10), but it is inferred above all from the parable of the vineyard owner (Matt. 20:1-15). Five times during a harvest day this employer hires workers, and he agrees with those hired in the early morning on the usual day's wages of a denarius. When the time for paying wages in the evening comes, each of the workers receives a denarius, regardless of the length of his labor. To the murmuring of those who have toiled the whole day long, the employer responds: "Friend, I am not doing you any wrong; did you not agree for a denarius [as pay]? Take what is yours and go; but I *will* to give this last man the same as you received. Am I not free to do as I will with my possessions? Or is your eye evil [i.e., are you envious] because I am generous?" It is explicitly stressed that this employer acts above reproach, legally speaking, and yet every hearer has the feeling that this justice is unjust. For again, undoubtedly behind the employer is concealed God, who declares without any restraint that he has the right to give rewards in the measure corresponding to his goodness. In this parable the emphasis lies solely on the point that no claim of any kind can be raised against God, that God's reward

is a gift of free goodness. To use Paul's language, God's reward is not based on an obligation, but God gives his reward out of gracious intention.

When Jesus nevertheless adopts the traditional talk of reward, this is undoubtedly because the demand for obedience to God's will would lose its seriousness if God did not react to man's actions. Of course the God of whose reward and punishment Jesus speaks is not the righteous judge who especially rewards special achievement (in Luke 18:9 ff. Jesus specifically rejects this), but the merciful Father who promises his love to the sinners who are converted, and whose love that seeks out sinners Jesus causes to become a reality. In the presence of this God there is no claim, but this God even now lets his salvation come to be a present reality in Jesus and promises heavenly reward to those who embrace this salvation in Jesus and conduct themselves on the basis of this salvation. That God forgives and that God recompenses is therefore a truth which belongs in Jesus' announcement and actualization of the divine salvation, and the special character of Jesus' preaching of reward and punishment is also conditioned by the divine salvation event which Jesus announces and actualizes. Only when we have understood what role Jesus ascribed to his own person in the context of his proclamation will we therefore be able entirely to grasp Jesus' preaching of God's action and his proclamation of God's will.

5. Jesus' personal claim

We have seen, in the consideration of his preaching of God's kingdom, his proclamation of God, and his interpretation of God's will, that Jesus ascribed to his person an important significance in the context of his proclamation of salvation. Of course, the question as to *what* role Jesus attributed to himself and what weight this personal claim had in the total context of his preaching is most sharply disputed. Indeed, all the gospels are written with the express intention of proclaiming the good news of Jesus Christ, the Son of God (Mark 1:1; cf. Matt. 1:1; Luke 3:22-23, 38), and this intention had already stamped the tradition even *before* the gospels, as is shown, for example, by the narrative about the baptism of Jesus in Mark 1:9-11 par. (see below). In view of this interest which marks the tradition, it is particularly difficult to determine which was the earliest tradition and which ideas and concepts could or must go back to Jesus himself.

a. JESUS' DEEDS

Therefore it is advisable not to start out with an examination of the honorific titles, but first to ask how Jesus spoke of his person and his work in the context of his proclamation of the coming of God's kingdom. There the first thing that strikes the eye is that Jesus is reported not only to have preached, but also to have performed certain deeds which evoked astonishment. Jesus himself points to these deeds in his answer to the Baptist (Matt. 11:4-5 par.; see above, p. 36), and the ruler Antipas, who was by no means kindly disposed toward Jesus, concurred in the rumor which he heard, which was circulating among the people, that Jesus' amazing deeds were to be explained by the fact that in him John the Baptist, who had been put to death by Antipas, had appeared again: "And King Herod heard [of Jesus], for his name had become well known, and people were saying that John the Baptist had risen from the dead and because of this the powers were at work in him . . . . When Herod heard this, he said, 'John, whom I had beheaded, has been raised'" (Mark 6:14, 16 par.). That Jesus performed deeds which people were bound to sense as extraordinary therefore is just as certainly attested by Jesus' own reference as by the assertion of contemporaries who stood at a distance from Jesus. But in fact we also have in the gospels a great number of reports of healings, cases of awakening the dead, and so-called "nature miracles" of Jesus, yet the opinions have always diverged over the historical worth and the significance of these reports. Now it is indisputable that these reports have their parallels in what people in Jesus' time told of miraculous deeds of saving deities, of the emperors, of certain pagan savior figures, but also, in somewhat different form, of Jewish teachers, and there are numerous analogies, especially in details, between these non-Christian miracle stories and those in the gospels. But it is equally obvious that certain kinds of miracle stories from the environment are not found at all, or are found only in isolated places, in the gospels (punitive miracles, self-help miracles, miracles of reward, miracles as demonstration of magical ability; exceptions that must be critically evaluated are in Matt. 17:24 ff.; Mark 11:12 ff. par.). But it particularly needs to be said that indeed many of the gospel accounts show a striking correspondence to the miracle stories of the surrounding world with their magical practices and the lack of a personal connection between the miracle-worker and the person healed (e.g., the healing of the blind man, Mark 8:22-26), while other reports hardly display any such features (as, for example, the healing of the withered hand, Mark 3:1-5 par.). This religio-historical observation agrees with the form-critical observation that those accounts which exhibit abundant "miraculous" features as a rule also teach nothing about Jesus and his message, while in the other accounts Jesus' deed affords the setting for a discussion of Jesus and his teaching. While it appears evident from these observations that the accounts of extraordinary deeds of Jesus in the gospels by no means bear the same character, it is equally clear that a part of the reports are firmly anchored in the earliest tradition by the fact that here Jesus in his distinctiveness and Jesus' preaching in a certain regard are set forth in the context of the narration of one of Jesus' deeds, and thus that Jesus, and not simply a miraculous event, is set before the gaze of the listener. If there can be no doubt about the historical reliability of such accounts, yet on the other hand it must remain questionable whether the reports that are primarily or exclusively interested in the miraculous event originally had anything at all to do with Jesus or at least represent cases of recasting a more original narrative. A certain answer to this question cannot be given in all cases, but in no case may the answer proceed from the presupposition that no claim to historical originality can be made for any account which goes beyond the experience that is known to us or that could be comprehended by ourselves. For the conception of the causal necessity from which there can be no exceptions is wholly foreign to ancient man, apart from isolated skeptics, and for Jesus, who reckons with God's sovereign power, such a conception is all the more impossible. If one takes this insight seriously, then for example the story of the centurion of Capernaum (Matt. 8:5-10, 13 par.) is seen to be an account in which Jesus' relation to his people and to the Gentiles and the question of faith toward Jesus are put into words, while the healing of the centurion's son (or servant) is reported without any interest in details. Therefore there is no hesitation in acknowledging the narrative as a report from Jesus' life, and the fact that this healing is performed from a distance, indeed without Jesus' speaking a single healing word, may not be used as an objection to this acknowledgment merely on the grounds that such an occurrence is contrary to our experience and is not rationally explainable. Conversely, however, the narrative of Jesus' expelling the demons from a possessed man, and sending them into a herd of swine which then runs into the sea and drowns (Mark 5:1-20 par.), shows us a very striking miraculous action of Jesus, one that is not altogether clear as to its meaning. But it does not disclose anything at all of the particularity of Jesus' person and proclamation. Therefore it must be described as very doubtful whether this account goes back to the earliest tradition and relates an occurrence from the life of Jesus. Yet, as we have already said, the question as to the historical reliability of the individual report cannot always be settled with certainty, and for the understanding of Jesus' personal claim, it also is unnecessary to ask how many astounding deeds Jesus did and what may be recognized or presumed as what happened in a particular case. The only thing decisive for our present context is the question of what meaning Jesus assigned to his deeds in the context of his proclamation of the coming of the kingdom of God.

First of all, it is clear that in Jesus' opinion his deeds can and should have no power of proof of any kind for his divine commission and for the decision concerning his person. This already appears from the fact that Jesus' adversaries can attempt to trace his power over the demons back to a league with the prince of demons: "With the help of the chief of demons he expels the demons" (Mark 3:22b par.); thus one by no means can unequivocally recognize that God is at work in Jesus' deeds. That Jesus' deeds possess no force of proof appears even more clearly from Jesus' rejection of the charge that he is in league with the prince of demons: "If I with the help of Beelzebub am driving out the demons, with whose help do your sons drive them out? Therefore *they* will be your judges" (Matt. 12:27 par.). For here Jesus recognizes without mincing matters that Jewish exorcists also have power over the demons similar to his, and with them precisely as with Jesus, one cannot know at once what is the source of their power. But Jesus not only affirms that his deeds have no demonstrative character; he even explicitly refuses to prove by any kind of deeds that God has sent him: "And the Pharisees went and began to dispute with him by demanding from him a sign from heaven and thus they put him to the test. And he sighed in the spirit and said: 'Why does this generation seek a sign? Truly, I tell you, no sign will be given to this generation'" (Mark 8:11-12 par.). Thus the adversaries wish to have an unequivocal proof that Jesus is sent from God, but Jesus unqualifiedly refuses to fulfill this demand. This is the way Mark at least has handed down Jesus' answer. Of course, according to the parallel tradition in the Sayings source, Jesus declares: "No sign will be given to this generation but the sign of Jonah" (Luke 11:29 par.). If the assumption, which has much in its favor, is correct that the Sayings source has preserved this saying of Jesus in a more nearly original version than Mark, it still is uncertain what was meant by "the sign of Jonah" on Jesus' lips (most likely: the Son of Man will appear to this generation, like Jonah to the Ninevites, as a preacher of judgment); but even in this version Jesus refuses to give a demonstrative sign which people were demanding of him as legitimation. According to Jesus' own statement, his deeds can be understood in their true nature only when one hears the message which accompanies his actions.

Now Jesus has plainly interpreted these actions: "If I by the finger of God am driving out the demons, then the kingdom of God has come to you" (Luke 11:20 par.). In Jesus' mighty acts God is acting, the coming kingdom of God is dawning. And precisely the same appears from the answer, already frequently cited, which Jesus gave to the Baptist's query from prison: "Blind men see and lame men walk, lepers are becoming clean and deaf men hear, and dead men are raised and the good news is being proclaimed to the poor; and blessed is the one who does not stumble at me" (Matt. 11:5-6 par.). Here not only is Jesus' activity portrayed as fulfillment of the Old Testament promise of salvation, but it is also explicitly added here that, in spite of these visible events, people can stumble at Jesus, that is, that they can also fail to recognize an eschatological saving event in these deeds and therefore also can fail to note that here God is causing his rule to become effective. And in a lament over the cities of Chorazin and Bethsaida Jesus says: "If the mighty deeds had occurred in Tyre and Sidon which have occurred among you, they would long ago have repented in sackcloth and ashes. But I say to you, it will be more tolerable on the judgment day for Tyre and Sidon than for you" (Matt. 11:21-22 par.; in Matt. 11:23-24 par. there follows a parallel utterance about Capernaum and Sodom). Thus Jesus had done mighty acts in the Jewish towns of Chorazin and Bethsaida (the gospels do not relate *these* deeds of Jesus), but the inhabitants had not felt prompted thereby to any kind of consequences, and Jesus thought that the inhabitants of the Gentile cities of Tyre and Sidon would have responded differently if such deeds of Jesus had come to their attention. Thus Jesus' deeds are unequivocal in their event character, but a person can perceive them without noting what actually is taking place. Jesus' miracles are proofs only for the person who is ready also to hear the interpretation of these miracles.

Therefore Jesus refuses to perform mighty acts whenever he is convinced that people are not ready also to listen to the meaning of his deeds. This is evident not only from his refusal to give a demonstrative sign, but especially from the account of his lack of success in Nazareth: "He came to his home town, and his disciples followed him. And when the sabbath came, he began to teach in the synagogue, and the crowd heard [him] and was amazed and said: 'Whence does he get these things, and what sort of wisdom is this that is given to him, and what sort are these wonders done by his hands? Is this not the son of the carpenter and Mary, and the brother of James and Joses and Judas and Simon? And are not his sisters with us?' And they were offended at him. And Jesus said to them: 'No prophet is honored in his own home town or among his kinsmen or in his family.' And he was unable to do any mighty deeds there, except for healing a few sick people by laying his hands on them. And he was amazed at their unbelief" (Mark 6:1-6 par.). Of course this narrative (which was made weaker quite early [cf. Matt. 13:58] because people were offended by it and which for that very reason must be regarded as historically reliable) does not mean to say that Jesus could do no miracles in his home town because in the absence of an echo he remains powerless—the qualification mentioned, that he healed a few sick people, argues against that. What is meant is rather that Jesus could not feel himself prompted to work wonders when he encountered in Nazareth such a fundamentally skeptical attitude toward his person. In Jesus' mighty deeds one can recognize who this wonder-worker is and what is happening through him, if one is ready to believe him, but without such belief Jesus' deeds are ineffective upon the people of his surroundings. Anyone who refuses to hear Jesus' call to repentance will also fail to benefit from marvelous deeds. Jesus makes this clear in the parable of the rich man and poor Lazarus: from hell the rich man begs Abraham to send Lazarus, who also has died, to his brothers on earth to call them to repentance, but Abraham answers: "If they will not listen to Moses and the prophets, they also will not heed even if one should rise from the dead" (Luke 16:27-31). Even the greatest miracle cannot teach anything to the person who is determined not to hear.

b. BELIEF IN JESUS?

But even if Jesus' miracles are only a reference to the happening of the kingdom of God and require interpretation, still they clearly show that Jesus ascribes to his person a decisive role in the eschatological saving event. We have also seen that the evangelist Mark described the resistance to Jesus by the residents of Nazareth as "unbelief" (Mark 6:6 par.). Did Jesus then demand belief in his person? This is unlikely, because though it is true that in the synoptic gospels faith is often spoken of, yet never in early tradition is anything said of "faith in Jesus" or "believing Jesus." Jesus speaks, rather, of faith in God and expects his disciples to have a faith which trusts God for the most impossible thing and does not let itself be shaken by anything: "If you had faith as a grain of mustard seed, you would say to this mountain, 'Be moved from here to there,' and it would be moved, and nothing will be impossible to you" (Matt. 17:20 par.); and when the disciples could not help a demon-possessed boy, Jesus said, "You faithless generation, how long shall I be with you? . . . All things are possible to one who believes" (Mark 9:19 par., 23). He rebukes the disciples who are frightened in the storm: "Why are you fearful? Have you no faith?" (Mark 4:40 par.). And Jesus calls the people who are anxious about food and clothing "people of little faith" (Matt. 6:30 par.). Thus for Jesus faith is the daring trust in God's concern and help to which Jesus would like to lead his disciples. But along with these, we find a number of sayings of Jesus in which faith in view of Jesus the wonder-worker is spoken of. To the Roman centurion in Capernaum who credits Jesus with being able to heal his son (or servant) with a mere word, Jesus says, "Truly, I tell you, I have not found such great faith in anyone in Israel" (Matt. 8:10 par.); Jesus commands the blind Bartimaeus, who with the cry "Son of David, have mercy on me!" asks Jesus for healing of his blindness, "Go, your faith has saved you" (Mark 10:52 par.). This is quite in harmony with Jesus' word to the ruler of the synagogue, Jairus, who had asked for healing for his daughter and whom people sought to dissuade from further pleading with the news of the daughter's death: "Fear not, only believe!" (Mark 5:36 par.). In fact, the early tradition, where it tells of a lame man who is lowered through the roof to Jesus, also speaks of faith in the same way: "When Jesus saw their faith . . ." (Mark 2:5 par.). Hence it has often been assumed that, in these contexts, faith is supposed to designate nothing but confidence in Jesus' miraculous power. Of course such belief in Jesus the wonder-worker would stand utterly without connection alongside the faith in God which Jesus calls for, and this is impossible in the light of Mark 9:19 par., 23, where the disciples' unbelief is clearly traced to the fact that the disciples have not let themselves be led by Jesus to real faith. Moreover, Matt. 7:24 par. ("Everyone who hears my words and does them is like a wise man who built his house upon the rock") and the rejection of the pronouncement of Jesus' mother's blessedness in Luke 11:28 ("Blessed rather are those who hear and observe God's word") show that Jesus expects that in listening to *his* word man comes to faith and obedience toward God. In fact, the acknowledgment anticipated by Jesus that in his driving out the demons God's kingdom is actualized (Matt. 12:28 par.) presupposes that in Jesus' actions one encounters, by faith, God's redemptive activity. Even if Jesus did not speak of faith in his person, still for him the encounter with God's eschatological kingdom depends entirely on the believing encounter with his actions and his teachings, in which God's eschatological redemptive activity is realized.

In harmony with this is the fact that Jesus explicitly spoke of the meaning of his coming and of his being sent by God. "Do not think that I have come to bring peace on the earth; I have not come to bring peace, but a sword . . ." (Matt. 10:34 par.); this says nothing else but that Jesus' coming produces a division among people according to their attitude toward Jesus. Luke 12:49 perhaps is also to be understood similarly: "I have come to bring fire upon the earth, and would that it were already kindled," i.e., the sending of Jesus has the effect of the judgment fire which separates wheat and chaff, but, in any case, here too an eschatological effect is attributed to Jesus' coming. Matt. 5:17 also shows that Jesus ascribes to himself an eschatological task: "Do not think that I have come to destroy the law and the prophets; I have not come to destroy but to fulfill" (see above, p. 53). Here Jesus identifies himself as the authorized and authoritative interpreter of the word of God and speaks of a divine mission: "I am sent only to the lost sheep of the house of Israel" (Matt. 15:24). In the light of all this, we cannot doubt that Jesus attributed to his commission and his work a central significance in the eschatological redemptive event which he proclaimed and brought.

C. JESUS THE PROPHET?

People have often sought to find justification for this interpretation of his mission by Jesus in the fact that Jesus claimed for himself the role of a prophet, and in favor of this assumption one can argue, on the one hand, that Jesus explains the negative attitude of his countrymen in Nazareth toward him with the proverb: "No prophet is honored in his own country and among his kinsmen and his family" (Mark 6:4 par.), and that Jesus said of his ultimate fate: "Today and tomorrow and the day after I must go on my way, for it cannot be that a prophet should perish away from Jerusalem" (Luke 13:33). On the other hand, one can point out that Jesus exhibits definite characteristics of prophetic behavior: the demand for repentance (Luke 13:3, 5); predictions of the future (Matt. 23:38 par.; Mark 13:2 par.); announcement of the imminent end (Mark 1:15 par.); and visions (Luke 10:18). Moreover, there can be no doubt that during his lifetime Jesus was regarded as a prophet (Mark 6:15 par.; 8:28 par.; 14:65 par.; Matt. 21:46; according to Luke 7:39 a Pharisee rejected this judgment because of Jesus' having something to do with a sinful woman). But it by no means follows from all this that Jesus thought of himself as a prophet. For the traditional formulations in Mark 6:4 par. and Luke 13:33 prove nothing about Jesus' own language, and the rest of the tradition contains not a single utterance in which Jesus describes himself as a prophet. Instead, Jesus plainly declared that he was not rightly understood with the designation of "prophet": "The men of Nineveh will arise at the judgment with this generation and condemn it; for they repented at the preaching of Jonah, and behold, something greater than Jonah is here" (Matt. 12:41 [RSV] par.; cf. also Matt. 12:42 par.). Thus it cannot be surprising that Jesus was convinced that the age of the prophets had ended with John the Baptist: "The law and the prophets [were in force] until John; from the days of John the Baptist until now the kingdom of God suffers violence, and men of violence plunder it" (Luke 16:16a; Matt. 11:12). Here Jesus clearly affirms that with his coming the time of the law and the prophets is ended, and this is in harmony not only with Jesus' claim to be proclaiming God's will definitively on his own authority ("But I say to you . . . ," Matt. 5:22, 28, 34; see above, pp. 52-53), but also with his bold thesis that his words will abide forever: "Heaven and earth will pass away, but my words shall not pass away" (Mark 13: 31 par.).

d. THE MESSIAH

Thus the question as to what significance Jesus ascribed to his own person in the context of his preaching of the coming of God's kingdom and of the will of God leads to the unequivocal recognition that in his teaching and actions Jesus saw God's eschatological redemptive activity realized, and therefore confronted the people whom he encountered with the decision whether they were ready to acknowledge this claim or whether they rejected it. Yet

the clarity with which this state of affairs may be seen is matched
by the lack of indication of what Jesus saw as the basis for this
claim and what further expectations were connected with this
claim. And the question is unavoidably posed whether Jesus did
not also clothe this claim in one of the forms which were available
in the *Jewish expectation of the end-time* of his day. This question
is already suggested because the gospel tradition has Jesus unequivocally using at least the titles "Son" and "Son of Man," and
unequivocally answering in the affirmative the question whether he
is "the anointed one." But it is also suggested because the Judaism
of Jesus' time had a very lively but also highly variegated expectation of the bringer of salvation, and it would be surprising, to say
the least, if in view of his so lofty personal claim Jesus had not been
confronted with these expectations.

Of course we should not forget that the Jewish expectation of the
coming kingdom of God or, more broadly speaking, of the final
judgment and salvation, by no means necessarily, and therefore by
no means always, was bound up with the expectation of an eschatological bringer of salvation. For example, of the Jewish writings
labeled "Apocrypha" in Christian Bibles, Tobit and Judith are not
acquainted with such a figure, and the same is true, among the
other Jewish writings of the last century before Christ, of the Book
of Jubilees or the "Ascension of Moses" (in this Pharisaic apocalypse composed in the first Christian decades, God himself appears to sit in judgment and to destroy Satan). But among the
people the expectation of an eschatological bringer of salvation
must have been so widely spread that "false" messianic figures
appeared and gained acceptance (cf. Acts 5:36-37), and that a warning had to be issued against the readiness to giving credence to
such figures (Mark 13:6-7; 13:21-22 par.). Numerous Jewish writings of the post-Old Testament times therefore are acquainted with
the expectation of a bringer of salvation, of course in very diverse
form, and these forms cannot always be sharply distinguished from
one another. Yet one can, with good reasons, distinguish three forms
of the expectation of a bringer of salvation in the Judaism of that
time: the Messiah, the king of the house of David; the eschatological
high priest from the house of Aaron; and the "Son of Man" coming
from heaven. In the synoptic gospels the expectation of a messianic
high priest is completely lacking while the other two forms of the
expectation of a bringer of salvation occur either directly or indirectly on the lips of Jesus. The question whether Jesus adopted
these forms of Jewish expectation of a bringer of salvation, or at

least had to come to grips with them, suggests itself therefore in the gospel accounts.

One will properly start with the expectation of an "anointed one," because Mark described his book as "good news of Jesus *Christ*" (1:1), and he reports Jesus' affirmative answer to the high priest's question whether he is "the anointed one, the son of the Blessed" (Mark 14:61-62 par.). The expectation of an "anointed one" (Hebrew *māshiah,* grecized *Messias,* translated into Greek *Christos,* Latin *Christus*) is relatively seldom attested in Judaism from the beginning of the second century B.C. down to the destruction of Jerusalem. Yet it is also found very emphatically as the hope of an earthly king, a son of David, the "anointed of the Lord," who will smash the political enemies of the Jewish people and will rule over the sinless holy people of God (thus in the Pharisaic "Psalms of Solomon" in the first century B.C.; text in C. K. Barrett, pp. 248-50). This expectation is further found as the hope of the "anointed one of righteousness" or the "anointed one of Israel," an eschatological prince, who however is not always clearly identified as David's descendant (thus among the pious of Qumran; see 4Q patr. 3-4; 1Q Sa II, 14; cf. Gaster, *Dead Sea Scriptures,* p. 329). This political hope of an eschatological earthly "anointed one" must have been very lively among the people, as the warnings in the gospels show (see above). One also sees it, above all, in the fifteenth petition of the Eighteen Benedictions which were to be said daily, whose wording, to be sure, is first attested with certainty from the time shortly after the destruction of Jerusalem: "Cause the shoot of David quickly to sprout, and let his horn be lifted up by thy help!" But recent studies have shown that the title "the anointed one" also appears in the context of other eschatological hopes, thus for the "Son of Man" (to be discussed later) in the pre-Christian "Similitudes" of the Ethiopic Book of Enoch (see in C. K. Barrett, p. 252), or for a prophetic figure who is described as a "messenger of joy" of the end-time, thus in an only recently published text from Cave 11 at Qumran. All this means that the designation "the anointed one" for the bringer of salvation indeed was used primarily for the political expectation of the end-time, but certainly also in other contexts, so that only the context can tell us about the precise meaning of the designation. It certainly was not necessary for Jewish expectation of the bearer of salvation in Jesus' time to use the title "the anointed one," yet the use of this title in this or that context was obviously suggested, and it would not be at all surprising if it should also have played a role in the context of Jesus' appearing on the scene.

The word "Christ" as a self-designation on the lips of Jesus does not occur in the synoptic gospels in the early texts (Matt. 23:10 and Mark 9:41 are clearly secondary). And the two passages in which Jesus is confronted with this title are historically very difficult. In the narrative in Mark 8:27-30 par. Jesus himself, in the vicinity of Caesarea Philippi, poses to his disciples the question of whom the people hold him to be, and receives the answer: "John the Baptist, others say Elijah, and others, one of the prophets." To the further question, "Whom do you consider me to be?" Peter answers, "you are the anointed one." The account then concludes with the remark, "And he warned them that they should tell no one of him." Two facts argue for the early date of this account: the indication of the place, which does not occur elsewhere in the synoptic gospels in connection with such a didactic report and shows Jesus far removed from the other places of his activity, and the conclusion of the account. The prohibition to repeat the confession of Jesus the Messiah is in harmony with the evangelist's view of the messianic secret which Jesus requires to be preserved (cf. Mark 3:12); it therefore hardly belongs to the original report. This command to silence however must have replaced the original conclusion of the story, and this breaking off of the original conclusion, the reaction of Jesus, which probably came to be regarded as no longer tolerable, likewise argues for the great age of the account. But when Jesus according to this account receives the answer to his question about the disciples' opinion of him that they held him to be the Messiah, this answer of Peter can only have had the meaning that the disciples expected that Jesus would appear as the ruler of the end-time sent by God, since the present Jesus in fact exhibited nothing of such lordly dignity. But even if it should be true that Peter's confession was uttered in this sense, the disciples hardly held to this, as their behavior in the passion narrative proves. Since the original conclusion of the account is not preserved, we also do not know how Jesus reacted to this confession. The conjecture has been suggested in various forms that Jesus' reaction to Peter's messianic confession is preserved in the saying of Jesus which follows shortly thereafter in Mark: "Get behind me, Satan, for your ideas are not those of God, but of men" (Mark 8:33). But this is untenable, because the first Christian community, which confessed Jesus as the Messiah, would never have transmitted unaltered an account in which Jesus rejected this confession as satanic. Thus the story of Peter's confession at Caesarea Philippi only lets us see that in the circle of Jesus' disciples such a confession was possible, at least at times, but teaches us nothing about Jesus' attitude toward this expectation of a bearer of salvation which was connected with him.

On the other hand, a direct comment of Jesus on this expectation is contained in the account of *Jesus' trial before the Sanhedrin* (Mark 14:53-65, esp. 14:61-62 par.). According to this account, after his arrest Jesus was brought by night into the house of the high priest, where the entire Sanhedrin was assembled, and there he was first accused of having predicted the destruction of the earthly temple and the building of a new temple not made with hands. When this accusation proved unusable because of the differences in what the witnesses said, especially since Jesus did not express himself on the matter, the high priest asked Jesus: " 'Are you the anointed one, the Son of the Blessed?' And Jesus said, 'I am, and you shall see the Son of Man sitting at the right hand of power and coming with the clouds of heaven.' Then the high priest tore his garments and said, 'Why do we need more witnesses? You have heard the blasphemy: what is your opinion?' And all of them condemned him, saying that he should be put to death." According to this account Jesus unequivocally answered the high priest's question in the affirmative and interpreted it with a prediction about the coming of the Son of Man. Of course the historicity of the report is much disputed: it is pointed out that the Christians could know nothing certain about what went on in the high priest's house, since none of the disciples was present at the proceedings; some emphasize that the nighttime hearing, the condemnation in the same session in which the hearing took place, and the condemnation for blasphemy without Jesus' having used the name of God would all contradict what we know of the rabbinical law governing trials; besides, the account in Mark 14:55-65 is said to be a disruptive insertion into the story of Peter's denial in Mark 14:53-54, 66 ff.; further, the account in Mark 15:1, "Early in the morning the chief priests, together with the elders and scribes and the whole Sanhedrin drew up a decision, and had Jesus bound and led away and handed over to Pilate," does not presuppose any prior nighttime condemnation by the Sanhedrin. But all these objections are hardly convincing (cf. also the commentaries on Mark 14:53-72). It is entirely likely that the first Christians, after they came to believe in the resurrection of the crucified One, could and did secure adequate reports about what happened at

Jesus' condemnation from members of the Sanhedrin; the points in the Markan account which conflict with the Pharisaic trial law are not weighty, because no one can say whether the detailed provisions of the codified Pharisaic law of the end of the second century A.D. already existed in Jesus' time and, if they did exist, were acknowledged as binding by the members of the Sanhedrin which, in the majority, was hardly pharisaically minded; the insertion of the account of the trial before the Sanhedrin into the story of Peter's denial corresponds to a literary method also used by Mark elsewhere (cf. only Mark 6:14-29 between 6:6-13 and 6:30-31), and therefore it does not prove that the account of the trial before the high priest in Mark 14:55-65 did not belong to the earliest tradition of the passion narrative. Thus if the objections against the great age and hence against the historical reliability of this account are by no means compelling, still the report that early in the morning the Sanhedrin "drew up" a decision and thereupon handed Jesus over to Pilate (Mark 15:1) of course arouses the suspicion that with his formulation, "They all condemned him as being worthy of death" (Mark 14:64), Mark has not entirely accurately described what took place. For even the further account of Jesus' trial before Pilate does not betray the fact that a formal judgment against Jesus had already been issued (esp. Mark 15:3, 13-14). But this contradiction disappears if we assume that the hearing before the Sanhedrin did not end with a formal condemnation of Jesus, but that this hearing was meant only to enable the members of the Sanhedrin to form a clear opinion in favor of surrendering Jesus to Pilate. If this conjecture is correct, then there is no need to call in question the historicity of the entire account of the proceedings against Jesus before the Sanhedrin, in its essential features.

In the context of this report now Jesus answers the high priest's question whether he is "the anointed one, the Son of the Blessed": "I am, and you shall see the Son of Man sitting on the right hand of power and coming with the clouds of heaven" (Mark 14:60-61). Of course the high priest's question was hardly worded in exactly the way Mark gives it, since "Son of God" was not a Jewish designation for the bearer of salvation (see below, p. 74). But in view of the political accusation with which the Jewish authorities must have delivered Jesus over to Pilate, it is highly probable that Jesus was asked about his position on the Jewish expectation of a royal "anointed one." Jesus' answer to this question is affirmative, and it elucidates this "yes" by saying that the Son of Man will sit at the right hand of God and will come with the clouds of heaven. It is obvious that in this answer Dan. 7:13 ("There came one with the clouds of heaven who was like a son of man") is combined with Ps. 110:1 ("The Lord said to my Lord, 'Sit at my right hand' "), which is applied to the eschatological Messiah. Some have described the combination of two biblical texts like these on Jesus' lips as just as inconceivable as the interpretation of the expectation of an "anointed one" by the expectation of the "Son of Man." But these objections unjustifiably presuppose that Jesus' thinking can only have moved along traditional lines. Mark 14:62 is rather an important indication that Jesus by no means rejected the expectation of an "anointed one," which indeed was not at all unequivocally fixed, yet he apparently did not see it in an adequately clear characterization of his mission and therefore did not use this title on his own initiative.

A notice which could be described as the only "non-Christian" notice about Jesus in the synoptic gospels, the *inscription on the cross,* shows that Jesus, even if he himself did not use the designation "the anointed one" to identify his personal claim, indeed must have made a claim which suggested this identification and thus also the high priest's question to him. This indication of the offense for which the penalty of crucifixion had been imposed on the criminal read, according to the earliest gospel, "The king of the Jews" (Mark 15:26). But this wording can be explained neither from Jewish presuppositions nor from Christian usage; for a Jew would have said, "The king, the anointed one" or, at the very most "the king of Israel" (cf. Mark 15:32 par.), and the Christians call Christ at the most "king of kings" (Rev. 17:14). On the other hand, the wording is easily explained as a Roman designation of the earthly ruler over the Jewish people (cf. Mark 15:2), and "the king of the Jews" occurs elsewhere only from the pen of the Greek historian Strabo and written for non-Jews by the Jewish historian Josephus (Josephus, Antiquities 14.36 and 16.311). Moreover, that "the Jews" was a non-Jewish and above all a Roman designation of the Jewish people is strikingly shown by an inscription, recently discovered at the Dead Sea but not yet published, on the shard of a wine tankard that came from Rome. The inscription reads: "The Jewish Herod." But if Jesus was condemned by Pilate as a claimant to the political rule over the Jewish people—and according to the inscription on the cross, this may be considered as certain as the fact of the crucifixion itself—then his preaching or his behavior must have given some kind of occasion for this accusation.

Of course it is certain that Jesus held no political aspirations.

When he was asked by the Pharisees about the justification for payment of the poll tax to the Roman emperor, because this poll tax was in dispute as a sign of the anti-godly subjection to the Romans, he thrust aside as unimportant this political problem which was important to the Pharisees, because only obedience to God is decisive (Mark 12:13 ff. par.) ; and Jesus did not promise a Jewish government in place of the Roman, but he demanded of his disciples service instead of the lordship customary among the Gentiles (Mark 10:42-43 par.). And in two sayings which cannot be explained with certainty, "I have come not to bring peace, but a sword" (Matt. 10:34), and "let him who has no sword sell his cloak and buy one!" (Luke 22:35-38), the word "sword" can only be used in a figurative sense (see commentaries).

e. THE SON OF DAVID

But above all, Jesus apparently rejected for himself the title "Son of David" for the expected political Messiah. It is true that it is reported in ancient tradition that a blind beggar cried out to Jesus for help with the words, "Son of David, have pity on me!" (Mark 10:47-48 par.), and it is entirely possible that this designation of the political savior was occasionally used with reference to Jesus. That Jesus belonged to David's family is an ancient and never-doubted Christian tradition (Rom. 1:3), which also underlies the later story of the birth of Jesus (Luke 2:1-7) and the similarly later genealogies (Matt. 1:2-17; Luke 3:23-38). To be sure the tradition does not tell us how Jesus reacted to being addressed as "Son of David," and we are lacking any indication that Jesus ever stressed his Davidic ancestry. It is even likely that he regarded this ancestry as unimportant. For according to Mark 12:35-37 par., Jesus himself posed the problem of how the expectation that the Messiah should be a son of David could be harmonized with the fact that in Psalm 110:1, obviously applied by the Judaism of that time to the Messiah, David calls the Messiah "my Lord." If this story goes back to Jesus (and there is much to argue that it does; see the commentaries on the passage), then the question, "David calls him [the Messiah] Lord, and how is he then his son?" can only be saying that Jesus rejects the religious meaning of the designation "Son of David" because the Messiah really is David's Lord and thus stands high above David. But then this clearly says that Jesus rejects for himself the expectation of a son of David who should fulfill the political hopes. Moreover, it follows that Jesus was unjustly condemned by the Romans under the charge of seeking to be a political claimant to power.

f. THE SON OF GOD

If Jesus thus made no political claims to lordship and further did not apply to himself the titles "the anointed one" and "the Son of David," still, as we have seen, he must have given occasion of some sort for such an accusation. According to the gospel tradition Jesus did in fact use two titles of honor for himself, that of the "Son," and that of the "Son of Man," and it must be asked whether from this fact the personal claim of Jesus in its real sense can be explained and the occasion for Jesus' condemnation as a political pretender can be made comprehensible.

It is beyond any doubt that the authors of all three synoptic gospels saw in Jesus the Son of God, as is already proved by the heavenly voice (reported by them in substantial agreement) at Jesus' baptism and transfiguration, "You are my beloved son" (Mark 1:11 par.; 9:7 par.). It is all the more striking that in the Synoptics, "Son of God" does not occur on the lips of Jesus at all and only once is attributed to Jesus on the cross by the jeering crowd: "He said, 'I am the Son of God' " (Matt. 27:43); but this is obviously an addition by Matthew. Thus Jesus certainly did not use the title "Son of God." This is only to be expected; for "Son of God" was not a Jewish designation of the hoped-for bearer of salvation, as the total absence of this designation in Jewish tradition shows. For this reason it is also historically extremely unlikely that Jesus was addressed by demon-possessed men as "Son of God" (Mark 3:11 par.; 5:7 par.) and that at the trial the high priest should have added to the question, "Are you the anointed one?" the phrase, "the Son of the Blessed" (see above, p. 71). Yet even the historical reliability of these reports would not nullify the thesis that Jesus did not call himself "Son of God."

Some have suggested that even without using this title, Jesus was conscious in a special sense of being God's Son, as is shown by his baptismal experience, by his way of addressing God, and above all by his self-designation as "the Son." Of course the narrative of *Jesus' baptism* (Mark 1:9-11 par.; see above, p. 31) can scarcely be employed biographically. It is true that it not only is certain that Jesus was baptized by John the Baptist, but it is also probable that at this baptism he had an experience that was crucial for his activity, since the shifting of such an experience to the baptismal event is not obvious from the content in meaning of this action.

The baptismal account adopted by Mark uses the words of God's address to the king in Ps. 2:7, which are applied to the Messiah: "You are my beloved son," in order to express by means of this heavenly voice the belief that at the baptism Jesus was installed by God in the position of his Son. But even if, as indeed can with good reason only be *surmised*, Psalm 2 should already have been applied to the Messiah by the Jews in Jesus' time, still the designation of the Messiah as "Son of God" was not Jewish, and therefore it is unlikely that this heavenly voice precisely repeats an experience related by Jesus, especially since elsewhere in the Jesus tradition there is no reference by Jesus back to his calling to be God's Son. It is by no means certainly attested even that Jesus called God "my Father" or addressed God thus in prayer. We know that Jesus addressed God as Abba (Mark 14:36 par.; Matt. 11:25 par.), but since Jesus also taught his disciples this way of addressing their prayers (Luke 11:2), it is not possible to interpret this form of address in the sense of "my Father" (although this interpretation is already given in Matt. 26:39, 42) and then to find therein a reference to Jesus' awareness of his sonship to God.

On the other hand, a serious problem is posed by the few texts which have Jesus speaking of "the Son." The saying, "Of that day and hour knows no one, not even the angels in heaven, nor the Son, but only the Father" (Mark 13:32 par.) is striking in two respects: it denies the exact knowledge by anyone, including Jesus as "the Son," of the date of the coming of God's kingdom, but it expresses this in the absolute formulations, not attested in Judaism, of "the Son" and "the Father." It is highly unlikely that early Christianity on its own accord attributed to Jesus such ignorance of the date of the coming of God's kingdom; on the other side, "the Son" is no more a Jewish designation for the bearer of salvation than is "the Father" for God, and thus Jesus could not at all have been understood at once if he had used these designations. The efforts to reduce the saying to a wording that is possible on the lips of Jesus, by eliminating the words "nor the Son, but only the Father," or only the words "nor the Son," are questionable even if not impossible. Therefore it cannot be determined in what wording this saying, whose complete fabrication in the community indeed is also hardly likely, goes back to Jesus, and therefore Mark 13:32 par. cannot serve as reliable documentation for Jesus' consciousness of being "the Son."

The saying in Matt. 11:27 par., unique in the synoptic tradition, "All things have been delivered to me by my Father; and no one knows the Son except the Father, and no one knows the Father except the Son and any one to whom the Son chooses to reveal him" (RSV), not only displays the same absolute usage of "the Son" and "the Father" which does not appear in the language of contemporary Judaism, but also employs the conception of mutual knowledge which is likewise unknown to Palestinian Judaism. Here too numerous proposals for alteration have been made in order to trace the saying back to a form plausible as Jesus' language, but none of these proposals is actually convincing, and the emergence of the saying first on Hellenistic Christian soil is the most illuminating explanation of the difficulties. Thus there remains, finally, the parable of the wicked tenants of the vineyard (Mark 12:1-12 par.), in which the owner of the vineyard first sends servants to collect the rent, but they all are driven away or killed. Finally he sends his only son, whom the tenants as inheritors likewise kill and cast out of the vineyard. The parable undoubtedly is not relating some occurrence that is possible in everyday life, but is an allegorizing portrayal of the behavior of God's people toward God's emissaries up to the rejection and killing of Jesus outside Jerusalem (cf. Heb. 13:12). Though this fact already shows that the parable looks back on the history of Jesus, still the figure of the only son and heir who is contrasted with the servants is understandable at all only for *those* hearers for whom "the Son" is a designation to be immediately related to Jesus, while in fact for the Jews in Jesus' time "the Son" was no more a comprehensible title for the bearer of salvation than was "the Son of God." Hence the parable in the form in which it is handed down certainly does not go back to Jesus, and if there should be concealed behind the parable as handed down a more original form which could stem from Jesus, we have no means of laying hold to reconstruct it. All this proves that we have no trustworthy report that Jesus thought of himself and occasionally confessed himself as being "Son of God" in a unique sense. Therefore the actual meaning of Jesus' personal claim cannot be clarified by the reference to his consciousness of sonship to God.

g. THE SON OF MAN

While the title "the Son" appears in the tradition of Jesus' sayings only in isolated cases, the designation "Son of Man" is found very frequently in the synoptic gospels, and indeed exclusively in sayings of Jesus. This restriction in the occurrence of the designation is striking and in no way argues in favor of the assumption that this title was a common form of expression for the faith of the primitive Christians which had established itself in the gospel tradition. In spite of this wide attestation of the title in the synoptic sayings of Jesus, however, the question is vigorously debated whether this title was used by Jesus himself or was first adopted by the primitive community, from whose belief then it made its way into the Jesus tradition. The answer to this question is so difficult because the concept can be variously explained, in terms of its source and meaning, and because in the sayings of Jesus it appears in various meanings which cannot easily be brought into harmony.

The expression "the Son of Man," which appears in the gospels, is strange and not quite comprehensible in Greek. In all likelihood it should be regarded as the all-too-literal translation of an Aramaic word combination of the language of Jesus and of the primitive community (bar-nascha = son of mankind = belonging to mankind) which means nothing but "man" or "the man." What is involved here is an ordinary term which usually is used only to designate the individual man. If Jesus should have used this Aramaic expression in a sense other than the usual one, and if the primitive community undoubtedly used it to designate a particular figure of a bearer of salvation, a figure which bears the title "Man," still, *this* meaning of the expression in the Aramaic language of Jesus or of the primitive community could have been understood only if "the Man" had already been employed in Judaism as a title in certain contexts.

This state of affairs is indeed disputed, but it can be rendered very probable. In the Old Testament the expression "the Man" appears only in the apocalypse of Daniel (about 165 B.C.) 7:13-14, where it is said: "I saw in the night visions, and behold, with the clouds of heaven came one like a man [literally 'a son of man'], and he came to the Ancient of Days and was presented before him. To him was granted power and honor and lordship, so that the peoples of every nation and language served him, and his kingdom will never pass away." This figure resembling a man stands facing four beasts which arise out of the sea, and these four beasts are further interpreted to mean four kings or four earthly kingdoms, but the "Man" is explained as "the saints of the Most High" (7:17-18, 22, 25, 27). There is no question that the book of Daniel thus interprets the figure of the "one like a man" collectively as the Jewish people in contrast to the heathen nations, but the conceptions, employed therein, of the four beasts and the "one like a man" show that "the one like a man" must originally have been an individual heavenly figure, and in this sense then the concept appears in the section customarily called "Similitudes" of the apocalypse of Enoch, fully extant only in the Ethiopic language (cf. excerpts from this apocalypse and from the Fourth Book of Ezra, to be mentioned below, in C. K. Barrett, pp. 237-38, 252 ff.). In spite of much dispute, there is no doubt that this section of the Enoch apocalypse is of Jewish origin and arose at the latest at the beginning of the first Christian century, and here now, as in the book of Daniel, there appears beside the "Ancient of Days" (i.e., God) a figure which looks like a man but then is called "this man" or simply "the son of man," but also "the elect one" and "the anointed one." He is a primeval, heavenly being and is to appear as judge of the world and to be placed by God on the throne of glory, and then the righteous will live with the son of man forever (Eth. Enoch 39.6; 46.1-4; 48.2-10; 49.2; 51.5; 52.4-6; 53.6; 61.5-8; 62.1-14). Since a Hebrew or Aramaic original must underlie this Jewish writing, the subject in this original was "the man" or "this man." From this it becomes clear that in certain apocalyptic-eschatological contexts people were speaking of the appearance and activity of "the Man," and that in this the Jewish hearer could at once note that the subject was an eschatological salvation-bringing figure. This figure came from God's world and could also, like the Davidic bearer of salvation, be described as "the anointed one" (Eth. Enoch 48.10; 52.4). This insight is confirmed by the apocalypse of Ezra (so-called IV Ezra) which emerged at the end of the first Christian century, in which the seer sees "something like a man" arising out of the sea; this man is then attacked, but he conquers all enemies and calls a peaceful army to himself. "The Man" is then explained as "that one whom the Most High for a long time has held in reserve, through whom he intends to redeem the creation," and it clearly is the task of this "man" to conduct the judgment of the world and to gather together the people of salvation (IV Ezra 13). Here too the figure of the eschatological judge and bearer of salvation who comes from God is compared with a man, but then is directly called "the Man," so that here too "the Man" is a designation of the eschatological judge and bearer of salvation. Since the famous scribe Rabbi Akiba (end of the first century) interpreted the "Man" of Dan. 7 to mean the Davidic Messiah (Bab. Talmud, Sanhedrin 38b), it seems certain that in Jesus' time "the Man" was known as a designation of the eschatological salvation-bearer who comes from heaven, without our being able to say whether this conception was very widespread.

The synoptic tradition has Jesus using this honorific name in three different connections. On the one hand, Jesus foretells the eschatological coming of the "Man" on the clouds of heaven in judgment, and in this context there is clearly an echo of Dan. 7:13. In the second place, he speaks of the "Man" as a present person. Finally, it is foretold of this present "Man" that he will suffer, die, and rise again. The peculiar thing in all this is that an explicit equation between the Jesus who is speaking and the "Man," which the evangelists on their own part presuppose and which the narrative context also occasionally suggests, appears in the sayings of Jesus only in isolated instances, and then undoubtedly always in parts of the text that are secondary (cf. Matt. 16:13 with Mark 8:27; Luke 22:48 par.). In view of this complicated and ambiguous tradition, in scholarly discussion there has long been an especially wide divergence of opinions over the question whether Jesus could and did use this concept and whether, if he did use it, he meant himself by it. Now when the concept "Man" also indisputably occurs in texts which cannot claim to be original (see for example Luke 21:36; compare Matt. 12:32 with Mark 3:29), there necessarily follows the implication that the question as to originality and the possible meaning of this concept on the lips of Jesus can be answered only by an unprejudiced testing of each individual text, and of course in our present context we cannot discuss all the texts.

Since the Jewish tradition expected the "Man" as a heavenly being for the end-time, the appearance of the concept in this application within the Jesus tradition is least astonishing. We have already met Jesus' announcement of the imminent coming of the "Man" in the saying, "You will not have finished with the cities of Israel before the Son of Man comes" (Matt. 10:23; see above, p. 33), and we have also seen that all the evidence argues that Jesus answered the high priest's question about his attitude toward the expectation of an "anointed one" in the affirmative and immediately elucidated his answer with the reference to the future sitting of the "Man" at God's right hand and his coming with the clouds of heaven (Mark 14:62 par.; see above, pp. 70 ff.). Of these two sayings, Matt. 10:23*b* of course only shows that Jesus expected the early coming of the "Man" as an event of the end of this world epoch, without an indication of a connection between the "Man" and Jesus. But the answer before the high priest indeed also does not establish any clear connection between Jesus and the "Man"; but in the context of the answer to the question, "Are you the anointed one?" the reference to the appearing of the "Man" makes sense only if therewith Jesus' "yes" to this question is elucidated, and thus something is said about *Jesus'* coming as "the Man." But other sayings of Jesus yield these facts likewise. On the one hand, Jesus gives warning with the reference to the uncertainty about the coming of a thief: "Therefore you be ready too; for at an hour when you do not expect it, the Son of Man comes" (Matt. 24:44 par.), and points to the suddenness of this coming: "For as the lightning flashes and shines from one end of heaven to the other, so will the Son of Man be in his day" (Luke 17:24 par.; similarly Luke 17:26-30 par.). In these sayings which let us detect the urgency of Jesus' expectation of the end, however, nothing is indicated about the connection between Jesus and the coming "Man." But it is a different matter in the saying in Mark 8:38 par.: "Whoever is ashamed of me and of my words in this adulterous and sinful generation, of him will the Son of Man also be ashamed when he comes in the glory of his Father with the holy angels." The comparison of this saying with the parallel tradition in the Sayings source ("Whoever confesses me before men, him will the Son of Man also confess before the angels of God; whoever denies me before men will be denied before the angels of God" [Luke 12:8-9 par.]) shows that originally the confession of Jesus was contrasted with the denial of Jesus and that the corresponding future reaction of the "Man" is attached to this response to the earthly Jesus. Even here a distinction is made between Jesus and the "Man," but at the same time it is obvious that the future reaction of the "Man" so precisely corresponds to a person's response to the earthly Jesus that there must exist so close a connection between this Jesus and the coming "Man" that the question of the identity of the two figures is at least suggested. Of course this identification is not explicitly made, and therefore it occurs only in a veiled way.

This strange state of affairs is remarkably matched by what may be discerned from Jesus' utterances about the present "Man." Even the saying, "The foxes have holes and the birds of the air have nests, but the Son of Man has no place to lay his head" (Matt. 8:20 par.), does not say clearly who is meant by the "Man"; but it cannot be talking about everyman generally, and the community did not elsewhere describe Jesus as the homeless one. Therefore in this saying Jesus can only be speaking of himself, and by the homelessness must be meant either his existence which was vagrant and which renounced the secure domestic life, or, less likely, the fact of his being rejected and opposed by the leading circles of his people. Now alongside this saying, which only obscurely speaks of the fate of Jesus as the "Man," is to be placed another saying which plainly refers to Jesus as the "Man": "To whom shall I compare this generation? It is like children who sit in the marketplace and cry to other children: 'We have piped for you and you did not dance; we have sung laments and you did not beat your breasts.' John came neither eating nor drinking, and people say [of him], 'He has a demon.' The Son of Man came eating and drinking, and people say [of him], 'Behold, a glutton and winebibber, a friend of tax collectors and sinners' " (Matt. 11:16-19*a* par.). Here the attitude of the Jewish contemporaries is compared with that of peevish children whom no game pleases: precisely so the contemporaries have rejected John the Baptist for his ascetic conduct and "the Man" for his behavior that is worldly and friendly toward sinners. This sharp contrasting of John the Baptist and Jesus does not correspond to the view of the primitive Christian community. On the other hand, the description of the criticism of Jesus corresponds to all that we know of the opposition to Jesus. Hence there is not the slightest reason for refusing to credit this saying to Jesus; but if this saying is from Jesus, it clearly follows that in the allusive form of speaking of "the Man" Jesus has contrasted himself in his present activity with the past activity of the Baptist.

This state of affairs is confirmed by the account of the healing of a lame man by Jesus (Mark 2:1-12 par.). We have already seen (above, p. 45) that according to this account Jesus defends himself against the accusation that he is blaspheming against God by his promise of forgiveness of sins to the lame man, with these words: " 'So that you may know that the Son of Man has power on earth to forgive sins'—he says to the lame man, 'I say to you, stand up, pick up your bed and go to your house' " (Mark 2:10). Objection has been voiced to the inclusion of this narrative in the earliest Jesus tradition, on the grounds that here the right of pronouncing the forgiveness of sins is attributed to the "Man," while such forgiveness of sins does not appear in the context of the Jewish Son-of-Man texts. One has further objected that it is inconceivable that Jesus would have used the title "the Man" in public (the people with whom he is talking are in fact Jesus' adversaries). But it is utterly unfounded to deny from the outset that Jesus could connect his commission, to cause God's readiness to forgive sins to become a reality, with his consciousness of mission, unless from the outset, but without any justification, one completely rules out the possibility of any such consciousness of mission. And it is equally unjustified to deny the possibility that Jesus could have spoken in public of himself as "the Man," especially since the text discussed above, Matt. 11:16-19 par., also presumably was uttered in public. But on the other hand, the combination "the Man upon earth" is meaningless, because it makes a point that is already obvious if it is speaking of man in a general sense, quite apart from the fact that Jesus would never have ascribed to all men the right to pronounce the forgiveness of sins (and the community also never did this!). Hence this saying about "the Man" can only come from Jesus, and it shows that Jesus could identify himself as the one working on earth as "the Man," whose dignity shows through in the claim to be able to pronounce God's forgiveness of sins just as much as it does in his ability to heal the lame man. The person who hears the narrative cannot fail to detect that in this saying it is Jesus who is meant by "the Man." Of course even in this context the justification of this claim is not proved by Jesus in a universally valid way, but can only be acknowledged by believing affirmation.

All these texts show with a great degree of certainty that Jesus not only adopted the Jewish apocalyptic expectation of the eschatological "Man" and connected it with the announcement of the imminent coming of God's kingdom, but he also connected this expectation of the "Man" with his own person in a new way, unexampled in the Jewish conceptual world, and at the same time introduced it into his own present time. This is certainly strange. For on the one hand this self-designation could not be immediately recognizable even to Jesus' hearers, because in fact the Aramaic word used by Jesus only means "the Man"; on the other hand, we have found that the connection between Jesus and the "Man" in many of the "Man" sayings is made clear only to a certain extent, while other sayings only allow such a connection to be inferred; and finally, it is quite seldom that Jesus speaks of "the Man" as a person of the present and thereby identifies his own life and activity among his hearers, while in Judaism the figure of the "Man" had been expected only as an eschatological figure. For these reasons, as was said earlier, it has frequently been denied that Jesus used this designation of the expected salvation-bearer at all, and some scholars, while ready to concede that Jesus indeed used this concept, think that he spoke of the "Man" only as a figure of the future who is not identical with his own person. From an unprejudiced consideration of the tradition, in contrast to these views, we may conclude that Jesus very probably spoke of himself in veiled fashion as the present and the coming "Man," and we now have to inquire into the meaning of this self-designation of Jesus. In so doing we must remember what we have discerned elsewhere of Jesus' announcement of the kingdom of God and of his personal claim.

Jesus proclaimed the imminent coming of the kingdom of God, but he also declared that in his actions and preaching "the kingdom of God has come to you." This presence of the kingdom of God is exclusively tied to the person of Jesus; it therefore is a hidden presence which only the believer can discern and which one can also overlook. Altogether in harmony with this, in his actions and preaching Jesus saw events of the end-time coming to pass and warned against mistaking this character of the event and thereby stumbling over his person. And Jesus finally made for his person a claim so high that some could misinterpret it as a striving for the expected eschatological royal kingdom and could denounce Jesus to the Romans for his political-messianic claim. But Jesus affirmed this charge only in the form that "the Man" would come on the clouds of heaven and would exercise judgment and lordship. But now Jesus' announcement that he is the present and coming "Man" is fully in harmony with these crucial features of his proclamation and with this claim for his person. When Jesus promised that "the Man" would soon come and pronounce his judgment upon men, each according to his response to the earthly Jesus, in this promise the extreme imminence of the eschatological event is presupposed just as is the unity, actualized through Jesus' person, of the present and the future salvation event. And when Jesus places the homelessness of the "Man" in the present alongside the right of the "Man," given by God, to pronounce the forgiveness of sins, this corresponds to *Jesus'* wandering life (Luke 13:33*a*) as well as to *Jesus'* pronouncement of the forgiveness of sins (Luke 7:47). And just as, according to Jesus' claim, the kingdom of God, whose dawning the Jews expected only of the future, contrary to all human expectation has already become effective in the present, and yet in so doing remains future, so, likewise contrary to all human expectation, according to Jesus' claim the "Man" has already come and become active, and yet it is only in the near future that he will manifestly appear to everyman in a cloud of heaven.

The necessary conclusion, however, from this agreement between Jesus' preaching of the kingdom of God and Jesus' personal claim on the one side and his "Man" claim on the other side is that Jesus' present reality as "the Man" could be a concealed reality only in the very same way in which the presence of the kingdom of God was discernible only to believers. But the idea of the "Man" was especially suited for this hidden dignity of Jesus in the present, capable of being proclaimed only in an allusive form, because in fact the term "the Man" acquires its special meaning of a title of honor only from the context and because at the same time it is made clear by means of this designation of the coming bearer of salvation who is at work in the present that it is not that political hope is to be satisfied, but that the consummation of the divine saving activity is to be proclaimed. Of course Jesus, contrary to all Jewish expectation, has this future completion of salvation already presented in his person, and by means of his present claim he confronted the people who met him with the decision whether they would acknowledge this in-breaking of God's future into their present and thereby let themselves be incorporated into the divine saving activity, or, by rejecting it, would shut themselves out of God's offer of salvation. Anyone who heard and acknowledged Jesus' claim to be "the Man," him God would meet as Father even now; but this person was also certain that in the near future the same Father would finally confront him, when "[the Man] will come in the glory of his Father with the holy angels" (Mark 8:38 par.).

Here we stand before the final riddle and mystery of Jesus' proclamation and his personal claim. Some have declared it inconceivable that Jesus could have identified himself with the figure of the future "Man," and, even more, that he could have spoken of the present activity of this eschatological "Man" with reference to his own person. Someone has recently asked, "How could a sane man have entertained such thoughts of himself?" (A. J. B. Higgins). But this question not only is wrongly posed; it also fails to see that this claim in no way involves a pathological or blasphemous overestimation of his human person by Jesus. With utter clarity Jesus rejected any veneration of his person: when a rich man asks him about the way to eternal life and in so doing addresses him as "good teacher," Jesus answers: "Why do you call me good? No one is good except one, God" (Mark 10:18 par.); and when a woman calls Jesus' mother blessed, Jesus counters: "Blessed rather are those who hear and observe the word of God" (Luke 11:28). Moreover, Jesus explicitly denied having any share in God's power and knowledge: the sons of Zebedee want to secure the places of honor beside Jesus at his coming in glory, but Jesus declares to them: "It is not in my power to give seats on my right or my left, but [it will be given] to those for whom it is prepared" (Mark 10:40 par.). Of the coming of the Son of Man he can only say that he will appear as unpredictably as a flash of lightning (Matt. 24:27

par.; perhaps Jesus also denied any knowledge of the day and hour of the end, but the original wording of the saying in Mark 13:32 par. is uncertain: see above, p. 75). But even if Jesus so plainly put himself beneath God in his human actuality, still he equally clearly knows God to be eschatologically at work in his actions and his preaching, and thus in his person, and the use in revised form of the Jewish "Man" expectation serves only to give expression to this knowledge. But precisely this dual attitude shows that Jesus does not set himself up, but knows himself to be God's eschatological representative, in whom God himself confronts man in action. With respect to this consciousness of mission on Jesus' part, the question whether such a consciousness can be attributed to a mentally healthy person is wrongly posed. For historical criticism cannot determine whether with this claim Jesus was right or not, and therefore it also has no right to deny the historical possibility that Jesus made and could make such a claim because this claim corresponded to reality. Historical criticism can only affirm that such a claim lies outside the possibility of testing in the realm of human experience and therefore is by its nature without analogy, but it is not therefore justified in denying the reliability of the tradition. Since otherwise no conclusive objections can be raised against the critically tested tradition of the "Man" sayings of Jesus, the historian must leave unanswered the question whether Jesus could rightly assert that in his person the expectation of the eschatological "Man" had become a provisional reality and will be fulfilled in his person in the near future in glory. But the person to whom Jesus' actions and preaching have become evidence that God has acted and spoken decisively through this man, and to whom the Easter message causes this belief to become certainty, will not be able to doubt that Jesus rightly identified himself as the "Man" who had come and would come, and he will understand this "hidden" claim as the appropriate form of expression for God's saving activity in the man Jesus.

This meaning of Jesus' "Man" claim however acquires its ultimate confirmation and deepening when we turn to the sayings of the "Man" which speak of the suffering of the "Man."

6. *Jesus' suffering and death*

a. THE PREDICTION OF JESUS' SUFFERING

That Jesus died on the cross is an undeniable fact, even though it is very difficult to determine how it could come about that Jesus was handed over to the Romans as a political pretender and was condemned and executed by the Romans, although his teaching and his behavior afforded no sufficient occasion for such an accusation. In our present context, however, it is not this problem of the history of Jesus that is important, but rather the question of how Jesus conducted himself in this event, whether he anticipated it and related it to his divine commission.

Of course the gospel tradition was convinced that Jesus had precise foreknowledge of his death. In the so-called *"predictions of the passion,"* of the Synoptics, therefore, Jesus teaches his disciples that "the Son of Man must suffer many things, and be rejected by the elders and the chief priests and the scribes, and killed, and after three days rise again" (Mark 8:31 par.; cf. 9:31 par.; 10:33-34 par.). It is evident from the formula-like and detailed character of these texts, which do not transmit any independent individual traditions, that these predictions of the passion with their detailed indications of Jesus' fate and their stressing of the divine necessity of all particulars of this event do not belong to the earliest tradition, but reflect the primitive community's belief that Jesus' suffering, in spite of its mysterious character (cf. Luke 24:20-21), corresponds to God's intention of salvation. But it can be inferred from early individual traditions that Jesus reckoned on an unhappy outcome of his activities. Even though it cannot be determined whether with the saying, "The Son of Man has no place to lay his head" (Matt. 8:20 par.; see above, pp. 80-81), Jesus was making reference to the rejection which he encountered, still the resistance to Jesus is clearly indicated by the saying, "Jerusalem, Jerusalem, which kills the prophets and stones those who are sent to it, how often I have wanted to gather your children together as a hen gathers her young under her wings, and you would not" (Matt. 23:37 par.). But two sayings which are connected in Luke 13:31-33 show that Jesus not only took note of such rejection as unavoidable, but also saw that it had to lead to a bad end for him. According to one of the sayings, in response to the warning that his ruler (Herod) Antipas wanted to kill him, Jesus said: "Go and tell that fox, 'Behold, I am driving out demons and performing healings today and tomorrow, and the third day I finish my course.'" According to the other, Jesus declared: "Today and tomorrow and the day after I must go on my way, for it cannot be that a prophet should perish away from Jerusalem." Accordingly, Jesus knew that in Jerusalem he would face a fate of death, and went to Jerusalem in spite of this.

And Jesus also spoke elsewhere of the fact that a violent end awaited him. When he is asked why his disciples do not fast, as do John's disciples, he answers: "Can the friends of the bridegroom fast, so long as the bridegroom is with them?" (Mark 2:19a par.). That with the word "bridegroom" Jesus is referring to himself is evident from the situation of the confrontation of his disciples and John's disciples, and it can hardly be denied that for him "the bridegroom" here is a designation of the eschatological bearer of salvation. But then it clearly says that the bridegroom is with his friends only for a limited time, and that the time of rejoicing will cease when he parts from them. Of course in this saying nothing is said of a *violent* separation of Jesus from his disciples, but this is clearly the case in Mark 10:35-39 par. To the request of the sons of Zebedee to be given the places at his right and his left when he comes in glory, Jesus counters with the question: "Can you drink the cup which I drink, or be baptized with the baptism with which I am baptized?" It is certain from Old Testament usage that the figures of drinking of the cup and of being baptized here must mean suffering and dying; and that this prediction by Jesus of his own suffering and death and of the suffering and death of the inquiring disciples represents an actual prediction and not a subsequently invented one is very probable, because the older Christian tradition knows nothing at all to report of a violent death of John the son of Zebedee. Thus Jesus here is reckoning on his own violent death; but then when he adds, in connection with the promise of the disciples' drinking of the cup and being baptized, "To sit at my right hand and my left hand is not mine to give, but [it will be given] to those for whom it is prepared," Jesus is equally clearly reckoning that the violent death awaiting him can only be the transition to a participation in the divine glory. That Jesus, to be sure, did not approach this unavoidable violent close of his life without anxiety is shown then in the isolated saying in Luke 12:50: "I must be baptized with a baptism, and how I am constrained until it is accomplished!" When this saying has Jesus shrinking from the fate of death that is thrust upon him, this so sharply contradicts the primitive Christian view of Jesus' way to death that we can hardly doubt that this saying belongs to the earliest Jesus tradition.

b. THE SUFFERING OF THE SON OF MAN

On the basis of these testimonies it may be regarded as certain that Jesus viewed his violent death as the way ordained for him by God, even though we obviously do not know whether he had always had this certainty or had only reached it in the course of his activity. But that poses the crucial question, in what sense then Jesus incorporated this death into his divine commission. The answer would be easier if the assumption, held in recent times in various forms, were correct, that the Judaism of Jesus' time had already connected the expectation of the eschatological "Man" from heaven with the figure of the suffering servant of God from Isa. 53 and that Jesus had adopted this view. But it is by no means proved that in Judaism in Jesus' time the conception of a "suffering Messiah" was known, and nowhere in the early Jesus tradition do we find clear reference to the suffering servant of God or even a quotation from Isa. 53. Since Judaism was not acquainted with a salvation-bringing figure who passes through suffering, but Jesus, in spite of his claim to be the "Man" sent from God who would appear as such in the future, reckoned on his violent death, the combination of the anticipation of suffering with the "Man" claim can only go back to Jesus himself.

Now as already mentioned, the gospel tradition also contains a series of *sayings of Jesus which foretell the sufferings of the "Man."* Since the faith of the community was especially interested in Jesus' foreknowledge of the sufferings, it is not surprising that many of these sayings can clearly be recognized as constructions of the community (cf. the "predictions of the passion": see above, pp. 86-87; further, Mark 9:9, 12 par.; 14:21 par.; Matt. 12:40 par.; 26:2; Luke 22:48). This also holds true, with great likelihood, for the saying in Mark 10:45 par.: "The Son of Man did not come to be served, but to serve and to give his life as a ransom for many." For the idea of the willing service of the "Man" is without parallel in the rest of the Jesus tradition, as is all the more true of the idea that the death of the "Man" would vicariously liberate "the many" from punishment. Hence it has often been assumed either that the saying which occurs in a similar context, "I am in your midst as a servant" (Luke 22:27), has preserved the original form of the saying of Jesus, or that only the first half of the saying in Mark, "The Son of Man came not to be served but to serve," goes back to Jesus. But in this context Luke presumably offers an independent tradition which does not represent a reshaping of the Markan saying; and if only the first half of the Markan saying should go back to Jesus, which is an unprovable conjecture, in this original version of the saying the subject would not have been the suffering of the "Man," and thus this saying in that conjectural original version teaches us nothing about Jesus' interpretation of his death. Therefore Mark 10:45 par. in its version as handed down hardly belongs to the earliest Jesus tradition, and in our present context of the question as to Jesus' interpretation of his sufferings, a hypothetical earlier version is without significance. Much the same is probably true also of the saying which Jesus utters in Gethsemane to his disciples, according to Mark, at the end of his struggle with the necessity of his death: "The hour is come; behold, the Son of Man is delivered into the hands of sinners" (Mark 14:41 par.). Here the subject is the "handing over" of the "Man," and this concept is used elsewhere for the abandonment to sufferings only in "Man" sayings whose character as original can hardly be assumed (Mark 9:31 par.; 10:33 par.; 14:21 par.). Hence it must remain doubtful whether Mark 14:41 par. in this form goes back to Jesus, but even if this should be the case, we could gather from the saying only the idea of the inevitability of the death of the "Man."

Luke 17:25, on the other hand, takes us further: "But first he must suffer many things and be rejected by this generation." It is evident from the context that "the Son of Man" is the subject of this sentence which is presupposed by Luke; the saying is incorporated into a collection of Jesus' words, coming from the Sayings source, on the eschatological coming of the "Man," and thus, by means of the word "first," the eschatological coming of the "Man" is supposed to be identified as the temporal consequence of the "many sufferings" of the "Man." In this saying, isolated in itself, no more precise declarations are made about the sufferings of the "Man," but the sufferings of the "Man" with his eschatological coming are placed, at least implicitly, in a temporal context. Recently it has frequently been asserted that the conjoining within this saying of the suffering and rejection of the "Man" with his eschatological coming cannot go back to Jesus, because the two conceptions are of different origin. But this argument is by no means convincing. Jesus' anticipation of his sufferings and his promise of the imminent coming of the "Man" are attested with adequate certainty, and therefore the combination of the two ideas in one saying is by no means impossible for Jesus. However, the absence of a more exact description of the sufferings of the "Man" (but cf. only Mark 8:31 par.!) argues in favor of the great age of this saying of Jesus. Hence if it is highly likely that Luke 17:25 goes back to Jesus, then here it is said of the "Man,"—and that means in the veiled way which is typical for this concept—that according to God's plan his great suffering must precede his coming in glory. From this it becomes clear that Jesus understood the sufferings awaiting him not as fate or a burden, but as part of his divine commission; but it is equally clear that no explanation is given for this divine necessity and no special, independent saving significance is attributed to Jesus' sufferings as over against his other deeds and his teachings. But that means that Jesus understood his sufferings not as the end but as a transition to the divine glory, as a presupposition of his coming as "Man" in the near future, and he intimated this in talking to his disciples.

Of course this expectation of Jesus so totally contradicts every form of Jewish expectation of the bearer of salvation (not only the political "Messiah" hope!) that it is entirely understandable that Peter as the disciples' spokesman tried to dissuade Jesus from this path: "Peter took him [Jesus] aside and began to rebuke him. But he turned, looked at his disciples, and rebuked Peter with the words, 'Get behind me, Satan; for your ideas are not those of God, but of men'" (Mark 8:32b, 33 par.). This narrative fragment, so sharply derogatory of Peter, which Mark has appended to the first "prediction of the passion," can hardly have first arisen in the community's tradition, but must give a historical recollection, and everything argues in favor of the view that here we are given a brief glimpse into the disciples' inability to understand Jesus' willingness for the way of God with him through suffering. But precisely this willingness of Jesus shows once more that his awareness of God's commission to him to be the present and coming "Man" was coupled with the willing submission to God's will and with the abiding consciousness of dependence upon God the Father.

C. GETHSEMANE AND THE LAST SUPPER

This insight is further confirmed by two texts which show us Jesus immediately in the presence of his approaching death. Of course the account of Jesus' struggle in *Gethsemane* with the necessity of his dying (Mark 14:32-42 par.) is historically very much disputed, since it must remain questionable whether the disciples could hear Jesus' prayer at all, since they are pictured as sleeping, and since the report moreover displays curious repetitions. Hence one will hardly be able to regard the account in all details as an exact rendering of what took place. Still, it is highly unlikely that the primitive church without any support in the historical tradition would have reported a struggle on Jesus' part over the inevitability of the fate of death and the disciples' complete failure in this situation of danger. Besides, there is the fact that the prayer in

Mark 14:36 par., "Abba, Father, to thee all things are possible; take this cup from me; yet not as I will, but as thou wilt," contains the way of addressing God which is typical of Jesus' language. Thus even though we may not build upon the wording in detail, yet the account as a whole shows that the disciples held in their memory the fact that immediately before his arrest Jesus struggled through to a complete submission to God's will, whereby Jesus' decision which can be discerned in Luke 17:25 is only confirmed.

What we can learn of *Jesus' last meal* with his disciples leads us still closer to Jesus' death. In view of the sharply divergent accounts, of course, it is extremely difficult here to arrive at a fairly certain historical insight, and therefore many scholars hold the opinion that the entire account of Jesus' last meal has been so much shaped by worship practices and by the faith of the Christian community, that we can no longer recognize anything about the words and thoughts of that evening. But when on the basis of the comparison of the various accounts we recognize that at the beginning of the tradition there must have existed a very simple account which is everywhere in agreement with the earliest Jesus tradition, then we are justified to assume that in this earliest recognizable account we come extremely close to the historical actuality of Jesus' last meal, even though we obviously cannot arrive at an official record (cf. also the commentaries on Mark 14:22-25). Of the four accounts of Jesus' last meal with his disciples (Mark 14:22-25; Matt. 26:26-29; Luke 22:15-20; I Cor. 11:23-26 on the basis of a tradition appropriated by Paul), Mark and Matthew on the one side, and Luke and Paul on the other, go together on the main points. Undisputedly Matthew has expanded the Markan text and therefore does not qualify as an independent witness. Hence if we compare only Mark and Luke-Paul with each other, opposite Mark's brief word about the bread, "This is my body," stands the addition in Luke and Paul, "which is given for you" or "which [is] for you," and then the command, "Do this in remembrance of me." Here there can be no doubt that Mark's short form is the most nearly original. However, in the saying about the cup, Mark and Luke-Paul diverge from each other completely. In Mark we read, "This is my blood of the covenant, which is poured out for many" (RSV). Paul offers, "This cup is the new covenant in my blood" (RSV), to which Luke adds, "which is poured out for you." Thus Luke has expanded the version which he has in common with Paul, but Mark's wording and that of Paul cannot be derived from each other. Thus one must decide which of the two versions is to be regarded as earlier, and many scholars here also regard the wording offered by Mark as more nearly original. Arguing against this, however, is the fact that the subsequent assimilation of the two sayings on the bread and on the cup to each other is significantly more probable than their subsequent differentiation, and the command to drink blood is hardly conceivable in Palestinian Judaism. Hence it is highly probably that the oldest attainable form of the cup-saying is preserved in Paul. Finally, after the two sayings about the bread and the cup, Mark further offers the sentence, "Truly, I tell you, I will no more drink of the fruit of the vine until that day when I drink it anew in the kingdom of God." Instead of this eschatological glimpse *after* the sayings about the bread and the cup, Luke offers *before* these two sayings Jesus' announcement (22:15-18) that he will no more eat the Passover meal until the kingdom of God, and that he will no more drink wine until the coming of the kingdom of God. Although many scholars think that Luke here offers an independent and very early account, there is significantly more to argue for the assumption that Luke has expanded the eschatological outlook contained in Mark to apply to the eating of the Passover meal and has placed it before the sayings about the bread and the cup. Thus, that in this case Mark has preserved the earliest version of the eschatological outlook is confirmed by Paul, who appropriates the account of Jesus' last meal and adds: "For as often as you eat this bread and drink the cup, you proclaim the Lord's death, until he comes." Thus Paul, too, knew that it was Jesus' intention that the last supper should point ahead to the coming of the kingdom of God.

If it therefore is likely that for the saying about the bread and the appended eschatological saying Mark has preserved the earliest tradition, but for the saying about the cup the same can be said of Paul, the question remains as to what meaning this earliest tradition has. According to Mark 14:12, Jesus' last meal was a Passover meal, and Matthew and Luke have adopted this chronological arrangement. The account appropriated by Paul and Paul himself, however, say nothing to suggest that a Passover meal is involved, and, taken by itself, the account in Mark of Jesus' last meal also contains no reference of any kind to the Passover meal; above all, any mention of the Passover lamb is lacking. For these and other reasons it is highly unlikely that Jesus celebrated his last meal with his disciples as a Passover meal, and hence we may not seek to understand the meaning of the words spoken at this meal in terms of the symbolism of the Passover feast, but are dependent on the wording of the utterances themselves.

Most unequivocal is the eschatological saying in Mark 14:25: "I will no more drink of the fruit of the vine until that day when I drink it anew in the kingdom of God." Here, in handing the cup with wine to the disciples, Jesus declares, in the form of an oath of abstinence, that he will drink no more wine until the kingdom of God comes. Thus in this meal we have to do with a *farewell meal* in which, as also later in their gatherings, the disciples are to drink wine together in the anticipation of Jesus' imminent coming as the "Man": when "the Man" comes, the disciples will celebrate the messianic banquet together with him. Thus Jesus' last meal with his disciples is supposed to unite the disciples with Jesus precisely when he takes his leave of them and to strengthen in them the certainty that they will again sit with him at the banquet when he appears in glory. This undoubtedly presupposes that even after Jesus' departure the disciples are to maintain such table fellowship with one another, even though the earliest account does not contain the explicit command to repeat it, as do Luke and Paul. The sayings about the bread and the cup are to be understood in that context of a fellowship meal which looks forward to the eschatological banquet fellowship.

According to Mark, the saying at the distribution of the broken bread reads, *"This is my body."* Since the breaking of the loaf of bread is a precondition of the distribution of the bread, Jesus' word refers only to the distribution of the broken bread. For the meaning of this saying on the lips of Jesus it would be crucially important to know what was the Aramaic wording, but this can only be surmised. On the most likely assumption, Jesus used an Aramaic word which means "self" as well as "body" (*guph*), so that the meaning of the sentence, which has been all too literally translated into Greek, was "This is myself." Thus in the context of the eschatological farewell meal Jesus is saying of the bread being distributed to the disciples, "This bread represents me." In the disciples' common eating of the bread distributed to them, they continue in fellowship with Jesus, and Jesus promises them that now and later, when they eat bread together, they are to remain in fellowship with him. Thus Jesus' imminent death is not to do away with the disciples' fellowship with him. His death is seen as part of his divinely willed way to eschatological glory.

But while the saying about the bread does not explicitly make reference to Jesus' death, this is clearly the case with the saying about the cup. According to Paul, this reads, *"This cup is the new covenant in my blood."* This saying also is uttered while the cup filled with wine is being passed around, and thus it does not mean the pouring of the wine, but the common drinking from the cup. Moreover, it is clear that Jesus is referring to the promise in the book of Jeremiah the prophet (31:31 ff.) : "Behold, the days are coming, says the Lord, when I will make a new covenant with the house of Israel and the house of Judah. . . . I will put my law within them, and I will write it upon their hearts; and I will be their God, and they shall be my people. . . . I will forgive their iniquity, and I will remember their sin no more" (RSV). Finally, it is evident that this covenant comes into being by means of Jesus' blood, i.e., by means of his death. But this says that Jesus promises the disciples, whom he invites to drink from the common cup for the last time before his death, that they are to share in the new divine covenant which his death brings about. It has often been thought that in this context Jesus' death is understood as an atoning death or a sacrificial death; but the saying about the cup in its earliest form suggests nothing of this. What is said is merely that Jesus' death initiates this covenant and, according to all that we know from elsewhere of Jesus' preaching, it is highly unlikely that Jesus' death here is to be evaluated and interpreted as a single isolated event and not rather as the consummation of the totality of God's actions in this man. Hence the most obvious assumption—we cannot be entirely certain—is that with the word about the cup Jesus means to say that his dying completes the making of God's new eschatological covenant with men which his entire activity and teaching have set in motion, and thus that through his death the dawning of God's kingdom in his person has finally become effective.

Thus Jesus was so keenly conscious of being in the service of God as the one to bring in the dawning kingdom of God that he entered upon the way to death imposed upon him by God and therein completed his mission. In this being delivered up to sinful men which was imposed upon him, and from which Jesus did not shrink, the love of God which in Jesus seeks out the sinner and encounters rejection comes to consummation and fulfillment. Even though Jesus very probably did not give any more specific interpretation of his death, still in the willingly accepted reality of this death a divine action appears, which the Christians later had to make comprehensible. And even if Jesus did not speak directly about his being raised by God—in any case we have no certain early witness for this—still he undoubtedly regarded his death as the transition to the coming which he anticipated as "the Man" from God, and thus confronted the Christians with the task of interpreting his person, his work, and his dying in the light of the experience of his resurrection, which at the time of the last supper still lay in the obscurity of the future. But this all says that the incorporation by earliest Christianity of Jesus' death and resurrection in the understanding of Jesus' person was sketched by Jesus in the interpretation of his death, and was not first inserted by the first community as something utterly strange and unexpected for the understanding of Jesus. Jesus did not explain his death, but he affirmed it as the end of his divine commission and therein was the present and coming "Man," who did not merely utter his claim with words and make it visible through deeds, but who also established this claim by his obedient actions to the very end. Hence Jesus' death is either the tragic end of an idealist and fanatic or an event which points beyond itself and which acquired its meaning through what happened beyond this death. Hence no understanding of Jesus which would answer to his own claim can ignore the testimony of the community which affirms this claim as having been confirmed by God's action and confronts us with the question of whether or not we are ready to acknowledge this divine confirmation.

CHAPTER II

THE FAITH OF THE PRIMITIVE COMMUNITY

1. *The Easter faith*

In the consideration of Jesus' utterances about his approaching death it has been established as probable that Jesus anticipated his death and interpreted it to his disciples as the transition into the glory of the "Man." But the disciples, in the person of Peter, had already earlier objected to this announcement (Mark 8:32*b*, 33 par.; see above, p. 90), and they obviously were unable, even at the last, to believe Jesus' predictions. After Mark had related that Jesus had been arrested by the people of the Sanhedrin under the guidance of the disciple Judas Iscariot, he added, "and all forsook him and fled" (Mark 14:50 par.). There is nothing in the further course of the earliest passion narrative to contradict this report. Only later was an attempt made to soften it. In Luke, Mark 14:50 is lacking; instead, in 23:49 he relates, in connection with Jesus' death, "But all his acquaintances . . . stood at a distance . . . "; and John 19:26 has the "disciple whom Jesus loved" standing beneath the cross. Hence there can hardly be any doubt that Jesus died on the cross forsaken by his disciples, and the earliest tradition knows also that a stranger named Joseph of Arimathea placed Jesus in a tomb (Mark 15:43 ff. par.). Therewith Jesus' work seemed to have collapsed, and his claim that through him God was achieving his eschatological salvation appeared to be proved false. This is the way the disciples must have felt it (Luke 24:20-21 later portrays this mood of the disciples), and this is the way it has been felt again and again by those readers of the gospels who were of the opinion that the account of the sealing of Jesus' tomb (Mark 15: 46 par.) is the last report that we can hear about Jesus. To be sure in Mark this account is followed by the report of the discovery by some women of Jesus' empty tomb, and in Matthew and Luke there are added to this some narratives about appearances of the risen Jesus. It is also historically indubitable that not long after Jesus' death his former disciples gathered themselves together again and proclaimed the resurrection of the crucified One. But as to what actually happened between the burial of Jesus and this emergence of a Christian community, opinions are widely divergent. Yet for understanding the person of Jesus and the primitive community it is essential to form a clear opinion on this question. Therefore we must ask what is attested with certainty, and on the basis of this information must attempt to form a clear conclusion.

a. PAUL'S ACCOUNT

We have two early accounts, which significantly differ from each other, about what happened in close connection, temporally speaking, with the burial of Jesus. The literarily earlier one is found in Paul's First Epistle to the Corinthians (15:3-8), where, on the basis of the tradition communicated to him, Paul enumerates those by whom the resurrected Jesus was seen. The other report is the concluding narrative of Mark's gospel (16:1-8) of two women who, two days after Jesus' burial, go to the tomb to anoint the body, find the tomb empty, and receive from an angel the information that he who was buried has arisen and has gone ahead of the disciples to Galilee. It is methodologically proper to take Paul's text as the point of departure, because we know that I Corinthians was written about the year 54/55 and Paul had already received the text he cites in 15:3 ff., while Mark must be later. The text reads: "For I delivered to you as of first importance what I also received, that Christ died for our sins in accordance with the scriptures, that he was buried, that he was raised on the third day in accordance with the scriptures, and that he appeared to Cephas, then to the twelve. Then he appeared to more than five hundred brethren at one time, most of whom are still alive, though some have fallen asleep. Then he appeared to James, then to all the apostles. Last of all, as to one untimely born, he appeared also to me" (RSV). Into the much discussed question of whether this tradition had been taken over by Paul as a unit or had been assembled from several component parts before his time or by him, we need not enter in this connection, where we are concerned only with the origin of the Easter faith. In any case, Paul enumerates all the people known to him who have seen the resurrected One, in order to prove by means of this enumeration that all the witnesses named attest the fact of the resurrection of the crucified One in the same way as he does (cf. 15:11: "Whether then it was I or they, so we preach and so you believed" [RSV]). Paul is just as clearly convinced that on the basis of this manifold testimony the resurrection of Jesus must be preached and can be believed ("But if it is preached of Christ that he has been raised from the dead . . ."; 15:12). Paul himself was transformed from a persecutor of the Christian community into a preacher of the risen One because the resurrected Christ had been shown to him, although he was not worthy of this grace (I Cor. 15:9-10; cf. Gal. 1:15-16). Because he has seen the resurrected One, he can proclaim the resurrection of Christ, and he presupposes that all the apostles can proclaim this same message because they have seen the resurrected One. According to these statements of Paul, there is belief in the resurrection of Jesus Christ and preaching of his resurrection because the resurrected One has been seen by the witnesses, last of all by Paul himself. Paul clearly does not assume that there are any other facts or reasons which could support the proclamation of the resurrection of Christ, but the same is also true of the tradition which he has appropriated, which according to linguistic indications must go back to the Aramaic-speaking primitive community. In other words, in this formula, whose delimitation is disputed—in the view that appears to me most likely, it goes only through the words "then to the twelve"—the expression of faith, "Christ died for our sins in accordance with the scriptures," is guaranteed as to its historical character by the statement "he was buried." Correspondingly, the expression of faith, "he was raised on the third day in accordance with the scriptures," is guaranteed as to its historical character by the statement, "he appeared to Cephas, then to the twelve." Thus in the opinion of the earliest community, the vision of the resurrected One by Peter and the twelve justifies the possibility of believing in the resurrection of the crucified One, just as Jesus' being buried compels one to assert the reality of Jesus' death, of which faith then confesses that it took place for our sins. Accordingly, both the earliest community and Paul mean to speak of an event when they confess, "Christ was raised on the third day in accordance with the scriptures," but for this confession they have no support other than the fact that the resurrected One has been seen by a number of witnesses. When in this connection Paul explicitly says of the group of five hundred brethren, whom he appends to the old formula, that most of them are still living, this can only mean that one could interrogate these still living witnesses. In this context Paul does not express himself as to how, in a more exact way, he conceives of the event of the resurrection of Christ. But in the further course of I Cor. 15 he speaks of the hoped-for resurrection of the Christians, and in that connection declares that "flesh and blood cannot inherit the kingdom of God" (15:50), and that at the resurrection the Christians will receive a "spiritual body" (15:44; cf. 49). From this we may infer with certainty that Paul cannot have been of the opinion that the resurrected Christ had been seen in his earthly body of "flesh and blood." We do not even have the possibility of establishing whether Paul was convinced that the tomb of the resurrected One was empty or not. For the old report of the primitive community which Paul quotes does not mention that the tomb had been found empty, nor does Paul add this circumstance. Thus neither for the earliest community nor for Paul is the mention of the empty tomb required in order to justify the belief in the resurrection of Christ on the third day. That Paul would not have omitted mentioning the discovery of the empty tomb if he had known of it, we must assume since in I Cor. 15:1-11 he means to adduce *everything* that supports belief in Christ's resurrection, in order then from this point of departure, acknowledged by all Christians, to be able to speak of the hope of resurrection for the Christians. The confession of the primitive community, appropriated by Paul and supplemented by means of all the reports known to him, is well-rounded and complete in itself and required no supplementing.

b. THE ACCOUNT OF MARK'S GOSPEL

Alongside this, we have the account in Mark 16:1-8, which according to the best manuscript tradition concludes the Gospel of Mark: "And when the sabbath was past, Mary Magdalene, and Mary the mother of James, and Salome, bought spices, so that they might go and anoint him. And very early on the first day of the week they went to the tomb when the sun had risen. And they were saying to one another, 'Who will roll away the stone for us from the door of the tomb?' And looking up, they saw that the stone was rolled back—it was very large. And entering the tomb, they saw a young man sitting on the right side, dressed in a white robe; and they were amazed. And he said to them, 'Do not be amazed; you seek Jesus of Nazareth, who was crucified. He has risen, he is not here; see the place where they laid him. But go, tell his disciples and Peter that he is going before you to Galilee; there you will see him, as he told you.' And they went out and fled from the tomb; for trembling and astonishment had come upon them; and they said nothing to any one, for they were afraid" (RSV). This account ends very curiously, even quite apart from the question, not to be treated here, whether the Gospel of Mark originally ended thus (see the commentaries on Mark 16:8). For the angel who gives the women the explanation of the shocking discovery of the empty tomb adds to this explanation in 16:7 the command to the disciples to meet Jesus again in Galilee. But the women do not heed this charge and tell no one at all anything of their experience. Now it is highly unlikely that the account in Mark 16:1-8 ended in so contradictory a fashion so long as it circulated independently; it is rather very likely that the angel's command to the women in 16:7, which points back to an earlier saying of Jesus in Mark 14:28 (see below, p. 101), was first inserted into the traditional narrative by the evangelist. That is to say, if one leaves out 16:7, a clearer connection results: the angel points to the resurrection that has occurred, and the women flee in fright and do not venture to tell anything.

This account of the discovery of the empty tomb, thus to be presumed as more nearly original, contains a number of difficulties. In view of the Palestinian climate, it is not conceivable that the women intend to anoint a corpse on the third day after death. Nor is it comprehensible that the women go to the tomb with the intention of anointing the body although they do not know who will roll away the heavy boulder in front of the tomb. Besides, among the Jews it was not the custom to use spices in caring for the dead. In view of these improbabilities, it is hardly possible to regard this account as historically reliable. Moreover, a closer examination shows that the account does not even aim in the first place to relate the discovery of the empty tomb by the women— the women are at first merely amazed at the tomb's being open and only have their attention drawn by the angel to the fact that the tomb is empty—but has its aim in the angel's message, that the buried Jesus is risen. Thus the narrative seeks to justify belief in Jesus' resurrection by means of the fact that an angel had announced to the women at the empty tomb the message of the resurrection of the crucified One. Hence, even in this narrative, belief in Jesus' resurrection is not guaranteed by a fact accessible to everyman independent of faith. Yet here a fact is reported—the discovery of the empty tomb—which lets the resurrection of Jesus become significantly more concrete than does the report of the resurrected One's having been seen by Peter and the other witnesses. Hence, according to the opinion of many Christians, the position with respect to the report of the discovery of the empty tomb of Jesus has a crucial bearing on whether or not one takes seriously the resurrection of Jesus as a divine occurrence. However, arguing against the historical trustworthiness of the account of the discovery of the empty tomb are not only the already mentioned historical difficulties, but above all, the fact that in the New Testament, outside Mark 16:1-8 and the reports in the other three gospels which are dependent on this text, nowhere do we find the slightest hint of the knowledge that Jesus' tomb had been found empty, or that it was even regarded as important to emphasize the tomb's being empty when people spoke of belief in Jesus' resurrection. Besides, we must note that in Mark's account it is not the fact of the empty tomb that is meant to awaken belief in the resurrection of the One who had been buried—even in early times efforts were made to explain this fact otherwise; cf. Matt. 27:64—but the angel's announcement, which attempts no sort of proof. Even if the discovery of the empty tomb of Jesus were significantly better attested than it is, in view not only of Paul but also of the rest of the New Testament outside the gospels, one would have to say that for the earliest Christians the "fact" of the empty tomb of Jesus obviously was not at all generally significant.

C. THE EARLIEST TRADITION

It would be incorrect to assume that the tradition (appearing first in Paul) that the disciples believed in the resurrected One because of the encounter with the risen Christ, and the account (first found in Mark) of the women's discovery of the empty tomb and the angel's announcement of Jesus' resurrection simply arose side by side, as two different and mutually independent traditions about the emergence of the Easter faith. In that case there would be nothing left for us to do but to attempt to determine with objective arguments which account is the more reliable. Instead, it can still be discerned even in the gospels that *the tradition of the discovery of the empty tomb has supplanted the more original tradition of the emergence of the Easter faith through the vision of the resurrected One.* Indeed, we have seen that the angel's instruction to the disciples to go to Galilee, where they would see Jesus, is found inserted into Mark's account of the discovery of the empty tomb. Thus here the tradition of the appearances of the resurrected One has been subsequently combined with the account of the discovery of the empty tomb, and a remnant of this tradition of the disciples' vision of the resurrected One is found also in Mark 14: 28. Here the prediction, "But after I have been raised up, I will go before you to Galilee," interrupts the narrative of the prediction of the disciples' taking offense at Jesus, although indeed then in the Gospel of Mark the disciples' meeting with Jesus in Galilee after the crucifixion is not mentioned. As therefore in Mark the awareness of the fundamental significance of the disciples' vision of the resurrected One is repeatedly shown, so also in Luke. For although Luke reports even more clearly than Mark of the women's discovery of the empty tomb in immediate connection with the account of the burial of Jesus (Luke 23:53; 24:3), we find, in his work (24:34) at the end of the now following narrative of the encounter of the resurrected Jesus with two disciples on the road to Emmaus, this statement on the lips of the disciples waiting in Jerusalem: "The Lord has truly risen and has appeared to Simon." Since Luke tells nothing of this vision of Peter, it is evident here also that the tradition of the fundamental significance of Jesus' having been seen by Peter has not been wholly supplanted. Thus the account of the discovery of the empty tomb undoubtedly developed only later and at the time of Paul obviously still was not known, but then already in the presynoptic tradition supplants the earlier reports that Peter and then other disciples came to believe in the resurrection of Jesus through the encounter with the resurrected One.

Thus the earliest tradition at which we can arrive relates that a short time after Jesus' death, Peter and the twelve, and then other people, saw the crucified Jesus as resurrected. There is no doubt that not only Paul himself ("When it pleased him who set me apart . . . , to reveal his Son to me," Gal. 1:15-16) but even the earliest community ("he was raised [that is to say, by God] on the third day in accordance with the scriptures," I Cor. 15:4) were of the conviction that Peter and the other witnesses had seen Jesus because *God* had intervened and had taken the deceased One up into his own life, into the life of the divine end-time. This *vision of the witnesses to the resurrection* undoubtedly was not an occurrence in which everyone who was present could share—we hear nothing of people who saw the risen Jesus without thereby becoming believers. We have also seen that Paul does not assume that Jesus appeared in his earthly body to the resurrection witnesses. Hence when people today describe the resurrection witnesses' seeing the risen Jesus as "visions" in the technical sense, this characterization presumably is a fitting hypothesis, which of course leaves unexpressed what is essential. For the crucial thing here is not what was the psychical nature of these visions of the witnesses, but whether Paul and the primitive community were rightly convinced that these encounters with the resurrected One were no "idle tale" (cf. Luke 24:11), that, instead, "God raised him on the third day and made him manifest" (Acts 10:40 RSV).

d. THE ESSENCE OF THE RESURRECTION FAITH

Historical research cannot give a compelling answer to this question, because no facts of the case can be accessible to it beyond the testimony of the witnesses to the resurrection. It can determine, however, that it was not by any means exclusively former disciples of Jesus who were convinced of his resurrection by the vision of the risen Jesus. Paul had been a persecutor of the Christians when, as he put it, "it pleased God to reveal his Son to me" (Gal. 1:13, 15-16); and Jesus' brother James, like the entire family of Jesus, had rejected him (Mark 3:21; cf. John 7:5), before the resurrected One showed himself to him (I Cor. 15:7). Both men, through an action on God's part which moved them spontaneously and from without, came to believe in Jesus' resurrection—at any rate Paul pictures it thus in his case, and we know nothing to the contrary for James. Further, in the case of the "more than five hundred brethren" (I Cor. 15:6), we can hardly assume that they all had earlier been in personal contact with Jesus. Besides all this, we must remember that Peter and the twelve (I Cor. 15:5) in fact had fled in despair and could come to a belief in Jesus' resurrection only through an unanticipated intervention from without. Hence even the historical scholar must grant that something has to have happened which suddenly awakened in all these men, who were in no way prepared for it, the conviction that God had shown them the risen Jesus although he cannot determine what it was that happened. For the first witnesses, of course, "this seeing was a seeing in faith, a believing seeing. Certainly not a seeing which faith engendered, but a seeing which engendered faith, in which unbelieving, stubborn, resisting hearts were conquered" (H. Grass). And these conquered men bore witness to the faith awakened in them, and on their testimony others of that time believed and others today can believe that God did not leave the crucified One among the dead. If this testimony is correct and God actually delivered the crucified One from the dead, then, but only then, Jesus' claim was proved justified, and his mission did not fail, but was confirmed by God. And only then was the first Christians' testimony of Jesus' resurrection justified and, to use Paul's words, they did not have to be subsequently described as "misrepresenting God, because we testified of God that he raised Christ, whom he did not raise"

(I Cor. 15:15 RSV). The experience of the disciples cannot ground the church's proclamation; only God's actual activity in Jesus can do that.

Hence it is important that we be clear about precisely what this belief in the resurrection of the crucified One, that had been awakened in them by the vision of the risen One, meant for these Christians. Here it is clear, on the one hand, that the first Christians were *not* thinking of a *return of Jesus to earthly life,* which then could or must have led to a new death of Jesus—this is the way the writer of the fourth gospel presents the raising of Lazarus (John 12:10). Instead, according to the belief of these Christians, the risen One has been elevated to the presence of God, and from there God has let him become visible; Paul later explicitly emphasizes that the risen Christ can die no more (Rom. 6:9); and still in the later portrayals of the appearance of the resurrected One it is assumed that he cannot simply be identified as the well-known Jesus of Nazareth in his human form (cf. Luke 24:16, 31; Matt. 28:16-17; John 20:14, 16). But that means, on the other hand, that for the faith of the primitive community *the resurrected One* as elevated to God's presence is already *in the eschatological glory* and therefore can send the gift of the eschatological spirit whose experience confirmed to these first Christians the reality of the resurrection: "This Jesus God raised up, and of that we all are witnesses. Being therefore exalted at the right hand of God, and having received from the Father the promise of the Holy Spirit, he has poured out this which you see and hear" (Acts 2:32-33). These sentences from Peter's speech after the bestowing of the Spirit on the first Pentecost are certainly a formulation of the author of Acts, but there are good reasons for assuming that in them the content of the primitive community's resurrection faith is correctly given.

Finally, this faith also included the expectation which Luke put into these words: "Him [Jesus the Messiah] Heaven must receive until the time for the restoration of all things of which God has spoken since ancient times by the mouth of his holiest prophets" (Acts 3:21). The belief in the exaltation of the resurrected One not only made the first Christians certain that Jesus had rightly claimed to be the promised bearer of the eschatological salvation; it also strengthened in them the expectation that the resurrected One would soon appear in full glory. But from this belief and this expectation there arose immediately the conviction that this divine truth must be proclaimed. Paul explicitly emphasizes the connection of resurrection faith and missionary commission (when it pleased

God "to reveal his Son to me, that I might proclaim him among the Gentiles," Gal. 1:16), and the book of Acts, certainly correctly, presupposes this connection even for the primitive community: "This one God has raised . . . , and he has commanded us to proclaim and to bear witness to the people that he is ordained of God to be judge of the living and the dead" (Acts 10:40, 42). Thus the proclamation of the resurrected One is unavoidably bound up with the belief in the resurrection of Jesus, and hence only the consideration of the primitive community's message about Christ will make their resurrection faith fully comprehensible to us.

2. The belief in Christ of the Palestinian primitive community

We do not have any sources which will allow us a direct look into the preaching and the faith of the primitive community. For the book of Acts, the only extant writing that tells of the beginnings of the Christian church, was written at least a half-century after the events, and its author undoubtedly was not an eyewitness of these events, but rather drew the picture which the Greek-speaking church at the end of the first century had of the beginnings of the church. It is true that there are good reasons for surmising that in his portrayal of the beginnings of the church, the author of the book of Acts made use of traditions which in part were very ancient, but the scope and even the wording of such traditions are difficult to determine in detail, and therefore any such assumption remains hypothetical. Along with this there exists further the possibility of moving, by way of inference, from the bits of tradition which Paul appropriated and from the changes within the synoptic tradition back to the conceptions and developments in the primitive community, but this too can be done only hypothetically. A further difficulty arises from the fact that the primitive community undoubtedly did not exhibit a unity. Already early there was in Jerusalem a Greek-speaking primitive Christianity alongside the Aramaic-speaking, and after the transition of the mission to the Gentile Christian territory there was also a Gentile Christian community. Since we can deduce the existence of these groups only from isolated reports, it often cannot be said with certainty in what stage of the development a concept or an idea arose; thus much remains hypothetical. Therefore the emergence and modification in the belief and preaching of the primitive community can be reconstructed only in broad outline and with a measure of uncertainty. But the attempt must be undertaken, because only against this background does the further development of the primitive Christian faith and thinking become comprehensible.

a. THE SON OF MAN

Jesus had been accused and condemned by the Roman procurator for political aspirations to rule, after the Jewish authorities had handed him over to the Romans with this accusation. This accusation appealed to the fact that Jesus had answered affirmatively the question about his position with respect to the expectation of an "anointed One" = Messiah, though to be sure he had reinterpreted it with the assimilation of the expectation of the "Man." Certainly Jesus had not incorporated the expectation of an "anointed One" into his own preaching but had related the expectation of the "Man" who in the future would come from heaven to his present activity *and* had spoken of his imminent appearance as "Man" in glory. This claim appeared to be proved false by Jesus' death on the cross; but the experience of Jesus' resurrection had convinced the disciples and other witnesses to the resurrection that Jesus' claim had indeed been true and had been confirmed by God. Hence one would expect that the primitive community would immediately have appropriated Jesus' self-designation as "Man" and his expectation of the imminent appearing of the "Man" in glory and made this the primary expression of its belief in the resurrected One. But this is done only in quite limited measure. Certainly the earliest community not only repeated Jesus' sayings about the "Man" but also enlarged them: the Son of Man's being betrayed and his rising from the dead (Mark 9:31 par.) ; the Son of Man has come to give his life a ransom for many (Mark 10:45 par.) ; the Son of Man will come on the clouds of heaven (Mark 13:26 par.) ; words spoken against the Son of Man can be forgiven, but not those spoken against the Holy Spirit (Matt. 12:32 par.) . But this enlargement remained limited to the transforming handing-on of Jesus' words. The community did not give expression to its belief in the risen Jesus by confessing or proclaiming the "Man."

It is true that the designation "the Son of Man" occurs *one time* outside the gospels in the context of the report on the primitive community and hence not on the lips of Jesus. We learn that Stephen, after his defense speech, full of the Holy Spirit, declared, "Behold, I see the heavens opened and the Son of Man standing at the right hand of God" (Acts 7:56) . It is hardly possible to give a certain answer to the much-discussed questions as to why the author of Acts, who did use the title "Son of Man" frequently in his gospel, employs the title in his second volume only in this passage, and why here, diverging from the language used in comparable passages in the gospels, he speaks of the Son of Man as standing, rather than as sitting. A plausible conjecture is that the Son of Man is mentioned only here because only in this case could the author of Acts say, in connection with the death of a Christian, that the resurrected One came to him as he would come to all men at the Parousia; and the Son of Man is described as standing because he rises to his feet to meet the dying Christian. But whether this conjecture is correct or not, the formulation in Acts 7:56 stems from the author of Acts, not from the primitive community's form of conception. Hence the note about the dying Stephen's vision does not argue against the statement that the primitive community did not use the title of "Man" to express its belief in the risen Jesus.

b. THE MESSIAH

Yet, we have clear indications that the earliest community spoke of the resurrected One as the "anointed One," i.e., the Messiah. In an ancient-sounding formulation, one which certainly has been taken over from elsewhere, at the end of Peter's address on Pentecost, we read: "Let the whole house of Israel therefore know assuredly that God has made him Lord and Anointed One, this Jesus whom you crucified" (Acts 2:36). And in the already mentioned discourse after the healing of the lame man, which likewise incorporates an ancient formulation, Peter says: "that the Lord may send the anointed One chosen for you beforehand, Jesus, whom the heavens must receive until the times for the restoration of all things" (Acts 3:20-21). And the confession of the primitive community appropriated by Paul also reads: "Christ died for our sins in accordance with the scripture . . . " (I Cor. 15:3). These fragmentary utterances clearly show that the primitive community confessed the resurrected Jesus as the present Messiah, whose appearing in glory they awaited. But now we read that God has *made* the crucified One the Messiah, which has led some to conclude that, according to the opinion of the primitive community, the already present Messiah who is active in the presence of God indeed is none other than the man Jesus who died on the cross, but that God appointed this man Messiah only by means of the resurrection. This would mean that for the primitive community the earthly life of Jesus cannot have had a messianic character. But there are two considerations arguing against such a conclusion. In the first place, the earliest community indeed also gathered together and repeated

107

those sayings of Jesus in which Jesus identified his activity and teaching as the dawning of the kingdom of God and thereby characterized it as "messianic." It undoubtedly was also aware of Jesus' interpretative "yes" to the high priest's question about Jesus' messianic dignity. Hence a view which regarded Jesus' life as "non-messianic" would have been a step back behind the claim of Jesus handed down by the primitive community itself. And there is the second fact, that not only does the confession of the primitive community handed down by Paul speak of *the Messiah's* having died in accordance with God's will as recorded in the scripture, but that we also know from elsewhere that people were already early concerned with demonstrating that the death of Jesus the Messiah was in accordance with scripture and hence a death willed by God: "Was it not necessary that the Christ should suffer and enter into his glory?" asks the unrecognized resurrected One in the ancient Emmaus story (Luke 24:26) ; and in an early prayer formula appropriated by the author of Acts we read: "In truth they gathered together in this city against thy holy servant Jesus, whom thou didst anoint, Herod and Pontius Pilate with the Gentiles and peoples of Israel, to do what thy hand and thy will had foreordained that it should happen" (Acts 4:27-28) . Thus, according to the belief of the primitive community, already as the earthly man Jesus was the "anointed one" predestined by God: "Jesus of Nazareth, whom God anointed with the Holy Spirit and with power, who traveled through the country doing good and healing all who were oppressed by the devil, for God was with him. . . . Him they killed by hanging him on a tree" (Acts 10:38-39) . According to the faith of the primitive community this man was elevated to the heavenly dignity of the Messiah, in order then shortly to appear as the Messiah of the end-time. This means that, for the believing primitive Christians, the messianic age and thus the final deliverance had begun, even though this presence of the time of salvation was only a hidden presence. But in spite of this hiddenness of the presence of salvation, this belief found its visible expression in the exultation with which the first Christians celebrated their common meals (Acts 2:46) .

C. THE SERVANT OF GOD

The primitive community however also expressed this faith in the present activity of Jesus as the Christ in still other forms. In the above-quoted prayer formulation in Acts 4:27, Jesus, the anointed One, is also described as God's "holy servant," and the same characterization of Jesus is found in Acts 3:13, 26 and 4:30, but nowhere else in the New Testament, while it appears frequently in later liturgical texts. Since this title, "the servant of God," is not characteristic of Luke's Christology and apparently is native to primitive Christian liturgical language, the conjecture is suggested that this designation of Jesus stems from very early tradition. It has often been assumed that thereby the primitive community meant to identify Jesus as the suffering "servant of God," following the language of Deutero-Isaiah, especially since in Acts 3:13, "the God of our Fathers has glorified his servant Jesus," reference presumably is made to the Greek text of Isa. 52:13, "my servant will be glorified." But this Greek formulation certainly does not stem from the primitive community, and in none of the four passages in Acts is reference made to the suffering of the servant of God. Since in Acts 4:25, also in the language of prayer and immediately before Jesus is named as "thy holy servant," "David thy servant" is spoken of, and since in Jewish prayers also David is spoken of as "God's servant," the assumption is much more likely that the designation "holy servant of God" was appropriated by the first Christians from the Jewish language of prayer familiar to them and was used to denote Jesus' commission by God. This could all the more easily happen since in Jewish apocalypses the designation "servant of God" occasionally occurs for the Messiah, e.g., "after this will my servant, the Messiah, die" (IV Ezra 7:29). In the primitive community this title, in its primary meaning, obviously identifies first of all the sending of the earthly man Jesus as the obedient servant of God, and not so much the office of the resurrected One. Hence it is understandable that this title as a designation for Jesus did not long continue in use, apart from formal usage in liturgical language. Of course its Greek form, as in fact it appears in the book of Acts, is ambiguous, because the Greek word employed there (*pais*) can designate a child as well as a slave, and hence the phrase "servant of God" could also be understood in the sense of "child of God." Greek-speaking primitive Christianity certainly soon understood the title in this sense, and in this sense the author of Acts could employ the ancient title handed down to him. But since the phrase was ambiguous, it soon was pushed into the background by the more unequivocal designation "Son of God."

d. THE SON OF GOD

Of course it is very difficult to say when the Christians began calling Jesus "Son of God." For we have in fact seen that "Son of

God" was not a messianic title and that Jesus himself very likely never used this designation (see above, pp. 74 ff.). But there are testimonies which very plainly point to a great age for this conception in Christian usage. As is widely acknowledged, at the beginning of Romans, Paul uses a formulation (Rom. 1:3-4) which he has appropriated and which must have run something like the following: "[Jesus Christ] born of the seed of David according to the flesh, appointed Son of God since the resurrection of the dead according to the Holy Spirit." Here the appointment to be Son of God since the resurrection is placed in point of time after the earthly messianic office of Jesus which is identified by the title "son of David." If in this way the messianic office of the earthly Jesus is understood as "a lowly first stage" (E. Schweizer), it undoubtedly displays a very early conception of the appointment at the resurrection of David's son Jesus to be God's son, and it most likely goes back to the very earliest primitive community (cf. the analogous conception of the appointment to be Messiah in Acts 2:36; see above, pp. 107-8).

That the early primitive community confessed Jesus as the Son of God appears also from Luke 1:32-33. Here, in the context of the certainly later narrative of the annunciation to Mary of the virgin conception, is found the promise: "This one will be called Son of the Most High, and the Lord God will give to him the throne of David his father, . . ." This promise is given a fully Jewish formulation: Jesus is to receive, as David's descendant, the everlasting kingdom on the throne of David, and, as a political ruler appointed by God, he is to bear the designation "Son of God." In this context "Son of God" is clearly a name bestowed on David's descendant by God: in II Sam. 7:14 the promise is made to David's descendant, "I will be a Father to him, and he shall be a son to me." Thus here also the idea is dominant that Jesus is appointed to be God's Son, but it is by no means evident when, according to this text, the appointment to be the Son is supposed to occur. In the Christian context the handing-over of David's throne indeed can only be related to the still awaited Parousia, but it is not necessary to assume that the naming as God's Son also is thought of as occurring only at this time. Hence the fragment appropriated by Luke in 1:32-33 likewise represents the primitive conception of Jesus' appointment to be Son of God. It takes us back into the earliest community.

This fragment from the primitive community, appropriated by Luke, already shows that the primitive community's naming of

Jesus to be God's Son must have arisen through the transferral of royal predicates from the Old Testament to the Messiah. This conjecture is confirmed by the *account of Jesus' baptism* (Mark 1:9-11 par.). Here after the baptism Jesus experiences the descending of the Spirit upon him and hears the heavenly voice: "You are my beloved Son, in you I have become well pleased." This address, which can hardly be used biographically (see above, p. 74), uses the words of the royal psalm 2:7 to designate Jesus as God's only Son, and the addition, "in whom I have become well pleased," means to say that God has now decided so to name Jesus. Thus the baptismal occurrence is understood here as an event in which the appointment to the dignity of sonship to God happened to Jesus. This also expresses the idea that only now has Jesus been made the Son of God, which again takes us back to earliest Christianity. We clearly see here how the primitive Christian description of Jesus as Son of God came about: the messianic interpretation of Ps. 2:7 lies at the root of this primitive Christian name of honor. Even though there is some likelihood that already in Judaism in Jesus' time this psalm had been related to the Messiah, the Christians seem to have been the first to derive from it the designation of the Messiah Jesus as "Son of God." Since the Christians believed in the exaltation of the risen Jesus to God, they could unhindered appropriate this designation which, used for a man, was offensive to Jewish ears, and on the basis of Rom. 1:3-4 we may assume that at first Jesus' appointment to divine sonship was thought of as coinciding with the resurrection, but that people then also bracketed Jesus' life with it and thus let the appointment to be the Son of God coincide with the baptism. In any case, with the title "Son of God" the first Christians were not describing Jesus' belonging in essence to God. They meant his eschatological office as bearer of salvation which is actualized in his life, death, and resurrection. This primitive Christian faith designation of Jesus has no connection of any sort with the pagan conceptions of "sons of Gods." When this description of Jesus then gained a central significance in Hellenistic Christianity, this of course is explained from Hellenistic Christianity's pagan environment, in which such conceptions in various forms played a great role.

e. THE LORD

But the primitive community found for its belief in the resurrected Messiah still another, new form of expression, which was of still greater significance for the transition of Christianity into the

Hellenistic world—the naming of Jesus as "Lord." That this title goes back to the earliest community is demonstrated with certainty by the Aramaic cry quoted by Paul, "Marana-tha" (I Cor. 16:22). This expression, taken over in the original language into Greek-speaking Christianity, can be translated in different ways, but there is wide agreement that it is to be translated "Our Lord, come!" especially since in Rev. 22:20 the cry which reads thus represents the Greek translation of it. Since it is likely that at the end of I Corinthians liturgical pieces from the beginning of the celebration of the Lord's Supper in the Corinthian community are being used, the cry "Our Lord, come!" was probably also employed in the observance of the Lord's Supper of the community in Corinth, and it is a logical inference that already in the Aramaic-speaking primitive community, this cry gave expression in the common observances of meals to the prayer for the early coming of the Lord Jesus in glory. Thus the first Christians gave the name "Lord" to the resurrected Jesus who was expected in glory in the near future, and thereby they expressed the belief that the now hidden resurrected One would one day appear as ruler. We have already met this expectation of Jesus' future appearing in might, in connection with the "Christ" title, and the adoption of the title "Lord" signified a strengthening of this expectation, especially since the discourse of the coming "Lord" also clearly indicates that his servants also will belong to the appearing Lord.

But does this say that, according to the belief of the primitive community, the resurrected Jesus was not yet the Lord, and *would* receive the position of Lord only at the eschatological appearing? It has often been argued thus, though a decisive argument against this view is the improbability that the community would have "regarded the exalted Lord as waiting inactively in heaven" (E. Schweizer). But there are also clear indications that the designation "the Lord" was used by the earliest community also as a designation for the earthly and the resurrected Jesus. On the one hand Paul uses the expression "the brothers of the Lord" (I Cor. 9:5; Gal. 1:19), which he himself can hardly have coined, because for him "the Lord" primarily denoted the resurrected One. Besides, the naming of Jesus' kinsmen as "those who belong to the Lord," attested in Palestinian Christianity of the later first century (see Hennecke-Schneemelcher-Wilson, I, 424), suggests that this naming of the earthly Jesus as "the Lord" goes back to the language of the Palestinian primitive community. On the other hand, the ancient formulation of Acts 2:36 says, "God has made him to be Lord and

Christ, this Jesus whom you crucified," and therewith gives expression to the early belief that at the resurrection Jesus had been *appointed* to the position of Lord as well as to that of Messiah. And finally, the Aramaic cry using "marana-tha" also shows that people addressed the exalted Jesus as "our Lord," and correspondingly, Paul uses an expression which in the Old Testament refers to God to describe the Christians as those "who call on the name of our Lord Jesus Christ" (I Cor. 1:2). Hence it is highly probable that the Palestinian primitive community already addressed the resurrected One as "our Lord," just as it described the earthly Jesus as "the Lord." Thus the Palestinian Christians knew and experienced the lordly dignity of the "Lord" as the present One, as a lordship which already now in the life of the Christians causes the eschatological salvation to become a reality, even though the full dawning of this salvation is yet to come.

Against this assumption that the Palestinian primitive community used the title of "Lord" for the earthly and the resurrected Jesus and anticipated the eschatological coming of the "Lord," numerous scholars have objected that the adoption of the title of "Lord" for Jesus could not be assumed for the primitive community, because for this Aramaic-speaking community no linguistic preconditions can be proved which could account for the emergence of this designation. They find the designation of Jesus as "the Lord" conceivable only in Greek-speaking territory. But this objection is not valid. Jesus undoubtedly was greeted during his lifetime with the salutation of courtesy, "Lord," and not only by Gentiles (Matt. 8:8 par.; Mark 7:28 par.), but also by Jews (Matt. 8:21; 18:21). However, this salutation in no way identifies Jesus as towering over an ordinary man, as is evident from the equivalent use of the salutations "Rabbi," i.e., teacher, and "Lord" (e.g., Matt. 8:19, 21). But this salutation of courtesy apparently early became the identification of Jesus as *the* Lord, to whom his disciples are obliged to give reverence as subject to him. This probably follows from the unusual and, at the same time, primitive language in the story of Jesus' entry into Jerusalem, where the disciples who are sent to fetch an ass are to say, "The Lord needs him" (Mark 11:3 par.). It follows, above all, from the Matthaean form of the saying of Jesus at the end of the Sermon on the Mount: "Not everyone who says to me, 'Lord, Lord,' will enter into the kingdom of heaven, but he who does the will of my Father in heaven" (Matt. 7:21). For in the obviously more nearly original version of this saying in Luke 6:46, "Why do you call me Lord, Lord, and do not do what I say?"

which could quite well go back to Jesus himself, the respectful salutation "Lord" is contrasted with the not at all obedient behavior of Jesus' hearers, while in Matthew this has become the reverent invocation of the judge of the world (the saying that follows in Matthew, in 7:22-23, clearly interprets 7:21 in this sense). This Matthaean reinterpretation of the saying clearly tells how the everyday predicate of respect has become the reverent salutation of the heavenly Lord. This development must have taken place very early, as the use of the name "Lord" in this sense in the Aramaic-speaking primitive community shows.

But finally, the possibility that this development can already have occurred in Aramaic-language areas also follows from an analogy which we now can demonstrate precisely in that Aramaic-language region. Only a few years ago an embroidered repetition of Genesis in the Aramaic language, from the first Christian century, found in Cave 1 at Qumran (the so-called Genesis Apocryphon) became known. Here we find the already known address of human persons as "my Lord" (2.9, 13, 24; 20.25; 22.18); but here we also find without linguistic distinction the designation of God as "Lord of the great ones," "Lord of the worlds," "Lord of heaven and earth," "Lord and ruler over all," and "Lord for all the kings of the earth" (2.4; 20.12-13, 15-16; 21.2; 22.16,21). Above all, God is addressed in prayer as "my Lord over all the worlds," as "my Lord God," or simply as "my Lord" (22.32; 20.14,15; cf. Gaster, pp. 256-67). Thus Aramaic-speaking Jews in the time of Jesus addressed God as "my Lord" (*māri*) with or without other identification and thus transferred to God the respectful address used in speaking to men who were felt to be superior. Hence the precondition, as far as language is concerned, was given, that the first Christians also transferred to the risen Jesus the respectful address as "my Lord" used with Jesus, and thus called on the resurrected One with this designation. The objection that the primitive community could not have done this because thereby they would have attacked mono-theism and placed themselves in opposition to Judaism is untenable in view of the clear documentation of the community's language and of the Jewish analogies. In addition, we must clearly under-stand that the Christian assertion of God's exaltation of the Jesus who died as a criminal was bound to be offensive to the Jews who rejected this assertion. Yet it was proclaimed without reserve by the first Christians. Hence we may be quite certain that the Aramaic-speaking primitive community confessed Jesus as its "Lord" and called on him as "our Lord."

f. THE MAN JESUS

This living faith of the primitive community in the resurrected Jesus Christ meant that the person of the man Jesus appeared in a new and more meaningful light for these first Christians. It has often been correctly emphasized that the earliest community, in view of its anticipation of the imminent end, could not have any interest in writing up a comprehensive account or even just collections of isolated reports or sayings of Jesus. In any case we have no possibility of knowing anything about any writing down of Jesus' words or of stories about Jesus before the recording of the so-called Sayings source, perhaps begun around the middle of the first century. But it undoubtedly would be a mistake to conclude that the earliest Christians had no interest in the person of the earthly Jesus and in his teaching. Arguing against this is the fact that, as the form-critical analysis of the synoptic material shows, already very early isolated stories about Jesus' deeds and isolated sayings or groups of sayings of Jesus must have been repeated. Further, the formula in I Cor. 15:3-4, which stems from the primitive community, clearly shows by its sentence, "Christ died for our sins in accordance with the scriptures and was buried," that people told of the death of Jesus, in context, as the introduction to the tradition about the Supper in I Cor. 11:23 shows, "In the night when he was betrayed." But above all it may be seen in *how* the deeds of Jesus were reported in the earliest gospel tradition (cf., e.g., the account in Mark 3:1-5 par. of the healing on the sabbath) that the narration of individual deeds of Jesus were needed for the preaching of the resurrected *Jesus.* Moreover, there was equal need to quote the sayings of Jesus in order to be able to give instruction and to answer ethical and theological questions within the community and in the debate with people who were to be won or who were hostile to the church. Thus the story of Jesus' statement about the obligation to pay the imperial head tax clearly was told because with it one could answer the perennially current question as to whether this head tax was to be paid or not (Mark 12:13 ff. par.). But not everything that is told of Jesus' words and deeds was related out of historical interest in the man Jesus; instead, the belief in the resurrection of this man compelled the testimony that God had raised this Jesus, "who went about doing good, healing all who were oppressed by the devil," and of whose deeds in Judea and Jerusalem the disciples were witnesses, "on the third day [after the crucifixion] and made him manifest" (Acts 10:38 ff.). Because people told of this man Jesus from the perspective of this belief in the resurrection of the man Jesus, there was never any report of Jesus which did not self-evidently presuppose that this Jesus was the "anointed One" sent by God. Hence it is not only inconceivable that the Christian community should ever have regarded Jesus as a mere prophet, but it is also obvious that people formed and re-formed the stories about Jesus' deeds and words from the perspective of this belief. It explains, for example, that we find side by side in the community's tradition two forms, the original form and one refashioned out of the community's faith, of the same saying of Jesus (cf., e.g., Luke 6:46 along with Matt. 7:21; see above, p. 113). Correspondingly, it is understandable that alongside Jesus' answer to the question, a live issue for the community, of the imperial head tax, there was handed down the legendary narrative, undoubtedly first developed in the community, of the coin in the fish's mouth, which seeks to give an answer to the question of the further obligation on the Christians' part to pay the Jewish temple tax (Mark 12:13 ff. par.; Matt. 17:24 ff.). This juxtaposition of ancient and later traditional material in the gospel tradition creates difficulties for us, who because of our intellectual situation must attempt to separate the historical reality of the pre-Easter Jesus from the faith image of the post-Easter community. Yet this difficulty did not exist for the Palestinian primitive community nor for Hellenistic Christianity. For to these Christians it was, in fact, the heavenly Lord whose earthly activity was being related, but of whom people were also convinced that he was at work as the living One in his community and was empowering them as believers to hand on, to share a lively understanding, and hence also to shape and reshape the Jesus tradition ("Where two or three are gathered together in my name, there am I in their midst," Matt. 18:20).

g. THE CRUCIFIXION

This understanding of the Jesus tradition growing out of the belief in the resurrected One not only led to the penetration into the Jesus tradition of the confession of Jesus as the Son of God. Above all, the Christians strove to understand the most puzzling event of Jesus' life, his death on the cross, in terms of God's will. In fact, the formula of belief of the primitive community handed on by Paul says, "Christ died for our sins in accordance with the scriptures" (I Cor. 15:3), and it is very likely that the saying, "The Son of Man came not to be served but to serve and to give his life as a ransom for many" (Mark 10:45 par.; see above, p. 88), had already been formulated in the Palestinian community. Thus the primitive community understood Jesus' death as a vicarious payment of human guilt and saw the Old Testament promise fulfilled therein. Recently there has been a great deal of discussion over how this expression of faith arose, and good arguments are presented both to assert and to deny that this belief in the saving efficacy of Christ's death arose by means of the transferral to Jesus of the utterances in Isa. 53 about the vicarious sufferings of the servant of God. Undoubtedly, philological arguments cannot prove compellingly that in the phrases in I Cor. 15:3 and Mark 10:45 par., most probably formulated by the Palestinian primitive community, the language of this chapter in Isaiah has an influence. Therefore the possibility cannot be ruled out that the earliest Christians first recognized the death of Christ as in harmony with God's saving intention and as foretold in the Old Testament, without thereby intending or being able to point to specific Old Testament texts. But if one realizes that "not only the resurrection but also the crucifixion of Jesus was understood as having messianic significance" by the first Christians, but that these Christians "could not fall back on a distinctive image of a suffering Messiah in order simply to transfer this image to Jesus" (E. Lohse), then it does appear very likely that the first Christians found the death of the resurrected Messiah Jesus "for our sins" and "for many" described in Isa. 53 (vss. 5-6, 12), and from this interpreted this death as in harmony with God's will and as a death for the sins of many.

This assumption becomes still more likely when one considers the wording of the saying about the cup in Mark's presentation of Jesus' last supper (Mark 14:24). Indeed, we have seen that Paul probably handed down the saying about the cup in the earliest version and that Mark's wording represents a revision (see above, pp. 91-92). Now this revision of the Markan version, "This is my blood of the covenant, which is poured out for many" (RSV), clearly is dependent, by virtue of the ideas of the pouring out of the blood and the vicarious dying "for many," on the description in Isa. 53 of the suffering servant of God. That is, here the interpretation of Jesus' death, which occurs vicariously for "the many" (= humanity), is clearly formulated in an analogy to the portrayal of the suffering servant of God. And one can only ask whether this was done already in the Palestinian community or first occurred in Greek-speaking Jewish Christianity outside Palestine. One will hardly be able to decide this with certainty, yet in view of the strangeness of the idea of drinking the blood it is more likely that this recasting of the saying about the cup was first undertaken in Greek-speaking Jewish Christianity. But regardless of how one may decide here, it is beyond doubt that already very early the primitive community felt constrained to explain the puzzling death of the Messiah in terms of its experience of his resurrection by God, and that it comprehended this death as God's sin-eradicating saving action.

The question has often been asked whether the primitive community did not thereby give to Jesus' death an interpretation which not only was foreign to Jesus' own preaching but also, by adducing the idea of the expiation of sins, incorrectly turned the gaze away from the coming salvation to man's past ruin and thus prepared the way for the Pauline "sin pessimism." But if Jesus himself regarded it as his commission to cause God's offer of the forgiveness of sins to become a present reality, and if Jesus viewed his death as the consummation of his divine commission, a crucial step is taken toward the primitive Christian interpretation of Jesus' death. The first Christians recognized that through the resurrection of the crucified One God had confirmed this shameful death as the consummation of his eschatological saving action in Jesus. They had to make Jesus' death understandable as *salvific* event, and one can rightfully say that "there was never a period, not even a very short one, after the resurrection, when the saving significance of the cross was not implicitly recognized" (R. H. Fuller). Hence it was not speculation but the experience of the divine event of Christ's resurrection which led to the understanding of Jesus' death as having happened for our sins. Of course the historian cannot answer the question whether this understanding of Jesus' death appropriately interprets the will of God in Christ or represents a distortion. From the perspective of belief in the divine reality of the resurrection of Jesus Christ, however, the question can and must be answered confidently in the affirmative.

3. *The belief in Christ in the Hellenistic community*

If with all this we have correctly described the belief in Christ of the primitive community in its essential features, so far as the sources allow this at all, still *one* question needs to be answered in this connection in order to be able somewhat adequately to survey the theological presuppositions of the thinking of later primitive Christianity. We need to achieve some clarity as to what further development or even what basic reshaping this belief in Christ of the primitive community underwent in the Greek-speaking Christian communities in Jerusalem and outside Palestine, but then also in the first Gentile Christian communities. Upon their forms of belief and traditions the various forms of belief of later primitive Christianity, primarily Paul and Johannine Christianity, build directly. But we have as few direct sources for Hellenistic-Jewish and Hellenistic-Gentile Christianity as for the Palestinian primitive community; therefore the forms of belief of these preliminary stages of the later Gentile-Christian primitive Christianity cannot be put forth except as hypothetical. It is true that just in recent times various attempts have been made to distinguish the views of Jewish-Hellenistic from Gentile-Hellenistic primitive Christianity, but all these attempts must make so many unproven assumptions that none of them can actually convince. Therefore here we shall refer to only two developments of the belief in Christ beyond the conceptions of the primitive community, for which some certainty can be claimed and the acquaintance with which is indispensable for an understanding of the theology of Paul and of the Johannine writings.

a. THE MISSION OF THE SON OF GOD

We have seen that the first Christians recognized Jesus as the Son of God and sought thereby to identify his eschatological office, given to him by God, as bearer of salvation, which was actualized in his life, death, and resurrection, but that Jesus' belonging to God was not to be expressed with this title (see above, pp. 109 ff.), But there is no direct road leading from this conception that is characteristic of the confession of the Palestinian Christian community to the utterances of Paul and John about God's sending his Son: "God sent his Son, born of a woman, placed under the law" (Gal. 4:4); "God sent his Son in the likeness of sinful flesh" (Rom. 8:3); "God gave his only Son" (John 3:16). In these formulations it is not the individual theology of these two Hellenistic-Christian theologians that is being expressed, but rather a conception common to pre-Pauline Hellenistic Christianity that comes to light. This is shown by the fact that this conception is found also in the Synoptics. In the parable of the wicked tenants of the vineyard (Mark 12:1 ff., par.;), which in the text as handed down cannot go back to Jesus (see above, p. 76), we hear of the owner of the vineyard who "had one, a beloved son," whom he sends to the tenants when his efforts with the sending of slaves comes to naught. It is undisputed that the vineyard owner of the parable stands for God, and therefore here, in the language of the parable the theme is the sending of the Son of God, who accordingly exists before he is sent. But in all these texts "Son of God" is clearly a designation of belonging to God and not only of an office given by God. However, when these Christians speak of the Son's belonging to God, they do not intend to be talking of divine "nature" or to speculate about the relationship of the Son of God to God, but they mean to confess that the Son of God is not one of God's creatures, but that he always belonged to God and had a part in what God was doing. Hence this belief in the Son's belonging to God implies that the Son had a part in the creation: for us there is *"one* Lord Jesus Christ, through whom are all things, and we through him" (I Cor. 8:6) ; "in him [the Son] are all things created, in heaven and on earth" (Col. 1:16) ; "through him [the Son] has he made the worlds" (Heb. 1:2; cf. also John 1:2). This belief likewise implies that at the resurrection the Son who had come into the world returned to the Father and shares in the Father's rule: "God has exalted him and given him a name that is above all names, that at the name of Jesus every knee should bow . . . and every tongue confess that Jesus Christ is Lord, to the glory of God the Father" (Phil. 2:9-11) ; "no one has ascended into heaven except the one who descended from heaven, the Son of Man" (John 3:13). Thus according to the conception of Hellenistic Christians, which was the underlying idea everywhere here, the Son of God is a being who belongs to God from time immemorial, who is sent from God's world into this world, and after completing his task returns to God's world and there receives a share in God's rule to the extent in which this rule has already become reality in the present down to the Parousia.

Clearly, the mythical figure of an emissary coming from God underlies this Hellenistic-Christian conception of the Son of God. There has been a great deal of debate over when and whence this mythical figure had been taken over by the Hellenistic Christians and related to the resurrected Christ. We can discern this common christological conceptual form of Hellenistic Christianity only by means of *a posteriori* conclusions, but we can hardly discover at what point in time the Christians took over this conceptual form and whether they took it over as a whole or little by little. With some degree of certainty, however, we may say that in this conception two religious ideas, which are related but were present in primitive Christianity's environment independent of each other, have flowed together. On one side, in Hellenistic Judaism, which however could thereby refer to the ideas of the Old Testament, the figure of Wisdom is active, which, formed before creation, proceeds from God's mouth, is God's instrument at creation and the likeness of God, which is sent to men but found no home there and returned to God in heaven, whence it again and again descends to the wise (cf. above all the Wisdom of Solomon, chap. 7 and 8). To a certain extent the appropriation of this Jewish wisdom speculation explains the Hellenistic-Christian idea of the heavenly Son of God, particularly in Paul's writings, but it cannot account for the conceptions of the Son's being eternally with God, of his hiddenness in this world, of his people's belonging to him, and much else besides (cf., e.g., John 1:2, 18; I Cor. 2:8; I Cor. 15:22b). But in the environment of early Christianity there is also a religious thought world in which, in the context of a dualism of heaven and earth, of above and below, of light and darkness, there appears in various forms the figure of the "emissary" which comes from the world of light, brings knowledge (Gnosis), and calls his own out of the world of darkness into the world of light (so-called Gnosticism). We cannot demonstrate this complex of ideas of the heavenly "emissary" in the context of a *single* source, but we may conclude with certainty from many indications that there must have been this religious thought world, and Hellenistic Christianity must already in the pre-Pauline period have appropriated the conception of the heavenly emissary as a form for expressing its belief in God's saving activity in Jesus Christ and combined it with Hellenistic-Jewish wisdom speculation. With the adoption of these conceptions the Hellenistic Christians created for themselves the possibility of describing the saving act of God in Christ really as *God's* saving act in Christ, and the great primitive Christian theologians clearly show the influence of this Hellenistic conception (especially Paul, the authors of the Johannine writings, of Hebrews, and of Ephesians). Of course along with the adoption of this Hellenistic conception, the danger loomed that the person of the man Jesus would be entirely too much pushed into the background by the figure of the divine emissary. We shall encounter the problematic produced therewith when we consider the proclamation of Christ as found in Paul and in the Johannine writings.

b. THE BEARER OF DIVINE POWER

But still another change in the picture of Jesus must have occurred in the Hellenistic-Jewish and Hellenistic-Gentile Christian communities. In the narratives of the synoptic gospels we frequently encounter portrayals in which the earthly Jesus appears as bearer of a divine power which visibly and essentially lifts him out from among all other men. Mark 5:1 ff. par. tells of Jesus' encounter with a demonically possessed man who with the help of the address "Son of the Most High God" seeks to ward off Jesus and whose demonic masters ask Jesus to send them into one of the herds of swine feeding nearby. When this wish is granted them, the herd plunges down the slope into Lake Gennesaret and drowns, while the once sick man now sits fully healed. But the swineherds and the residents of the surrounding localities ask Jesus to leave their region. Here Jesus appears not only as the man who by his word can drive out demons (thus Mark 1:23 ff. par.), but as a powerful being who in the same way is able to work blessing and curse and whom people therefore would rather not have in their vicinity. A similar picture is yielded by the following story in Mark. Here the narrative of a woman ill with a hemorrhage is set in the context of the account of the raising of Jairus' daughter (Mark 5:21-24, 35-43 par.), in which Jesus performs the miracle of raising the dead only by means of his word. This woman, whom many physicians had not been able to help, approaches Jesus in a throng of people, touches his garment from behind, because she is convinced that such a touch would bring her healing, "and immediately her hemorrhage dried up, and she noted in her body that she was healed of her scourge. And Jesus immediately noticed in himself that power had gone out from him, turned in the crowd, and said, 'Who touched my garments?' " The woman confesses the truth and receives from Jesus the promise that from now on she will remain healthy (Mark 5:25-34 par.). Here all the more it is not Jesus' word nor even his conscious action; here it clearly is rather a power radiating from Jesus even into his clothing which performs the healing, and Jesus is seen as the possessor of a supernatural miraculous power which belongs to him by his very nature. The account of Jesus' walking on the lake (Mark 6:45 ff. par.) yields a similar conclusion. For here Jesus, walking on the water, comes to the disciples who are struggling against the wind in a boat on the lake, and speaks to them with the identifying word, "It is I; be not afraid," and then gets into the boat with them, whereupon the wind settles. Here also Jesus is shown as a being who has at his disposal physical possibilities over which no other man can have control, and it is even plainly said that the disciples thought Jesus was an apparition until he identified himself to them.

This conception, that Jesus already as man was a supernatural being equipped with uncanny powers, who occasionally disclosed his real manner of being, emerges especially clearly in the story of the transfiguration (Mark 9:2 ff. par.). For here, in fact, it is explicitly said of Jesus that he was "transfigured" and that as a result of this transformation his heavenly nature became visible to the disciples. This nature is shown in his wearing heavenly garments, in the cloud of the divine presence that surrounds him, and in his ability to talk with the departed Elijah and Moses, who are thought to be in heaven. The heavenly voice, "This is my beloved Son, listen to him!" does not address Jesus but the disciples, and therewith also those who hear the story, and it indicates that in this transfiguration and this heavenly manner of appearance the transfigured One's sonship to God is made known. And just as Jesus lets his true nature be seen by means of his transfiguration, so also he can equally suddenly stand before them again as the Jesus well known to the disciples.

In all these texts appears a conception, foreign to Judaism but familiar to Hellenism, of a natural, native gift of power, to which corresponds the epiphany, the becoming visible of the divine being before the eyes of certain men. In pagan Hellenism people knew the conception of men who have divine powers and abilities and are able to demonstrate them by means of miraculous deeds, and this conception had also made its way, in diluted form, into the Jewish-Hellenistic contemplation of Old Testament figures. Hellenistic Christians adopted these conceptions to give expression to the belief that God sent the man Jesus, without forming any ideas about how this divine nature of Jesus is to be explained.

C. THE SPIRIT AS POSSESSION AND THE BIRTH OF JESUS WITH-
   OUT A HUMAN FATHER

Yet eventually this question was also posed, and two conceptions were afforded Hellenistic Christians to make this divine nature of Jesus comprehensible, both of which, to be sure, are heard only occasionally. On the one hand, people were convinced that at baptism Jesus received the *divine Spirit as a possession,* so that from that time on he had this Spirit at his disposal. At least according to the understanding of the Hellenistic Christians and then also of the author of Mark's gospel, the baptismal narrative says (Mark 1:9-11 par.) that the Spirit which descended on Jesus as a dove remained with him; John 1:32 stresses this explicitly, and one can even translate Mark 1:10 to read, "He saw the Spirit descend as a dove into him." And when Jesus' saying, "Anyone who speaks blasphemously against the Holy Spirit will never be forgiven," is related by the gospel writer to the charge of Jesus' adversaries, "he has an unclean spirit" (Mark 3:29-30), it is presupposed here that Jesus is *in possession* of the Holy Spirit.

Alongside this, undoubtedly already in Hellenistic Jewish Christianity, the conception grew that Jesus was born of a human mother without the assistance of a man. This conception, more alluded to than explicated in Luke 1:26 ff., in no way thinks of a begetting by divine seed, as would correspond to the pagan idea, but of the begetting of the child by a divine creative act (in Hellenistic Judaism something similar was told of the motherhood of certain women of the Old Testament). In Luke, Jesus' sonship to God (Luke 1:32: "he will become great, and will be called son of the Most High") thus is traced back to a special creative act of God at his begetting and nothing is said yet of a physical sonship to God. But then when Matthew simply formulates: "His [Jesus'] mother Mary, who was betrothed to Joseph, before they came together was found pregnant by the Holy Spirit" (Matt. 1:18; cf. 1:20), this formulation approaches the conception of a physical sonship to God, and subsequently (but only beyond the New Testament) the idea of the begetting of Jesus without a father was understood in this sense.

To be sure, as already mentioned, these two attempts to render Jesus' essential sonship to God *understandable* are only slightly attested in the New Testament, because people at first apparently did not everywhere feel the need to develop further ideas at all about Jesus' essential sonship to God which was being proclaimed. On the other hand, there can be no doubt that in Hellenistic Jewish Christianity and Gentile Christianity before Paul and the emergence of the gospel writings, people also began to make the person of the man Jesus understandable to themselves by the assumption of his essential sonship to God, which was expressed in an unlimited ability to work miracles and in the capacity to change his appearance. If the knowledge of this development is indispensable for the understanding of the Gospel of John, still in the consideration of John's gospel the question will be thrust upon us whether *this* further development of the belief in the Son of God who has appeared in Jesus does not contain at least the danger, even more strongly than does the idea of the heavenly emissary, that the humanity of Jesus in its reality is no longer taken entirely seriously.

But the primitive community not only created the presuppositions for the thinking of the great theologians of primitive Christianity by means of the further development of the belief in Christ on the basis of its experience of the resurrection of the crucified One. It learned, at the same time with the emergence of this belief, to understand itself as the community of the risen Christ. Therefore we must explore the rise of the primitive *community,* if we wish to get an overview of the presuppositions for the theological thinking of Paul and of the Johannine writings in their essential features.

4. *The church's self-awareness*

We do not know for sure where the first witnesses saw the risen Jesus, and therefore we also do not know for sure where the witnesses to the resurrection first came together. But it is very likely that the appearance to Peter and the twelve took place in Galilee (Mark 14:28 par.; 16:7 par.), and it is equally likely that the appearance to the five hundred brethren (I Cor. 15:6) occurred in Jerusalem. If these assumptions are correct, one will have to conclude that, at the time of the appearance to the five hundred brethren, the Galilean witnesses to the resurrection had already moved to Jerusalem, and in fact the book of Acts takes for granted that the witnesses to the resurrection first gathered in Jerusalem (Acts 1:12-15) and that there, at the Jewish Feast of Weeks, after the Passover at which Jesus was killed, a larger group of Christian believers was assembled and had a decisive experience of the Spirit (Acts 2:1-13). This historical picture of the book of Acts, according to which the primitive community developed from the center at Jerusalem, has been called into question in two respects. On the one hand it has been assumed that the Jerusalem community of Christians arose at all only years after the one in Galilee; even three years after his conversion Paul is said not to presuppose a community in Jerusalem, since he does not mention it in Gal. 1:18. On the other hand, it has been conjectured that from the very first there were *two* centers of Christianity, in Galilee and in Jerusalem, and the Jerusalem community came to the fore only in the course of the years. Now it is not impossible that from the outset or at least already very early there were Christian communities in Galilee, which had arisen independent of Jerusalem and also developed independently; but we know absolutely nothing concrete of such communities, and therefore we also do not know which faith perspectives were dominant in such communities and whether they had any influence on the development of primitive Christianity. We must also observe that according to Gal. 1:18 Paul knows only *one* place where after his conversion he would have been able significantly to come in contact with the Christian community. On the other hand, it is an arbitrary assumption that Peter and James should have worked in Jerusalem more than three years after Jesus' death (thus Gal. 1:18-19) without any Christian community having been formed, and it is equally unjustified to assume that the author of the book of Acts was unable to learn anything more at all that was reliable about the beginnings of the Christian church. It rather is still the most likely assumption that in fact the first witnesses to the resurrection very soon returned from Galilee to Jerusalem and joined themselves to the resurrection witnesses there. Of course we can only conjecture why this return took place, but it may reasonably be assumed that the fact of Jesus' crucifixion and resurrection (not his appearance!) in Jerusalem was just as much the occasion for it as the self-understanding of these first Christians, which we shall discuss presently.

a. THE SELF-UNDERSTANDING OF THE PRIMITIVE COMMUNITY

Hence the crucial question is: What interpretation did the resurrection witnesses who returned to Jerusalem, and the disciples of Christ who gathered around them, give to their fellowship, and what religious life forms corresponded to this self-understanding? The book of Acts takes for granted that the first Christians participated in the temple prayers, spent time in the temple otherwise as well, and obeyed the law (Acts 2:46; 3:1; 5:12, 42; 10:14) ; nothing is said, to be sure, of participation in the temple sacrifices. This picture in Acts of the first Christians' obvious clinging to the religious customs and the law-abiding conduct of their religious environment is confirmed by the fact that in Jerusalem at the so-called Apostolic Council, some sixteen or seventeen years after he became a Christian, Paul encountered the demand that Gentile Christians be circumcised, and, afterward, in Antioch met the Jerusalemite view that Gentile Christians may not have fellowship at table with Jewish Christians. In the same way, some sayings of Jesus in the Synoptics, which are strictly true to the law and which contradict Jesus' critical attitude (cf. above, pp. 51-52) , prove that there were at least some circles in the primitive community which practiced a consistent clinging to the traditional observance of the law and demanded similar conduct of all followers of the risen Christ (cf. Matt. 5:18 par., 19; 23:2, 3*a*; 23:23 par.; 24:20) . Hence one may assume with good reason that the Jerusalem Christianity of the first years held fast to the Jewish observance of the law and to the religious usage of the Jews. Yet a difference within the primitive community probably was soon revealed, when the preaching of Christ laid hold also upon Greek-speaking Jews from the Diaspora in Jerusalem. Even though the speech put in the mouth of Stephen in Acts 7:2 ff. can hardly be adduced as a source for the thinking of this leader of the Greek-speaking Jewish Christians of Jerusalem (see the commentaries), still the hostility of the Jews toward these Hellenistic Jewish Christians (Acts 8:1, 3-4; 11:19) proves that *these* Jewish Christians offered a greater offense to the Jews than did the Aramaic-speaking primitive community. Hence the report that among these Hellenistic Jewish Christians there was an outspoken rejection of the temple cult (Acts 6:11-12; 7:48) is very illuminating, and even the accusation against Stephen, that he had set himself against the law (Acts 6:13-14), is in essence probable, because in Antioch the Hellenistic Jewish Christians who were driven out of Jerusalem in connection with the persecution of Stephen also preached to Gentiles "the glad tidings of the Lord Jesus" (Acts 11:20). This could hardly have been successful if at the same time they had demanded circumcision and, along with it, fulfillment of the entire Jewish law. Thus presumably already very early there was formed an attitude of varying strictness with respect to the traditional Jewish legal piety in the Aramaic-speaking and the Greek-speaking Jewish Christianity in Jerusalem, and according to a very likely assumption, the account of the choice of the Hellenistic "Seven" (Acts 6:1 ff.) also betrays a certain opposition between these two groups of the primitive community (see the commentaries).

From these facts the conclusion has frequently been drawn that the primitive community understood itself as one of the numerous special groups within Judaism which actually was distinguished from the rest of the Jews only by the fact that it could bear witness to the resurrection of the crucified Jesus and hence summoned to belief in this eschatological saving act of God with respect to his people (cf. Acts 2:24, 31-32). There were, in fact, in the Judaism of that time various groups (Pharisees, Sadducees, Essenes, Qumran people) each of whom regarded themselves as the true Jews and who in part, as for example the Qumran people, denied the rest of the Jews the right still to regard themselves as the people of God. Hence in fact the conjecture is obvious that the primitive Christian community was also first regarded by the Jews as a special group, and support is given to this conjecture by the fact that the author of Acts puts in the mouth of the Jews the designation "sect" (*hairesis*) for the Christian community (24:5, 14; 28:22). One can also cite facts which appear to support the assumption that the primitive community itself regarded itself as such a special group. The book of Acts takes for granted that the Christians of the primitive community attributed to themselves the designation "the Way" (9:2; 19:9, 23; 22:4; 24:14, 22), and this designation by a group for itself in distinction from all other forms of Jewish understanding of the law is found elsewhere only in the Qumran group (1QS 9.18; 10.21; cf. Gaster, pp. 68, 128). One can point out further that the primitive community identified itself as "the saints" and "the elect," as may be inferred from Paul, the Synoptics, and the book of Acts (cf. Rom. 15:25-26; I Cor. 16:1; II Cor. 8:4; Acts 9:13, 32—Mark 13:20, 22, 27 par.; Rom. 8:33), and both titles appeared with the Pharisees and in Qumran as a designation of the special chosen group in contrast to the rest of the Jewish people (I Macc. 1:46; Tob. 12:15—Wisdom of Sol. 4.15; 4 QpPs 37.II.5; cf. Gaster, pp. 253-55). But both titles also occur in Judaism as a designation for the entire elect people of God (Wisdom of Sol. 18.9; Ps. Sol. 17.36; see in Barrett, *Background*, pp. 248-49—"Lord, thou didst will that this people should be thy chosen people," Asc. Mos. 4.2). Consequently the self-designations of the primitive community as "the saints" or "the elect" are no certain evidence of their claim to be the special chosen group of the Jewish people.

But now there are two clear circumstances which argue against this understanding of the self-predication of the primitive community. In the first place, in the primitive community as with Jesus, there is lacking the idea, known from the prophets and claimed by the Pharisees and the Qumran people, that their group is the holy "remnant" of the people of God, alone preserved by God for the end-time. Jesus rather spoke of the "new covenant" which God would establish through his death (I Cor. 11:25; see above, p. 94), and, by means of the circle of "the twelve" gathered around his person, expressed the claim of God on the *entire* nation of the twelve tribes. Quite in harmony with this the primitive community understood itself as the members of the new eschatological fraternity which God had created in Jesus: "you are sons of the prophets and of the covenant which God made with your fathers" (Acts 3:25). This fraternity had the task of calling the entire people of salvation into this covenant: "Let all the house of Israel assuredly know that God has made him Lord and anointed One, this Jesus whom you crucified" (Acts 2:36). It is in this sense, also, then, perhaps first in Hellenistic Jewish Christianity, that Jesus' saying about the cup at the last supper (I Cor. 11:25) was recast in such a way that now the theme is the making of a covenant in favor of the "many" (= the people generally; "This is my blood of the covenant which is poured out for many," Mark 14:24; see above, p. 91). Thus the primitive community was persuaded that through Christ God had begun in their midst the new eschatological covenant of salvation which should embrace the entire nation.

Still another fact points in the same direction, namely that the primitive community described itself as "community (or even church) of Jesus" or "community of Christ." This appears from Jesus' saying to Peter which in Matthew's gospel is inserted into the narrative of the messianic confession at Caesarea Philippi (see above, pp. 69-70) : "Blessed are you, Simon, son of Jona, for flesh and blood have not revealed it to you, but my Father in heaven. And I say to you that you are Peter, and on this rock I will build my church, and the gates of Hades will not prevail against it. I will give you the keys to the kingdom of heaven, and whatever you loose on earth will be loosed in heaven" (Matt. 16:17-19). We have seen that this promise to Peter can have developed only in the Christian community, but the language and the structure of the saying show clearly that the Aramaic-speaking primitive community was expressing its self-understanding in this saying. The saying is peculiar and important primarily because here the existence of the "community" of Jesus Christ in the present and the fundamental significance of Peter for the existence of the community willed by Jesus are asserted. Now it is not immediately clear, and hence it is disputed, which Aramaic expression underlies the Greek word *ekklesia* which occurs in Matt. 16:18, but in all likelihood it takes up the Old Testament concept of the "divine community" (*qahal*, Aramaic *qehala*). Already with the choice of this concept, the primitive community expresses its claim that those who believe in Christ represent the people of God and thus have taken the place of the old people of God. But this people of God is characteristically no longer identified as "God's community" but as "Jesus' community" or "Christ's community," because through the resurrection and exaltation of the crucified Jesus to be the Messiah, the eschatological people of God under the leadership of the Messiah has come into being. In this community of Jesus, the role of administrator is ascribed to Peter, who by his decisions about what is allowed or not allowed, and by his binding or forgiving of sins, authoritatively determines access to the community of Jesus and therewith also opens or closes the prospect of participation in the coming kingdom of God. When this function in accordance with the will of Jesus Christ is attributed precisely to Peter, there is indeed reflected therein not only Peter's leading role in the primitive community, which is also discernible elsewhere (Gal. 1:18; Mark 16:7; Acts 1:15, and frequently in Acts 1–12), but above all the fact that Peter was the first to see the resurrected One, and hence probably also the first to proclaim Jesus' resurrection (Acts 2:14 ff. presupposes this). Because the community is the community of the resurrected Messiah and because in this resurrection of Jesus God has caused his eschatological salvation to begin, on the consummation of which at the coming of God's kingdom one waits, therefore "all who confess Jesus as the Christ, and only these, . . . are the eschatological community of salvation" (L. Goppelt).

b. THE SEPARATION FROM THE JEWISH COMMUNITY

This self-understanding of the community, however, means that the primitive community, regardless of how self-evidently it remained in the context of Jewish legal life and of Jewish religious practice, knew itself in principle to be separated, as the *new* community of God, from the Judaism that surrounded it, and further knew itself to be commissioned to call everyone to join this new community. But now this fundamental attitude also very early led to the situation wherein the members of the primitive community also visibly distinguished themselves from the rest of the Jews.

This distinction had already arisen from the fact that in the primitive community the effective *power of the eschatological Spirit* was experienced. As is well known, the book of Acts tells, in 2:1 ff., of an event which took place fifty days after the Passover of Jesus' death, at the time of the Jewish Feast of Weeks, and at which the whole company of those who up to that time had come to believe in Jesus' resurrection experienced the Holy Spirit descending upon them and enabling them to speak "with other tongues," which then was observed as a speaking in foreign languages by the rest of the Jews from all over the world. It is widely acknowledged that in the account of the book of Acts, the report of an ecstatic experience of the first Christians at the Jewish Feast of Weeks, in which the ability of Spirit-prompted, ecstatic "speaking in tongues" was exhibited for the first time, has been fused with the conception of a speaking in foreign languages (cf. the commentaries on Acts 2:1-12 and I Cor. 14). Obviously it is not possible for us to determine whether the date given is correct for this first experience of being enabled to speak under the impulse of the divine Spirit, but there is no serious argument against it. And it is certain that the interpretation of this event as a case of speaking in foreign languages is not correct. On the other hand, we can hardly doubt that from earliest times the primitive community was convinced that the Spirit of God which was promised for the end-time was active in their midst (cf. the quotation of Joel 3:1 in the form given in Acts 2:17a; see the commentaries on this passage; further, Acts 4:31; 10:44-46; 13:2; Mark 13:11 par.), and the emergence of prophets (Acts 11:27-28; 13:1; 15:32) was in harmony with this. This conviction and the experience of the activity of God's Spirit in the entire community of believers in Christ already *were bound* more or less to lead to a visible separation of the Christ community from the rest of the Jews.

But what was true for the community was true also for the individual Christians. For the Christ community had practiced, from very early times, *baptism* as the rite of admission into the community. Not only does the book of Acts take this for granted from Pentecost onward (Acts 2:38, 41), but it also appears from the fact that Paul, who must have become a Christian two or three years at the most after the death of Christ, assumes that he has been baptized like every Christian (Rom. 6:3; I Cor. 12:13). In view of the absence of other patterns, it is highly probable that the primitive community took over the rite of water baptism from the disciples of John the Baptist; and from this it is also probable that from the first this rite purported to impart the forgiveness of sins by means of washing and at the same time admitted one to the community. This is the way Acts 2:38, 41 represents it, but adds that those baptized received the gift of the Holy Spirit; and Paul also assumes that every baptized person has received the Spirit of God (I Cor. 12:13). Now it has been doubted that, from the first, baptism was thought of as bound up with the bestowal of the Spirit, because Mark and Matthew still contained no reference to the general bestowal of the Spirit on the community, and the book of Acts also tells of isolated cases of the separation of baptism and the bestowal of the Spirit (10:44, 47-48; 8:12; 11:15-16; 19:2-6; cf. also 18:25). But the absence of references to the general bestowal of the Spirit on the community in Mark and Matthew proves nothing, because it is not otherwise in the Gospel of Luke, although in the book of Acts the same author represents the idea of the bestowal of the Spirit on all Christians at baptism. The passages in Acts which presuppose a separation of baptism and the bestowal of the Spirit (and these are to be evaluated quite differently in each case; see the commentaries on these passages) proceed precisely from the view that normally baptism and reception of the Spirit belong together. In addition, there is the fact that from the very beginning baptism undoubtedly was performed "in the name of Jesus," i.e., with the pronouncing of the name and hence with the invocation of Jesus (Acts 2:38; 8:16; 10:48; cf. I Cor. 1:13), and the relating of the baptized person and the risen Jesus, who had given and continued to give the Spirit to his community, also had to mean for the individual baptized person an entering into a relationship with the Spirit of the risen One. Thus the fact that all members of the primitive community were baptized likewise signified a visible separation from the rest of the Jewish community.

But the community had still another religious practice which separated it from the Jewish community—*the common meal*. The book of Acts, in its comprehensive portrayals of the life of the first Christians, says: "They continued steadfastly in the apostles' teaching and in fellowship, in the breaking of bread and in prayers" (2:42); "Daily they attended the temple together, and, breaking bread in their homes, they took their food rejoicing and with generous hearts" (2:46). Thus at the gathering of Christians in private homes bread was broken and of course also eaten, and these common meals took place with rejoicing. In these few indications there is lacking any reference to the drinking of wine and any reference back to Jesus' last meal or even to Jesus' death. Hence it has often been surmised that this celebration of a meal of the first Christians was only an eschatological common meal which had nothing to do with Jesus' last supper and the words of institution spoken there, but therefore was also completely separate from the Lord's Supper of the Pauline communities which had reference back to this last supper of Jesus. But this is a very unlikely conjecture, because the eschatological saying of Jesus, repeated by the primitive community ("I shall not drink of the fruit of the vine again until that day when I drink it new in the kingdom of God," Mark 14:25 par.), clearly assumes that the primitive community knew that it was to continue to drink wine at its common meals, and because the cry, "Our Lord, come!" presumably used at the common meals (I Cor. 16:22; see above, p. 112), likewise presupposes that in keeping with Jesus' will people assembled in the hope of being soon reunited with the risen Lord. But if people invoked the risen Lord at the common meals, then such meals were a worship observance which the primitive community solemnized along with its participation in the Jewish religious life and in which undoubtedly only the members of the community could take part. The designation "breaking of bread" used for this observance appears to be a Christian neologism, but we do not know why people thus named the observance, which certainly did not consist exclusively of the breaking of bread.

C. THE TWELVE AND THE APOSTLES

Still another element joined the members of the primitive community as over against the Jews who rejected the message of the resurrection of the crucified One and hence separated them from the Judaism to which they felt themselves to belong and which, by means of their preaching, they would call to the community of the new covenant. At first the primitive community undoubtedly had no fixed order. Peter appears to have represented the community to the outside world, as is taken for granted in Gal. 1:18 as well as in the book of Acts (3:12; 5:3, 29; 8:14). Somewhat later then we hear of the "elders" in the Jerusalem community (Acts 11: 30; 15:22-23). The emergence of such a group at the head of the community indeed lets us see that the primitive community was establishing itself over against the Judaism surrounding it, yet nothing actually can be discerned from this about the self-understanding of the primitive community, particularly since, for example, a community organization that in certain respects is kindred to it is also found in the Qumran group, which in no way thereby meant to separate, or did separate, from Judaism. On the other hand, the peculiar self-understanding of the primitive community which was establishing itself over against Judaism is shown in the role played by "the twelve" and "the apostles" in the primitive community. After Peter, the *circle of the twelve,* installed by Jesus as representatives of his call to the entire nation, had seen the resurrected One (I Cor. 15:5), and according to the account in Acts this circle belonged to the earliest community (1:13-14). Since we hear somewhat more than a decade later of the execution in Jerusalem of James, who belonged to the circle of the twelve (Acts 12: 1-2), the conjecture is justified that this group of the twelve played a role in the Jerusalem community as witnesses to the resurrection and indeed as witnesses to the earthly life of Jesus as well. The passing on of Jesus' prediction that at the Parousia the twelve would judge the twelve tribes of Israel (Matt. 19:28 par.) proves, moreover, that people in the primitive community attributed to the twelve an eschatological role with respect to the rest of the Jews. Of course this role of the twelve in the primitive community can only be inferred from these indications, and hence the same is true of the primitive community's consciousness of being commissioned to proclaim to the rest of the Jews the testimony of the resurrection of Jesus Christ. Already at the time of the so-called Apostolic Council (*ca.* A.D. 48), the twelve no longer played a decisive role in the primitive community. Neither in Gal. 2:1-10 nor in Acts 15:1-29 are they mentioned, and for later primitive Christianity they appear to have had no crucial importance.

But it was of abiding significance for the further development of the primitive church and of Christianity generally that *"the apostles"* were to be found in the primitive community in Jerusalem. In Galatians, Paul says that immediately after his calling by means of the vision of the resurrected One, who also made him an apostle (thus I Cor. 15:8-9), he could have gone to Jerusalem "to the apostles [who were there] before me." But he emphasizes that he did not do this, but only three years later went to see Peter in Jerusalem; "but I saw no other of the apostles, except James, the Lord's brother" (Gal. 1:17-19). From these words it clearly appears that "the apostles before him" belonged to the Jerusalem community and that Peter was the most important member. Whom else Paul counted among the apostles is disputed, but it may be said with great probability that for him the other members of the group of twelve also qualified as apostles; since the twelve were the first witnesses to the resurrection after Peter and must already have been in Jerusalem very early, and since three years after his call Paul takes for granted "the apostles" in Jerusalem, but on his visit meets only Peter, one of the twelve, it may hardly be thought that he does not count the twelve among the apostles (cf. Gal. 1:17-19; I Cor. 15:5). Yet it can hardly be determined with certainty whether in the ambiguous clause, "I saw no other of the apostles, except James, the Lord's brother," Paul counts James among the apostles; and it likewise cannot be said with certainty whether Barnabas was numbered with the apostles (cf. I Cor. 9:5-6; Acts 14:14). But undoubtedly according to Paul men otherwise unknown to us, like the Jewish Christians Andronicus and Junias (Rom. 16:7), belonged among the apostles. Thus the circle of the apostles was in no case limited to the twelve; on the other hand, according to Paul's conviction it was definitively closed, since in I Cor. 15:7 he speaks of an appearance of Christ to "all the apostles," after which followed only his own vision of the resurrected Christ which also made him an apostle. Hence while on the basis of the facts mentioned it can no longer be said with certainty who and how many belonged to the "apostles before Paul," still Paul lets us see clearly what is for him the distinguishing mark of an apostle: he must be called to the mission by the resurrected One himself (I Cor. 9:1; 15:9-10; Gal. 1:16-17). Thus it is not simply the vision of the resurrected One that makes one an apostle (the "five hundred brethren" of I Cor. 15:6 are not apostles!), but the special call. We do not know how this apostolic circle arose in the first period of the primitive community, because our sources are silent about this, and the opinions about it are widely divergent. But it is clear that it was the task of the apostles to bear witness to the resurrection of Jesus of Nazareth that had been revealed to them, and for the sake of this testimony of the event of the resurrection one had to adhere to the primitive community, in whose midst were to be found the apostles.

Now of course in this respect Paul, on the basis of the call that had come to him through the resurrected One, places himself on an equal footing with the Jerusalem apostles, and hence he emphasizes that he did not at first go to see the Jerusalem apostles. But then after three years he did go to Jerusalem and visited Peter for two weeks and, in addition, met James, the Lord's brother. Even though it is not certain that by his choice of words in Gal. 1:18 ("I went up to Jerusalem to get acquainted with Cephas") Paul is saying that he wished to get information from Peter, still it is a likely assumption that for Paul the personal contact with Peter was important also because Peter as a disciple of the earthly Jesus could tell something of this Jesus. When Paul relates then in Gal. 2:2 that fourteen years later he laid his preaching to the Gentiles before "those who were of repute" (RSV) in the Jerusalem community, among whom in addition to James the Lord's brother were also Jesus' disciples Peter and John (Gal. 2:9), "lest I should run or had run in vain," this account is found in the context of a statement in which Paul wishes to prove the essential independence of his apostolic office from men and above all from the Jerusalem apostles (Gal. 1:1, 11; 2:8-9, 11). When Paul nevertheless regards the recognition of his non-law-observing preaching of the gospel by the "pillars" of the Jerusalem community as necessary so that his missionary labor should not be in vain (cf., with regard to the expression "run in vain," Phil. 2:16!), this can be understood only if Paul was of the conviction that the connection with "those of repute" in the Jerusalem community is indispensable for every community of Jesus Christ. Paul had received his apostolic office and with it the commission to bear witness to the resurrection of Jesus Christ from the resurrected One himself; hence for him the necessity of a connection with "those of repute" in Jerusalem, among whom must have been also the former disciples of Jesus and present Jerusalem apostles (Peter and John in fact are named!), can only be based on the fact that here alone was to be found the tradition of the earthly Jesus on which every Christian community was dependent. Even if the restriction of the name of apostle to the twelve, as the book of Acts expressly represents it, is a later limitation which we encounter for the first time in the Gospel of Mark, and thus at least twenty years after the Apostolic Council (Mark 6:7, 30 par.), still the primitive community in Jerusalem already very early could claim to be the community of the apostles which mediated the connection with the tradition of the earthly Jesus. Greek-speaking Jewish Christianity as well as Gentile Christianity preserved this connection by appropriating the apostolic tradition and shaping and developing it out of their own experiences of faith and for their own needs. This special character of the original community as the community of the apostles of Jesus Christ justified its unique significance, indispensable for all Christians. But this special character also brings with it the fact that the decline of the original community in Jerusalem in the Jewish-Roman war—in A.D. 66 the Jewish Christians of Jerusalem emigrated to Pella in Trans-Jordania and from then on no longer played a significant role—had no important consequences for the Christian church which in the meantime had made its way into the Mediterranean world of the Roman Empire. "That is to say, it belongs to the very nature of the office of apostle to be unique and not transferrable" (O. Cullmann), because for later primitive Christianity, what was of abiding importance was not the persons of the apostles, and even less the "mother community," but the knowledge of God's act in Jesus of Nazareth and his resurrection. The Gentile Christian church appropriated this tradition and under the leadership of the divine Spirit interpreted and wrote it down and thus preserved the mission of the apostles.

At the transition from the Palestinian apostolic community to the later Gentile Christian primitive Christianity stands Paul, according to his own estimate the "least of the apostles" (I Cor. 15:9) and yet the first theologian of Gentile Christianity. From him alone we have precise knowledge of his theological thought; hence his epistles form for us the temporal center of New Testament theology.

CHAPTER III

THE THEOLOGY OF PAUL

1. *The historical position of Paul*

a. EFFECT AND SOURCE OF PAULINE THOUGHT

In addition to the gospels and the book of Acts, the New Testament contains a number of writings in epistolary form and the Revelation of John. The epistles that begin with the author's name of Paul comprise not quite three fifths of this non-narrative part of the New Testament. This very statistical relation prompts in the reader the impression that Paul was the most significant and most influential thinker in primitive Christianity. And this impression is strengthened by the fact that Paul is the only one among the authors of New Testament writings of whose person and history we learn anything more outside his own writings. This would hold true even if I Peter should stem directly or indirectly from Peter, because we know hardly anything further about Peter's activity after the time of his leading role in the first community. If a Gentile Christian author of the late primitive Christian times wrote I Peter, which is highly probable, then the author of this epistle is otherwise just as little known to us as are the authors of the other "catholic epistles" and of the Revelation of John (cf. any introduction to the New Testament). But from Paul's epistles we can get to know a significant section of Paul's activity as missionary, and the book of Acts, even though it is not everywhere able to give us a reliable account, allows us to place these reports in a coherent setting. The great scope of the Pauline corpus of letters and the uniqueness of what we know about the person of Paul thus set the Pauline letters apart from the rest of the New Testament and lead to the view that Paul's theological thought not only forms the temporal center of the New Testament, but also decisively dominates the development of primitive Christian thought. When people began in the nineteenth century to separate the preaching of the historical Jesus from the evangelists' presentation, and in the process significant differences between the theology of Paul and the preaching of Jesus emerged, the impression was strengthened that Paul had played the decisive role in the reshaping of the preaching of Jesus into the Christ faith of the primitive church. It was only natural then that the post-Pauline writings in the New Testament also were interrogated essentially with a view to determining to what extent the ideas of Paul continue to work in them or fail to do so. In the meantime, of course, it has been recognized, as we have seen, that very substantial presuppositions of Pauline thought had already been created in the Palestinian and, above all, in the Hellenistic primitive community, and it has also been recognized that in various places in his epistles Paul employs formulated traditions which form for him the points of departure of his theological argument. On the other hand it has become evident that we have in the New Testament and in the time immediately connected with it a whole series of writings which presuppose the theological thought of Paul or are presented directly as Pauline (Ephesians, the Pastoral Epistles, Hebrews, I Peter, Ignatius of Antioch), but that numerous writings betray no sort of Pauline influence or are in some way set in opposition to Paul—thus the gospels and the book of Acts, James, II Peter, the Johannine epistles, Revelation, and I Clement (in spite of his use of Paul's letters). Thus upon closer examination the impression that Paul forms the center of the New Testament and has decisively influenced the development of later primitive Christianity does not prove true.

And yet there can be no doubt that Paul played a very substantial role in the development of primitive Christianity. This is unconditionally true of Paul's missionary activity; for even though Christianity spread independently of Paul in many parts of the Roman Empire, as in Syria, Egypt, and Rome, still, according to all that we know, Paul was *the* missionary of primitive Christianity who with a definite decision brought the gospel to non-Jews and drew the theological and practical inferences from this task. If we may take seriously the missionary principle which he asserted, of preaching only where Christ was not yet named (Rom. 15:20), then he was the first one to establish Christian communities in Asia Minor, Macedonia, and Greece, and he concerned himself with the proper growth of these communities even after his departure, through the sending of epistles and in part also through his companions. But Paul was capable of this historically decisive achievement because—and for our purposes this is the more important consideration—he had been a Jewish rabbinical scholar and therefore became *the first theological thinker* in Christianity. It is in this that his real significance lies, and if his impact in the context of primitive Christianity and in the first period afterward was slighter than the first impression would suggest, still his epistles were collected very early—presumably already by the end of the first century—and from the very first belonged to the canon of the Christian church which was being formed. This fact had the effect that from the end of the second century onward his theological ideas constantly influenced Christian thought and in several cases decisively turned it in a new direction.

Thus if Paul's significance in the context of the development of primitive Christian thought lies in the fact that he was the first Christian theologian, still this indisputable fact must not be allowed to lead us into reading the Pauline epistles as dogmatic texts or to approach them with theological inquiries which are alien to them. Paul was a theologian, but he was theologian as missionary, and therefore his theological thinking is to a large extent determined by the *discussion with his communities* and with divergent opinions which come to his ears from the communities. This by itself ensures that his reflection is not systematic in nature, but is connected with the missionary task. But for our acquaintance with Paul's thought, there is the additional fact that his reflection is not preserved for us in systematic presentation, but in epistles which were written for specific readers and to specific situations. This means that Paul is counting on readers who know the presuppositions of the arguments advanced and therefore also can understand allusions which we are not able with certainty to interpret. But above all, this means that Paul did not need to say to his readers everything that would have to be said in a particular connection, and on many points which in themselves are essential he does not say anything at all, because they are undisputed and can be assumed to be acknowledged by the readers. Hence it is requisite in the interpretation of Paul's epistles to reckon with the fact that many individual statements must remain incomprehensible. The absence of certain ideas or their merely incidental mention by no means should be taken to mean that Paul considered these ideas unimportant, or that he perhaps deliberately rejected them. Rather, the exegete must carefully note the historical situation out of which and to which the individual trains of thought are written, and must also be open to the possibility that individual views of Paul changed in the context of his activity.

And we must take still another historical presupposition of Paul's theological thought into consideration if we wish to interpret Paul appropriately. Paul in fact at first had been a convinced *Pharisee,* who in Jerusalem was a pupil of a famous rabbi (Phil. 3:5; Gal. 1:14; Acts 22:3). But he was also a *Jew of the Diaspora* (Acts 22:3), who was acquainted with Hellenistic education at least to the extent that this resulted of itself from association with non-Jews in a Hellenistic city: cf. only the quotation from Menander in I Cor. 15:33 and the reference to sport customs in I Cor. 9:24-25. Hence we can expect Paul in his theological formulations to use not only Palestinian-Jewish but also Hellenistic-Jewish and Hellenistic-pagan concepts and ideas, and this is in fact the case. Hence it is undoubtedly mistaken to explain Paul's theology one-sidedly, in terms of one of these historical presuppositions, especially since Palestinian and Hellenistic Judaism were not at all sharply separated entities. But it is difficult to determine in detail from which religio-historical presuppositions Paul proceeds in a particular context, and for this reason many an exegetical question cannot be answered with certainty.

b. THE SOURCES

Even the question of which sources can be used in setting forth the Pauline theology is disputed. Surely it cannot seriously be doubted that the author of the book of Acts has only a very imprecise view of Paul's thought and often, in the discourses attributed to Paul, puts in his mouth ideas which are not in harmony with basic Pauline ideas (above all in the speech on the Areopagus, Acts 17:22 ff.), so that Paul's speeches in the book of Acts cannot be considered as sources for the presentation of the theology of Paul. On the other hand, opinions are widely divergent over how many of the thirteen letters in the New Testament handed down under Paul's name go back to Paul and hence can be employed by us as sources for the theology of Paul. The divergence from the rest of the letters of Paul is most evident in the so-called "Pastoral Epistles," i.e., the epistles to Timothy and Titus, and indeed precisely in the religious terminology and in basic theological ideas, so that these epistles can hardly have Paul as their author. Even the assumption that a secretary of Paul wrote them following Paul's instructions cannot explain the profound substantive differences between the Pastoral Epistles and Paul. A similar judgment very probably is to be made about Ephesians also. For in this writing which is not addressed to any particular community, and which in extraordinary fashion adopts and reshapes ideas and formulations of the Colossian epistle, not only is there a language which is decidedly different from Paul's usage, but the theological content of the epistle, above all in the estimate of the church and of the apostles and in the lack of a genuine eschatological expectation, stands in such sharp tension with Paul that this writing too cannot have been composed by Paul (see any introduction to the New Testament). The Pauline origin of Colossians and of II Thessalonians is also doubted by many students of the question. The arguments adduced in favor of this position (see any introduction to the New Testament), however, are by no means compelling, and although certain difficulties remain, one may still regard these two epistles as stemming from Paul. This means that available to us as sources for the presentation of Paul's theology are nine epistles of Paul (Romans, I and II Corinthians, Galatians, Philippians, Colossians, I and II Thessalonians, and Philemon), which were written between the years 50 and 60. It is certain that the Thessalonian epistles are the earliest of these, and of the remaining, so far as they can be dated with certainty, Romans is undoubtedly the latest, written some six years later than the Thessalonian epistles, which were composed in about the year 50. The Corinthian epistles are to be placed in the interim, and the Galatian epistle also belongs in this interim, although we cannot be certain in what relation in time it stands to the Corinthian epistles. On the other hand, it is much disputed, and scarcely to be decided with certainty, whether the epistles that stem from an imprisonment of Paul, i.e., those to the Philippians, the Colossians, and Philemon, also date from the years 50-56 and then would have to have been written during an Ephesian imprisonment, or were written in a later imprisonment, after the appearance of the Roman epistle, in Caesarea or Rome. But in view of this uncertainty it also is hardly possible to use these epistles as witnesses for a late form of Pauline thought. Instead, we know literary utterances of Paul only from the brief series of years of his activity in Europe and western Asia Minor (from six or, at the most, ten years), and neither in the emergence of his thinking—his call lies some eighteen years before the earliest extant epistle—nor in any kind of developments of his theology do the sources allow us a certain insight.

2. *The present as the time of salvation*

When one tries to present the various forms of theological thought in the New Testament according to their own inward coherence and not on the basis of a scheme imposed upon them from without, one must ask in each case about the fundamental concerns dominating the respective theological thought form. If for Jesus the preaching of the imminent kingdom of God was the point of departure (also emphasized by the gospel writers), Paul's point of departure is closely related to this basic outlook of Jesus. Of course this is an insight which does not present itself at first glance, and hence it is not acknowledged on all sides. In fact, Paul himself summarizes the faith of the Christians thus: "If you confess with your mouth Jesus as Lord and believe in your heart that God has raised him from the dead, you will be saved" (Rom. 10:9), and he says of his preaching: "We preach Christ as crucified" (I Cor. 1:23). These sentences do say that the message of the crucified and resurrected Jesus Christ is the most important concern of the Pauline proclamation. On the other hand, the rediscovery of the biblical message of salvation by Martin Luther has started from the insight that Paul does not proclaim the wrathful God, but the justification of the sinner by God out of grace through faith, and hence this idea of Paul certainly has rightly been called "the center of the Pauline message" (H. D. Wendland). Nevertheless, neither the preaching of the cross and the resurrection of the Lord Jesus Christ nor the doctrine of justification by faith alone is the suitable point of departure for a historically appropriate presentation of Pauline theology. Both Paul's message about Christ and his doctrine of salvation can rightly be understood only when one recognizes that Paul fundamentally sees the present as the time of the beginning eschatological saving activity of God; in other words, when one recognizes that Paul, like Jesus, starts out from the belief in the imminence of the eschatological consummation of salvation.

a. THE EXPECTATION OF THE IMMINENT CONSUMMATION OF
   SALVATION

This state of affairs does not immediately strike the eye so clearly as with Jesus, because Paul only rarely uses the concept of the *kingdom of God* which was so important for Jesus. Of course in some passages where the concept of the kingdom of God occurs in Paul's writings, he clearly takes for granted that entrance into the kingdom of God is a future event which coincides with the final judgment: "Those who do such things will not inherit the kingdom of God" (Gal. 5:21; similarly I Cor. 6:9-10; 15:50); the present patience and the faith of Christians are an "evidence of the righteous judgment of God, that you may be made worthy of the kingdom of God" (II Thess. 1:5 RSV). All these passages show that in Paul's opinion also, Christians are promised participation in the coming kingdom of God and thus in God's glory ("that you walk worthy of God, who calls you into his kingdom and glory," I Thess. 2:12). However, not only are these references to the coming kingdom of God uncommon, but along with them there also are found in Paul some expressions about the kingdom of God in which one can be of the opinion that with this concept Paul means to describe the present existence of Christians: "The kingdom of God is not eating and drinking, but righteousness and peace and joy in the Holy Spirit" (Rom. 14:17); "the kingdom of God (shows up) not in word but in power" (I Cor. 4:20); the three Jewish Christians Aristarchus, Marcus, and Jesus Justus "are all fellow-workers with relation to the kingdom of God" (Col. 4:11). Now of course it is by no means certain that in these passages Paul is thinking of the present existence of the kingdom of God and not rather of the advance working of the future kingdom of God in the present. But regardless of which way one interprets them, these passages show that for Paul, similarly as for Jesus, the kingdom of God is not *only* a matter of hope. Thus though Paul only seldom employs the concept of the kingdom of God, nevertheless the appearance of this concept is an indication that for him also the anticipation of God's future saving activity is important, and in fact it can easily be observed that in *all* his epistles apart from the little epistle to Philemon, Paul refers to the imminent end or the coming end event. In the earliest of the extant epistles, Paul not only speaks about the sudden coming of the (Last) "Day" as "a thief in the night," but he clearly is calculating that the risen Lord at his resurrection "will descend from heaven, and the dead in Christ will rise first; then we who are alive, who yet remain, will be caught up together with them in the clouds . . ." (I Thess. 5:2,4; 4:15-17). Paul here expects in his lifetime to experience the parousia, i.e., the coming of the Lord at the end of time, just as he does in I Corinthians: "The time is foreshortened" (7:29); the last trumpet "will sound, and the dead will be raised incorruptible, and we shall be changed" (15:52). While Galatians, II Corinthians, and Colossians only speak of the coming day of the Lord, of the appearing of the Lord, of the coming resurrection of the dead, and of the coming inheritance of the kingdom of God (II Cor. 1:14; 4:14; Gal. 6:9; Col. 3:4), without explicitly referring to the *imminence* in time of these eschatological events, Philippians, which cannot be dated with certainty, says, "The Lord is at hand" (4:5). But in Romans, written later than II Corinthians and Galatians, Paul again says plainly that "our salvation now is nearer than when we first believed," and expects the final events as so immediately imminent that he can formulate it thus: "These [the unbelieving Jews] have now been disobedient toward the [divine] mercy shown to you, so that they also *now* may receive mercy" (13:11; 11:31). Along with this Paul shows again and again that he expects the near future to bring the judgment day (Rom. 2:5; 13:12; I Cor. 3:13; 5:5) or the day of Christ's appearing (Phil. 1:6; 3:20; I Thess. 2:19; 3:13; I Cor. 15:23), the reception of salvation (Rom. 5:9, 11:26; I Cor. 3:13, 15), the resurrection of the dead in Christ (I Cor. 6:14; 15:22; II Cor. 4:14; Rom. 8:11), and "being with Christ" (I Thess. 4:17; 5:10; II Cor. 13:4), but also the final decay (Rom. 2:12; 8:13; II Thess. 2:10; Gal. 6:7-9). Correspondingly, we find in Paul rare but clear references to the anticipated events of the end-time (I Thess. 4:15-17; II Thess. 2:3-10; I Cor. 15:22-28, 51-53; II Cor. 5:1-4, 10), We shall have to return to the significance for Paul of these apocalyptic (in the narrower sense) eschatological conceptions (see below, pp. 235 ff.); but in view of all these texts there can be no doubt that Paul is basically molded in his thinking by the expectation of the imminent consummation of salvation.

b. THE PRESENCE OF SALVATION

However, Paul equally stresses his conviction that the present is already the time of salvation: "Behold, now is the accepted time, behold, now is the day of salvation" (II Cor. 6:2). *Now* the righteousness of God attested by the law and the prophets has been revealed, *now* through Christ we have received the reconciliation, "now there is no condemnation for those who are in Christ Jesus," now the mystery hidden from eons and generations has been revealed to the saints of God (Rom. 3:21; 5:11; 8:1; Col. 1:26). Correspondingly, the present is described as the fulfilled time, in which God sent his Son (Gal. 4:4), and in which for the Christians "the ends of the ages have come" (I Cor. 10:11). Therefore it is said of the Christians: "You were justified in the name of the Lord Jesus Christ," "We are saved by hope," "For freedom Christ has made us free" (I Cor. 6:11; Rom. 8:24; Gal. 5:1). Thus according to Paul, God's action in Christ in the past has already caused eschatological salvation to become effective; with the sending of Christ the time of salvation has dawned. Of course this presence of salvation is provisional, and Paul not only emphasizes that "we are saved by hope" (Rom. 8:24), but also says of himself: "I do not judge concerning myself that I have laid hold" (Phil. 3:13), and speaks of the Christian community as "those who have the first fruits of the Spirit" and of whom it is also true that "we groan inwardly as we wait for the redemption of our body" (Rom. 8:23). Hence there can be no doubt that with the assured expectation that the time of final salvation will soon come with the appearance of Christ, Paul combines the certainty that through God's action in Christ the eschatological salvation has already begun.

Thus Paul took over the eschatological expectations of contemporary Judaism, but in consequence of the primitive community's belief in the resurrection of Jesus Christ has reshaped it so that a contradictory conjunction of future expectation and belief in the present eschatological salvation results. This impression is confirmed when we note the concepts of time which Paul employs to describe the present. From Judaism Paul adopts the contrast of "this world-age (eon)" and the "coming world-age." He frequently speaks of "this eon" as a present reality, in which the Christian lives and which threatens him (Rom. 12:2; I Cor. 1:20; 3:18; similarly "the present age," Rom. 8:18), and he explicitly names the demons, the "world elements," and Satan as the rulers or the god of this eon (I Cor. 2:6, 8; Gal. 4:3, 9; Col. 2:20; II Cor. 4:4). In the same sense Paul can speak of "this world [cosmos]" (I Cor. 3:19; 1:20; 5:10), and can expressly emphasize, "The form of this world is passing away" (I Cor. 7:31). Thus like apocalyptic Judaism he considers the present as part of the perishing world-age which is estranged from God (" the god of this eon has blinded the thoughts of the unbelievers," II Cor. 4:4), and therefore this world-age can be described as "the present evil eon" (Gal. 1:4). Of course it is curious then that Paul does not speak of the "coming eon," but calls the anticipated future characterized by salvation the "kingdom of God" (Gal. 5:21; I Cor. 15:50), the "coming [parousia] of Christ" (I Cor. 15:23; I Thess. 2:19; 3:13; 4:15; 5:23; II Thess. 2:1, 8-9), the "revelation of the Lord" (I Cor. 1:7; II Thess. 1:7), the "revelation of the sons of God" (Rom. 8:19), and the "revelation of the coming glory" (Rom. 8:18). This shows clearly that Paul is not interested in an apocalyptic division of time, but in the final salvation wrought by Christ. Hence Paul not only can say of the present that it belongs to the evil eon which is passing away, but he can also confess: "Jesus Christ has given himself for our sins, that he might rescue us from the present evil eon according to the will of God and our Father" (Gal. 1:4) and correspondingly declare of the Christians: "[God] has delivered us from the power of darkness and transferred us into the kingdom of his beloved Son" (Col. 1:13). Therefore the Christians can be challenged: "Be not conformed to this eon" (Rom. 12:2), but there likewise exists for them the danger that in spite of their having died to the elements of the world, they will behave "as though they were living in the world" (Col. 2:20). Thus it is clear from this perspective also that for Paul the present evil eon still exists and signifies a danger, but that God's decisive act in Christ has occurred for the overcoming of this eon, and that on the basis of this divine act the Christians are liberated from the powers of the present eon and already now can live in the kingdom of Christ.

Thus Paul clearly starts out from the basic outlook that his present is decisively determined by the sending of Christ, his death and his resurrection, which have introduced God's eschatological action. The Christ event brings about the basic turning point in God's dealing with the world, because the eschatological kingdom of Christ has dawned, although the present evil eon still continues and Christ's appearance in glory and hence the arrival of God's kingdom in glory are still delayed. Therefore for Paul world history is not, as it is for the Greeks, a repetitive cycle, but he sees history as issuing from God and moving toward a divine goal which signifies the end of world events: "From him and through him and to him are all things" (Rom. 11:36); "For us [there is] one God, the Father, from whom are all things, and for whom we exist" (I Cor. 8:6); "Then the end, when [Christ] will deliver the kingdom to God the Father" (I Cor. 15:24). However, this world event that is moving toward God's conclusion for it also is not divided into several periods, as in Jewish apocalyptic, but has its turning point exclusively in Christ, whom God sent "when the fullness of time had come" (Gal. 4:4), and in whom "it pleased all the fullness [of God] to dwell and through him to reconcile all things to him [Christ]" (Col. 1:19-20).

C. ADAM AND CHRIST

Now Paul sees this eschatological event which has been introduced by God's action in Christ as bound up in a twofold way with history *before* Christ. First, he places Adam and Christ in parallel: as belonging to Adam all men must die *because* they all sin (Rom. 5:12, 15, 18); "As in Adam all die, so in Christ will all be made alive" (I Cor. 15:22); "As we have borne the image of the earthly [man], we shall also bear the image of the heavenly

[man]" (I Cor. 15:49). Here humanity before Christ clearly is seen as a unity belonging to Adam only in the hopelessness of its being a prey to death and to this extent exclusively in its alienation from God and its lostness; in the context of this conception, the coming of Christ signifies the appearing of the divine life: "If, through the transgression of one, death gained dominion through the one, how much more will those who have received the abundance of grace and the gift of righteousness reign in life through the one Jesus Christ" (Rom. 5:17).

But this almost elemental conception, which seemingly portrays a stark fate for pre-Christian humanity, is broken by Paul in a variety of ways. In the first place, according to Paul the rule of death over mankind in Adam is by no means eliminated even since Christ's coming; until the Parousia Christians also, like all other men, still must die: "If we die, we die unto the Lord" (Rom. 14:8; cf. Phil. 1:21; I Thess. 4:13; I Cor. 11:30; 15:6,18). Only when Christ appears "is death, as the last enemy, destroyed" (I Cor. 15:26). Thus death's dominion over mankind still continues, as the old eon still continues. Further, it is true that the Adam humanity is indeed generally in a state of being prey to the fate of death, but death affects all men "because they all have sinned" (Rom. 5:12d; see below, pp. 178 ff.). Thus the death of every single man is the consequence of the sin of each individual and hence of his guilt (cf. Rom. 3:19-20a). But above all, Paul inserts, into the contrast of the humanity descended from Adam and humanity since Christ, the law of Moses as "having come in between": only through the coming of the law of Moses does the sinful behavior of men become guilt, and do men actually become transgressors who are gravely guilty (Rom. 5:13, 14a, 20). That is to say, Paul breaks the contrast of Adam and Christ, which appears as elemental fate and leaves out of consideration God's historical action prior to Christ, with a reference to the intervening law of Moses. He shows therewith that for him the time between Adam and Christ cannot be described simply as the period in which all men as sinners fell prey to death.

d. THE HISTORY OF ISRAEL AND THE CHRIST EVENT

In other words, Paul sees the eschatological event as connected with the history of Christ in yet another way. The sending of Christ when the time was fulfilled signifies the righteousness of God becoming revealed without law (Gal. 4:4). But this eschatological action of God is "attested by the law and the prophets"

(Rom. 3:21; cf. Rom. 1:2). As here the pious men of Old Testament history appear as the ones who foretell God's eschatological saving act, so Paul says that certain events of Israelite history "happened to those [people] as an example, but they were written down as a warning to us to whom the ends of the eons have come" (I Cor. 10:11). Quite in harmony with this, after Paul has cited the Old Testament expression (Gen. 15:6) about the faith of Abraham which was reckoned to him as righteousness, he says: "Not for his sake alone was it written that 'it was reckoned to him,' but also for our sake to whom it is to be reckoned, we who believe on the one who raised Jesus our Lord from the dead" (Rom. 4:23-24). Thus certain events of Old Testament history are identified as prefigurings of the Christ events and in accordance with God's will have been written down for the sake of the Christians. Finally, in harmony with this also is the fact that according to Paul the miraculous event of the water-yielding rock that followed the people of Israel in the wilderness is connected with the Christ happening: "And the rock was Christ" (I Cor. 10:4).

Corresponding to the preparation, demonstrated by Paul in examples, of the eschatological Christ salvation in events of the history of Irael are two lines of this history which Paul draws to Christ. *Abraham* appears as the believer, who was justified because of his faith and to whom it was promised that, like him, all believers, whether Jews or Gentiles, will be justified because of their faith: "But the Scripture foresaw that God would justify the Gentiles by faith, and proclaimed to Abraham in advance the glad tidings that 'in you all peoples will be blessed.' Hence those [men] of faith are blessed together with believing Abraham" (Gal. 3:8-9); Abraham "is the father of all who believe without being circumcised, so that righteousness is reckoned to them, and the father of the circumcised who are not merely circumcised but also walk in the footsteps of the faith of our father Abraham which he had while he was [yet] uncircumcised" (Rom. 4:11-12). Paul does not mention any other men who before the "coming" of faith (Gal. 3:23), like Abraham, believed, and from this some have wanted to deduce that, for Paul, Abraham is only a timeless example and not a figure of the Israelite prehistory of the revelation of Christ. But this is not correct, because Paul clearly reckons that the divine promises were entrusted to the Jews, and that "many did not believe them" (Rom. 3:3), yet by no means all were unbelieving. Besides, in Rom. 9:7-8, Paul explicitly separates from the totality of Abraham's descendants according to the flesh ("they are not all children because they are seed of Abraham") those who are "children of the promise" and hence are actually acknowledged by God as "Israel." Further, the expression "With most of them God was not pleased" (I Cor. 10:5), said of the Israelite people in the wilderness, takes for granted that not all the Israelites of the wilderness period were among those with whom God was not pleased. Thus Paul sees, from Abraham on through the history of Israel, a preparatory saving activity of God being achieved, which "is written down for our sake" (Rom. 4:23), and was written beforehand "for our instruction" or "to admonish us" (Rom. 15:4; I Cor. 10:11), even though this preparatory saving activity of God is not described as a continuous occurrence.

Beside this line from Abraham to Christ and the Christians, Paul draws a second *line from Moses to Christ,* and this line is purely negative. "The law came in, to increase the trespass" (Rom. 5:20); "Before faith came, we were confined under the law, kept under restraint until faith should be revealed. So that the law was our custodian until Christ came" (Gal. 3:23-24 RSV). The covenant of Mount Sinai led into bondage (Gal. 4:24). But even though "the law brings [only] wrath" (Rom. 4:15), because "by works of the law no flesh will be justified before him [God]" (Rom. 3:20), still even this maleficent occurrence is a sign in advance pointing to the eschatological salvation in Christ, because "the law was our custodian until Christ came, that we might be justified by faith" (Gal. 3:24 RSV), and because "Christ is the end of the law" (Rom. 10:4).

Thus it is clear that Paul sees all the lines of divine activity since the creation as running toward Christ and that therefore for him the Christ event represents the beginning of the divine eschatological salvation that has been planned from time immemorial. But since Paul also maintains that the perishing evil eon is not yet at an end, there results his peculiar basic outlook, that *the old eon still exists and yet the end-time has already begun.* From this state of affairs it is clear that Paul has reshaped in paradoxical fashion the traditional Jewish conception of the two mutually exclusive eons. He does not sketch a speculative periodization of history, but sees his present from the perspective of the belief that God sent his Son when the time was fulfilled, "that we might receive the adoption as sons" (Gal. 4: 4-5). That is to say, Paul recognized in faith that "now is the day of salvation" (II Cor. 6:2), but he also knows that "the time is shortened" and "the form of this world is passing away" (I Cor. 7:29, 31). And therefore he is persuaded that already in the perishing eon the end-time has begun. Thus one could say that for Paul's belief the two eons exist together in his present, that the time between Christ's resurrection and his Parousia represents an "interim," for the end of which the believer yearns. God's eschatological saving activity has brought about this state of affairs, and therefore Paul sees the being of the Christian from the perspective of this "interim period." Hence Paul's theological thought is concerned with comprehending the Christ event as an eschatological event within the world-age that is passing away, and with describing the existence of the Christian from that perspective.

e. PAUL'S CALL EXPERIENCE

The correctness of this description of the basic outlook dominating the theological thought of Paul is shown by a look at Paul's experience of his call. We know about the so-called "conversion" of Paul only from a few allusions in his epistles (Gal. 1:12-16; I Cor. 9:1; 15:8; Phil. 3:6-7; possibly II Cor. 4:6), since the three accounts in the book of Acts at the most add supplementary reports on the external story (Acts 9:1-19; 22:4-16; 26:9-18). To be sure the usual description of Paul's call experience as "conversion" is erroneous because even before this experience Paul had been a strictly law-observing Jew who did not need to make any sort of accusations against himself (Phil. 3:6), and because Paul in fact as a Christian held to the God of the fathers (Rom. 15:8). Paul looks back on his pre-Christian time as a time which meant "gain" for him (Phil. 3:7), and he is not in the least aware of somehow having come to doubt his Jewish legal piety or otherwise having been prepared for a more open attitude toward Jesus. Paul rather had been in his Jewish period "an extremely zealous person for the traditions of my fathers" (Gal. 1:14), and this means that he had striven by observance of the pharisaically interpreted law to stand "with respect to the righteousness that is according to the law blameless" in the sight of God (Phil. 3:6). But the Christians asserted, contradicting the law, that a crucified man, who according to the law was cursed by God (Deut. 21:23 is cited in this sense in Gal. 3:13), had been raised by God: "He was crucified in weakness, but he lives by God's power" (II Cor. 13:4). Still as a Christian Paul describes the preaching of the crucified Messiah as an "object of indignation for the Jews" (I Cor. 1:23), and this indignation prompted him to "persecute and oppress the church of God above measure" (Gal. 1:13; cf. I Cor. 15:9). In view of his violent resistance to God's action in Christ, it is, in the judgment of the Christian Paul, a sign of pure divine grace that "it pleased God to reveal his Son to me" (Gal. 1:15-16) and to call him to be an apostle (I Cor. 15:9-10). About this revelatory experience at Damascus Paul only says: "Christ was seen by me" (I Cor. 15:8; cf. 9:1), and this vision of the resurrected One convinced him that God had installed the man Jesus who was born of the seed of David to be the Son of God with power (Rom. 1:3-4), and thus that the preaching of the Christians, in spite of what had been been for Paul up until then its blasphemous character, was right. Now Paul knew that God in fact had sent his Son when the time was ripe, and that Christ was raised as the firstborn from the dead (Col. 1:18; Rom. 8:29). With this belief was given the conviction that the end-time had broken in through God's action in Christ, but at the same time the certainty that the Lord Christ is exalted to the presence of God brought with it the hope in the final appearing of the Lord in glory: "Our citizenship is in heaven, whence we also await the Lord Jesus Christ as savior, who will transform our lowly body, that it may be made like his glorious body, by the power to subject all things to himself" (Phil. 3:20-21). Now Paul had to understand the present as the dawning end-time of salvation, as the in-breaking of the end-time into the eon which is passing away, and it was his task as thinker to understand the divine action in Christ as well as the being of the Christians from the standpoint of the faith experience, that in Christ God had wrought the final salvation, but that the final consummation, with the appearance of Christ in glory, was yet to come. Hence Paul describes the Christ event as a historical action of God, and hence he sees the Christians in the context of *this* historical actuality. In order to comprehend Paul's theological thought, we must inquire as to this historical action of God in Christ and this being of the Christians in God's history.

3. The Christ event

a. THE SENDING OF THE SON OF GOD

At the beginning of the epistle to the Romans, Paul sums up the content of the gospel of God which was committed to him for proclaiming, with a confessional formula of the primitive community which he presumably had somewhat recast (see above, p. 110), in the following fashion: "Paul . . . , called apostle, set apart for the proclamation of God's good news . . . , [which treats] of his Son, who is born of the seed of David according to the flesh, who is installed to be the Son of God in power according to the Holy Spirit since the resurrection from the dead, [namely] Jesus Christ, our Lord" (Rom. 1:1-4). This characterization of Paul's good news to a community which he had not founded is distinctive in that not only do the two most important predicates of honor for Jesus Christ, namely Son of God and Lord, occur here, but also in the description of the Son of God his earthly ancestry is mentioned as well as his heavenly dignity. In this characterization of Jesus Christ some have liked to see described the "two sides" of the existence of the Son of God and have wanted to see in this a first step in the direction of the early church's doctrine of the divine and human natures of the Son of God. But that would undoubtedly be a false interpretation of this Pauline text. Indeed, Paul is speaking here, as the formulation and the temporal addition "since the resurrection" show, not of a static being, but of an event. The Son of God was born as a member of the tribe of David; therein consists his earthly origin. This son of David has been raised from the dead by the working of God's Spirit and thereby designated the powerful Son of God, who now as "our Lord" sends out his apostle, in order to awaken believing obedience among the Gentiles (Rom. 1:5). Thus here Paul is describing how the Son of God, who had become man, now through an act of God has been exalted to be the *mighty* Son of God and thus Lord. Thus the Son of God has experienced a history, and to preach of this history is the commission of the apostle Paul.

This basic outlook of the Pauline message of Christ is confirmed by the "Christ psalm" which Paul has appropriated in his Philippian epistle (Phil. 2:5-11): "Have among yourselves such a mind as [one is to have] in Christ Jesus, who was in the form of God, [but] did not exploit the being equal with God, but emptied himself, by assuming a servant's form and entering into equality with men and being found like a man in appearance. He humbled himself by becoming obedient even as far as death, indeed, death on the cross. Hence God also has highly exalted him and given him a name which is above all names, that at the name of Jesus every knee should bow, [of things] in heaven and on earth and under the earth, and every tongue confess that Jesus Christ is Lord, to the glory of God the Father." The assumption today is widespread that this hymn does not originally come from Paul, but that it had arisen in the primitive community and had been appropriated and slightly expanded by Paul (see the arguments in the commentaries). Of course this thesis is not as certain as those who hold it assert, since we know nothing at all that is certain about the prevailing principles of primitive Christian poetry and Paul very possibly could himself have produced this poetic work using traditional formulations. But whether Paul is adapting to his own purposes a hymn that he has appropriated or is himself speaking in traditional language, in any case he is giving expression in this "psalm" to his view of Christ: Jesus the Christ was in essence like God, but in obedience to God was ready to surrender this likeness to God and to assume the human form of existence, which means being enslaved to the powers of this world. In obedience he even descended further, to the shameful death on the cross. For this reason God has exalted the humiliated One even above his previous divine nature and has given to him the highest name, the name of Lord, so that now all beings in the world should confess Jesus Christ as Lord and thereby honor God. It is evident that here, too, a *history* is being related. Paul is not interested in precisely describing the divine being and the human existence of Jesus Christ. He is interested in the fact that the one who belonged to God, who is not here called Son of God, of his own free will took on the full actuality of human existence and, moreover, submitted to the crucifixion. And he is interested in the fact that this one who became man has been installed by God in the heavenly dignity of Lord and now can claim worship from all the beings in the world. Thus this history of Jesus Christ, as Paul describes it here, consists of the stages of being with God (pre-existence), being man, and exaltation (post-existence); hence the time of Jesus' being man is only a part of this way of the heavenly Lord.

We saw earlier that Hellenistic Christianity connected the Hellenistic conception of the heavenly emissary with Hellenistic-Jewish wisdom speculation and in this way created for itself the possibility of describing vividly the action of God in Jesus Christ (see above, pp. 119 ff.). Paul concurs in this conceptual form, but in so doing he is not interested, in the context of the Philippian epistle, in the details of the divine being of one who became man, but only in two points: the man Jesus who died on the cross came from God and in obedience to God went to the limit in surrendering his divine origin; and this man Jesus who died on the cross is now, through an act of God, the heavenly Lord to whom every being must bow. In this connection Paul does not make it clear whether this worship of Christ by all beings is already occurring in the present, and according to I Cor. 15:23-24 this was hardly his opinion. It is sufficient for him to know that this was God's intention in the installation of Christ in the dignity of Lord, and he is sure that this intention will be fulfilled in the near future. But what is crucial has already happened with the resurrection, not explicitly mentioned here, and the exaltation of Christ to the position of Lord; Christ has conquered the powers (Col. 2:15), and for Christians he is already the Lord, "through whom all things [are], and we through him" (I Cor. 8:6). Thus Paul sees the historical reality of the man Jesus as a part of an action of God which embraces the entire span of the world-age; this action's end and aim took its beginning in the raising of Christ and will find its consummation in the appearing of Christ from heaven (I Cor. 15:20, 23).

b. JESUS AND CHRIST

But the actual meaning of this message of the descent and exaltation of Christ only becomes evident when we consider the individual honorific titles which Paul uses for Jesus Christ. Here it is shown immediately that the two concepts "Jesus" and "Christ" have no theological significance. Paul seldom uses the personal name *"Jesus"* alone, and in these cases he denotes with it in the same way the earthly Jesus ("If we believe that Jesus died and rose again . . . ," I Thess. 4:14) and the resurrected One: ". . . to wait for his Son from heaven, whom he raised from the dead, Jesus, who saves us from the coming wrath" (I Thess. 1:10). But the same holds true also for the combination "Lord Jesus" (cf. I Cor. 11:23 with Rom. 10:9), and all this shows that, when Paul speaks of "Jesus," for him this name is the designation of the person of the man Jesus, who is also the resurrected One.

Curiously, though, it is hardly different with the concept *"Christ."* Of course Paul was aware that "the anointed one" was a Jewish title for the bearer of salvation which the primitive community had used for Jesus, but it appears that he uses the word only once in this sense: in the enumeration of the peculiar gifts given by God to the Jews, the last item is: "and from them [comes] the Christ according to the flesh" (Rom. 9:5). For the rest, Paul uses "Christ" only as a proper name, both by itself and in the combination "Jesus Christ" or "Christ Jesus," and recent studies have shown that only stylistic reasons are the cause for the alternation among these three forms of his usage. Even the name "Christ" was used by Paul for the pre-existent One ("they drank from the spiritual rock that followed them, but the rock was Christ," I Cor. 10:4), the earthly One (Christ "was crucified in weakness," II Cor. 13:4), and the resurrected One ("fellow heirs of Christ, . . . that we also should be glorified with [him]," Rom. 8:17). Paul thus shows by the way in which he employs "Jesus" and "Christ" as equivalent proper names that he is always conscious that the *man* Jesus has been raised by God. Perhaps it also is not accidental that Paul does not use "Jesus" for the pre-existent One, because his taking seriously the historical concreteness of the man Jesus forbids the projection of this name back into the pre-existence. But Paul can speak without any distinction of the pre-existent, the earthly, and the resurrected Christ; he obviously takes seriously the unity of God's action in all three stages of the history of Christ.

C. THE "FINAL MAN"

While in Pauline usage the name "Christ" has lost the confessional character which this title had in the primitive community, the title "Son of Man," which was handed down in the primitive community, to be sure only in the words of Jesus, is no longer used by Paul at all. Since Paul is writing only to Gentile Christian communities, this is altogether understandable, because the Greek expression "the Son of Man" was bound to be incomprehensible to Gentile Christians. But this absence of the concept by no means says that Paul left aside the expression concerning the person of Jesus which was intended by this concept. On the contrary, this is not at all the case. That is to say, in a number of passages Paul contrasts the man Adam with the man Christ (see above, pp. 146-47). While in this contrast the effect of the sinful act of the *one* man is compared with the effect of the obedience of the other man (Rom. 5:12-19), still it cannot at once be discerned from this that the man Jesus Christ in this comparison is not simply to be designated only as an earthly man just like the man Adam. The remark about Adam, inserted at the beginning of this text, "who is the type of the future [Adam]" (vs. 14c), to be sure calls Christ the "future Adam" and therewith identifies him as the "man" who is expected for the *end-time* (cf. the title for the bearer of salvation, "the coming one," in Matt. 11:3); yet this parenthetical remark is not developed further. In I Cor. 15:22 Paul contrasts the humanity belonging to Adam with the men belonging to Christ: "As in Adam all die, so in Christ will all be made alive"; but in this Christ is not described as "man." On the other hand, in I Cor. 15:45, 47-49 the conception underlying these two texts becomes evident. From 15:35 on, Paul is concerned with showing that in addition to man's earthly body there is also a "spiritual" body, and for this purpose he refers to the succession of the two "men": "Thus it is also written: 'The first man Adam became a living soul, the last Adam a life-giving spirit.' . . . The first man [was] as an earthly [man] from the earth, the second man [was] from heaven. As the earthly [man], so also [are] the earthly [men], and as the heavenly [man], so also [are] the heavenly [men]. And as we have borne the image of the earthly [man], so shall we also bear the image of the heavenly [man]." Here Adam as the first and earthly man is clearly set in contrast to Jesus Christ as the last Adam or the second, the heavenly, man. From the first and the second Adam proceed lines of humanity whose kind of being corresponds to the founder of their line. However, even in this text Paul does not more precisely develop this parallelism of the two "men" and the lines of humanity that belong to them. Instead, he presupposes it as familiar and accepted, and from it derives the certainty that those who belong to the second man, the Christians, will bear a "spiritual body," the image of the heavenly "man." But now in the context of this contrast of the first and the second man, Christ clearly is no longer conceived of as earthly man, even of a special kind, but as a heavenly being who bears the name "man." What all this says is this: in these three texts Paul employs, with varying application, the contrasting pair of the earthly, first man and the eschatological, heavenly, second man, and in so doing touches the Jewish anticipation, adopted by Jesus, of the eschatological "man," the "Son of Man." For with Paul also in these contexts, "man" is a designation of the figure of the heavenly bearer of salvation of the end-time, as in the expectation of the "man" who would appear on the clouds of heaven in Jewish apocalyptic and with Jesus (see above, pp. 77 ff.) .

Nevertheless, the way in which Paul employs the concept of the heavenly man in contrast to the first man Adam rules out the possibility that in so doing Paul is directly dependent on the Jewish apocalyptic or the gospels' "Son of Man" tradition. For there the setting in parallel of the first and the second man is lacking, as is the conception of the respective lines of humanity belonging to these "men." But the Jewish-apocalyptic figure of the "man" is on its own part undoubtedly an eschatological reshaping of the "primeval myth, widespread in the Near East, of the first man and the king of Paradise" (M. Schenke), who as the "primal man" embraces all humanity or, in another version of the myth, the totality of those who are saved. Apocalyptic Judaism had appropriated this pagan conception of the primal man in an eschatological variation as the expectation of the "man" of the end-time, and Hellenistic Judaism had employed the conception to describe the primeval mediator of creation who stands in contrast to the first earthly man, Adam. Hellenistic Christianity and, with it, Paul concurred in this Hellenistic-Jewish use of the myth of the heavenly "man." But Paul interprets this conception of the heavenly "man" in a strictly eschatological sense, in order in this way to describe the solidarity of Christians with the already present and anticipated bearer of salvation of the end-time and their expected participation in his glory. It is true that Paul says that the "last man" came "from heaven" (I Cor. 15:47), and thus presumably is thinking *also* of the earthly man Jesus when he speaks of the "last man" (cf. also what is said in Rom. 5:19 about the "obedience of the one"). But the real interest in Paul's use of this mythical conception lies in Jesus Christ who has been raised and is expected in glory, who has become a "life-giving spirit" and whose heavenly "image" the Christians are to bear when at his eschatological appearance they have put on his glorious body (I Cor. 15:45, 49; cf. Phil. 3:20-21). Thus Paul appropriates from the tradition the myth of the heavenly final man, but he does not use it to describe speculatively the figure of the earthly or of the resurrected Jesus Christ; instead, it enables him to make a predication about salvation: because the Christians belong to the heavenly "man," they have a share in the conquest of death wrought by him and in his life in the Spirit of God. "We shall bear the image of the heavenly [man]" (I Cor. 15:49): this is the certainty which Paul wants to express when he speaks of the heavenly "man" Jesus. But this title, also, did not have central significance for Paul's proclamation of Christ.

d. THE LORD (KYRIOS)

On the other hand, in Paul the designation *"the Lord"* (*kyrios*) for Jesus Christ occurs frequently, and we have already seen that in the Christ hymn of the Philippian epistle, Paul described it as God's aim in his working through Jesus Christ that "every tongue should confess that Jesus Christ is Lord, to the glory of God the Father" (Phil. 2:11). Since, quite in keeping with this, the confession "Jesus is Lord" is named as the characteristic form of expression of the faith of the Christians (Rom. 10:9; I Cor. 12:3), the assumption is certainly justified that this designation of honor is especially characteristic of Paul's view of Christ. Paul had found the way of invoking Jesus as "Lord" already in the language of the Hellenistic-Christian community. Here the Christians are characterized as those "who call on the name of our Lord Jesus Christ" (I Cor. 1:2), and in the Hellenistic-Christian community people spoke of the "Lord Jesus" when they related anything from his life: "The Lord Jesus, in the night in which he was betrayed, took bread . . ." (I Cor. 11:23). In fact, Paul also presumably found the Aramaic cry *maranatha* ("our Lord, come!" I Cor. 16:23) already in use in the Hellenistic-Christian community. Thus for the Hellenistic-Christian community Jesus was already the Lord as the earthly One, the resurrected One, and the coming One, and the calling on the "name of our Lord Jesus," the report about his life, and the prayer for his eschatological coming all belong in the context of the gathering of the community, i.e., in the worship service of the pre-Pauline Hellenistic community. But correspondingly also, in the communities founded by Paul, Jesus is called on as Lord, reports are given from his life, and his coming is hoped for and prayed for (I Cor. 12:3; "as I also delivered to you," I Cor. 11:23; I Cor. 16:22; 11:26), so that one can rightly say that for Paul, "the Lord" denotes Jesus Christ to whom the community prays in worship, and who therefore encounters the community in worship.

But it would be mistaken to deduce from this observation that for Paul the title of Lord acquires its real meaning from this worship event. It is fully certain that calling upon Jesus Christ as Lord is common Christian tradition, but in Paul it acquires its real meaning from the fact that Paul knows himself and hence the Christians in general as slaves of this Lord. "He who was called in the Lord as a slave is a freedman of the Lord. Likewise he who was free when called is a slave of Christ" (I Cor. 7:22 RSV); "render a slave's service to the Lord Jesus Christ!" (Col. 3:24); "Anyone who in this way [i.e., in righteousness, peace, and joy in the Holy Spirit] renders a slave's service to Christ is well-pleasing to God and approved among men" (Rom. 14:18) —these utterances show that according to Paul's conviction the Christian has entered into slave service of the Lord Christ and must live out of this reality. Here Paul proceeds from the assumption that man is always enslaved to a power that stands above him: "Do you not know that you are slaves to the one to whom you submit in obedience like slaves, whether it is sin, leading to death, or righteousness, leading to righteousness?" (Rom. 6:16; see below, p. 186). But Christ with his death has paid a "cash price" for the Christians, and thereby has acquired them as his possession: "you are bought with a price" (I Cor. 6:20; 7:23); "For this purpose Christ died and became alive again, that he might be Lord of the dead and of the living" (Rom. 14:9); "You belong to Christ" (I

Cor. 3:23). As one who has been called by Jesus Christ to be an apostle, Paul knows himself in a special sense to be a "slave of Christ Jesus" (Rom. 1:1; cf. Gal. 1:1), but in this sense can also name himself together with Timothy (Phil. 1:1). That Jesus Christ is Lord therefore describes for Paul in a comprehensive sense the existence of the Christian which has been altered by the encounter with the Lord Jesus: "If you confess with your mouth Jesus as Lord and believe in your heart that God has raised him from the dead, you will be saved" (Rom. 10:9).

But even if the confession of Jesus Christ as Lord basically describes the situation of the believing Christian, still this confession also at the same time is an utterance about Jesus Christ himself. Now Paul plainly says that "Christ died and became alive again, that he might be Lord of the dead and of the living" (Rom. 14:9), and according to the Christ hymn in the Philippian epistle, God has exalted the crucified One and has "given him the name that is above every name, that . . . every tongue should confess that Jesus Christ [is] Lord" (Phil. 2:9-11). Thus since the resurrection Jesus Christ is Lord through God's act; this position as Lord, however, is related not only to the Christians, but also to the whole cosmos, the entire world. At the end of the hymn in Philippians, Paul says plainly that "every knee, of heavenly and terrestrial and sub-terrestrial beings, should bow and every tongue confess that Jesus Christ [is] Lord" (Phil. 2:10-11); and because God, through Christ on the cross, "has disarmed and made an open spectacle of the powers and principalities, triumphing over them in him [Christ]" (Col. 2:14-15), Christ is "the head of every power and principality" (Col. 2:10). Thus the Christians have a share in the event which has brought about the new eon, if they submit to the lordship of Christ: "Our Lord Jesus Christ, who has given himself for our sins, that he might deliver us from the present evil eon according to the will of God and our Father" (Gal. 1:4).

But the words just quoted show a further important state of affairs: it is God's own will that is wrought in Christ's redemptive act, and the reverent submission of all powers to the Lord Jesus Christ takes place "to the glory of God the Father" (Phil. 2:11). Hence for Paul the acknowledgment of Jesus Christ as Lord not only says that the Christian knows himself to be included in God's salvation: "The same Lord over all is rich toward all who call on him; for everyone who calls on the name of the Lord will be saved" (Rom. 10:12-13). According to Paul's conviction, one can really submit to God himself at all only when one obediently acknowledges the Lord Jesus Christ: "Thanks be to God, who has given us the victory through our Lord Jesus Christ" (I Cor. 15:57). Thus the confession of Jesus Christ is the expression of the certainty of having been saved by God himself.

But even though in the confession of Christ the Lord, Paul is thinking in the first place of the resurrected One, still he undoubtedly uses this title also to speak of the earthly Jesus: "The Lord Jesus, in the night in which he was betrayed, took bread . . ." (I Cor. 11:23) ; (the Jews) "killed the Lord Jesus and the prophets" (I Thess. 2:15) ; "God has raised the Lord and will also raise us" (I Cor. 6:14). He uses the expressions "the cross of our Lord Jesus Christ" (Gal. 6:14), and "the brothers of the Lord" or "the Lord's brother" (I Cor. 9:5; Gal. 1:19), and appeals to the instructions of the Lord in the latter's lifetime (I Cor. 9:14; 7:10, 12). Even if these formulations at least in part bear a traditional character, they cannot be thrust aside as unimportant. Paul rather takes them seriously, as is shown by the fact that he occasionally even calls the pre-existent Christ "Lord": "You know the grace of our Lord Jesus Christ, that he, being rich, yet for your sakes became poor" (II Cor. 8:9). The fact that this usage occurs so seldom in Paul lets us see that Paul has projected the designation of Jesus as "Lord" backward from the resurrected One onto the earthly Jesus and then onto the pre-existent One. But precisely this is characteristic and important. For it shows with full clarity that when Paul speaks of the resurrected Lord he is always thinking also of the man Jesus, and that for him there is an unbroken unity between the man Jesus and the resurrected Lord.

e. THE SON OF GOD

This unity is most clearly shown in the way in which Paul employs the concept "Son of God" for Jesus. The concept occurs relatively seldom in Paul, but very emphatically. In this usage Paul undoubtedly is not influenced by the pagan conception of the physical begetting of the child of God by a God. Instead, he takes for granted the normal human birth of the Son of God: the gospel speaks "of his Son, who is born of the seed of David according to the flesh" (Rom. 1:3) ; "God sent his Son, born of a woman" (Gal. 4:4). Thus Paul places crucial worth on the full humanity of the Son of God: "God sent his Son in the form of sinful flesh" (Rom. 8:3). But this talk of the "sending" of the Son also shows that for Paul Jesus Christ was already God's Son before he was born as a man, and the one born as a man remained, even as man, God's

Son: "We were reconciled with God through the death of his Son" (Rom. 5:10) ; "I live by faith in the Son of God who loved me and gave himself for me" (Gal. 2:20). Since his resurrection the Son of God is "installed as the Son of God with power" (Rom. 1:4), God can reveal him as the resurrected One (Gal. 1:16), and "send the Spirit of his Son into our hearts" (Gal. 4:6). Thus through the resurrection the Son of God has come into his heavenly power—Paul speaks of "reigning as king" with reference to the resurrected Son of God (I Cor. 15:25, 28)—and therefore the Christians may believe that God has "transferred" them "into the kingdom of his dear Son" (Col. 1:13). But the resurrected One will appear from heaven (". . . to await his Son from heaven, whom he raised from the dead, Jesus," I Thess. 1:10), and then will the Christians "be conformed to the likeness of his Son, that he may be the firstborn among many brethren" (Rom. 8:29). Thus with the adopted title "Son of God" Paul describes the whole "history" of Christ from pre-existence to the Parousia, and thus far this concept not only most comprehensively reflects the fact that Paul sees God's action in Christ as a full unity, but also most clearly points to the connection between God's action and the Christ event.

Indeed, again and again in his utterances about the Son of God, Paul speaks of God's acting through the Son: God sends the Son, is reconciled with us through the death of his Son, installs the Son to be the Son of God in power, reveals him to Paul, transfers the Christians into the kingdom of his Son, sends the Spirit of his Son into their hearts, and causes them to wait for the Son of God from heaven (Rom. 8:3; Gal. 4:4; Rom. 5:1; 1:4; Gal. 1:16; Col. 1:13; Gal. 4:6; I Thess. 1:10). Here God is always the actual subject of the event, and thus "Son of God" "in Pauline usage is the designation of the bearer of salvation under the aspect of his belonging to God" (W. Kramer). That God the Father himself is working salvation in that which has happened and will happen through Jesus Christ is what Paul wants to emphasize when he speaks of the Son of God.

Indeed, Paul shows even more clearly what this means for the Christians. He emphatically calls to the attention of the community in Rome how heavily God is personally involved in the activity of his Son: "God did not spare his own Son, but delivered him up for us all" (Rom. 8:32) ; "God demonstrates his love for us, in that while we were still sinners, Christ died for us. . . . That is to say, if we as enemies were reconciled with God through the death of his Son, so much more, being reconciled, we shall be saved by his life"

(Rom. 5:8, 10). Thus also there is emphasis placed on the "kingdom of his dear Son" (Col. 1:13). But now this by no means signifies that Paul sees in the Son of God nothing but an instrument without a will of his own in the hand of the Father. Instead, the Son appears rather as the obedient fulfiller of the will of God. This obedience is not only stressed in the hymn in Philippians: "And being found in the form of appearance of a man, he humbled himself and became obedient unto death, indeed, even unto death on the cross" (Phil. 2:7-8). This obedience is also set in contrast with Adam's disobedience: "As through the disobedience of the one man the many were made sinners, so also through the obedience of one the many will be made righteous" (Rom. 5:19). As Paul can say: "Jesus was delivered up [by God] for our transgressions" (Rom. 4:25), so also: "I live by faith in the Son of God, who loved me and gave himself up for me" (Gal. 2:20; also cf. Rom. 5:8 with 14:15).

f. the formula "through christ"

This conviction, that God acts through the Son in that the Son obediently does the Father's will, leads to the formula frequently employed by Paul, "through Christ." On the one hand, with this formula Paul can express the belief that through the man Jesus, God has wrought salvation in the past, allows Christians in the present to share in this salvation, and will perfect it at the Parousia: "Through Christ God has been reconciled to us" (II Cor. 5:18); "Being justified by faith we have peace with God through our Lord Jesus Christ" (Rom. 5:1); "God has not destined us for wrath, but to obtain salvation through our Lord Jesus Christ" (I Thess. 5:9 RSV). Correspondingly, with this formula, though without mentioning God at the same time, Paul speaks of Christ's having secured salvation for us or having called us into his service: "Much more [= much more certainly] we, who now have been justified through his blood, shall be saved from wrath through him" (Rom. 5:9); "Jesus Christ, our Lord, through whom we have received grace and apostleship, to awaken the obedience of faith among all nations for the sake of his name" (Rom. 1:4-5). On the other hand, Paul speaks of admonitions and thanksgivings of the Christians which take place "through Christ": "I admonish you . . . through the name of our Lord Jesus Christ" (I Cor. 1: 10); "First, I thank my God through Jesus Christ for you all" (Rom. 1:8). But in these passages there is no idea that Christ acted on his own or independently of God, nor could Paul arrive at the idea that the connection between the Christians and God required a mediating agency in between. Quite to the contrary, the formula "through Christ" specifically makes God's action and the relation of the Christian to God concrete. Paul speaks of God's universal activity through Christ: "For us [there is] *one* God, the Father, from whom everything [comes] and we to him, and *one* Lord, Jesus Christ, through whom everything [happens] and we through him" (I Cor. 8:6); cf. also "Paul, apostle . . . through Jesus Christ and God, the Father" (Gal. 1:1). With this Paul clearly shows that without exception God's whole way of acting in creation and saving work is fulfilled in the work of Christ. And because the relation of the Christian to God is thus entirely established by Christ, Christ is not the mediator of salvation, but the Christian's only way to God: "All God's promises are in him [the Son of God Jesus Christ] yes; therefore through him also [sounds forth] the [answering] Amen to the glory of God through us" (II Cor. 1:20). All this says that the formula "through Christ" expresses especially emphatically the view that Jesus Christ as Son of God fully belongs together with God, so that the Christian may be firmly convinced that in Jesus Christ, God the Father himself is confronting him.

g. THE "LIKENESS OF GOD"

Surely Paul by no means intends with this confession to equate the Son of God with God. This is shown in the occasional adoption of the title "likeness of God" for Christ: "The God of this eon has blinded the thoughts of the unbelievers, so that they should not see the light of the gospel of the glory of Christ, who is the likeness of God" (II Cor. 4:4); in God's beloved Son "we have the redemption, the forgiveness of sins; he is the likeness of the invisible God, the firstborn of the whole creation" (Col. 1:14-15). In these utterances, "likeness of God" clearly denotes the Son of God, who in the creation as well as in the new creation—II Cor. 4:4 presumably refers to Paul's call—makes God's actions visible, represents the invisible God to men. There is no doubt that Paul thus transfers to Christ a characterization of divine Wisdom as it was common in contemporary Judaism; Wisdom "is a reflection of the eternal light, a flawless mirror of the divine work and an image of his goodness" (Wisdom of Solomon 7.26). The source of the concept in itself makes extremely unlikely an equation of the Son of God with God, and indeed Paul evidently uses this concept because with it he can say clearly that in God's Son God himself confronts us, yet at the same time remains the invisible one.

It is evident, further, from the fact that Paul avoids calling Christ "God" that he has no idea of equating them. The two passages I Cor. 3:23 and 11:3 show this quite clearly: all things are yours, "but you are Christ's, and Christ is God's"; "I want you to know that Christ is the head of every man, but the man is the head of the woman, but the head of Christ is God." In both cases the reference to Christ's connection with God is not actually necessary in the context; when Paul in both cases adds that Christ is dependent on God, apparently he is concerned with emphasizing that the relation of Christians to Christ precisely sets forth the true relation to God. In view of these texts, then, it cannot be doubted that the much debated blessing in Rom. 9:5 ("from them [the Israelites] comes Christ according to the flesh—the God who is over all is blessed forever, Amen") can refer only to God, although the syntax would allow a reference to Christ. That here God must be meant is confirmed by the usage of Paul, who without exception employs the word "God" for God the Father and who moreover could not characterize the "Christ according to the flesh" as the "God over all." Therefore it holds true without qualification that Paul avoids calling Christ "God."

Finally, that Paul does not equate the Son of God with God appears also from the fact that he sees the work of the Son as oriented to the Father and has his task bounded by God's eternity. The hymn in Philippians indeed describes it as the aim of the worship of the "Lord Jesus Christ" by all the powers of the world, brought about by the exaltation of Christ, that "the glory of God the Father" may be increased (Phil. 2:11). Altogether in harmony with this, Paul says that "Christ has accepted you, to the glory of God" (Rom. 15:7), and the Christians' thanksgiving which ascends to God because of God's saving act in Christ "is to be superabundant, to the glory of God" (II Cor. 4:15). There is frequent mention that the Christians' being attached to Christ leads to a life *for God:* "You have died to the law through Christ's body, so that you might belong to another, to the one who was raised from the dead, in order that we might bear fruit for God" (Rom. 7:4); "Through the law I died to the law, that I might live for God; I am crucified with Christ; yet *I* no longer live, but Christ lives in me" (Gal. 2:19-20; cf. also Rom. 6:10-11). Consequently what Christ does in obedience to God serves God's glory and is intended to bring men to God. And therefore Paul also expects that after this aim is achieved, at the final Parousia Christ will surrender the lordship to God alone: "Christ [arose] as the firstfruits, then at his coming those who belong to Christ [will arise]. Then [will] the end [be], when he delivers [or 'has delivered'] the kingdom to God and the Father, when he has overcome every rule and every lordship and power. . . . But when all things are subjected to him, then will the Son himself be subjected to him who subjected all things to him, that God may be all in all" (I Cor. 15:23, 24, 28). One can hardly decide whether in this ultimate hope Paul antici-pates that the Son will completely give up his position as Lord—I Thess. 4:17 can be cited against this: "And so shall we ever be with the Lord"—or whether Paul takes for granted even for this final consummation the Christians' belonging to their Lord as con-tinuing—in addition to I Thess. 4:17, also Rom. 8:17 could argue for this: "if we suffer with him, we shall also be glorified with him [Christ]." But it is after all questionable whether Paul is at all interested in such speculative thinking through to the end; for the aim of his statements undoubtedly is only the proclamation that Christ leads us to God for time and eternity and that when Christ shall have appeared in glory, the Christians will "through Christ stand under the perfected lordship of God" (W. Thüsing).

But therewith it becomes evident that Paul's proclamation of Christ, regardless of how obviously it presents utterances about Christ which are meant to be understood in the literal sense, in so doing still does not have in view any speculations about a heavenly figure, but seeks first of all to proclaim the divine salvation wrought by God through the man Jesus Christ and his resurrection. To be sure it has been objected against such an understanding of the Pauline proclamation of Christ that Paul shows no interest of any kind in the man Jesus, moreover that he equates the resurrected Jesus with the Holy Spirit and therefore shows his indifference toward the person of Jesus; furthermore, his sayings about the pre-existence and the anticipated eschatological coming of the resur-rected One must be characterized as speculative. But these objec-tions do not correspond to the facts.

h. THE HUMANNESS OF JESUS

We have already seen (above, p. 160) that Paul stresses the full birth of the Son of God, and it is very likely that, in view of his conception of the heavenly pre-existence of the Son of God who was born of a woman, he knew nothing of Jesus' having been be-gotten without a father. Of course this can only be inferred. But it is curious that Paul mentions hardly anything from the life of this man Jesus and also cites only isolated sayings of the "Lord" (I Cor.

7:10; 9:14; I Thess. 4:15). This fact has been combined with the saying in II Cor. 5:16: "Hence from now on we know no man according to the flesh; even though we had known Christ according to the flesh, now we know him no longer," and from both the conclusion has been drawn that for Paul the earthly Jesus was of no significance. Now it certainly is mistaken to cite II Cor. 5:16 in this connection. For in this text Paul does not at all deny any interest in the earthly Jesus for his person (the subject is not "Christ according to the flesh," but knowing Christ in the way of the flesh) ; instead, Paul pushes aside as unimportant for the Christian a purely human, intra-worldly relation to Jesus. Paul also occasionally refers to the conduct of the earthly Jesus, as at the last supper (I Cor. 11:23) ; the imitation of Christ by Christians is set in parallel to the imitation of Paul by Christians (I Cor. 11:1; I Thess. 1:6) ; "I admonish you by the meekness and gentleness of Christ" (II Cor. 10:1) undoubtedly points to the conduct of the earthly Jesus, and the same holds true for Rom. 15:2-3: "Let each of you please his neighbor for good, that he may be edified; for Christ also did not please himself, but rather, as it is written: 'The reproaches of those who reproached you have fallen upon me.'" Hence one may undoubtedly assert that Jesus as an earthly man was by no means unimportant to Paul. That Paul so seldom *quotes* Jesus' sayings, though of course he frequently alludes to such sayings without pointing out that it has to do with a saying of Jesus (as in Rom. 12:14; 13:9; Gal. 5:14), is at once understandable when one knows that the Lord's words indeed possess for Paul an ultimate authority (cf. I Cor. 7:10), but that Paul also as one commissioned by Christ makes the claim throughout of being able to render an authoritative decision (I Cor. 7:25, 40: "But I think that I have the Spirit of God"). Consequently, Paul refers to the earthly Jesus and his words where he sees the possibility of doing so, but his real interest lies in the conclusive fact of Jesus' death on the cross and his having been raised by God. For in this event the powers are conquered and God's salvation has become effectual (Col. 1:22; 2:14-15; Rom. 8:3), and therefore Paul designates the cross of Christ as the actual content of his proclamation (I Cor. 1:23-24) : "You foolish Galatians . . . , before whose eyes Jesus Christ has been placarded as crucified" (Gal. 3:1). But it is the cross of the man Jesus (the Jews "have killed the Lord Jesus and the prophets," I Thess. 2:15) in which God has wrought salvation, and for Paul's proclamation this man is of crucial importance, even though the reference to his life and teachings in detail plays no great role, at least in his epistles.

i. CHRIST AND THE SPIRIT

But did not Paul equate the resurrected One with the Holy Spirit and thereby show that for him the person of Jesus Christ has been dissolved into the Holy Spirit? This question is raised by the observation that Paul can, to a large extent, make the same utterances about Christ and the Holy Spirit. Furthermore, there is the Pauline sentence, "The Lord is the Spirit" (II Cor. 3:17). Now it is in fact true that Paul also traces many of Christ's effects back to the Spirit: God's love comes to us through the Spirit and through Christ (Rom. 5:5; 8:39); we have peace in Christ and in the Holy Spirit (Phil. 4:7; Rom. 14:17); Christ and the Spirit give life (Rom. 6:23; II Cor. 3:6); Christ as well as the Spirit dwells in Christians (Rom. 8:10, 11), and so on. But along with this we must also observe that Paul can make distinctive assertions only of the Holy Spirit: the pouring out of the Spirit into our hearts (Rom. 5:5); the Spirit as the earnest (Rom. 8:23); the Spirit dwells in us (I Cor. 3:16), and so on. Other utterances are possible only of Christ, namely all those that presuppose a personal relation between Christ and the Christians: "Three times I have besought the Lord" (II Cor. 12:8); "The Lord . . . will descend from heaven . . . , we shall be caught up on the clouds to meet the Lord in the air, and so shall we ever be with the Lord" (I Thess. 4:16-17); "Who will accuse us? Christ Jesus, who died, rather who rose again, who is at the right hand of God, who also intercedes for us?" (Rom. 8:34); "We await [from heaven] as savior the Lord Jesus Christ, who will refashion our lowly body to be like his glorious body by the power which enables him to subject all things to himself" (Phil. 3:20-21). Hence it cannot be said that Paul equated Christ and the Holy Spirit. Paul rather strictly maintained the personal confrontation of Christ and the Christians; while he can speak of the Spirit in personal terms ("the Spirit intercedes for us," Rom. 8:26; "all this is wrought by one and the same Spirit, who bestows on each one as he wills," I Cor. 12:11), but does not think of him as person: he speaks of having and receiving the Spirit, I Cor. 7:40; Gal. 3:2; of quenching the Spirit, I Thess. 5:19; and in the well-known benediction in II Cor. 13:13, alongside the "grace of our Lord Jesus Christ and the love of God" there stands "the participation in the Holy Spirit." Correspondingly, Paul can speak of the "Spirit of God" in the same way as of the "Spirit of Christ": in Rom. 8:9 they are in immediate conjunction. And we find "the Spirit from God" (I Cor. 2:12) along with the "help by the Spirit of Jesus Christ" (Phil. 1:19).

Furthermore, this conclusion is not called in question by the much-discussed sentence, "The Lord is the Spirit" (II Cor. 3:17). For this sentence in no way intends to assert the identity of Christ and the Spirit, particularly since immediately after this sentence Paul speaks of the "Spirit of the Lord" (= Spirit of Christ) and of the "Lord of the Spirit" (= Christ). The sentence, "The Lord is the Spirit," is meant in the context rather to interpret the preceding Old Testament citation (cf. the commentaries on this passage). In this quotation ("as soon as he turns to the Lord, the veil is taken off," Exod. 34:34) the subject is "the Lord," and with the explanatory sentence, "The Lord is the Spirit," this "Lord" is interpreted to mean the Spirit, but this Spirit is at once understood as "the Spirit of the Lord" who bestows liberty. Thus according to the context Paul intends to say with the sentence, "The Lord is the Spirit," that Christ bestows the Spirit of sonship who frees us from the law of death (cf. Rom. 8:15, 2), and thus in this sentence he is talking about the Spirit of Christ and not of the identity of Christ and the Spirit. Thus even though he can make many statements in the same way about Christ as about the Spirit, Paul never forgot that the Christian stands facing his personal Lord Jesus Christ, and knows himself to be taken into service personally by the resurrected Lord.

When Paul in spite of this also speaks of God's saving action through the Spirit and in so doing makes many statements which he can likewise make of God's action in Christ, this not only has its basis in tradition—the formulation of the primitive community appropriated by Paul in Rom. 1:4 (see p. 110) indeed even speaks already of Christ's installation as Son of God in power according to the Holy Spirit—but is objectively conditioned. Through the Holy Spirit God has raised the Son of God who descended to the death on the cross, and since then the Holy Spirit is active through God and Christ: "designated the Son of God in power according to the Holy Spirit since the resurrection from the dead" (Rom. 1:4); "the last Adam has become a life-giving spirit" (I Cor. 15: 45b); "God has raised the Lord and will raise us by his power" (I Cor. 6:14), to be compared with which is "in the power of the Holy Spirit" (Rom. 15:13). This Spirit is bestowed on the Christians in the believing acceptance of the preaching and of baptism (Gal. 3:2; I Cor. 12:13); "the love of God is poured out into our hearts by the Holy Spirit who is given to us" (Rom. 5:5); and Paul metaphorically identifies this gift of the Spirit that has been given to the Christians as a "firstfruits gift" (Rom. 8:23) or as an "earnest" (i.e., a first installment: II Cor. 1:22), and thereby makes it clear that through the Holy Spirit the salvation of the end-time is already bestowed on the Christians in advance. The gift of the Spirit enables the Christians to recognize their adoption into the position of sonship to God: "But that you are sons—God has sent the Spirit of his Son into our hearts, who cries 'Abba, Father'" (Gal. 4:6); "You have received the Spirit of adoption. In him we cry 'Abba, Father'; the Spirit testifies to our spirit that we are children of God" (Rom. 8:15-16). The Christian lives by this gift of the Spirit: "The Spirit assumes our weakness" (Rom. 8:26), and precisely as one who has received the Spirit the Christian waits for the perfection of being with Christ: "We who have received the firstfruits of the Spirit groan inwardly while we wait for the redemption of our bodies" (Rom. 8:23). For "as long as we are in the [earthly] body, we are away from the Lord" (II Cor. 5:6), although we "have received the earnest of the Spirit" (II Cor. 5:5), but "we know that he who raised up Jesus will also raise us with Jesus and will bring us with you into his presence" (II Cor. 4:14). The Spirit, whom the Christians have received and through whom God in Christ wrought salvation, thus connects the Christians with the absent Lord "until he comes" (I Cor. 11:26), and thanks to the Spirit the Christians lack none of the gifts of grace while they must wait for the coming of the Lord: "You do not lack any gift of grace while waiting for the revelation of our Lord Jesus Christ" (I Cor. 1:7); "There are varieties of gifts, but the same Spirit" (I Cor. 12:4). Thus the Spirit imparts to the Christians, who in faith have received a share in the event of the end-time, but still wait for full fellowship with the exalted Lord, the reality of the future salvation in their present entirely personally. Also the Pauline juxtaposition of Christ and the Spirit shows that Paul's expressions about Christ describe the salvation which God in Christ, at the beginning of the time of final deliverance, has wrought, is working, and will work.

j. THE PRE-EXISTENCE OF CHRIST

But why then does Paul also speak of the pre-existence of Christ? This declaration indeed appears not to be connected with the present reality of being a Christian, because it goes back behind God's action in the sending of the Son of God as the man Jesus, and some have sought therefore to see in this statement Paul's adopting a Hellenistic-Christian conception which is purely speculative and endangers the real humanness of Jesus. Now in fact there can be no doubt that Paul appropriated this conception from Hellenistic Christianity (see above, pp. 119-20) . But it is also evident that in so doing he is by no means pursuing a speculative interest. That is to say, generally speaking Paul mentions the pre-existence of Christ only in passing (Gal. 4:4; Rom. 8:3–I Cor. 10:4–Phil. 2:6-7; II Cor. 5:21; 8:9–I Cor. 8:6), and he goes into the matter somewhat more specifically only where he must defend the cosmic significance of Christ against its denial by heretics: "He is the image of the invisible God, the firstborn of all creation, for in him are created all things in heaven and on earth, visible and invisible, whether thrones or dominions or principalities or powers. All these are created through him and for him, and he is before all things, and in him the universe has its coherence" (Col. 1:15-17a) .

But if Paul therefore speaks of the pre-existence of Christ, of his mediation in creation and his working before the incarnation in Jesus, without any speculative interest, and attempts no sort of description of the existence of the pre-existent One, still here he is speaking particularly strikingly in *mythical language,* and nowadays such mythical language is frequently characterized as incomprehensible to modern man and as a conceptual form which we must give up if we wish to make Paul's proclamation of Christ in its real intention understandable to ourselves. Of course Paul is speaking just as much in mythical language when he speaks of the humiliation of the One who was in the form of God and of his exaltation by God to the position of heavenly Lord. But in the conception of Christ's pre-existence, the mythical character of this statement is still more evident, because the abiding sense of this statement is not immediately clear to us. We cannot here comprehensively discuss the demand, made in view of such mythical statements, for "demythologizing" (R. Bultmann) . We must, however, inquire into the substantive reasons which prompted Paul to adopt such mythical language. Indeed, the statement about Christ's existence with God before his incarnation is no more and no less "mythical" than the confession of the raising of the crucified One from death, of his exaltation to God, of the sending of the Holy Spirit by the resurrected One, of the expectation of his imminent appearing in glory, and of the gathering of Christians around him. In all these cases, in fact, the subject is the action of a divine being, God or Christ who does not belong to this world, in the context of time and space in *this* world, and the conception of such involvement of other worldly powers in this world is rightly characterized as "mythical." Now one may in fact ask whether such mythical conceptions, which are bound to the world view of ancient man, are still comprehensible to us today and hence can still be used by us today. To this question one will have to answer that the proclamation of God's action in Jesus Christ at all events speaks of an intervention of the eternal God in the history of this world and therefore *cannot* refrain altogether from mythical discourse without giving up the crucial affirmation. But if this is correct and is conceded, then the mythical discourse about the resurrection and exaltation of the crucified One is therefore not only comprehensible to us, but appears to us to be an unavoidable affirmation, because this proclamation of the resurrection and exaltation of the crucified One indeed offers the interpretation of an experience, namely of the vision of the resurrected One by the witnesses and of the guidance of the community of the resurrected One by the Spirit of God which he has sent.

But is it not a different matter with Paul's mythical discourse about the pre-existence of Christ? Here, indeed, we do not have an interpretation in mythical language of an experience. Instead, here is the assertion of an event which neither has a point of support in the experience of the Christians nor gives a comprehensible and necessary expression to the confession of God's eschatological saving action in the man Jesus Christ and his resurrection. But of course even though it is true that, in what he says about the pre-existence of the incarnate Son of God, Paul is following a conception of Hellenistic Christianity, we can further recognize that two important substantive reasons are guiding him in the adoption of this conception. (1) Paul has invoked the resurrected Christ as "Lord" and is conscious of owing him unconditional obedience (II Cor. 12:8; 10:5), and in this way he behaves in relation to Christ in the same way as he, as a Jew, had behaved in relation to God. But in spite of this relation to Christ, he also continued to be firmly convinced that it holds true for Christians also that even though there are many gods and many lords, "still there is for us [only] *one* God, the Father, from whom all things [come] and we unto him" (I Cor. 8:5-6). For Paul the Christian, this meant that the glory is due only to this one Creator (cf. Rom. 1:25). His demand that the belief in Christ must not call monotheism in question now is fulfilled by the mythical conception of the Son's belonging eternally to the Father, of the incarnation of the eternal Son of God, and of his installation in the heavenly position of Lord. For in this way, in fact, he is speaking of *God's* action when he speaks of the Son who shared in the Creation, was disclosed in

God's action among the fathers, and was born of the seed of David according to the flesh. In his doing so the myth in no way delineates the "being equal with God," but it gives expression to the confession that in the "Lord" Jesus Christ we encounter God himself. (2) Paul is equally firmly convinced that Jesus Christ has wrought an eschatological salvation. Thus he confesses of himself: "The God who said, 'Let light shine out of darkness,' has caused the light to shine into our hearts, that we may perceive the glory of God in the face of Christ" (II Cor. 4:6), and says of Christians in general: "God has not destined us for wrath, but to obtain salvation through our Lord Jesus Christ, who died for us" (I Thess. 5:9-10 RSV). These two quotations alone show that Paul intends decisively to emphasize that in Christ God himself effects salvation, and he says still more clearly that "God shows his love toward us in that Christ died for us, while we were yet sinners" (Rom. 5:8). It is essential for Paul that salvation actually comes from God, the creator of the world, and this faith also finds expression in the conception appropriate to that time, that the eternal Son of God who comes from God and has returned to God effects salvation.

Thus the mythical talk about the pre-existence of the Son of God, which gives expression to the belief in *God's* saving action in the man Jesus, has its essential roots in a central concern of faith and not in speculative curiosity. One is obliged to ask whether the concern of faith which stands behind the Pauline affirmation of the pre-existence of the Son of God can be expressed today in another form which is more suited to our conceptions; but one must not neglect this concern of faith if one tries to understand and maintain Paul's proclamation of Christ in its ultimate significance. That God himself has begun in the man Jesus and his resurrection the salvation promised for the end-time—to proclaim this is Paul's single concern when he speaks of Jesus Christ. And for this reason, the full meaning of this proclamation can become clear only when we turn to the Pauline conceptions of lostness and salvation.

4. The lost condition of man in the world

"When the fullness of time had come, God sent his Son . . . , that he might redeem those under the law, that we might receive the adoption as sons" (Gal. 4:4-5); "The law of the spirit of life in Christ Jesus has made you free from the law of sin and death" (Rom. 8:2); God "has canceled and set aside the handwriting which was against us with its requirements, by nailing it to the cross;

he has disarmed the principalities and powers and publicly exposed them, by triumphing over them in him [Christ]" (Col. 2:14-15). These assertions, cited by way of example, about the salvation wrought by God in Christ refer in various ways to the state of being without salvation from which God in Christ liberates one, and we must be acquainted with this desperate condition in which, according to Paul, man finds himself, if we wish rightly to understand the Pauline message of salvation in Christ.

Paul sees man in "this world," from which he cannot escape and whose time yet is only limited (I Cor. 5:10; 7:31). This world, it is true, is created by God (Rom. 1:20; cf. I Cor. 8:6), but through Adam's sin death has come into the world, and since then God has subjected the creation to perishability (Rom. 5:12b; 8:20). Dominant in the world now are the "elements of the world" and spiritual powers which Paul calls "rulers of this eon"; indeed, he describes the devil as "the god of this eon" (Gal. 4:3; Col. 2:20; I Cor. 2:6, 8; II Cor. 4:4). Through this dominion of the demons and the devil in this world, men stand under the power of these rulers of the world: "When we were children, we were enslaved under the world elements," it is said in Gal. 4:3 of pre-Christian humanity (cf. Gal. 4:9). This means that men are kept alienated from God (I Cor. 2:12; Gal. 6:14). But now Paul not only speaks of the world in which men find themselves, but much more frequently uses the designation "the world" (kosmos) for men themselves: "What the law says, it says to those under the law, so that every mouth may be stopped and the whole world may be responsible before God" (Rom. 3:19). For men who are identified as "world," it is characteristic that they do not want to acknowledge God, although they know of him: God's "invisible nature since the creation of the world can be seen with the reason in his works . . . , so that they are inexcusable, because they have known God, but did not glorify him as God or give him thanks" (Rom. 1:20-21); "Since in the time of God's wisdom the world through wisdom did not know God . . ." (I Cor. 1:21). Accordingly, the humanity identified as "world" lets itself be determined by "the elements of the world and not by Christ" (Col. 2:8; cf. the contrast of "godly sorrow" and "sorrow of the world," II Cor. 7:10), and such reliance on itself on the world's part in relation to God Paul calls "boasting in the presence of God" (I Cor. 1:27-29). Paul accordingly sees man as standing ever before God ("so that your faith may not rest in the wisdom of men, but in the power of God," I Cor. 2:5), but the man who is in the "world" worships "the creature instead of the creator" (Rom. 1:25), and is thereby estranged from his destiny: "We have one God, the Father, from whom all things come and we unto him" (I Cor. 8:6). This picture of man takes just as seriously the fact that man is God's creature as that he has always evaded the acknowledgment of this reality of creation.

a. MAN AS FLESH

Paul characterizes the man who is in the world by means of a whole series of concepts, but the understanding of these is made very difficult by the fact that Paul does not have a fixed and unambiguous terminology. Above all he sees man placed in the antithesis of "flesh and spirit," and since this antithesis occasionally appears to coincide with that of physical and spiritual man ("If you live according to the flesh, you will die; but if in the spirit you put to death the deeds of the flesh, you will live," Rom. 8:13), it has often been thought that Paul is influenced by the Hellenistic antithesis of body and soul and that he understands "flesh" in the sense of "fleshly substance." But upon closer consideration of the concept "flesh" this proves not at all the case. In isolated cases Paul employs this word without any value judgment, altogether in the Old Testament sense, for earthly man in his creaturely givenness, as: "I conferred not with flesh and blood" (Gal. 1:16); the Son of God "was born of the seed of David according to the flesh" (Rom. 1:3). But in most cases in Paul, "flesh" stands in contrast to the divine Spirit or to God and then denotes the whole man: "In other words, while jealousy and strife [rule] among you, are you not then fleshly, behaving in a human way?" (I Cor. 3:3); "We glory in Christ Jesus and do not trust in the flesh," i.e., in Jewish-religious advantages (Phil. 3:3). Now according to Paul's assertion, men who as "flesh" stand over against God are without exception sinners: "When we were in the flesh, our sinful passions, which came into being through the law, were at work in our members, so that we were bearing fruit unto death" (Rom. 7:5); "God sent his Son in the likeness of sinful flesh and because of sin, and condemned sin in the flesh" (Rom. 8:3). What does "flesh" mean in this context and how does Paul conceive of the connection between flesh and sin?

Paul often speaks of the flesh as of a personal power which stands opposite man in hostility. It is true that "to be in the flesh" can simply describe the earthly existence (" . . . insofar as I now live in the flesh . . . ," Gal. 2:20; "as those who walk in the flesh," II Cor. 10:3), but likewise also the state of being ruled by sin:

"When we were in the flesh, our sinful passions . . . were at work in our members" (Rom. 7:5). To live "in harmony with the flesh" is identical with "to live in sin": "If you live according to the flesh, you will die" (Rom. 8:13; cf. II Cor. 10:2). Now since Paul also can speak of "being fleshly minded" (Rom. 8:6) and of the "desires of the flesh" (Gal. 5:17), and disputes the obligation of man "to the flesh" ("We are not debtors to the flesh, that we [must] live according to the flesh," Rom. 8:12), it is an obvious assumption that Paul sees the flesh as an evil power, a demon, which seeks to rule man. But this assumption is refuted by the discovery that Paul can use "flesh" and "body" entirely interchangeably. The hope that "the life of Jesus may be manifest in our body" stands beside the hope that "the life of Jesus may be manifest in our mortal flesh" (II Cor. 4:10, 11), and "absence in the body" corresponds to "absence in the flesh" (I Cor. 5:3; Col. 2:5). Thus also "body and spirit" can just as well denote man as a whole as "flesh and mind" (I Cor. 7:34 alongside Rom. 7:25). Thus flesh is the identification of man in his earthly corporeality.

Nevertheless for Paul "flesh" and "body" do not simply coincide: "flesh" is limited to man in his mortal actuality: "Flesh and blood will not inherit the kingdom of God" (I Cor. 15:50); "body," on the other hand, can also describe the existence of the resurrected Christian: "it will be raised a spiritual body" (I Cor. 15:44); God "will also make alive our mortal bodies" (Rom. 8:11). Though Paul can speak also of the "*body* of sin," that is, of the "old man," which must be destroyed ("Our old man is crucified with him, so that the sinful body might be destroyed and we might no longer be slaves to sin," Rom. 6:6; "If in the spirit you put to death the deeds of the body, you will live," Rom. 8:13), yet there is no "life according to the body" as there is a "life according to the flesh." Flesh denotes man only in his earthly corporeality, limited to this life, and precisely this man, who is in the flesh and is living according to the flesh, is, according to Paul, a sinner.

However, this sinfulness on the part of fleshly man is not the consequence of the fact that man has a fleshly body which leads him astray into sin. Even though Paul occasionally expresses himself as though this were his meaning ("but I am fleshly, sold under sin," Rom. 7:14), such an interpretation would be a misapprehension. Paul expressly emphasizes that man can live in the flesh without therefore also being obliged to sin: "Walking in the flesh, we do not contend according to the flesh" (II Cor. 10:3); "we are not indebted to the flesh, to live according to the flesh" (Rom. 8:12).

And according to Paul even Christ bore "sinful flesh" (Rom. 8:3) and yet remained without sin (II Cor. 5:21; I Cor. 15:3). Thus man is not a sinner because he has a fleshly body. This statement is supported by the observation that Paul knows no dualism within man which sets a better "inner man" in opposition to the baser corporeality. This is not immediately evident to the observer of Pauline theology, because Paul uses a whole series of concepts for the "inner man" which he does not clearly distinguish from one another, such as soul, mind, heart, conscience, and even spirit; but all these concepts are clearly used in such a way that the "inner man" does not stand any nearer to God than the flesh: "The psychical man does not receive the things of the (divine) Spirit; for him they are foolishness, and he cannot understand them" (I Cor. 2:14); "God has given men up to a reprobate mind, so that they do what is unseemly" (Rom. 1:28); "In accordance with your hardness and your impenitent heart you are storing up for yourself wrath on the day of judgment" (Rom. 2:5).

To be sure there are three much-discussed texts in Romans that could lead to the assumption that Paul does know an "inner man" that stands closer to God. But upon closer examination, these texts also do not allow an interpretation in this sense. "Since the creation of the world God has been seen by the (eye of the) understanding in his invisible nature, namely, his eternal power and deity, in the things that are created, so that they are without excuse, because they knew God, but did not honor him as God or give him thanks . . . " (Rom. 1:20). This passage undoubtedly says that through reason men were given the possibility of knowing the creator by means of a consideration of the creation. But according to Paul men have not used this capability, given to men by God, of a knowledge of God from the creation, in order actually to know God; instead, they have suppressed this possibility given to them, so that precisely through this "spiritual" capability given to them they have become guilty. And the sentence found in Rom. 2:15: Men "show that the law's work is written in their hearts," is a conclusion from the proposition that the Gentiles, when without knowledge they perform the works of the Jewish law, give themselves legal guidance, and therefore are responsible before God for what they do, just as the Jews are. Thus in both cases Paul shows that in actuality man does not grasp the possibility, given to him by God's creation, of existence in God's presence, and that therefore, in spite of these "spiritual" capacities, "all have sinned and come short of the glory of God" (Rom. 3:23).

Most striking, finally, is the famed portrayal of the man who does not do what he wills and who therefore must say of himself: "In the inner man I rejoice in God's law, but I see another law in my members, which contends against the law of my mind and makes me captive through the law of sin which is in my members" (Rom. 7:22-23). Since the days of the church fathers it has been disputed of whom Paul is speaking with this "I," but according to the interpretation most probable in the context Paul means man as he exists "in the flesh," that is, every man as the Christian sees him (see the commentaries on this passage). Now here it is undoubtedly taken for granted that man as "inner man" would like to do God's will, but that the sin in his flesh compels him to commit sin, so that nothing remains for him but the despairing cry, "Wretched man that I am, who will deliver me from this body of death?" (7:24; cf. 7:14 ff.). But the distinctive thing about this portrayal of the despairing situation of man is that, on the one hand, sin and the flesh are made responsible for the committing of evil (vss. 17, 18a, 20) and the "inner man" rejects this doing of evil (vs. 22), but that for the rest, willing and doing have the same "I" as subject ("I do not do the good that I will; instead, the evil that I do not will, this is what I do," vs. 19). Thus the desperate situation of this man consists precisely in the fact that he is unable to do what he recognizes as his obligation in view of God's law and therefore would like to do. Thus even here, in spite of the dualistic-sounding terminology, man is seen as a unity, as "fleshly, sold under sin" (vs. 14). If therewith in this text the intention to do good and man's awareness of his own failure are more strongly emphasized than elsewhere in Paul, this presumably is explained by the fact that here man is viewed consistently through the eyes of the Christian who knows himself already to be saved from this desperate situation. But this peculiarity of the portrayal in Rom. 7:14 ff. cannot call in question the proposition that here, also, Paul sees the whole man as "flesh" and likewise as sinner.

This man, who is ruled by the powers of this world and as "flesh" is obedient to sin, now is characterized by the fact that he "boasts": "God has chosen the folly (= the fools) of this world to put to shame the wise . . . , that no flesh shall boast before God" (I Cor. 1:27, 29). "Since many boast in accordance with the flesh, I too will boast," i.e., Paul reluctantly, aware of the folly of it, follows the example of such human conduct (II Cor. 11:18). Such "boasting with respect to human connections" (I Cor. 3:21) is characteristic of the "flesh" and is based on man's holding to his own tradition and his own ideas: the Colossian heretics are "puffed up without reason because of their fleshly mind" and therewith intend an "indulgence of the flesh" (Col. 2:18, 23). In so doing man resists God ("The mind of the flesh is enmity against God," Rom. 8:7) and follows "the lusts of the flesh" (Gal. 5:16; cf. 5:13). Thus Paul describes the man who lives "after the flesh" not at all differently from the man who lives in the "world," and can fully equate being ruled by the "flesh" with devotion to the "world": "are you now ending with the flesh?" corresponds to "how do you now turn again to the weak and beggarly elements [of the world]?" (Gal. 3:3; 4:9); and of the Christians' past it is said: "When we were children, we were in bondage to the elements of the world," just as it is true of them that "when we were in the flesh, our sinful passions, which came into being through the law, were at work in our members, so that we were bearing fruit unto death" (Gal. 4:3; Rom. 7:5). The man who is characterized by the "flesh" is thus the man who lets himself be ruled by the powers of this world. Further, the concept "flesh" thus does not simply describe the existence of man as a fate which is given with his very nature, but it characterizes the action of man who stands before God and, instead of acknowledging God, trusts in himself. For Paul sees man always in a slave-master relationship, either to God or to sin: "When you were slaves to sin, you were free from righteousness. . . . But now you are free from sin and have become slaves of God" (Rom. 6:20, 22). Thus for Paul flesh is "the mark of man as he is distinguished from God" (A. Schlatter) and it characterizes man, not according to his existence, but according to his historical conduct in the world that is passing away.

b. THE UNIVERSALITY OF SIN

When Paul in this sense asserts the sinfulness of all men ("All have sinned and come short of the glory of God," Rom. 3:23; "the Scripture has concluded all things under sin," Gal. 3:22), as a rule he simply sets this forth as an existing fact: "I am fleshly, sold under sin" (Rom. 7:14). But once he also speaks of the beginning of this human existence under sin (Rom. 5:12-19). To be sure, even in this connection he is not guided by an interest in explaining the origin or emergence of sin. His aim in this passage is, rather, to place in contrast with the universality of the sin that has come into the world through *one* man the life that is brought through the *one* man Jesus as the much greater gift of God. In this context the subject is the beginning of sin: "As through *one* man sin entered into the world and death through sin and thus death passed to all men, because all have sinned . . ." (Rom. 5:12) . This much-debated sentence has no grammatical conclusion, but is taken up again after a long interruption: "Thus as [it came] to condemnation for all men through one transgression, so also to the justification of life for all men through one righteous act" (vs. 18) . In the introductory clause in vs. 12 as well as in vs. 18, where it is taken up again, it is first of all clearly said that Adam's sinful deed brought sin into the world and, as its consequence, death, because "death is the wages of sin" (Rom. 6:23) , i.e., because Adam's sin had the effect of the imposition by God of death as punishment. When Paul then adds that thus "death passed upon all men" (vs. 12c), it is said therewith that since Adam's being punished with death, all men must die. One could interpret this statement to mean that Adam, through his sinful deed, brought the penalty of death upon all men (cf. also vs. 17: "For if through the transgression of the one, death gained its dominion through the one . . . ") . In this way, then, without any further explanation the collective punishment of all men would be asserted as a consequence of the sinful act of the first man (so-called "inherited death") . But in vs. 12d Paul adds: "because all have sinned," and with these words he places beside the assertion that since Adam's death all men must die the explanation that every man must die because of his own sin. This combination of the two ideas, "since the punishment of sinful Adam all men must die" and "every man must die for his own sin," appears to be contradictory; but here Paul is simply following a Jewish conception according to which Adam incurred the connection of sin and punishment, but every man earns this punishment through his own sin. "Though Adam first sinned and brought premature death upon all, yet each individual one of those descended from him has brought upon himself future misery and again every individual one of them has chosen for himself future glory" (Syriac Baruch 54.15) . Thus Paul by all means is representing the idea of the death caused by Adam, but by no means that of inherited sin, because he, in full agreement with Jewish thinking, maintains the responsibility of every man before God for what he does; cf. also Rom. 1:20-21: men are "inexcusable, because they knew God, but did not give honor to God."

Thus again we see that Paul does not regard man's being subject to the powers of this world and to sin as fate, but as guilt for which man is responsible. But Paul understood man's being dominated by the powers of this world and by sin in a thoroughly radical sense, in that he expresses the universality of sin not as a judgment of experience, but as a judgment of faith. For the sentence, "All have sinned and come short of the glory of God and are freely justified by his grace through the redemption that is in Christ Jesus" (Rom. 3:23-24), clearly goes from the fact, certain in faith, that man's deliverance is possible only through God's redemption in Jesus Christ (cf. also Rom. 8:2), back to the proposition that without this redemption all men are sinners and are subject to death. It is true that Paul avoids in any way inquiring behind Adam's deed for this universality of sin which for him as a Christian is indubitable. "He stops with the idea that sin came into the world through the act of sinning" (R. Bultmann). On the other hand, Paul gives clear expression to the conviction that all men since Adam without exception have fallen victim to sin, in that he sees this condition and man's being in the flesh together: "I am fleshly, sold under sin" (Rom. 7:14).

But even with this formulation the actual universal sinfulness of men is not derived by Paul from anything other than sin itself. Paul only says concretely and specifically that man as "flesh" is always a sinner. Hence Paul cherishes no doubt as to man's *responsibility* for his *actual sinning*. Paul can certainly speak in strongly personal form of sin: sin comes into the world and rules there (Rom. 5:12, 21; 6:12), it makes men its slaves (Rom. 6:6, 17, 20) and pays with death as its wages (Rom. 6:23), it revives, deceives, and slays man and to this end misuses the law (Rom. 7:9, 11). This personifying way of talking about sin is in keeping with Paul's using the Greek word for "sin" only seldom in the sense of "sinful act" (as in Rom. 7:5; I Cor. 15:17; Gal. 1:4); on the contrary, as a rule he speaks of "the sin" which makes man its slave. But this slavery is worked out concretely in man's actions, and man is responsible for these. "Do not present your members as unrighteous instruments of sin" (Rom. 6:13), Paul admonishes the Christians, who formerly had presented their members "as servants of impurity and lawlessness, for the aims of lawlessness" (Rom. 6:19). Men in fact knew of the invisible God and hence are inexcusable, and this holds true for all men, and moreover for Jews in particular: "They have a zeal for God, but not in a rational way; indeed, they do not understand God's righteousness and have sought to establish their own [righteousness] and [thus] have not submitted themselves to God's righteousness" (Rom. 10:2-3). Man, whether Gentile or Jew, resists God's will; for "the mind of the flesh is enmity against

God, for it does not submit to God's law and cannot. But those who are in the flesh cannot please God" (Rom. 8:7-8).

Obviously it can be asked, and it has often been asked, how Paul can speak of man's responsibility before God when man yet as flesh is sold under sin and cannot go further than the cry, "Wretched man that I am, who will deliver me from this body of death?" (Rom. 7:24). Of course in answer to this question one can point out that Paul nevertheless leaves open the possibility that "Gentiles, who do not have the law, by nature do the works of the law" (Rom. 2:14), and that Paul says of Abraham that he "honored God" and that such faith was "accounted to him for righteousness" (Rom. 4:20 ff.; cf. also 4:9-11). But it is not at all certain that with these references Paul intended to adduce exceptions to the assertion that "all have sinned . . . and are undeservedly justified by his [God's] grace" (Rom. 3:23-24), because even among the Gentiles who may "do the works of the law," on the day of judgment "their thoughts will accuse or defend them" (Rom. 2:15-16) and because Abraham was not justified on the basis of his own achievement. Paul presumably knows no actual exception to the universal sinful condition of man, even when he speaks of men who "keep the demands of the law" (Rom. 2:26). When he nevertheless maintains the responsibility and therefore the guilt of man, he can do this first of all because according to his conviction, all men in fact have known God and in spite of this have not acknowledged him (Rom. 1:20-21) and have let themselves be deceived and led astray by sin (Rom. 7:11, 13). Thus for Paul man's responsibility and guilt are beyond doubt, because he does not trace man's sinning to "a quality necessarily inherent in man" (R. Bultmann), but exclusively to the sinning itself.

C. LAW AND GUILT

This responsibility becomes more reasonable by virtue of Paul's bringing into his argument the law, which first actually establishes man's guilt. This is by no means done arbitrarily, but compulsorily, because for Paul as a Jew the Jewish law had been God's only way of salvation, and he must now regard this way of salvation as a false way: I was "blameless as to the righteousness on the basis of the law. But what was gain to me, this I regard as loss for the sake of Christ" (Phil. 3:6-7). In spite of this experience, Paul maintains that "the law is holy, just, and good," that "the law is spiritual" (Rom. 7:12, 14), and counts the gift of the law to the Israelites as one of the advantages which God has granted to his people (Rom. 9:4). But the law itself points beyond itself: law and prophets testify in advance of the righteousness without law (Rom. 3:21), and "Moses writes that [only] the man who practices the righteousness based on law will live on the basis of that righteousness," while the righteousness that is of faith says that one need not seek Christ in heaven or in the underworld, "but what does it say? The word is near you, in your mouth and in your heart, that is, the word of faith which we preach" (Rom. 10:5-8, with an appeal to several Old Testament texts). Hence Paul can explicitly declare that with the coming of faith, the time of the law was at an end, and "Christ is the end of the law, unto righteousness for everyone who believes" (Gal. 3:25; Rom. 10:4). That means that for the Christians the law as a way of salvation no longer exists, but it also unavoidably poses the question as to what role the law which comes from God has played and perhaps continues to play in God's plan of salvation. To this question Paul gives a threefold answer.

(1) The law requires fulfillment of God's demand proclaimed in it, and indeed unconditional fulfillment: "Again I testify to everyone who is circumcised that he is under obligation to keep the whole law" (Gal. 5:3; cf. 3:10). But there is no man, neither Jew nor Greek, for whom it would not be true that "all have turned aside, and have become unfit; there is no one who does good, no, not one" (Rom. 3:9, 12), and hence Paul can deduce from this verse from the Psalms and similar quotations: "We know that what the law says, it says to those who are under the law, that every mouth may be stopped and the whole world may be accountable to God" (Rom. 3:19). The law indeed shows man God's will ("In the inward man I delight in the law of God," Rom. 7:22), but it is not able to help man in following God's will, because sin misuses the law and deludes man, and man is too weak to resist this delusion: "Sin used the commandment as a point of attack, deceived me, and killed me by it [the commandment]" (Rom. 7:11); "For insofar as the law, being weak because of the flesh, was helpless, God sent his Son . . . and condemned sin in the flesh" (Rom. 8:3). Thus the law confronts man with God's will, but is incapable of preserving him from the deceitful power of sin and hence of preventing the fact that for the man who "would do good, evil is at hand" (Rom. 7:21). Thus the law only brings it about that man must see that indeed and in truth he is a sinner and hence is guilty: "But where there is no law, there also is no transgression" (Rom. 4: 15); "for through the law comes knowledge of sin" (Rom. 3:20b).

Because man knows God's will and yet, yielding to the power of sin, does not fulfill it, he is a transgressor, who must confess himself guilty before God (Rom. 3:19*b*).

(2) Paul of course makes one noteworthy exception to this rule: "Until the law, sin was in the world, but sin is not imputed when the law is not present; but death ruled [in spite of that fact] from Adam to Moses even over those whose sin was not like Adam's transgression" (Rom. 5:13-14). Here a distinction is made between men since the coming of the Mosaic law, who like Adam transgressed an explicit divine commandment, thereby became guilty, and received death as the wages of sin, and the men between Adam and Moses, who knew no such divine commandment, hence could not transgress it and thereby become guilty, but in spite of this sinned and therefore had to die, although their sin was not "imputed." It is puzzling why Paul, in the context of his placing Adam and Christ in parallel as originators of death and of life, comes to speak of the peculiar position of men between Adam and Moses, and it is even more inexplicable to what extent, in Paul's opinion, these men stand before God differently from the Gentiles "who have not the law and are a law unto themselves" (Rom. 2:14), and the Israelites since Moses, who indeed all sinned and had to die. But even though this subordinate Pauline idea remains incomprehensible to us, still precisely the emphasizing of this exception by Paul shows that, apart from this special case, in Paul's opinion all men must apprehend that they are sinners, because the law showed them God's will, without being able to help them to fulfill it.

(3) But Paul goes a step further: he describes this inability of the law to bring men to God as arising out of God's intention. The law is not at all given directly by God himself; in this, God rather has employed the mediation of angels and of Moses (Gal. 3:19). The law, moreover, "came in on the side" (Rom. 5:20), and thus it did not, as the Jewish interpretation had it, introduce the decisive period of salvation; the time of the law is rather an episode. But this episode had a twofold aim in God's will: Men were to be kept under supervision, in prison, by the law until the coming of faith: "Before faith came, we were guarded, shut up unto faith which should be revealed. Hence the law was our overseer until Christ" (Gal. 3:23-24). At the same time, through its prohibitions the law would cause transgressions to multiply: "The law came in, that it might multiply the transgressions" (Rom. 5:20); "it was added for the sake of transgressions" (Gal. 3:19); "When we were in the flesh,

our sinful passions, which came into being through the law, were at work in our members" (Rom. 7:5). Through this misuse of the law, sin is supposed to be unveiled in all its fearfulness: "Has that which is good [i.e., the law] now brought me death? By no means. It was rather sin [that brought me death], that it might be evident as sin, producing death in me through that which is good, so that through the commandment it became sinful beyond measure" (Rom. 7:13). Thus, because salvation comes through Christ, the law cannot at all be given in order to bestow life: "If the law had been given with the ability to make alive, then there would indeed be a righteousness based on the law" (Gal. 3:21); "I do not nullify the grace of God; for if righteousness [had come] through the law, then Christ would have died in vain" (Gal. 2:21). The formulation, "the commandment [which is to lead] to life" (Rom. 7:10), on the other hand, points only to the law, without considering the intervention of sin. Thus the ultimate aim of the law is, in accordance with God's will, to point out to men that they can become righteous before God only by faith and not by works of the law: "Hence the law was our overseer until Christ, that we might be justified by faith; but since faith has come, we are no longer under an overseer" (Gal. 3:24-25). Hence Paul can say to the Galatians: "You once did not know God, and served those that by nature are no gods; but now you have known God, or rather have been known by God—how can you turn again to the weak and beggarly [world] elements, which you want again to serve?" (Gal. 4:8-9), and can warn them with these words against the adoption of circumcision and therewith subjection to the law (Gal. 5:2; 3:2).

Thus the law is also counted among those powers which hold man in the world and try to hinder his turning to God; for the law also leads men astray into self-glorying: "You who boast in the law dishonor God by breaking the law" (Rom. 2:23). Paul dares not only to describe this state of affairs, that the law leads man away from God, but to trace it to God's will, because he can understand all events ultimately only as arising from God's saving intention and as in harmony with his plan of salvation. In this divine source *and* aim of the law, then, is grounded the fact that the law, which could not lead man to salvation, yet continues to be preserved as a clue to the divine will for the Christians (see below, p. 227). Thus, in accordance with God's will, it is only by means of the law that man actually becomes a transgressor and thus guilty, "that every mouth may be stopped and the whole world may be guilty before God" (Rom. 3:19). But therewith also is created the precondition for the intervention of divine grace: "The law came in, in order to make the transgressions abundant; but where sin abounded, grace was much more abundant, so that, as sin reigned in death, so also through righteousness grace might reign unto eternal life through Jesus Christ our Lord" (Rom. 5:20-21).

5. *Salvation in Jesus Christ*

Thus Paul quite certainly sees man in a hopeless situation which finally allows him nothing but to break out in the cry: "Wretched man that I am, who will deliver me from this body of death?" (Rom. 7:24). But this view of man does not arise out of any sort of reasoned pessimism or dualism, but is the consequence of the certainty that the Christians are freed from this situation by God and that every man can be freed from it. Thus the picture of man which Paul draws is only the other side of his message of the redemption of man by Christ. Paul repeatedly speaks of the fact that now everything has changed: "But now God's righteousness has been revealed without the law" (Rom. 3:21); "Therefore there is now no condemnation for those in Christ" (Rom. 8:1); "The mystery hidden from the eons and the generations is now disclosed to his saints" (Col. 1:26; cf. also Rom. 3:26; 5:9, 11; 7:6; I Cor. 15:20; II Cor. 6:2; Col. 1:22; and above, p. 144). And as Paul can describe the lost condition of man with various metaphorical conceptions, so he also speaks of the salvation that has now become a reality in various forms of conceptions, all of which describe the same divine event from various sides.

a. DELIVERANCE AND REDEMPTION

The most general concept is that of "deliverance," usually translated as "salvation." Man as sinner is in fact confronted by "perdition": "do not let yourselves be frightened by the adversaries; which for them is a sign of perdition, but for you of salvation, and that from God" (Phil. 1:28), and hence Paul contrasts those who perish with those who are saved (I Cor. 1:18; II Cor. 2:15; Phil. 1:28). But Paul can say to the Christians: "God has not destined us for wrath, but to obtain salvation through our Lord Jesus Christ" (I Thess. 5:9 RSV). Thus he speaks frequently of the deliverance which awaits the Christians: the gospel "is a power of God unto deliverance for everyone who believes" (Rom. 1:16); "if with your mouth you confess Jesus as Lord and believe in your heart that God has raised him from the dead, you will be delivered" (Rom. 10:9).

Rom. 13:11-12 shows that Paul expects this deliverance at the coming of Christ in glory that is anticipated in the near future, that is, at the imminent end: "Now is our deliverance nearer than [at that time] when we first believed. The night is far along, the day has come near" (on the "day," cf. I Cor. 1:8; I Thess. 5:2). But Paul speaks not only of the *expectation* of the future deliverance; he also closely connects this future with the present: "We await the redemption of our body; for in hope we are saved" (Rom. 8:23-24), and accordingly says: "Behold, now is the accepted time, behold, now is the day of deliverance" (II Cor. 6:2). For the Christian the coming salvation is an assured gift already in the present, because it is grounded in Christ's death and resurrection in the past: "How much more shall we, who now have been justified through his blood, be delivered from wrath through him. For if we, who were enemies, were reconciled with God through the death of his Son, how much more shall we as reconciled be delivered by his life" (Rom. 5:9-10). The deliverance of the Christian, which he assuredly expects at the approaching end of the world, thus is for him already a present reality, because God's decisive saving act has happened and in the present the Christian already receives a share in this salvation event of the past. At the same time, this general concept, "deliverance," already makes it evident that the Christian's state of being saved corresponds to the fact that the Christian knows himself to be set in the time between the resurrection and the anticipated coming of Christ in glory and therefore, in spite of his life in the old eon, already has a share in the dawning of the coming eon. Of course it is only in the specific concepts related to salvation that we can discern what this state of being delivered means in terms of contents.

b. LIBERATION FROM THE SPIRITUAL POWERS

We are already led somewhat further by the conception of liberation. According to Paul's conviction, man is always a slave and therefore unfree: "Do you not know that you are slaves to that one to whom you make yourselves available for obedience as slaves, in your obeying this one [lord], whether it is sin, unto death, or obedience, unto righteousness?" (Rom. 6:16), and therefore it is only a question of who is the master of the slave. In this world man is in himself slave to many lords which seek to draw him away from God: sin (Rom. 6:6, 20), the law (Rom. 6:14-15; 7:5-6), and the elements of the world (Gal. 4:3, 8). Christ has freed and will free men from all these masters. Paul can express this truth quite

generally: Christ "has become for us wisdom from God, righteousness and sanctification and redemption" (I Cor. 1:30) ; "Where the
Spirit of the Lord is, there is liberty" (II Cor. 3:17) ; "We who
have the firstfruits of the Spirit groan inwardly in the expectation
of the redemption of our body" (Rom. 8:23). What this liberation
means concretely for men first becomes discernible, however, where
Paul speaks of the liberation from the slavery to the individual
"lords."

Most comprehensive are the statements about the liberation from
the world elements, the spiritual powers. Indeed, according to
Paul, in this world men stand inescapably under the power of the
demons and the devil, which keep men from God and thus from
the godly life (see above, p. 173). But by the sending of Christ
God has "disarmed the powers and principalities and made a public
exposure of them, by gaining the victory over them in him [Christ]"
(Col. 2:15). In other words, Jesus Christ himself became a slave
of the powers of this world: "he emptied himself, taking on the
form of a slave" (Phil. 2:7) ; "God sent his Son in the likeness of
sinful flesh" (Rom. 8:3), and because Christ appeared "in the likeness of men" (Phil. 2:7), "none of the rulers of this eon knew
[the wisdom of God]; for if they had known it, they would not
have crucified the Lord of glory" (I Cor. 2:8). But thus the
powers of this world wrongly thought that they could exercise
their power of death even over Jesus Christ; but this did not come
true; instead, "Christ is risen from the dead, and become the firstfruits of those who were asleep" (I Cor. 15:20; cf. Col. 1:18), and
thus through the cross and resurrection of his Son, God has disarmed the powers and "made peace through him, by the blood of
his cross, on earth as in heaven" (Col. 1:20). Since then Christ is
"the head of every lordship and power" (Col. 2:10), even though
the powers are not yet destroyed (cf. I Cor. 7:5; 10:20; Gal. 4:9).
Because Christ has conquered the powers, the Christian may be
convinced that Christ "has given himself for our sins, that he might
deliver us from this present evil age" (Gal. 1:4) ; for God "has
rescued us from the power of darkness and transferred us into the
kingdom of his dear Son" (Col. 1:13). As the Christian is certain
that the powers are disarmed (cf. also Rom. 8:37-38), so also he is
certain that at Christ's appearing in glory, which is expected in the
near future, "at the name of Jesus every knee shall bow, of things in
heaven and on earth and under the earth, and every tongue shall
confess that Jesus Christ is Lord, to the glory of God the Father"
(Phil. 2:10-11). Then when Christ "has destroyed every lordship

and every principality and power, . . . the last enemy to be destroyed is death" (I Cor. 15:24 ff.; cf. also the destruction of the antichrist, II Thess. 2:8). Then will "the creation also be set free from slavery to perishability into the glorious freedom of the children of God" (Rom. 8:21).

This circle of ideas, complete in itself, which echoes in many passages in the letters of Paul but is cited in more detail only where the significance of Christ's death and resurrection for the whole world is not seen and Paul therefore must contend against this devaluation of God's act in Christ (that is to say, with respect to the Colossians), is undoubtedly especially alien to the present-day Bible reader: Satan and the demons are figures inconceivable to us, and we can hardly imagine that the historical event of the death and resurrection of Jesus Christ should have basically changed the situation of the whole world, and indeed its ultimate fate. Moreover, the idea that the demons were deceived by the incarnation of Jesus Christ, and hence were robbed of their power by the cross and the resurrection of their Lord who was unknown to them, seems to give a questionable form to the belief in the saving act in Christ. Now one will be able to understand the idea that the demons were deceived by the incarnation of the "Lord of glory" (I Cor. 2:8) only when one assumes that Paul knew and appropriated the Gnostic myth of the descent of the redeemer through the heavens, during which the rulers of the various heavens were deceived by the redeemer's disguise (cf. the adoption of this myth in the Great Church's "Epistula Apostolorum" of the second century, chap. 13 of the Coptic text, and in the Gnostic "Ascension of Isaiah," also from the second century, chap. 10:7-31 and chap. 11:22-32; both texts in translation in Hennecke-Schneemelcher-Wilson, I, 197-98; II, 659-62). To be sure it is by no means evident from I Cor. 2:8 that Paul *intended* to say that Christ by means of his incarnation wished to deceive the demons as to his true nature—the idea of the intentional deception of the devil was held beginning with the early church fathers and continuing down to Luther, and is inferred in part from Paul's allusion. But even if Paul is supposed to have spoken only of a deception of the demons that actually occurred, this idea is hardly a suitable form of expression for the belief that in Christ, God has robbed the world powers of their might. Yet the foreignness of this entire circle of ideas continues to exist for us, even if we leave aside this individual conception, which in fact is only a subordinate idea. We should, to be sure, think twice before we simply thrust aside these ideas which are so important for Paul.

The conception that a world hostile to God is guided by personal beings (Satan, demons) undoubtedly belongs to the ancient picture of the world, one that is still real today for many people, but which we are no longer able to share. Still, after the experiences of the last decades, we can hardly simply deny that the resistance against God the Creator and the reality of the seductive power of evil extends far beyond the individual man or even isolated groups of men, that there is a reality of evil into whose power the individual man sees himself helplessly delivered. But since we cannot deny this, God's saving action in Jesus Christ cannot have decisive significance unless the power of evil also were thereby affected to the very core. Hence the Pauline message of the "disarming of the powers" undoubtedly is an important statement, not only for Paul, but intrinsically, even though this statement appears not to be personally significant for the individual believer in the same measure as Paul's statements about God's redemption in Christ, which we shall discuss in the following pages.

The Pauline message of the disarming of the powers is strictly bound to the historical situation of the Christian as it is recognized in faith. For as unequivocally as Paul confesses that the demons are conquered by Christ's death and resurrection, and as sure as Paul is that the Christians therefore are saved from the present evil eon and the power of darkness (Col. 2:15; Gal. 1:4; Col. 1:13), just as clearly does Paul know that the form of this world is yet to pass away (I Cor. 7:31), and that therefore the devil and the demons still represent a danger, even for the Christian, who after all still lives in the flesh (II Cor. 4:3-4; Gal. 4:9; I Cor. 7:5; 10:20). Thus the Christian can be certain that the power of evil will not have the last word, because the powers are to be destroyed and God will be all in all (I Cor. 15:24, 28; II Thess. 2:8), and he can be confident that no power in the world can snatch him away from God's love in Christ (Rom. 8:38-39; 5:9-10; I Thess. 1:10; 5:9). But this destruction of the power of evil is yet to come, as certain as it is that it will come, and therefore now it holds true for the Christian: "Let us not sleep, as do the others, but watch and be sober!" (I Thess. 5:6). Thus the Pauline discourse about God's victory in Christ over the spiritual powers describes with the utmost seriousness the historical situation of the Christian in the present between the resurrection and Christ's appearing in glory, and to this extent it has for us also an abiding significance.

C. LIBERATION FROM THE LAW

Of course the Pauline message of liberation from the law appears to us to be significantly more central. For Paul as a former Jew, the law is the power which bids man do God's will, and therefore Paul regards all the time down to the coming of Christ as the time of the law (Gal. 3:23). But Paul the Christian had to recognize that the law keeps man in prison, awakens sinful passions in him or prompts him to self-justification before God, and in both cases makes him a slave who must serve the world elements (Gal. 3:23; 4:3-5, 9; Rom. 6:14-15; 7:4-6; 9:31-32; 10:3). The law was not capable of giving life to man, and by works of the law no man can be justified before God, so that man under the law can only come to the cry: "Wretched man that I am, who will deliver me from this body of death?" (Gal. 3:21; Rom. 3:20; 7:24). Of course this question is immediately answered by Paul: "Thanks [be] to God, through Jesus Christ our Lord" (Rom. 7:25a); and accordingly Paul proclaims to the Galatians who desire to be subject to the law: "Christ has redeemed us from the curse of the law, by becoming a curse for us"; "God sent his Son, born of a woman, placed under the law, that he might redeem those [men] under the law, that we might receive the adoption as sons" (Gal. 3:13; 4:4-5). But this redemption from the law signifies freedom: "For freedom Christ has made us free"; "you, brethren, are called to freedom" (Gal. 5:1-13). And for Christians quite generally it is true that "You are not under law, but under grace"; "You have died unto the law through [entering into] the body of Christ" (Rom. 6:14; 7:4); "Since faith came, we are no longer under [the dominion of] the guardian" (i.e., the law), because "Christ is the end of the law unto righteousness for everyone who believes" (Gal. 3:25; Rom. 10:4). Thus here, too, two periods of the divine dealing with the world are clearly set in sequence: until the coming of Christ and of faith, men stood under the curse of the law, because "cursed is everyone who does not abide by all that is written in the book of the law, to do it" (Gal. 3:10). Christ has put an end to this curse, in that he himself "has become a curse for us, because it is written, 'Cursed is everyone who hangs on a tree'" (Gal. 3:13). Thus Paul interprets Christ's death on the cross as a vicarious taking upon himself of the curse of the law, which necessarily affected men who were disobedient to the law; and Paul portrays this vicarious bearing of the law's curse as a redeeming of men from this curse.

There has been much puzzling over how this figure of redemption is meant in detail; how the captivity, the price paid, the recipient of this payment, etc., are to be understood. But it is utterly uncertain whether such a question may be raised at all, since Paul also can speak of the redemption of Christians without thereby thinking of the liberation from the curse of the law: "You are bought with a price" (I Cor. 6:20; 7:23). He apparently is thinking only that men formerly lived in slavery to the powers of the world and therewith also to the law, and now are set free from this slavery and, corresponding to the image of the slave, "are redeemed" (i.e., "bought free") : by Christ's humbling himself so far that he vicariously bore the curse of the law which did not apply to himself, he broke the power of this curse and set men free from the power of the law that cursed them, "that we might receive the promise of the Spirit through faith" (Gal. 3:14*b*). Because in Christ's death and resurrection God wrought *eschatological* salvation ("When the time was fulfilled, God sent his Son, . . . to redeem those [men] under the law, that we might receive the adoption as sons," Gal. 4:4-5), therefore, with the in-breaking of the coming eon into this perishing world, through Christ's death and resurrection the law is also deprived of the power to enslave men and to impose a curse upon them. The curse of the law, which would have had to strike the disobedient man, is taken away by Christ's vicarious dying and his resurrection. But therewith it is shown that the actual state of being lost, which affects the man who is enslaved under the law, is the curse of the law, the "guilty" sentence of the man who is under the law's demands; and the freedom from this curse, brought about by Christ, is by its very nature freedom from the guilt which is pronounced by this curse. Therefore only when we inquire into the liberation from guilt will we understand in its ultimate meaning Paul's message of the redemption of man by Christ.

d. liberation from sin and guilt

That is to say, Paul sees the enslaving dominion of sin over man as bound up closely with the law as the lord that enslaves man in the world. Thus he can say of man under the law: "When the commandment came, sin revived, but I died" (Rom. 7:9-10) and therewith can describe the fact that man always stands under the death-dealing power of sin so long as he is under the power of the law (cf. also Rom. 7:5). But he can also declare to the Christians: "Sin will not rule over you; indeed, you are not [any longer] under the law, but under grace" (Rom. 6:14). Thus Paul sees sin first of all as a power to which men are subject as slaves (see above, p. 180) and which exercises its rule through death (Rom. 5:21; cf. also 6:23). But Christ has also *set us free from slavery to sin:* "But you are freed from sin and have become slaves to God" (Rom. 6:22); "For the law of the spirit of life in Christ Jesus has made you free from the law of sin and death" (Rom. 8:2). How has Christ broken the power of sin over man? When Christ became man, he assumed "sinful flesh" and thereby committed himself to the sphere of sin's power (Rom. 8:3), without himself doing sinful deeds: "Him who knew no sin he has made to be sin for us" (II Cor. 5:21). Sin has also delivered this man up to death: "In that he [Christ] died, he died for sin once for all" (Rom. 6:10*a*); but Christ did not die as a "slave to sin unto death" (Rom. 6:16), but "for our sins," "for us," "for all," "for the ungodly" (I Cor. 15:3; I Thess. 5:10; Rom. 5:6, 8; II Cor. 5:14; *et passim*). In this death of Christ thus is shown God's love (Rom. 5:8), and because God acted here "for us ungodly ones" (Rom. 5:6), it may therefore be said of this death: "God sent his Son in the likeness of sinful flesh and because of sin and condemned sin in the flesh" (Rom. 8:3). Paul did not say more precisely how he conceived of this condemnation of sin, this disarming of sin by the death of Christ, but the idea probably is that this death could not befall a sinner, and hence it struck the sin which had no rights over this man (cf. the commentaries on Rom. 8:3). God indeed did not let this death be the last word, but raised the One who died on the cross and therein as well showed himself to be the conqueror of the power which brought Jesus to death, namely sin: "Who is it that condemns? Is it Christ Jesus, who died, yes, more, who is raised, who is at the right hand of God?" (Rom. 8:34); "We know that Christ, who was raised from the dead, dies no more; death has no more dominion over him" (Rom. 6:9). Thus if God has "condemned sin in the flesh" (Rom. 8:3), then, since Christ's death and resurrection, sin is no longer lord over the flesh and it is possible "to walk not according to the flesh" (Rom. 8:4). Thus also with respect to the power of sin Christ's death introduces a new world epoch, the time of the final salvation, but here too it is true that the old eon has not yet passed away and the power of sin is not yet destroyed. Hence the Christians have died to sin and are freed from slavery to the power of sin (Rom. 6:2, 18), but sin can still exercise its dominion "over your mortal body, so that you obey its desires" (Rom. 6:12). The message of the liberation from the power of sin thus is also set in the context of

the Pauline message of the overlapping of the two eons and therefore can only become fully comprehensible when we inquire about
the Pauline view of the state of being of the Christian in this age of
final salvation.

Certainly we have gained a partial view of the Pauline message
of the redemption of man from sin only when we have spoken of
the liberation from the power of sin. Indeed, we have already
seen that for Paul, man's most desperate misery is the guilt into
which sin plunges man. Because all men have sinned, "every mouth"
is "stopped and the whole world" is "guilty before God" (Rom.
5:12d; 3:19; cf. 3:9, 23; 5:20; see above, pp. 178 ff.). But in Christ
"we have redemption, the forgiveness of sins" (Col. 1:14). To
be sure, it is only in this passage in Colossians, whose genuineness
is disputed, that Paul so undisputedly says that God in Christ has
made the guilt of sin ineffective through forgiveness. But alongside
this image of forgiveness, taken from the personal association of
men, Paul uses a number of other images in order to express the
message of the removal of the guilt of sin by God: "Now there is
no [more] condemnation for those in Christ Jesus" (Rom. 8:1);
"God reconciled the world to himself in Christ, in that he did not
reckon their shortcomings to them" (II Cor. 5:19); "how much
more shall we, who now have been justified by his blood, be saved
from wrath through him" (Rom. 5:9; cf. I Thess. 1:10); "He has
forgiven us all our trespasses, he has canceled and set aside the indictment that stood against us, with its demands, by nailing it to the
cross" (Col. 2:13-14). In these texts, alongside the conception, stemming from the religious sphere, of deliverance from the divine
wrath, we encounter above all, in varied application, the juridical
image of acquittal and remission of guilt. The conceptual world of
legal decisions then is also the most important thought form in
which Paul expresses his message of the removal of the guilt of sin
by God in Christ, and in the context of the so-called doctrine of
justification also the idea of the forgiveness of sins occurs again.

e. JUSTIFICATION

It is in the polemical contexts of Romans and Galatians that
Paul goes into this message of divine justification in the most detail.
The so-called "theme" of Romans (the gospel "is the power of
God for salvation to everyone who believes, first to the Jews and
[then] to the Greeks; for in it God's righteousness is revealed out of
faith to faith, as it stands written: 'Those who are righteous by
faith shall live,'" Rom. 1:16-17) finds its fundamental exposition

in Rom. 3:21-30: "But now is God's righteousness apart from law revealed . . . , but God's righteousness through faith in Jesus Christ for all who believe. For there is no distinction: all have sinned and come short of God's glory and are justified without merit by his grace, through the redemption in Jesus Christ. Him has God set forth as an expiation in his blood, [which is grasped] through faith. Thereby God's intention was to cause his righteousness to become effectual, by forgiving the sins committed earlier, in the time of God's patience; God intended thereby to cause his righteousness to become effectual in the present time, that he himself might be just and might declare righteous him who has faith in Jesus . . . . That is to say, we hold that a man is justified by faith without works of the law. Or is God only [the God] of the Jews? Is he not [the God] of the Gentiles also? Yes, of the Gentiles also, if there then is one God who will justify the circumcised on the grounds of their faith and the uncircumcised through their faith." In what follows, this message is illustrated by the figure of believing Abraham, and then there is the quite general statement: "To one who trusts him who justifies the ungodly, his faith is reckoned as righteousness, as David also calls the man blessed to whom God reckons righteousness without works; 'Blessed are those whose transgressions are forgiven and whose sins are covered; blessed is the man to whom the Lord does not reckon sin' " (Rom. 4:5-8). Similarly in Gal. 2:15-16: "We, who by nature are Jews and not sinners of the Gentiles, yet knew that man is not justified by the works of the law, but through faith in Christ Jesus, we have believed in Christ Jesus, that we might be justified by faith in Christ and not by works of the law, because by works of the law no flesh shall be justified." And here also Abraham is named as an example of faith: "As Abraham believed God and it was reckoned to him for righteousness. Thus you see that those who are of faith are Abraham's sons. But the Scripture foresaw that God would justify the Gentiles by faith, and therefore proclaimed the gospel beforehand to Abraham: 'In you shall all the nations be blessed.' Hence those who are of faith are blessed together with believing Abraham" (Gal. 3:6-9). And still a third time Paul speaks still more explicitly of justification, after he had spoken in the Philippian epistle of the fact that he had learned to regard the irreproachable law-righteousness of his Jewish past as loss for the sake of Christ: "But now I count all things as loss because of the superlative worth of the knowledge of Christ Jesus my Lord, for whose sake I have suffered the loss of everything, and count it as refuse, in order to gain Christ and to be found in him, that I might have, not my own righteousness by the law, but the righteousness that is by faith in Christ, the righteousness that is from God on the basis of faith" (Phil. 3:8-9) .

But Paul also frequently speaks briefly elsewhere of the justification of the Christians or of justification by faith (Rom. 5:9, 18; 8:30, 33; 10:4, 10; I Cor. 1:30; 6:11) and of "God's righteousness" (Rom. 3:5; 5:17; 10:3; II Cor. 5:21) , and the often-held view, that Paul's doctrine of justification is a mere "polemical doctrine" and hence not a central expression of his message of salvation, cannot be maintained in view of the dominant position of this doctrine in the Pauline epistles. Quite to the contrary, we can easily see that the doctrine of justification represents the basic and most highly personal form of expression of the Pauline message of God's eschatological saving action.

To be sure this form of the Pauline doctrine of salvation has its historical roots partly in the discussion with the Jewish doctrine of salvation which Paul had held as a Pharisee and which now was being held, from a Jewish and extreme Jewish-Christian side, counter to the Pauline proclamation of salvation in Christ. Indeed, this polemical character of the Pauline utterances about justification is unmistakable, because Paul emphasizes that the divine justification is imparted to man "apart from works of the law" or "apart from the law" (Rom. 3:20-21, 28; 4:6; Gal. 2:16; 3:11) and therefore "without [human] merit" (Rom. 3:24) and without "my own righteousness by the law" (Phil. 3:9) . This polemical antithesis also explains the paradoxical formulations: "Man is justified by faith" or "To the believer his faith is counted for righteousness" (Rom. 3:28; 4:5) , which have repeatedly led to the misunderstanding that in place of the human works of the law Paul demands human faith as man's achievement in advance for the divine justification. But Paul's doctrine of justification has its historical presupposition also in the fact that in the Judaism of the last pre-Christian centuries, in the appropriation of Old Testament ideas the concept of "God's righteousness" had been used in the sense of God's gracious faithfulness which maintained his covenant: "If I stumble, through the wickedness of my flesh, my right will remain eternally through God's righteousness" (1 QS 11.12; cf. Gaster, p. 132) ; "Thy righteousness and goodness, Lord, are made manifest in thy mercy toward those who have no treasury of good works" (IV Ezra 8:36) . Furthermore, it has been widely asserted that the Pauline doctrine of the justification of the sinner by grace had already been prefigured in certain circles in Judaism, primarily in

Qumran. But the fact that in these circles similar statements occur ("Only through thy goodness is man justified," The Hymns 13.16-17; cf. Gaster, p. 187) must not deceive us as to the fact that Judaism in the time of the New Testament indeed is thoroughly acquainted with the idea that man is dependent on God's grace. But this idea presupposes the necessity of radical obedience to the law and does not know, as Paul does, God's eschatological delivering action which alone makes possible the salvation of sinful man.

For this now is Paul's basic statement in this context: God's righteousness is disclosed or has been revealed (Rom. 1:17; 3:21), God has demonstrated his righteousness (Rom. 3:25-26), and this in the present. God's righteousness is revealed in two ways: through the gospel, i.e., by the proclamation of the gospel (Rom. 1:16-17), and now also, to the believer, through the redemption in Christ Jesus, through whom God has demonstrated his forgiveness (Rom. 3:21-24, 25). Thus God has acted in the present time in Christ and continues to act through the gospel, and thus causes his righteousness to be manifest. To understand this idea correctly, three questions must be cleared up: (1) What does "righteousness of God" mean with Paul? (2) What role does Jesus Christ play in connection with the revelation of the righteousness of God? (3) How are justification and faith related?

What does "righteousness of God" mean?

Paul uses the concept "righteousness of God" relatively seldom (Rom. 1:17; 3:5, 21-22, 25-26; 10:3; II Cor. 5:21; somewhat differently in Phil. 3:9), but always as a set phrase whose meaning is not indicated by the mere wording, but only by the traditional import of this term together with the observation of its employment in the context of the Pauline doctrine of justification. The phrase "righteousness of God" is used in apocalyptic Judaism, as we have seen, to denote the faithfulness of God, who graciously maintains his covenant. Thus in Paul also "righteousness of God" is not a statement about God's nature, but about God's action. When Paul speaks of "righteousness of God" he does not intend to describe how one must conceive of God, but to relate that God has acted in a way entirely different from the way in which men can imagine. Man, especially the pious Jew, thinks that he can and should establish his own righteousness by fulfilling the demands of the law, he can achieve *his* righteousness through the fulfilling of the law (Rom. 10:3; Phil. 3:9); "Israel, who pursued the law of righteousness, did not attain to the law" (Rom. 9:31). Since his becoming a

Christian, Paul has learned to see that his irreproachable righteousness of the law has been "loss" for him, that it is not possible to create his own righteousness out of the law, because "by works of the law no flesh shall be justified before him [God]" (Phil. 3:6-7, 9; Rom. 3:20). God has now rather caused his righteousness to become evident, God has revealed himself as the one who acts justly and declares righteous, without his demanding works of the law or bringing them into consideration. God's righteousness has become manifest "through faith in Jesus Christ for all who believe" (Rom. 3:21-22, 26-27). On the basis of this statement it is clear, first, that "God's righteousness" denotes an action of God which has become manifest in the present, which is not merely proclaimed, but has occurred and therefore is proclaimed (cf. Rom. 10:8-10; I Cor. 1:23-24, 30; Col. 1:22-23). It is clear, further, that this divine action "justifies the man who has faith in Jesus," for which Paul can also say: "To him who does no works but believes on him who justifies the ungodly, his faith is counted for righteousness" (Rom. 3:26; 4:5). Thus God's righteousness comes to pass in God's declaring the ungodly righteous.

There has always been a great deal of discussion about whether Paul speaks only of a "pronouncing righteous" or of a "making righteous" by God. In reality this is an idle dispute. It is true that the verb used by Paul in itself means nothing more than "declare righteous, pronounce righteous"; cf. also the contrast of "pronounce righteous" and "condemn" in Rom. 8:33-34; further, I Cor. 4:4: "I am not aware of anything against myself, but I am not thereby acquitted. It is the Lord who judges me" (RSV). But for Paul, God's action that acquits is a creative action which causes the godless to become righteous and makes the sinner into a "new creation": in II Cor. 5:17, 21, "If anyone is in Christ, he is a new creation; the old has passed away; behold, the new has come into being," is in parallel with "He has made him who knew no sin to be sin for us, that we might become the righteousness of God in him." And as in Rom. 5:1 Paul says, "We have peace with God," as a consequence of being justified by faith, so he says of himself, having turned away from the righteousness of the law: "I . . . not having my own righteousness which is of the law, but that [righteousness] which is through faith in Christ, the righteousness from God on the basis of faith" (Phil. 3:9; cf. also Col. 2:13-14). Indeed, for Paul God is the one "who gives life to the dead and calls into being that which does not exist" (Rom. 4:17), and therefore God's judgment is an event and his pronouncement of righteousness has "the character of power" (E. Käsemann; cf. Rom. 1:17). Thus if for Paul "God's righteousness" denotes God's saving action which in the present end-time declares sinful man righteous and thus is a newly creative force, then what is meant thereby becomes fully comprehensible, to be sure, only when we observe the connection of this divine action with Jesus Christ and the precondition of faith for the pronouncement of justification.

Christ and justification

Paul describes God's justifying action as an action of love which comes to pass in Christ's death: "For when we were yet weak, at this time Christ died for the ungodly . . . . But God shows his love toward us in that while we were yet sinners, Christ died for us. How much more shall we, who now have been justified by his blood, be saved from [the coming] wrath through him" (Rom. 5:6, 8-9). This says clearly, first, that God's love for us sinful men caused Christ to die for us; it says equally clearly that this death has brought it about that we were now declared righteous by God and may have the firm assurance that in the final judgment we can stand in the presence of God's wrath. But it cannot be discerned from this text how we are to conceive of Christ's death for us, as the fulfillment of God's love, as bringing about the justification of the ungodly. The much disputed basic statement in Rom. 3:21-30 (see above, p. 194) gives at least some allusions in this direction.

Since 3:24-26 not only makes a poor grammatical connection with 3:23, but also displays an unusually large number of words and conceptions which do not occur elsewhere in Paul, it is very probable that in these verses Paul has appropriated a traditional formula of the faith, which of course he interprets in his own sense. Because important concepts in this passage do not occur again elsewhere in Paul, it is difficult to determine their exact meaning; yet the translation (see above, p. 194) and interpretation presupposed in the following could be justified in detail only on the basis of the Greek text (ambiguous and disputed above all are the two words in vs. 25 translated as "expiation" and "forgiveness, passing over"). If the translation "expiation" is correct, then Paul is declaring here that God's action which frees men from their guilt came to pass by God's setting forth Christ as "expiation" through his blood, i.e., through his death. Since the concept "expiation" denotes a cultic action which intends, through a sacrifice, through rites of purification, or through other expiatory performances, to remove the defilement of a man or a group of men before a deity, this Pauline concept in this passage has often been understood to mean that Christ dies a vicarious sacrificial death and with the help of this sacrifice offered to God expiates men's guilt before God. But according to Paul God himself is the one who acts in Christ's death, and God of course cannot offer himself a sacrifice; besides, according to the faith of the primitive church and also of Paul, Christ's death was not at all a final death, as one would have to assume for a sacrificial death. Thus Paul is thinking rather of the purification of man from guilt by God, when he calls the death of Jesus God's "expiation": Jesus' death on the cross is indeed the lowest level of the humiliation of Christ Jesus (Phil. 2:8). That Christ died for us while we were yet sinners is contrary to all human probability (Rom. 5:6, 8), but precisely this is the way of the love of God, "who did not spare his own Son, but gave him up for us all" (Rom. 8:32).

But now Paul also indicates what God intended to achieve with this vicarious death of the Son of God on the cross, through which he caused his love to become effective as expiation (vs. 25b, 26): God intended to cause his righteousness to become effective "through the forgiveness of the sins which were committed earlier, in the time of forbearance," and thus to be just and to justify those who believe. If the translation "through forgiveness" fits the meaning of what Paul intended—and there is much to argue for this— then the aim of God's expiatory action which is actualized through Jesus' death is the forgiveness of sins which humanity had committed up to this time. Through Jesus' death God wrought the forgiveness of sins and therewith the acquittal of the ungodly (Rom. 4:5); God has nailed the bill of indictment to the cross and thereby canceled it, and "has made us alive with him [Christ], by forgiving us all our trespasses" (Col. 2:13-14). Paul nowhere says that God *had* to act in this way and therefore Christ *had* to die, that Christ had to suffer the penalty in our place, as the church's theology later worked it out. It is not Paul's aim to make comprehensible why God acted thus and not otherwise; he only intends to describe, in the conceptual forms of his Jewish past, God's saving action that eradicates the guilt of sin, because God has laid on him the obligation of proclaiming the good news of the saving power of the gospel in which God's righteousness is made manifest for everyone who believes (I Cor. 9:16; Rom. 1:14-17). But that confronts us with the definitive question as to the significance of faith in the context of this divine act of justification.

Faith and justification

In his statements about God's act of justification Paul repeatedly points out that this act applies to all who believe: the gospel "is a power of God unto salvation for all who believe, first the Jews and [also] the Greeks. For in it God's righteousness is revealed from faith to faith, as it stands written: 'But the just by faith shall live'" (Rom. 1:16-17); "But now God's righteousness has been revealed apart from the law . . . through faith in Jesus Christ for all who believe . . . . God has set him [Christ] forth as the expiation through faith in his blood . . . . We affirm that a man is justified by faith apart from the works of the law" (Rom. 3:21-22, 25*a*, 28); "The Scripture foresaw that God would justify the Gentiles by faith" (Gal. 3:8, *et passim*). Now Paul can, as we have seen, also use the formulation: "To the one who believes in him [God] who justifies the ungodly, his faith is counted for righteousness" (Rom. 4:5), so that the impression arises that faith plays the role of an achievement which God acknowledges and rewards. But it is easy to see that this easily misunderstood manner of expression is occasioned by the adoption of the quotation from Gen. 15:6 ("Abraham believed God, and it was reckoned to him for righteousness"; see Rom. 4:3, 22-23; Gal. 3:6) and is already set right in the context of Rom. 4:3-5 by the fact that it speaks of a reckoning "by grace" (cf. also Rom. 3:24). Paul rather understands faith unequivocally as a consequence of the divine saving action in Christ: faith comes about on the basis of preaching and of the sending of the preacher: "But how shall they believe on him of whom they have not heard? And how are they to hear without a preacher? And how is one to preach unless [someone is] sent? As it is written, 'How beautiful are the feet of those [messengers] who proclaim the glad tidings of good things!' But not all have heeded the glad tidings" (Rom. 10:14-16); similarly, in II Cor. 5:18-19 it is said in the context of the message of reconciliation: "God has been reconciled to us through Christ and has given to us the ministry of reconciliation . . . . In Christ God was reconciling the world to himself . . . and set forth the word of reconciliation among us." Consequently, faith is first of all assent to the preaching that is heard: through Christ "we have received grace and apostleship, to [awaken] the obedience of faith among the Gentiles" (Rom. 1:5); "If with your mouth you confess Jesus as Lord and in your heart believe that God has raised him from the dead, you will be saved" (Rom. 10:9).

Accordingly, Paul can say in the same way: "We have believed in Christ Jesus, that we might be justified by faith in Christ and not by the works of the law" (Gal. 2:16), as he can refer the Corinthians to "the gospel which I preached to you, which you also received, in which also you stand, through which also you are saved, if you hold fast to the word which I proclaimed to you, unless you have believed in vain" (I Cor. 15:1-2). Thus since faith undoubtedly is the acknowledgment of the Christian message, Paul can occasionally also use faith and knowledge interchangeably (Rom. 6:8-9): "We know that, as long as we are at home in the body, we are away from the Lord; for we walk by faith, not by sight" (II Cor. 5:6-7).

But faith in Paul's sense is by no means adequately described therewith. *Faith* in its actual nature *is* not intellectual acknowledgment of a state of affairs, but *obedience:* "You . . . have become obedient from the heart to the standard of teaching to which you were committed" (Rom. 6:17 RSV); "not all obeyed the gospel" (Rom. 10:16 RSV); corresponding to the clause, "your faith is proclaimed in all the world" (Rom. 1:8 RSV) is "your obedience came to all" (Rom. 16:19). Hence Paul can describe his divine commission as "grace and apostleship with the aim of the obedience of faith among all nations" (Rom. 1:5). If faith as obedience thus denotes the totality of being a Christian, yet at the same time it is posed as provisionally in opposition to the eschatological seeing: "We walk [now] by faith, not by sight" (II Cor. 5:7) and is characterized as hope: "If you abide in faith, firm and unshaken, and do not let yourselves be turned aside from the hope of the gospel which you have heard" (Col. 1:23); "In hope we are saved; hope that can be seen is not hope. For if one sees something, why does he still wait [for it]? But if we hope for what we do not see, we wait in patience" (Rom. 8:24-25). In this sense Abraham appears as the prototype of faith, because he "believed in hope against [all] hope, that he would become the father of many nations . . . . But toward the promise of God he did not waver in unbelief, but was strong in faith, glorified God, and was firmly convinced that God was able to do what he had promised. Hence it was also reckoned to him for righteousness" (Rom. 4:18, 20-22). Altogether in harmony with this, then, it is said about the faith of the Christians: "In the Spirit, on the basis of faith, we await the righteousness hoped for. For in Christ Jesus neither circumcision nor uncircumcision counts for anything, but [only] faith working through love" (Gal. 5:5-6).

Thus faith is the response of the man who has encountered in the preaching of the gospel the message of God's saving action at the end of time which produces righteousness and who obediently embraces the grace of God which is offered in this message: "We have heard of your faith in Christ Jesus and your love which you have toward all the saints because of the hope laid up in heaven for you, of which you have heard beforehand through the word of the truth of the gospel, which is present with you . . . since the day in which you heard and came to know the grace of God in truth" (Col. 1:4-6). Thus faith is no human achievement, no "work," but a "free act of obedience" (R. Bultmann), on the basis of which the believer knows himself to be "delivered from the present evil eon according to the will of God and our Father," because "Jesus Christ has given himself for our sins" (Gal. 1:4). On the basis of this act of obedience the believer at the same time knows himself to be "transferred into the kingdom of his dear Son, in whom we have redemption, the forgiveness of sins" (Col. 1:13-14). Only the believer can know that God "willed to demonstrate his righteousness in the present time, . . . that he might be righteous and might justify him who has faith in Jesus" (Rom. 3:25-26); but where there is no faith, nothing at all can be said of God's justifying action. Of course this very state of affairs includes the fact that God alone "gives us the victory through our Lord Jesus Christ" (I Cor. 15:57), and therefore precisely the believer knows very well that boasting "is excluded. By what law? That of works? No, by the law of faith" (Rom. 3:27). Only he who believes comprehends that "God's righteousness is revealed . . . for *all* who believe" (Rom. 3:21-22), and that "since in the time of the wisdom of God, the world did not know God through wisdom, God resolved through the folly of what we preach to save those who believe" (I Cor. 1:21). He who believes knows himself to be transplanted into the time of salvation that has been begun through Christ's cross and resurrection, but he also knows that such a saved condition is in effect for him only so long as he lives in such faith: "You are cut off from Christ, you who [wish] to be justified by the law; you have [then] fallen from grace" (Gal. 5:4).

Thus Paul's message of the justification of the sinner by faith also describes the existence of the Christian in the present as the end-time in its inception, while the old eon is hastening to its end. This is confirmed by *the juxtaposition of expressions about present and future* with reference to the justification event. We hear frequently of justification that has already been received: "Since we have been justified by faith, we have peace with God"; "we who now are justified through his blood"; "the Gentiles . . . have attained righteousness, the righteousness that is by faith"; "you are washed, sanctified, justified" (Rom. 5:1, 9; 9:30; I Cor. 6:11; cf. Rom. 5:17; 8:30; II Cor. 5:21). But justification is equally clearly expected of the future: "thus through the obedience of the one will the many be made righteous"; "if God is one, who will justify the circumcised by faith and the uncircumcised through faith"; "in the Spirit, on the basis of faith, we await the hope of righteousness" (Rom. 5:19; 3:30; Gal. 5:5). Accordingly, Paul can say of himself: "Not that I have already attained or am already perfect, but I press on, to lay hold, for I have been laid hold upon by Christ Jesus. Brethren, I do not consider myself already to have laid hold" (Phil. 3:12-13). That is to say, with all the grateful confession of the justification that has already taken place, the ultimate justification remains the hoped-for gift of God. God's action that justifies man has occurred and for the believer is the assured present, as a gift of grace already received; but since there exists the possibility of falling from grace (Gal. 5:4), the condition of standing finally before God without reproach reads thus: "If you abide in faith, firm and unshaken, and do not let yourselves be turned aside from the hope of the gospel which you have heard and which has been proclaimed to every creature under heaven" (Col. 1:23). Hence we must ask what role is played by the present behavior of the Christian, the "faith that works through love" (Gal. 5:6), in the context of the final justification of God.

f. RECONCILIATION

But first we must refer to one last image with which Paul describes the liberation of man in the world, the message of reconciliation. Paul uses this conception somewhat in detail only twice, both times in clear conjunction with the idea of justification: "God shows his love toward us in that while we were yet sinners, Christ died for us. How much more shall we, who have been justified through his blood, be saved from wrath through him. For if we who were enemies were reconciled to God through the death of his Son, how much more shall we as reconciled be saved by his life" (Rom. 5:8-10); "If anyone is in Christ, he is a new creation; the old has passed away; behold, the new has come into being. But all this [comes] from God, who has reconciled himself to us through Christ and has given to us the ministry of reconciliation, which has as its content that 'Through Christ God reconciled the world to himself, in that he did not reckon their trespasses to their account, and entrusted to us the word of reconciliation.' Now we are ambassadors in the service of Christ, in that God issues his admonition through us; in Christ's service we beg, 'Be reconciled to God! Him who knew no sin he has made to be sin for us, that in him we might become the righteousness of God'" (II Cor. 5:17-21). Other than in these two passages in which Paul speaks emphatically of reconciliation, he mentions this conception only once in passing: "If their [i.e., the Jews'] rejection [effects] the reconciliation of the world, what does their acceptance effect but life from the dead?" (Rom. 11: 15). In addition, he spoke in hymnic form of the reconciliation of the universe: "In him [Christ] all the fullness was pleased to dwell and through him to reconcile all things to him, by making peace through the blood of his cross—through him [to reconcile] what is on earth and what is in heaven. You also, who once were estranged and aliens in your minds, in evil works, he now has reconciled in his body of flesh by means of his death" (Col. 1: 19-22). While the idea of justification was an image from the legal realm, the image of reconciliation comes from the sphere of personal association; reconciliation presupposes that an enmity exists between men, which is removed by the readiness of one of the angered sides (or of both sides) to bury the enmity, precisely through a being reconciled. Judaism also is familiar with the idea of the reconciliation of the angered God, but here it is the guilty men who petition God for reconciliation, as for example in II Macc. 1:5; 8:29, where the same word for "to be reconciled" is used as in Paul. But Paul, who speaks of God's wrath and God's enmity against men (as in Rom. 1:18; 5:9-10), but likewise of the enmity of men toward God (Rom. 8:7; Col. 1:21), unmistakably says that God has reconciled himself with men or with the world. Thus God has buried the enmity and made peace (Col. 1:20; Rom. 5:1), through Christ's death. Paul also clearly says that Christ died for us, that thereby the guilt of sin is removed and that thus we have the certainty of being preserved from God's coming wrath. Thus here also the cross of Christ is the way which God has chosen when he wanted to set aside the enmity between men and himself, and here also it is true that the Son of God "loved me and gave himself for me" (Gal. 2:20). But Paul does not say more; in Paul there is nothing said, not even by allusion, of a "satisfaction" by

Christ toward God or even of the necessity of Christ's atoning death for the reconciliation of God, as the church's teaching has extended Paul's ideas since the days of the church fathers but especially since Anselm of Canterbury (11th century).

But it is true that the association of the two figures of justification and reconciliation in all three major Pauline passages makes it clearly evident that in Paul's mind reconciliation expresses, just as does justification, the removal of the separation of man from God that is caused by human guilt. But the personal figure of reconciliation gives still clearer expression to the fact that the personal relationship of man to his divine Lord is disrupted by guilty man and moreover cannot be put in order again, but that this broken relationship has been restored by God. Hence a part of the event of reconciliation necessarily is the "ministry of reconciliation," i.e., the preaching of reconciliation under commission from Christ, and the human response to the plea, "Be reconciled to God!" Indeed, even more clearly than with justification, it is true that no one can know anything of reconciliation and therefore preach about it who has not acceded to the plea for acceptance of the reconciliation and "accepted this grace of God" (II Cor. 6:1), that is, believed that God has been reconciled with us (cf. the context of Col. 1:21 and 22). To be sure Paul speaks of reconciliation, as has correctly been pointed out, only in the verb form of the past, or, at the most once (Rom. 11:15), of the present. For the reconciliation has indeed already taken place, when God acted in Christ's death as the one reconciling himself with the world (Rom. 5:10a), and Christ has "died for sin once for all" (Rom. 6:10a). And yet the message of reconciliation also describes the historical reality of the life of the believers in the end-time which has begun and is not yet consummated. For God's reconciling action which has become reality in the past in Christ's death is not complete, because the "ministry of reconciliation" still must exhort, "Be reconciled to God," because God's making peace is intended to embrace the whole world (Col. 1:20), but the message has not yet reached all men. The historical character of God's reconciling action is also shown in the fact that the belief in the reconciliation that is received must be maintained (II Cor. 6:1; Col. 1:23), and the ultimate deliverance from the divine wrath, hoped for as certain, is yet to come (Rom. 5:10). The message of reconciliation also thus describes the provisional character of the divine gift of salvation that is received in faith and confronts us with the question as to the present reality of the Christian life in the context of Pauline theology.

6. God's gift of salvation and the task of the Christian

a. THE PRESENT REALITY OF THE CHRISTIAN LIFE

As we have seen, Paul uses a number of figurative conceptions to describe the liberation of man from slavery to the powers of this world, to the law, and to sin, and the liberation from guilt by God's eschatological action in Jesus Christ. They all give expression to the belief that the man to whom this divine action has been proclaimed and who has opened himself in faith to the truth of this joyous message is thereby transferred into the reality of the time of final salvation which has begun. But in the discussion of these various conceptions of Paul, the question has remained unanswered of how Paul conceived more precisely the reality of the life of the believer which is rendered possible by this divine saving action, and untouched remained the question of how, according to Paul, incorporation into this divine saving action comes about. If we pursue these questions, we quickly note that to a large extent Paul describes the present reality of the Christian life and becoming a Christian with concepts and ideas other than those which we have encountered up to now in the consideration of Paul's message of salvation. This can be discerned especially well in the epistle to the Romans, whose first five chapters speak almost exclusively of the sinfulness of humanity, of the justification of the sinner by faith, of reconciliation, and of the gift of life through Christ's coming. Yet already in Rom. 5:5, alongside these there suddenly appears the Holy Spirit who is given to the Christians, of whom chap. 8:2 ff. then speaks in detail. Equally unexpectedly, chap. 6 mentions baptism, in which the Christian dies with Christ, and from this state of having died Paul infers the obligation of the Christian to serve righteousness and not sin. In this connection Rom. 6:11, 23 speaks of life "in Christ Jesus" (cf. 8:2, 39) ; Rom. 12:5 speaks of the "one body in Christ" which the Christians represent; and already in Rom. 7:4 there was mention of "having died through the body of Christ." All these conceptions also occur repeatedly elsewhere in the letters of Paul, and it must be asked how they are related to Paul's doctrine of salvation which has already been considered and in what sense they describe the state of being a Christian.

Paul had concluded his statements about the superabundance of the righteousness brought by Jesus with the affirmation: "As sin reigned in death, so also grace is to reign through righteousness to eternal life through Jesus Christ our Lord" (Rom. 5:21). But then he vigorously rejects the question attached to this affirmation, "Shall we continue in sin, that grace may abound?" with the declaration, "How can we who are dead to sin still live in it? Or do you not know that we who were baptized into Christ Jesus were baptized into his death? Thus we are buried with him by baptism into death, so that, as Christ was raised from the dead by the glory of the Father, so also we walk in a new life" (Rom. 6:1-4). Here Paul can argue by referring to a state of affairs which obviously is self-evident for all Christians; this shows that for Paul the statement, "Being justified by faith we have peace with God through our Lord Jesus Christ," (Rom. 5:1), which holds true for all Christians, can be carried forward without further ado in Rom. 6:2 ff. by means of the expression, for us utterly unexpected but familiar to the Romans, that Christians have died to sin, because they are baptized into Christ's death and with Christ are buried and transferred into a new life through this baptism. Baptism into the death of Jesus and having died with Christ (Rom. 6:3, 8) accordingly for Paul denotes the same reality as being justified by faith, which signified peace with God (Rom. 5:1). In order to understand this connection, we must inquire into the meaning of baptism in Paul.

Baptism and the body of Christ

Paul found *baptism* already present as the rite of admittance for incorporation into the Christian community, and he himself was baptized (Rom. 6:3). He also takes for granted that all Christians are baptized and have received the divine Spirit at baptism. "Indeed, we all were baptized in one Spirit into one body" (I Cor. 12:13), and he interprets the baptism that is performed by immersion as washing, which imparts forgiveness of sins; after an enumeration of vices he says: "You were formerly such people; but you have been washed, you have been sanctified, you have been justified in the name of the Lord Jesus Christ and in the Spirit of our God" (I Cor. 6:11); "you are buried with him [Christ] in baptism, in him you are also raised by faith in the working of God who raised him from the dead. And you who were dead through the trespasses and the uncircumcision of your flesh, you has he made alive with him [Christ], by forgiving us all our trespasses" (Col. 2:12-13). Paul shares this understanding of baptism with the community (see above, pp. 131-32), but it at once becomes evident that Paul connects this understanding with his basic theological outlook: in I Cor. 6:11 the washing in baptism is equated with the justification by God, and in Col. 2:13-14 the forgiveness of sins in baptism is accounted for with the cancellation of guilt through the cross. But Paul now has explained the event in baptism by means of two further ideas which he presumably found already present in Hellenistic Christianity, but in which certainly his own particular understanding of baptism finds expression.

Baptism introduces the baptized person into the "body of Christ": "For as the body is one and has many members, but all members of the body, though they are many, form *one* body, so also [is] Christ; that is to say, we all have been baptized through one Spirit into *one* body, whether Jews or Greeks, whether slaves or free men, and all have drunk of *one* Spirit. . . . You are Christ's body and each on his own part a member" (I Cor. 12:12-13, 27) ; "As many of you as are baptized into Christ have put on Christ; there is neither Jew nor Greek, neither slave nor free, neither male nor female [any longer]; you are all one in Christ Jesus" (Gal. 3: 27-28) . Thus baptism is not only a rite of admittance in the sense that the man who comes to faith, through the acceptance of baptism with its purification from sin and its bestowal of the Spirit, is joined to the Christian community in unequivocal fashion and shows thereby that he now "in the midst of a crooked and perverse generation" belongs or at least wishes to belong to the "blameless children of God" (Phil. 2:15) . Baptism, with the help of the divine Spirit, rather makes the baptized person a member of the "body of Christ" and thereby introduces him into a human company in which earthly distinctions no longer have any meaning because everyone has "put on Christ" in the same way. These statements show that for Paul baptism has a real effect: anyone who is baptized belongs to the body of Christ and has put on Christ.

Of course the conception of the *"body of Christ"* does not occur in Paul very frequently and is nowhere more precisely explained; Paul apparently can take it for granted that the Hellenistic Christian communities to whom he is writing know this conception and understand it at once (Rom. 7:4; 12:5; I Cor. 10:16, 17; 11:27, 29; 12:13, 27; Col. 1:18, 24; 3:15). He uses the conception of the body in this context in a twofold sense. On the one hand the Christian community is compared with a body, that is, an organism, and the individual Christian accordingly has his task in the community as one of its various members, which together form the body: "For as we in *one* body have many members, . . . so are we many *one* body in Christ, but members in relation to one another" (Rom. 12:4-5) ; "Just as the body is one and has many members, but all the members of the body, being many, form *one* body. . . . Indeed the body is not *one* member, but many" (I Cor. 12:12a, b, 14). On the other hand, through baptism the Christians are introduced into the already existing body of Christ, and the Christians in their totality are directly identified as "Christ's body" or "Christ" (I Cor. 12:12-13, 27; Gal. 3:27-28; see above, pp. 207-8; "Is not the bread which we break a participation in Christ's body?" I Cor. 10: 16). To be sure Paul uses the figure of the body as an organism only to characterize the duty of cooperation which is placed upon every Christian as a member of the body alongside other members: "God has fitted the body together . . . , that there may be no division in the body, but that the members may have the same concern for one another" (I Cor. 12:24-25; cf. Rom. 12:3 with 12: 4). That is to say, in this context the idea of the organism serves only to make the admonition concrete, by calling the attention of the Christians to the consequences of their belonging to the body of Christ, but it does not describe the actual nature of the body of Christ. But according to the other statements, the body of Christ is a reality which is given with the state of being a Christian: without regard to earthly origin and differences of sex, the members of the body of Christ form a unity: "but you are Christ's body and members each one of the other" (I Cor. 12:27). Paul can equally well give the designation of "Christ" or "the body of Christ" to the reality that is given with being a Christian: if the community divides into groups, then "Christ is divided" (I Cor. 1:13); when the lack of regard for one another on the part of community members hinders their eating together, and it therefore "is impossible to eat the Lord's supper," then such inconsiderately feasting Christians make themselves "guilty of the body and blood of Christ," because they "do not discern the body" (I Cor. 11:20, 27, 29). How really this belonging to Christ's body means for Paul the participation in Christ himself is further shown in the Pauline argument against a Christian's consorting with a prostitute: "Do you not know that your bodies are members of Christ? Shall I now take Christ's members and make them members of a prostitute?" (I Cor. 6:15; cf. the commentaries on this passage). And finally, it is to be noted that Paul also can say of the incorporation into the body of Christ through baptism: "You have put on Christ" (Gal. 3:27). Now it is true that the source of the figure of putting on Christ cannot be explained with full certainty, but it is very probable that the idea is that Christ enfolds the baptized person as a garment, and in this case the figure of putting on Christ comes from the same intellectual sphere as that of the body of Christ. For the juxtaposition of the statements "you have put on Christ" and "you are all one in Christ Jesus" (Gal. 3:27-28) on the one hand and "As the body is one . . . , so also is Christ; for we are all baptized into one body" (I Cor. 12:12-13) on the other hand plainly shows that Christ is conceived of as the one universal man who like a garment embraces the many individual men who come into relationship with him and together with them forms the universal personality of the Christ, the "body of Christ." Since Paul, as we saw earlier (above, pp. 155 ff.), describes Christ as the final or heavenly man and this designation probably goes back to the pagan conception of the primal man in a Jewish remolding, the image of the body of Christ presumably is likewise a further development of the idea of Christ as the "heavenly" or "final man." But even if the question of the source of this conception of the body of Christ for the time being cannot be answered with certainty, still it is not at all doubtful that Paul understands the Christian's belonging to the body of Christ as a participation in the eschatological saving event which has begun through Christ, i.e., he describes the effect of baptism as entrance into a company of people which belongs to Christ and has a share in the final salvation that has already begun.

Further, it cannot be questioned that "body of Christ" specifically means *the Christian community*. For just as according to Paul the individual is incorporated by the divine Spirit into the body of Christ, so also the divine Spirit in the community imparts to the individuals the most widely diverse gifts of grace (I Cor. 12:4-11), and correspondingly Paul speaks explicitly, in conjunction with the statements about the body of Christ (I Cor. 12:12-27), of the "church," in which there are the most varied functions: "And God has set some in the church, first apostles, second prophets, third teachers, then mighty deeds, then gifts of healing, helpers, administrators, various kinds of tongues" (I Cor. 12:28). While in this passage the equation of "body of Christ" and church may be recognized from the context, in Colossians it is explicitly stated: "He [the Son of God] is the head of the body, the church"; ". . . for his body, which is the church" (Col. 1:18, 24). In these passages "church" clearly denotes the whole of Christendom, and this is undoubtedly the basic meaning of the concept in Paul, as is proved above all by the usage, "the church of God": in I Cor. 10:32 "Jews, Greeks, and the church of God" are placed side by side, and Paul twice tells of having persecuted "the church of God" (I Cor. 15:9;

Gal. 1:13), while in Phil. 3:6 he speaks only of persecution of "the church" (cf. also I Cor. 11:27).

This designation of the Christian community that is taken over from the primitive community (see above, pp. 129-30), following Old Testament usage, understands the Christian community as the true, the eschatological, people of God: "Peace upon the Israel of God" (Gal. 6:16); "We are the circumcision, who hold worship in the Spirit and glory in Christ Jesus" (Phil. 3:3). To be this people of God, "he has called us not only from among the Jews, but also from among the Gentiles" (Rom. 9:24), but this people of God becomes visible in the individual Christian communities, and hence Paul can speak in the singular of "the church of God which is in Corinth" (I Cor. 1:2; II Cor. 1:1; cf. Rom. 16:1) as well as in the plural of "the churches" or of "every church" (Rom. 16:4; I Cor. 4:17; 11:16; etc.). But in place of "church of God" we also find in the same sense "the church of Christ" ("all the churches of Christ greet you," Rom. 16:16), "the church in Christ" ("I was unknown by sight to the churches of Judea in Christ," Gal. 1:22), or "the church of the Thessalonians in God the Father and the Lord Jesus Christ" (I Thess. 1:1; II Thess. 1:1). Thus the Christian community is the "church of God" because Christ is her Lord: in the community "there are diversities of service and [only] one Lord" (I Cor. 12:5).

Precisely corresponding to this is the conception of Christ as the "head of the body, the church" (Col. 1:18). To be sure apart from Ephesians (1:22; 4:15; 5:23), which certainly does not come from Paul, this conception occurs within the Pauline epistles only in Colossians (see further Col. 2:10, 19), and people have repeatedly seen therein one of the features which prove Colossians to be non-Pauline. But this is hardly correct. For if the church is the body of Christ and Christ is the Lord of this body, then it is perfectly natural to describe Christ as the *head of the body*. It is all the more natural if the figure of the head is used in the sense of the lordship over the body: "The head, from which the whole body is guided and held together by means of the ligaments and tendons and [thus] grows with a divine growth" (Col. 2:19). Accordingly, Paul can just as well say that Christ, the mediator of creation, through his resurrection has become "Lord" of all worldly powers: ". . . that at the name of Jesus every knee of heavenly, earthly, and subterrestrial [beings] should bow and every tongue confess: 'Jesus Christ is lord'" (Phil. 2:10-11; cf. I Cor. 8:6), as he can describe Christ as "the head of every power and authority" (Col.

2:10). The dominion of Christ in which the resurrected One has been installed (see above, pp. 157 ff.) has made him head and Lord of all powers as well as head and Lord of his community. Thus, membership in the body of Christ, which is wrought by baptism, is grounded in God's eschatological saving action in Christ's death and resurrection, as well as is the justification and reconciliation through Christ in which God causes the believer to share. Yet the inner connection of this statement (i.e., that the Christian is incorporated into the body of Christ through baptism with the message of justification on the basis of God's eschatological saving action in Christ) becomes entirely understandable only when we turn to the other sphere of thought with which Paul describes the effect of baptism in a special way.

Dying with Christ

Baptism also signifies a "dying with Christ." "Or do you not know that we who were baptized into Christ were baptized into his death? Thus we are buried with him by baptism into his death, that as Christ was raised from the dead by the glory of the Father, so we also might walk in a new life. For if we have grown together with the form of his death, so shall we also [have grown together] with the [form of his] resurrection. We know that our old man has been crucified as well, that the body of sin might be destroyed, so that we should no longer render slaves' service to sin. . . . But if we have died with Christ, we believe that we shall also live with him" (Rom. 6:3-6, 8); "You are buried with him [Christ] in baptism; in him you are also raised through faith in the power of God, who raised him from the dead; and you, who were dead through the trespasses and the uncircumcision of your flesh, you he has made alive with him, by forgiving us all our trespasses" (Col. 2:12-13). In these texts Paul says plainly that the person baptized is dead, that his "old man," his "body of sin," is slain and destroyed. Of course this state of having died, in however real a sense it is meant, cannot be intended to denote the cessation of the earthly existence of the baptized person; corresponding to the old man's having died is rather the walking in a new life (Rom. 6:4), or the having-been-made-alive with Christ (Col. 2:13). In Romans, moreover, this new life in the present is bound up with the hope of a "living with" in the future (Rom. 6:8), while in Colossians we read that the Christians "are raised together in Christ through faith" (2:12), which then likewise corresponds to the hope that at Christ's appearing the Christians also "will appear with him in

glory" (Col. 3:4). Now it is by no means an obvious thing to interpret the rite of immersion in water as a dying and a coming to
new life or being awakened. Therefore some recently have thought
that the Pauline understanding of baptism is not connected with
the baptismal rite at all, that Paul was rather speaking of the
dying of the Christian in order to express the change in lordships
which the Christian experiences when in faith he detaches himself
from the dominion of sin and entrusts himself to the dominion
of Christ, and that Paul brought this idea into connection with
baptism only secondarily. But this is very unlikely; for on the one
hand, the idea of dying with Christ is by no means explained
on the basis of this assumption, and on the other hand, it remains
incomprehensible then why Paul speaks of being buried together
through baptism (Rom. 6:4; Col. 2:12). Since apart from these two
passages, the fact that Jesus was buried is mentioned only in the
primitive community's formula in I Cor. 15:4 and it occurs in this
connection without any reference to Christians as a mere indication
of the reality of Jesus' having died, the reason that Paul speaks
precisely of "being buried with him by baptism into [Jesus']
death" must be that being buried together in fact clearly signifies
the same event as having died with Christ (Rom. 6:4, 8). But this
implies that immersion at baptism must have been interpreted by
Paul as a being buried and hence as a dying, and it is also evident
that this dying is understood as a dying "with Christ" (Rom. 6:4;
Col. 2:20). But this conception of having died and having been
buried with Christ in baptism and of having been transplanted
into a new life with Christ can hardly be explained without the
assumption that the idea, attested in Hellenistic mysteries in various forms, that through certain rites the initiate is given a share
in the fate of the God who dies and comes to life again, has already
been adduced in the pre-Pauline Hellenistic Christian communities
to interpret baptism and that Paul has adopted this interpretation.
If the emergence of the understanding of baptism as a dying with
Christ thus can hardly be explained without relying on Hellenistic
mystery conceptions, it can of course be seen equally clearly that
Paul employed this interpretation in a sense which has only the
conceptual form in common with the nature-oriented understanding of dying with the deity in the mysteries.

First it is to be observed that Paul can also speak of dying with
Christ without any reference to baptism. Thus in Rom. 7:4: "Therefore, my brethren, you too have died to the law through the body
of Christ"; but the Pauline usage of "body of Christ" allows us to

understand this statement only to mean that the Christians have died to the law by being taken into the body of Christ, the community, when they died to the law, which had them enslaved, by receiving the Spirit of God; cf. the continuation of the passage: "But now we are discharged from the law, dead to that which held us captive, so that we [now] . . . serve in the new life of the Spirit" (Rom. 7:6). Even if in this statement Paul should also be thinking of dying with Christ in baptism—of course there is nothing of that idea to be found here—still the crucial statement, that by being joined to Christ the Christian has died to the law, is entirely possible for him without his alluding in any way to the process of being immersed in water at baptism. Accordingly, Gal. 2:19-20 says: "That is to say, through the law I died to the law, in order to live to God; I am crucified with Christ. But thus I am no longer living; instead, Christ is living in me. But insofar as I now am [still] living in the flesh, I live in faith in the Son of God . . . ." Here it is said of Christians—the "I" does not describe Paul alone—that they are crucified with Christ and thereby are dead to the law, because by means of the law Christ was brought to the cross (Gal. 3:13) and through his resurrection he has robbed the law of its power (Gal. 4:4). Even here baptism is not mentioned; on the other hand, it is clearly said that faith in the Christ who died for us was crucially involved in this dying and coming to new life of the Christian. And in the same epistle then Paul can say in similar fashion: "Those who belong to Christ Jesus have crucified the flesh with the lusts and passions. If we live in the Spirit, let us also walk in the Spirit" (5:24-25). "By it [the cross of Christ] the world is crucified to me and I to the world. For neither circumcision nor uncircumcision counts for anything, but new creation" (6:14-15). But in II Corinthians above all Paul has described the being of the Christians as follows: "The love of Christ impels us who judge that one died for all, and thus all have died. And he died for all so that those who live no longer live for themselves, but for him who died for them and was raised . . . . Hence anyone who is in Christ is a new creation; the old has passed away; behold, the new has come to be" (II Cor. 5:14-15, 17). This clearly says that Christ's dying has the consequence for all that all have died. This having died with Christ also brings about a new life, a new creation "in Christ," and in this assertion likewise there is no reference to baptism. However, in what follows Paul states that God has brought about this death and the new creation, he who reconciled himself to us through Christ and through the preaching has called on us to accept this reconciliation (see above, pp. 203 ff.) . Here not only are the dying and the new creation with Christ grounded in our belonging to Christ and not in baptism, but it also is clear that God's reconciling act in Christ, which faith accepts, has as its consequence the sharing in the death and the new creation with Christ.

These texts of the letters of Paul which ground the Christians' dying and new life with Christ in God's historical redemptive act and do not mention baptism clearly show that for Paul the rite of baptism does not effectuate this dying with Christ and this new creation, but that baptism can only be the visible expression for a more comprehensive event. But a second fact reveals still more clearly that it is only an entirely external connection that joins the Pauline understanding of baptism as a dying with Christ with the conceptions of the mystery religions. Paul says: "We are buried with him [Christ] by baptism into death" (Rom. 6:4) , or: "[you are] buried with him in baptism" (Col. 2:12) , and thereby obviously interprets the immersion in the baptismal waters as a being buried with Christ. But he does not say: "You have died with Christ in baptism," or any such thing, but: "we are baptized into his [Christ's] death," when we "were baptized into Christ" and "we have died with Christ" (Rom. 6:3, 8) . And quite in accordance with this, it is also said only that "we are buried with him by baptism into his death, that, as Christ was raised from the dead . . . , we also walk in newness of life" (Rom. 6:4) , or "[you are] buried with him in baptism, in him are you also raised together through faith in the power of God, who has raised him from the dead" (Col. 2:12) . In other words, neither the dying with Christ nor the being transplanted into a new life nor the being raised with Christ is placed by Paul in the same point of time with baptism. The reason for this also is fully clear, as Paul expressly emphasizes in the context of the statements about baptism in the epistle to the Romans: "Christ, who was raised from the dead, dies no more . . . . For in that he died, he died for sin once for all; but in that he lives, he lives for God" (Rom. 6:9-10) . For Paul Christ's death and resurrection are unique occurrences of the distant past which cannot be repeated; but the Christians have died with Christ, when they believed the message of God's reconciliation, let themselves be baptized, and thus were incorporated into the body of Christ, and that at a time which was far removed from Christ's death and resurrection. Christ's death on the cross and the Christians' dying with Christ thus by no means coincide in point of time. The

Christians rather have obtained in their present time a share in the past event of Christ's death and resurrection. And Paul nevertheless speaks of an actual dying with Christ and of an actual transference into a new life, not merely of an imagined or sympathetically shared experience.

How is this conceived? We have already seen that in Rom. 6:3-4 Paul directly names baptism into Christ's death and the dying with Christ as a description of the same reality of which he has spoken in the epistle to the Romans up to that point: that is, the experience of being justified through faith in God's saving act in Christ's death and resurrection (see above, p. 207). We have also seen that in II Cor. 5:14 ff. the dying and the new creation of all is grounded in the dying of one for all, because in this dying God has reconciled himself with us and through the word of reconciliation has urged us, "Be reconciled to God" (see above, p. 214). In Col. 2:11 ff. the being buried with Christ in baptism and being raised together in Christ is pictured as grounded in the fact that by the eradication of the guilt of sin by means of Jesus' crucifixion God has forgiven our sins and thus has made us alive with Christ. As the plea for the acceptance of reconciliation in II Cor. 5:20 presupposes faith, so also in Col. 2:12 it is expressly said, "You are raised with him through faith in the power of God." Quite similarly, in Gal. 3:26-27, the statement, "you all are sons of God through faith in Christ Jesus," is justified with the clause, "for all of you who are baptized into Christ have put on Christ." Thus it is the believer who embraces God's justifying and reconciling action in Christ's cross and resurrection and therefore submits to baptism and in baptism experiences the dying with Christ and the new life in Christ as a reality affecting him personally. The one baptized does not have a share in the past death of Jesus on the cross, but in the effects of this death, because the crucified One has risen and therefore the effects of his death for us can be appropriated by the believer in the present as the eschatological saving event. It is not that baptism effects the dying with Christ and transfers one into a new life, but that the believing Christian, when he is baptized and thus is buried with Christ, comes to understand that he has died with Christ and has been transferred into a new life. Thus baptism does not effect anything other than faith does; both bring it about that the person who is baptized as a believer belongs to Christ and thereby is delivered "from the present evil eon in accordance with the will of God and our Father" (Gal. 1:4).

The Holy Spirit and "being in Christ"

In the context of Paul's statements about baptism, however, we encounter now two further conceptions which afford a still better view of the Pauline understanding of the present existence of the baptized believer: "We are all baptized in one Spirit into one body" (I Cor. 12:13), and "You all are sons of God through faith in Christ Jesus" (Gal. 3:26). To take up first Paul's mention of the Spirit, it must be noted that Paul speaks in altogether the same sense of *"the Holy Spirit"* (Rom. 5:5; 9:1), "the Spirit of God" (Rom. 8:9, 14), and "the Spirit of Christ" (Rom. 8:9; Phil. 1:19), and we saw earlier that the gift of the Holy Spirit, which the Christian receives as down-payment of the coming glory, for Paul establishes the Christian's tie with the exalted Lord until he comes (see above, p. 169). It is characteristic further that Paul equally well can say that the Christians have received the Spirit at baptism (I Cor. 12:13) or can trace the reception of the Spirit to faith: "I should like to know only one thing of you: did you receive the Spirit on the basis of works of the law or on the basis of believing hearing?" (Gal. 3:2). Thus the Spirit is the concrete reality through which the believer has obtained a share in the eschatological salvation which has begun through Christ's resurrection. From this it follows that for Paul the Christian's changed situation is expressed in that he "is a servant in a new Spirit and not in the old letter" (Rom. 7:6), and that it can be said of him that he walks "not after the flesh, but after the Spirit" (Rom. 8:4) and is "led by the Spirit" (Gal. 5:18). Since the Spirit is the first installment of the coming final consummation, he can certainly empower the Christian to do miraculous deeds (I Cor. 2:4; I Thess. 1:5; Rom. 15:19), particularly the ecstatic speaking in tongues (I Cor. 14:2). But Paul does not place the emphasis here; he traces all abilities which a Christian is able to employ in the community back to the working of the Spirit (I Cor. 12:7-11) and sees the criterion for these abilities in the edification of the community, not in the demonstration of the working of the Spirit as such (I Cor. 14:4, 12). For him in this connection the emphasis lies in two points: "We who have the same Spirit of faith in accordance with the saying in Scripture, 'I believed, and therefore I spoke,' also believe and hence also speak, since we know that he who raised Jesus will also raise us with Jesus" (II Cor. 4:13-14; cf. Gal. 5:5; Rom. 8:11). That is, the Spirit enables the Christian for faith and for hope in the final deliverance; indeed, the Spirit gives the certainty that the Christians have been adopted as sons of God ("You have received the Spirit of adoption as sons. In him we cry, 'Abba, Father.' The Spirit himself testifies to our spirit that we are God's children," Rom. 8:15-16; cf. Gal. 4:6) and will be heirs of God (Gal. 4:7; Rom. 8:17). And the second point is this: the Spirit makes possible the overcoming of the flesh and the life in accordance with God's will: "If in the Spirit you put to death the deeds of the body, you will live" (Rom. 8:13; cf. Gal. 5:25; 6:8); "But I say, walk in the Spirit, and then you will not fulfill the lusts of the flesh" (Gal. 5:16). Of course in the context of these statements about the power of the Spirit over the flesh imperatives repeatedly emerge, and we shall have to return to the question of the conditional character of this possession of salvation of the Christian (see below, pp. 224 ff.). The second of the conceptions mentioned above, with which Paul describes the present existence of the baptized believer, is the formula *"in Christ."* It has long been thought that with this term and the corresponding expressions "in Christ Jesus" and "in the Lord" Paul intends to describe the "mystical" unity between the Christians and the resurrected One, and hence uses the spatial image of "being in Christ" (in Phil. 3:8-9 the "to gain Christ" and "to be found in him [Christ]" are parallel to each other), particularly since Paul can also say, conversely, "I no longer live, but Christ lives in me" (Gal. 2:20). On the other hand, some have disputed that this formula has a local meaning at all and have wanted to see it as merely describing a relationship. We shall be able to arrive at a proper understanding of this form of expression which is characteristic of Paul, however, only when we recognize that the formula is used by Paul with varied meanings and by no means always in the sense of a formula. Thus for example Paul can use "in Christ" in an almost instrumental sense and hence can describe the divine saving action through Christ thus: "In Christ God was reconciling the world to himself" (II Cor. 5:19); "We are freely justified by his grace by means of the redemption in Christ" (Rom. 3:24; cf. Gal. 3:14; Rom. 8:39). Thus "in Christ" can simply have the meaning of "Christian": Paul sends the slave Onesimus back to his master "no longer as a slave, but as much more than a slave, as a beloved brother, especially for me but how much more for you, both in the flesh and in the Lord" (Philemon 16), and this designation then distinguishes Christians from non-Christians (I Cor. 7:39; Gal. 1:22; Rom. 16:7-8, 11). The local meaning, which undoubtedly is to be detected here, also certainly is voiced when "in Christ" describes membership in the "body of Christ," i.e., in the

Christian community: "We, being many, are *one* body in Christ" (Rom. 12:5); "you are all one in Christ" (Gal. 3:28; cf. Rom. 16:12; Gal. 5:6).

If, in all these cases, "in Christ" denotes the Christian's relation to the eschatological saving event and the Christian community that is founded thereby, still in numerous contexts Paul undoubtedly uses this expression with the import of a formula, and in these cases the preposition "in" does not primarily have a local meaning, but identifies the Christian's connection with Christ and the Christ event. Thus "in Christ" describes the new creation which has been bestowed on the believer through God's act in Christ: "If anyone is in Christ, he is a new creation" (II Cor. 5:17); "Of him [God] are you in Christ Jesus, who from God has become for us wisdom, righteousness, sanctification, and redemption" (I Cor. 1:30); "We live, if you stand fast in the Lord" (I Thess. 3:8; cf. I Cor. 4:15; Phil. 1:1). But above all with this expression Paul characterizes the new life of the Christian which is established by being joined to Christ and dying with Christ: "Thus reckon yourselves as dead to sin, but alive to God in Christ Jesus" (Rom. 6:11); "Him who knew no sin he has made to be sin on our behalf, that we might become the righteousness of God in him" (II Cor. 5:21; cf. also Gal. 2:4; Phil. 2:24). But now it is characteristic that Paul then also on the one hand uses this concept in a hortatory sense, usually in the form "in the Lord": "Stand fast in the Lord, my beloved" (Phil. 4:1); "I commend to you Phoebe . . . , that you may receive her in the Lord as is worthy of the saints" (Rom. 16:1-2; cf. Phil. 3:1; 4:4); on the other hand he sees the hoped-for final salvation of the Christians as grounded "in Christ": "There is therefore now no [more] condemnation for those in Christ Jesus" (Rom. 8:1); "But I press toward the goal, toward the prize of God's upward call in Christ Jesus" (Phil. 3:14; cf. 4:7). Since Paul can use the form of expression "in Christ" also to denote God's saving action in the past (see above), this conception also identifies the historical being of the Christian in the end-time that has begun, before the anticipated consummation of salvation.

When Paul finally unequivocally bases the present time of salvation, which is described with the words "in Christ," on faith ("You all are sons of God through faith in Christ Jesus," Gal. 3:26), the assumption that with the formula "in Christ" Paul intends to characterize a mystical communion of the believer with Christ undoubtedly is proved to be erroneous. The texts which above all have given occasion for this false assumption are to be explained otherwise. This is obvious in Gal. 2:20: "I no longer live; Christ lives in me," when one notes what follows, where it is said of the life of the Christian in the flesh: "I live in faith in the Son of God, who loved me and gave himself for me." According to this, the believer knows that the dead and risen Christ is his Lord and rules his life, and therefore he can confess: "Christ lives in me"; cf. also Rom. 8:10: "If Christ is in you, the body is dead because of sin, but the spirit is life because of righteousness." That is to say, because Christ rules by the Spirit in the Christian, he can do righteous deeds. Hence what is said about the Christians' being "in Christ" also does not show that Paul was a mystic, but describes the believers' belonging to the "man of the end-time" Christ who embraces them, and it therefore is likely that what is said about "being in Christ," as well as the figure of the "body of Christ," owes its emergence to the conception of Christ as the universal personality (see above, p. 210) .

The Lord's Supper and the transformation into glory

Finally, this judgment, that Paul does not hold a "mystical" theology, cannot be rendered uncertain by two conceptions which have often been cited in the sense of a mystical interpretation of Paul. Curiously, Paul speaks of the Lord's Supper only in I Corinthians (10:16-17; 11:20 ff.) , and in fact in both passages because the Corinthians did not pay attention to the peculiarity of the Christian observance of the meal. This fact itself shows that Paul manifestly—other than with baptism!—can speak extensively of the faith and life of the Christians without even mentioning the Lord's Supper at all. The participation in the Lord's Supper, even though it presumably was self-evident for all Christians in the Pauline communities ("Now when you come together," I Cor. 11:20) , therefore is hardly constitutive for the Christian existence in Paul's mind. Moreover, it is likely that in addition to the community's observance of the Supper there were services of the word, in which non-Christians also could participate (I Cor. 14:23) , while the Lord's Supper consisted of a common meal of the baptized Christians (I Cor. 11:33) , at which prayer was offered over a cup of wine, all drank from this cup and all ate of a loaf of bread that was divided among them (I Cor. 10:16-17; 11:26) . Paul speaks plainly of eating the bread and drinking the cup of the Lord (I Cor. 11:26-27; 10:17) , but we do not know in what way this communal eating of a loaf of bread and the common drinking from a cup were combined with the meal that was taken communally (I Cor. 11:20-21,

33), and the frequently proposed thesis that this eating of the bread and drinking of the wine took place after the common meal, as a cultic observance separate from the meal, is utterly unprovable.

Some have asserted, further, that Paul interprets the common eating of the bread and drinking of the wine as a partaking of the body and blood of Christ and therefore traces illnesses and deaths in the community to the unworthy eating of these "elements" conceived of as having magical effects (cf. I Cor. 10:16; 11:29-30). But this in no wise corresponds to Paul's statements. "Is not the cup of blessing which we bless a participation in the blood of Christ? Is not the bread which we break a participation in the body of Christ? For *one* bread [is eaten], *one* body are we the many; indeed, we all partake of the *one* bread" (I Cor. 10:16-17): with these words Paul intends to emphasize that the participants in the Lord's Supper enter into personal communion and sit at the same table with the risen Lord (I Cor. 10:21), and from this he draws the inference that the Christians cannot also sit with demons at their table. Thus even the context here shows that in the reference to the Lord's Supper the only thing that concerns Paul is the fellowship with the Lord. Moreover, the Greek word translated above as "participation" has only the meaning of a partaking in common and cannot denote "consumption." It is to be noted, finally, that elsewhere Paul always uses the expression "blood of Christ" to refer to Christ's salvation-bringing death (Rom. 3:25; 5:9; Col. 1:20), and the expression must also have this meaning in I Cor. 10:16; 11:27; that is, Paul interprets the common drinking of the blessed cup as an obtaining of a share in Christ's saving death and its effects. Altogether in keeping with this, it may be seen that for Paul, "body of Christ" always denotes the community of the resurrected One (see above, pp. 208-9), and in I Cor. 10:17 it is even explicitly said that the common eating of the one bread corresponds to the common membership in the body of Christ.

Hence while I Cor. 10:16-17 speaks clearly against the assertion that Paul understands the drinking of the cup and the eating of the bread at the Lord's Supper as an eating and drinking of the body and blood of Christ, in I Cor. 11:20 ff. also the point is not the inadequate regard for the "elements" of the Lord's Supper by the community—Paul knows nothing at all of such—but rather the neglect of a sharing in the food and consequently a "not discerning the body [of Christ]" (11:29). Here also Paul speaks only of eating the bread and drinking the cup, and he does not trace the illnesses and deaths in the community to the "unworthy" eating of

Christ's body and blood—Paul nowhere speaks of this—but to the judgment of God upon those Christians who "unworthily" partake of the bread and the cup at the Lord's Supper, that is, do not maintain the fellowship with the members of the community who "have nothing," and thereby "despise the community of God" (I Cor. 11:26, 30, 27, 31-32, 22). Thus according to Paul the Lord's Supper brings it about that the Christian, who knows of the reality of the community of the risen Lord and hence about his body, obtains a share in the salvation which God has wrought and is working in Christ's death and in the creation of the community of the resurrected one. For Paul the Lord's Supper is by its very essence a "proclamation of the Lord's death until he comes" (I Cor. 11:26) ; that is, in the Lord's Supper there is proclaimed to the believer, who is awaiting the imminent coming of the Lord (in fact, the cry, "Our Lord, come!" in I Cor. 16:22 probably belongs to the observance of the Lord's Supper; see above, p. 112) , the salvation which has become reality in Christ's death, and as a member of Christ's body, he receives in faith anew a share in this salvation. Since through faith and being baptized the Christian has already been incorporated into Christ's body, the participation in the Lord's Supper can only confirm the received salvation, not first impart it. Hence the Lord's Supper also is tied to faith and brings one into connection with the salvation of the end-time, and thus has no mystical, timeless effect.

The second conception which is incorrectly adduced to support a mystical interpretation of Paul's preaching is expressed in II Cor. 3:18: "But we all behold with unveiled face the glory of the Lord and are thus transformed into the same image from glory to glory, as [proceeding] from the Lord of the Spirit." This curious sentence describes the present existence of the Christians in contrast to the Jews, upon whose hearts a veil lies and who therefore are blind to the message of their own Scriptures and do not recognize Christ (II Cor. 3:14-15) ; the Christians, on the other hand, behold the glory of the Lord. This statement would be strange, if for no other reason, in that Paul here says of all Christians what he confesses a little later in the same epistle of his own vision of Christ at his call: "God has shined into our hearts, so that the knowledge of the glory of God became clear in the face of Jesus Christ" (II Cor. 4:6) . Yet here the statement goes much further: this vision of the glory of the Lord by the Christians leads to the transformation of the Christians into this glory and to the assimilation to the image of the glorified Lord. These two ideas, that already in the present the Christians are assimilated to the glory of the Lord and that such transformation is occasioned by the vision of the Lord, are without parallel in the letters of Paul, but on the other hand have their clear parallels in Hellenistic mysticism, for which the vision of the deity signifies the way to transformation into the divine nature. But even though in this passage Paul went further in the adoption of mystical conceptions than anywhere else in his epistles, still the context of these statements shows that Paul intends to express something other than the wording suggests at first glance. For, in the first place, at the end of the sentence this vision of the glory of the Lord is clearly attributed to the activity of "the Lord of the Spirit." That is to say, this salvation is not based on human endeavor, but is the operation of the risen Lord. Further, Paul can mean this vision of the glory of the Lord only in a very provisional sense, since in II Cor. 5:7 he expressly emphasizes that the Christians "walk by faith, not by sight," and describes the Christians' state of being saved as hope which does not see (Rom. 8:24). But above all, shortly after the "mystical" sounding statement in II Cor. 3:18, in II Cor. 4:10, 17, he characterizes the existence of the Christians as a "bearing-about of the death of Jesus in our body," and contrasts with the "present slight affliction" the promised "eternal weight of glory." That is, in spite of the undoubtedly "mystical" language of the sentence in II Cor. 3:18, even here Paul undoubtedly is not thinking of a present substantial deification of the Christians, but is describing, in an extravagant and hence easily misunderstood fashion, their being "away from the Lord" (II Cor. 5:6), as a being on the way, wrought by the Spirit, as a state of having already come nearer to the goal (cf. also II Cor. 4:16; Phil. 3:14).

Thus Paul described the justified Christian, who has died with Christ and is transferred into a new life, as a new creation, as dead to sin, as alive to Christ, as assured, through the Spirit, of the future resurrection. It is not without reason that some have wanted to infer from these and similar statements that Paul regarded the Christian as a sinless man who has "crucified the flesh, together with its passions and lusts" (Gal. 5:24) and for whom therefore there is no more condemnation (Rom. 8:1). But two facts clearly argue against this inference: in the letters of Paul are repeatedly found admonitions to the Christians not to risk the received salvation, and it is equally clearly said to the Christians that even they can be rejected in the judgment. How can these statements be brought into agreement with the picture of Christians which we have found in Paul?

b. INDICATIVE AND IMPERATIVE

In numerous passages in Paul, *indicatives and imperatives* are found side by side. After Paul has affirmed in Rom. 6:11: "So also you consider yourselves to be dead to sin, but alive to God in Christ Jesus," he adds: "Thus sin is not to rule in your mortal body, that you should obey its appetites" (6:12), and then in what follows, repeatedly sets the two possibilities before the eyes of the Roman Christians: "As you have put your members at the disposal of lawlessness, as servants for uncleanness and lawlessness, so now put your members at the disposal of righteousness as servants unto sanctification" (6:19). The statement, "Those who belong to Christ Jesus have crucified the flesh together with its passions and appetites," is immediately followed by the demand: "If we live in the Spirit, let us also walk in the Spirit" (Gal. 5:24-25; cf. also Col. 3: 3, 5). Correspondingly, Paul can make the same statement indicative and imperative: "All you who are baptized into Christ have put on Christ" (Gal. 3:27), alongside, "Put on the Lord Jesus Christ and do not be concerned for the flesh, so that lusts [arise]" (Rom. 13:14); "You have become imitators of us and of the Lord, when you received the word in much affliction with the joy of the Holy Spirit" (I Thess. 1:6) alongside, "Be imitators of me, as I [am an imitator] of Christ" (I Cor. 11:1). The two are combined in the most paradoxical fashion in the metaphorical statement of I Cor. 5:7: "Cleanse out the old leaven that you may be a new lump, as you really are unleavened" (RSV). Corresponding then to this immediate conjoining of indicative and imperative is the fact that in all his epistles—with the exception of the personal letter to Philemon—Paul combines admonitions with the statements about God's saving action on behalf of the Christians: "Thus, brethren, we are not debtors to the flesh, to live according to the flesh; for if you live according to the flesh, you will die . . ." (Rom. 8:12, 13*a*); "He who thinks he is standing should take heed, lest he fall. Only a human temptation has befallen you . . ." (I Cor. 10:12, 13*a*); "By working together [on the communication of the message of reconciliation], we exhort you, that you will not receive the grace of God in vain" (II Cor. 6:1); "Thus as long as we have time, let us do good to all men" (Gal. 6:10); "Only walk worthy of Christ" (Phil. 1:27); "If now you are risen with Christ, seek what is above, where Christ is seated at God's right hand; seek what is above, not what is on the earth" (Col. 3:1-2) ; "Finally, we beg you and admonish [you] in the Lord Jesus that you [walk] as you have learned from us, how you must walk and please God, as indeed you also are walking" (I Thess. 4:1) ; "So stand firm, brethren, and hold to the traditions about which you have been taught" (II Thess. 2:15) .

Thus it undoubtedly is incorrect to say that Paul thought of the Christians as sinless. But are not these admonitions in irreconcilable conflict with all that Paul has said about the new creation of the Christian and the Christian's being dead to sin? This has often been said, and the most diverse explanations have been attempted, many of which, however, have not been able convincingly to explain the juxtaposition of indicative and imperative. A proper explanation must start out from the fact that Paul calls for the battle against sin at all only because the Christian has been freed from the compulsion of sin (cf. the "therefore" in Rom. 8:12; Gal. 6:10; Col. 3:5; II Thess. 2:15; and the "since . . . really" in I Cor. 5:7) . Thus for Paul the Christian undoubtedly is not a "poor sinner" who cannot do anything but commit sin; but neither has the liberation of the Christian from the power of sin transformed the nature of the Christian so that he could no longer sin. Instead, Paul can say of himself, "I am not aware of any guilt," but immediately adds, "but I am not thereby acquitted" (I Cor. 4:4) and accordingly warns the Corinthian Christians who think that "everything is permissible for me": "but I will not let myself be enslaved to anything" (I Cor. 6:12) . In spite of all his liberation from the power of sin, the Christian remains subject to temptation ("for fear that somehow the tempter had tempted you and that our labor would be in vain," I Thess. 3:5 RSV; cf. I Cor. 10:13) , and for the Christian there still exists the possibility of falling into grave sin: "Let us not practice fornication . . . , let us not tempt Christ . . . , let us not grumble. . . . Hence he who thinks he is standing should take heed, lest he fall" (I Cor. 10:8-12) ; "So put to death the members on the earth, unchastity, uncleanness, passion, evil appetite and covetousness, which is idolatry" (Col. 3:5-6; cf. Rom. 13:12-13) . Because the Christian can fall into temptation and sin, Paul considers it entirely conceivable that even a Christian may be rejected by God: "I beat my body and keep it in subjection, lest I should preach to others and myself be lost" (I Cor. 9:27) ; "When we are judged we are being chastened by the Lord, so that we may not be condemned together with the world" (I Cor. 11:32; cf. I Cor. 4:4;

Rom. 14:23a). In other words, in his estimate of the ethical situation of the Christian, Paul by no means starts out from the experiences which he has had by himself or, particularly, with his communities, but from the belief in God's saving act in Jesus Christ at the end of time. From this there results for him a dual state of affairs.

The Christian knows that God has delivered him from the present evil eon and has transferred him into the kingdom of his dear Son, that through Christ's death God has cleansed him of sin and has reconciled himself with him, that by receiving the Holy Spirit he is incorporated into the body of Christ and in the Spirit can fulfill the just demands of the law (Gal. 1:4; Col. 1:13; Rom. 3:24-25; 1 Cor. 12:13; Rom. 8:4). All this has actually happened, the Christian is actually "free from the law of sin and death" (Rom. 8:2), and he has crucified the flesh and lives in the Spirit (Gal. 5:24, 25a); with the help of the Spirit he can call on God as "Abba," and in this he notes that God has accepted him as a son (Gal. 4:6; Rom. 8:15b, 16). All this is reality, but only for the believer; for only as a believer does the Christian know of God's saving act, only as a believer can he let himself be led by the Spirit. If on the other hand the Christian places himself again under the law, he loses the freedom which he as a believer, as "in Christ," possesses (Gal. 5:1; Rom. 8:1-2). Because the new creation, the liberation, is God's act, which can be and remain actual only in faith, the maintenance of faith is the condition of freedom, but therefore also the loss of freedom is possible with the weakening or the loss of faith. The very connection of salvation with faith therefore makes the admonition, "Watch, stand fast in faith" (I Cor. 16:13) indispensable.

To be sure this Christian, who in faith knows himself to be delivered from the present evil eon, still continues to live in the old eon that is passing away. As a believer and one who has been endowed with the divine Spirit, he has died to the world, but he still lives in the flesh; Satan, sin, the law, all are indeed conquered in Christ's death and resurrection, but not destroyed, and therefore not ineffective, even with respect to faith. In the Spirit the Christian has the down-payment of salvation, he is justified and adopted as God's son, but he can succumb to temptation, he can obey the flesh instead of the Spirit, he can fall from grace. His being saved, his final salvation, consequently, depends on his letting the Spirit rule over him, his remaining a servant of righteousness, his offering his body as "a living sacrifice, holy, acceptable to God," and thereby performing a "spiritual worship," and not being "conformed to this eon" (Rom. 12:1-2).

All of this shows that the juxtaposition of indicative and imperative is for Paul, in view of the existence of the believer in both eons, a necessary, an indispensable, antinomy. The indicative describes the eschatological salvation in which the Christian in faith has obtained a share; it says that the believer is newly created and shaped by God's saving actions in past and present and by the assured hope of the anticipated early consummation of salvation. But the imperative characterizes the Christian as threatened by the old eon which is coming to an end and by its powers, and hence as responsible for holding firm to the deliverance that he has received. Indeed, the Christian can "fulfill the just demands of the law" if he "walks not according to the flesh, but according to the Spirit" (Rom. 8:4). But therefore he must be reminded of the message of salvation which he has received as well as of the ethical instruction which he also has received (I Cor. 15:1-2; 11:2; I Thess. 4:1; Gal. 5:21). Because the Christian can "fulfill the just demands of the law" (Rom. 8:4), he is subject to God's demand of love, which is expressed in the law and is valid for Christians also: "The law is fulfilled in *one* word: 'Thou shalt love thy neighbor as thyself'" (Gal. 5:14; cf. Rom. 13:8-10). Thus Paul affirms the moral demands of the law, but the command of the Lord Christ stands above the law (cf. I Cor. 9:8-9, 13, alongside 9:14), and thus as the ultimate norm Paul cites, where it is possible for him to do so, not the law but the command of the Lord (I Cor. 7:10, 25), which he paradoxically can identify as the "law of Christ" (Gal. 6:2; cf. I Cor. 9:21). Even where Paul cites the law as the norm for Christians, he has not forgotten that the Christian is "not under law, but under grace" (Rom. 6:15); "freedom *from* the law as the way of salvation is at the same time freedom *for* the law as command with regard to substance" (W. Schrage).

If thus in fact the imperative is just as appropriate and necessary as the indicative in the context of the Pauline doctrine of salvation, still the important thing is that objectively the imperative always only follows the indicative. What the believing Christian does he does not by his own strength but because of the divine salvation which has come to him ("What do you have that you have not received?" I Cor. 4:7), and the imperative does not admonish one to gain his salvation, but to hold fast and not to lose the salvation that has been received. Hence the affirmation, "It is God who works in you according to his will, both to will and to do," is the motivating presupposition for the admonition, "Work out your own salvation with fear and trembling" (Phil. 2:12-13). Thus, along with the warning against falling, Paul also can express to Christians the certainty: "Only a human temptation has befallen you; but God is faithful, and he will not let you be tempted beyond your powers, but with the temptation will also provide a way of escape, that you may be able to bear it" (I Cor. 10:13).

C. JUDGMENT ACCORDING TO WORKS

Finally, the fact that Paul speaks of man's being judged according to his works also shows that the imperative, that is, the reminder of the task posed for Christians to "stand perfect and complete in all the will of God" (Col. 4:12), necessarily belongs to Paul's message of salvation. Paul can speak of "God's judgment" quite generally: God "will reward every man according to his works; to these who in the patient doing of good works seek glory and honor and immortality, [he will give] eternal life; but to those who are selfish and do not obey the truth, but rather obey unrighteousness, wrath and fury [will be given]" (Rom. 2:6-8). And quite in keeping with this is what he says about the day "in which God will judge the secrets of men," and the "day of wrath and of the revelation of God's righteous judgment" (Rom. 2:16a, 5b, cf. I Cor. 1:8; 5:5; I Thess. 1:10). But since Paul elsewhere clearly says, as we have seen (above, p. 195), that it is not possible to be acquitted by God on the basis of works of the law (Rom. 3:20, 28; Gal. 2:16), some have doubted that Paul could even be thinking of Christians when he speaks of the coming judgment day. But because of their unconditional formulation, the statements just cited in Rom. 2:6-8, 16a, 5b, admit of no other interpretation than that here Paul is anticipating God's judgment upon all men, even upon Christians. This interpretation is confirmed by the texts in which Paul plainly speaks of a judgment of God or of Christ upon Christians: "We must all appear before the judgment seat of Christ, so that each one may receive good or evil, according to what he has done in the body" (II Cor. 5:10 RSV); "Indeed, we all shall stand before the judgment seat of God" (Rom. 14:10; cf. I Thess. 4:6; I Cor. 3:12-13; 4:4). Paul, who does assert that the Christian is justified (I Cor. 6:11; Rom. 5:9a) and stresses that "there is therefore now no condemnation to them that are in Christ Jesus" (Rom. 8:1) and that Jesus "delivers us from the wrath to come" (I Thess. 1:10; cf. Rom. 5:9b), everywhere takes for granted that the Christians still can be rejected by God: I have sent Timothy to you "in order to learn of your faith, for fear that the tempter had somehow tempted you and our efforts would be in vain" (I Thess. 3:5) ; "Do not destroy, by what you eat, that [brother] for whom Christ died" (Rom. 14:15; cf. Gal. 5:4; I Cor. 6:8-9; 8:11; 10:12; and the passages listed above on pp. 225-26). However strange it may at first appear, in view of the Pauline gospel of the justification of the sinner by grace apart from the works of the law—there can be no doubt that Paul anticipates the divine judgment upon men on the basis of their deeds and does not except Christians from this expectation.

But now this contradiction is by no means to be explained by saying that Paul dragged along from his Jewish past the conception of judgment according to one's works, although it no longer fitted into the framework of his doctrine of salvation. For he has decisively reshaped the Jewish conceptions.

Paul consistently distinguishes between the plural, "works," by which he designates the autonomous action of man, by which man can gain no standing before God (cf. Rom. 13:12; Gal. 5:19) , and the singular, which describes the action of the Christian: "The work of everyone will be made manifest; for the day will bring it to the light, because it will be made manifest by fire, and the fire will test how the work of each one has been done" (I Cor. 3:13) ; " . . . in the conviction that he who has begun a good work in you will complete it unto the day of Jesus Christ" (Phil. 1:6; cf. II Cor. 9:8; Gal. 6:4; etc.; the parallel concept "fruit" is likewise found only in the singular, for example in Rom. 6:22; Phil. 1:11). At the judgment God will not ask about works, fruits, achievements, but about "the fruit of righteousness through Jesus Christ" (Phil. 1:11), and this means, to put it in another way, God will ask about the "proof" (Rom. 5:4; II Cor. 9:13; I Cor. 11:19). Hence Paul can say of himself: "Thus one should regard us as servants of Christ and stewards of the mysteries of God. But in this it is [only] required of the stewards that one be found trustworthy" (I Cor. 4:1-2). Hence the Christians' task is not the performing of works, but striving for the verification: "I strain, I press toward the goal, the prize, which consists in the upward call from God in Jesus Christ" (Phil. 3:13-14).

Paul does not ask about the "how" of the reward, nor even about the "how" of the condemnation. He is sure that there is a condemnation, and that there are those who are condemned (Phil. 1: 28; I Cor. 1:18; II Cor. 2:15; II Thess. 2:10), and, as we have seen, he reckons with the possibility that even Christians may fall victims to corruption. But he makes no further statements about the condition of being under condemnation; the fate of non-Christians is not a subject of reflection for him. When he speaks of the judgment according to one's works, he is emphasizing that God knows no "respect of persons" of any kind (Rom. 2:11) and that therefore the commissioned apostle as well as every other Christian must be conscious of the seriousness of the judgment (I Cor. 4:4-5; II Cor. 5:10). But neither does he picture in detail the salvation bestowed upon the saved; instead, he only describes it in comprehensive terms as eternal life, glory, deliverance, being with Christ, being at home with the Lord (Rom. 2:7; 5:21; Gal. 6:8; Rom. 2:10; 8:18; Col. 3:4—Rom. 13:11; I Thess. 5:9—II Cor. 13:4; Phil. 1:23 —II Cor. 5:8, etc.).

But above all, Paul looks toward the judgment upon Christians with confidence: "God has not destined us for wrath, but to obtain salvation through our Lord Jesus Christ" (I Thess. 5:9 RSV); "How much more shall we, who now have been justified by his blood, be saved from wrath through him" (Rom. 5:9); "Rejoice in the Lord always . . . , the Lord is at hand" (Phil. 4:4-5). The basis for this confidence is evident: the God who holds judgment is indeed the God who through Jesus Christ saves the sinners: "If God is for us, who is against us? . . . Who will raise any charge against God's elect? Is it God, who justifies? Is it Christ Jesus, who died, indeed, who rose again, who is at the right hand of God, who also intercedes for us?" (Rom. 8:31, 33-34); "You await the revelation of our Lord Jesus Christ; he will also confirm you to the end, that you may be blameless on the day of our Lord Jesus Christ" (I Cor. 1:7-8).

But therewith it becomes evident that Paul saw the *expectation of the judgment in the context of the message of salvation*. This is true in two respects.

Knowing of the inevitability of the divine judgment before which man cannot stand causes man to open himself to receive the message that only God's saving action in Jesus Christ can save him from being lost: "Do you think . . . that you will escape the judgment of God? Or do you scorn the riches of his goodness and patience and forbearance? Do you not know that God's goodness is guiding you to conversion?" (Rom. 2:4); "I find for myself that when I want to do good, evil is present with me . . . . Wretched man that I am, who will deliver me from this body of death?" (Rom. 7:21, 24). But not only does it hold true for every man in a quite general sense that being reminded of the imminent condemnation in the judgment must make him ready to receive the message of deliverance; it also holds true for the Christian that the recollection of the possibility of "falling from grace" was bound to prompt him to strive to hold fast to the deliverance that was received: "I Paul say to you: if you have yourselves circumcised, Christ becomes of no benefit to you" (Gal. 5:2) ; "I pommel my body and subdue it, lest after preaching to others I myself should be disqualified" (I Cor. 9:27 RSV) ; "If we tested ourselves, we should not be judged; but if we are judged by the Lord, this serves for our chastening, so that we may not be condemned along with the world" (I Cor. 11:31-32). Now if the certainty of divine judgment is maintained and taken seriously, the divine saving action in Christ appears as the only deliverance, which must unconditionally be grasped and held.

But the decisive thing is this: God's judgment will condemn the world because the world is guilty before God (I Cor. 11: 32; Rom. 3:19), "estranged and hostile in mind, doing evil deeds" (Col. 1:21 RSV). But this is no longer true of the Christians: "There is therefore now no more condemnation to those who are in Christ Jesus. For the law of the spirit of life in Christ Jesus has made you free from the law of sin and of death . . . . God sent his Son in the form of sinful flesh and for sin and [thus] condemned sin in the flesh, that the just demands of the law might be fulfilled in us, who do not walk in accordance with the flesh, but in accordance with the Spirit" (Rom. 8:1-4). This plainly says that the Christian does not do God's will by his own strength, but that the divine Spirit bestowed upon him fulfills in him (or through him) God's righteous demands, and thus that it is the divine Spirit that is really acting in the Christian. And Paul describes the same state of affairs in paradoxical fashion in Phil. 2:12-13: "Therefore, my beloved [because Christ has humbled himself to death on the cross and therefore has been exalted to the position of Lord], work out your salvation with fear and trembling; for God is working in you the willing and the doing according to his good pleasure." Thus the Christian can strive for his salvation, because God himself guides his willing and working, because God himself is acting through the Christian. The salvation that is given to the Christian first makes it possible for him to fulfill God's will, and therefore at the judgment the Christian is asked about the work that he has done, not about his achievement; that is, he is asked only whether he has made a place in what he has done for God through the Holy Spirit. Hence God justifies the Christian solely on the basis of faith, even though he asks about the work (Rom. 3:30; 14:23b) ; for in fact the believer actually is living in faith only when he lets himself be ruled by the Spirit and thus puts to death the deeds of the body (Rom. 8:13b), and the hope in God's righteousness is valid only for the "faith that works through love" (Gal. 5:6). Thus though there may be in the preaching of Paul a contradiction, formally speaking, between justification by faith alone and the judgment according to work—it is the same God who out of grace intends to justify the sinner at the end of time, if the sinner submits in faith to the message of God's eschatological saving action in Jesus Christ, and who asks about "obedience to Christ" (II Cor. 10:5) and passes judgment on whether the Christian in such service to Christ appears "well-pleasing to God and approved by men" (Rom. 14:18). The antinomy that God is righteous *and* gracious dominates the biblical faith in God; in the last analysis, it is this antinomy which becomes visible in the formal contradiction in Paul between justification by faith and judgment according to work; and we can affirm this anomaly as valid for ourselves also and therefore appropriate or reject it, but we cannot reduce it to a system free of logical contradictions.

d. DIVINE PREDESTINATION

If the reference to God's judgment according to work thus intends only to strengthen the Pauline message that God alone provides in Jesus Christ the liberating salvation, this same purpose is served also by the few allusive sentences in which Paul speaks of divine predestination. Since the days of the church fathers the view has been repeatedly read from the Pauline arguments about the ultimate fate of Israel in Rom. 9–11 that God in his wrath has predestined certain men for perdition and in his mercy certain ones for eternal bliss (cf. above all Rom. 9:18, 22-23). But an exposition that pays close attention to the context—nowadays there is hardly any difference of opinion about this—shows that these statements in their entirety do not at all intend to speak of the problem of divine predestination, of the election or reprobation of men. Instead, they seek to answer the much more narrowly restricted question whether the unbelief of most Jews toward the gospel, which deeply troubled Paul, means that God "has rejected his people" (Rom. 11:1), although the message of the gospel as the saving power for every believer was addressed first to the Jews and only then to the Greeks (Rom. 1:16). Paul's answer to this question, that in spite of Israel's unbelief God has not rejected his people, but that the present unbelief of the Jews is only God's roundabout way, first to win the Gentiles and then the Jews, cannot engage us here in detail (cf. the commentaries). But it is undoubtedly true that the few statements which Paul makes about God's plans for mankind cannot be fitted into a doctrine of double predestination of man to salvation or to perdition. Paul indeed emphasizes with all clarity that God is free to harden and to exercise mercy: "Thus he [God] shows mercy to whom he will [show mercy], and hardens him whom he will [harden]" (Rom. 9:18; cf. 9:11-12, 22-23; 11:7-10); but he also plainly says that the Jews, who now are unbelieving, can yet come to believe (Rom. 10:1; 11:13-14, 23) and that the Gentiles who came to believe can again lose this faith (Rom. 11:20, 22). Hence the subject in these chapters in Romans is not God's finally pronounced decisions about the destiny of mankind, but the fact that God can make such decisions and that man as God's creature may not dispute his right to do so: "O man, who are you to contend with God?" (Rom. 9:20).

But even though Paul did not teach any doctrine of divine predestination, yet in some few passages he did speak of *God's plan for the Christians*. In I Thess. 5:9-10, in the context of admonitions to watchfulness in view of the imminence of the day of judgment, he says: "God did not destine us for wrath, but to gain deliverance through our Lord Jesus Christ, who died for us that we, whether we wake or sleep, should live with him." Similarly, in II Thess. 2:13-14 we read of the Christians: "We are bound to give thanks to God always for you, brethren beloved by the Lord, because God chose you from the beginning [this is probably the correct textual reading] to be saved, through sanctification by the Spirit and belief in the truth. To this he called you through our gospel, so that you may obtain the glory of our Lord Jesus Christ" (RSV). Already in these two texts the deliverance of the Christians by Christ is attributed to God's decision, already made "in the beginning," which then led to the calling of the Christians and thus to their being saved. Paul calls this divine decision to call the Christians God's "election": "God has elected what is foolish in the world . . . , God has elected the despised, even that which is nothing, to reduce to nothing that which is something, so that no flesh might boast in God's presence" (I Cor. 1:27-29); "We know, brethren beloved by God, your election, because our preaching of the gospel did not come to you in word only, but also in power and in the Holy Spirit, and with great assurance" (I Thess. 1:4-5). Now in the only passage where he speaks somewhat more in detail of this election, Paul gives the following expression to this conviction that the Christians were privileged to hear the gospel and to believe it because God had chosen them for that purpose: "We know that to those who love him, God causes all things to work together for good, to those who are called according to [divine] purpose. Those whom he foreknew he also predestined to be conformed to the likeness of his Son, that he should be the firstborn among many brethren; and those whom he predestined he also called, and those whom he called he also justified, and those whom he justified he also glorified" (Rom. 8:28-30). Here the assured conviction that the ultimate deliverance will be given to the Christians as those called and justified by God (cf. Rom. 8:32!) is given certainty by the declaration that the calling of the Christian, which causes God's saving action to become for him a personally experienced reality, goes back to God's electing determination. But in this the decisive thing for Paul is the aim which God was pursuing with such a determination and the calling of the Christians which followed from it: the called ones were to be assimilated to the likeness of Jesus Christ, by means of their call and the bestowal of the Spirit they are adopted as sons of God (Rom. 8:15; Gal. 4:6) and thus have become brothers of the Son of God. For Paul the hope, given therewith, of the Christians' participation in the glory of the risen Son of God ("He will remake our lowly body to be like his glorious body," Phil. 3:21) is so certain that in Rom. 8:30 he can already say: "Those whom he justified he also glorified!" But at the same time Rom. 8:28-29 clearly shows that Paul is not speaking of the divine election and predestination out of speculative interests, but wishes in this way to give expression to the joyous certainty of faith that God in Christ will lead those who are called to a sure deliverance.

But in this connection it is important to note two things: in these contexts Paul nowhere speaks of the men to whom God's call has not come or who have rejected it, and nothing is said of a divine resolve to *condemn* these other men. On the other hand: even though God has called those whom he has chosen in advance, for Paul no unconditional certainty of salvation is given therewith; even the one who is called can in fact fall away from faith and be rejected: "If you [wish to] be justified by the law, you have fallen from grace" (Gal. 5:4; cf. 1:6; 3:2-3; I Cor. 10:12, etc.). "Even the believer can fall. How is this related to the eternal constancy of the divine counsel? Paul did not reconcile these two principles with any mediating ideas" (A. Schlatter). For here also Paul stands by the truth, recognized in faith, that it is the righteous God who out of grace offers his saving act in Christ, and here also we must accept the contradiction arising thereby and can only gratefully affirm, as the basis of our certainty of salvation, the Pauline proclamation of God's determination to call those who are saved—or reject it as incomprehensible.

e. THE FINAL CONSUMMATION

Thus Paul maintained the *two* truths, that "God has called us as those whom he has prepared beforehand for glory" (Rom. 9: 23-24), but also will cause "tribulation and distress" to come "upon every soul of man who does evil, the Jew first and also the Greek" (Rom. 2:9). This combination of two truths which are in tension with each other is matched by the fact that Paul also fails to give an answer that is free from contradiction to the question, now finally set before us, of the final consummation. In all his epistles Paul undoubtedly anticipated the coming of the risen Christ in glory (the "advent," Greek "Parousia") and therewith the inbreaking of the consummation of salvation as very close at hand (see above, pp. 143-44), but only seldom did he refer more in detail to the anticipated events of the end (I Thess. 4:15-17; II Thess. 2:3-10; I Cor. 15:22-28, 51-53; II Cor. 5:1-4, 10). The attempts to arrange the eschatological events mentioned in these texts and also occasionally elsewhere (I Thess. 3:13; Rom. 16:20; Gal. 4:26-27; I Cor. 6:3; Phil. 3:21) in a continuous sequence have not been successful, and it is highly questionable whether Paul intended any such systematic apocalyptic arrangement at all.

The destruction of the powers of the world and "being with Christ"

Instead, in this connection Paul's interest obviously lies in two areas:

When Christ appears from heaven with all his angels, all principalities and powers, together with Satan and, as the last enemy, death, will be destroyed (I Thess. 2:19; 3:13; 4:15-16; II Thess. 1:7; 2:1, 8; I Cor. 15:23-25; Rom. 16:20). "But when all things have been subjected to him [Christ], then will the Son himself be subjected to the one who subjected all things to him [i.e., God], that God may be all in all" (I Cor. 15:28). The expectation of Christ's coming in glory accordingly includes the assured hope that the *powers of this world* which were robbed of their power by God's saving act in the life, death, and resurrection of Christ, but not yet destroyed, then are *finally to be put out of commission*, that then God alone will assume dominion, so that then "neither death nor life nor angels nor rulers nor things future nor powers nor height nor depth nor any creature will be able to separate us from the love of God in Christ Jesus our Lord" (Rom. 8:38-39). This assumption of power by Christ and finally by God himself and therewith the elimination of all powers hostile to God is for Paul the crucial presupposition for the hope of the ultimate salvation which nothing more can shake, and all individual apocalyptic conceptions only serve to lend expression to this assured hope.

When Christ appears from heaven, "the dead in Christ will rise first, then we, the living who remain, shall also be caught away into the air with them to meet the Lord, and so we shall ever be with the Lord" (I Thess. 4:16b, 17). In this earliest extant formulation of Paul's hope of the consummation of salvation, there appears as a description of the final salvation the assurance of being *"with Christ."* Paul frequently used this expression to describe the hope of salvation: "We shall live with him by the power of God which is already bestowed upon you" (II Cor. 13:4; cf. I Thess. 4:15; 5:10; Phil. 1:23; Col. 3:4); and thereby he showed that for him the ultimate salvation in its essential nature did not consist in the gift of divine glory (Rom. 5:2; 8:18, 21; I Cor. 15:43; II Cor. 4:17; Col. 1:27; 3:4; I Thess. 2:12; II Thess. 2:14) and thus in receiving eternal life (Rom. 2:7; 5:17, 21; 6:22-23; II Cor. 2:16; 5:4; Gal. 6:8) and imperishability and immortality (I Cor. 15:53-54), although this description of the final salvation is valid in its full scope for Paul. In its essential nature the final salvation hoped for by Paul consists rather in the nevermore ending and nevermore imperiled communion "with Christ" and through him with God the Father, who has made us for fellowship with himself: "For us [there is only] *one* God, the Father, from whom [come] all things and to whom our own being leads" (I Cor. 8:6; C.K. Barrett, *I Corinthians,* p. 192); cf. also I Cor. 1:9: "God is faithful, by whom you were called to be partakers in his Son Jesus Christ our Lord."

Paul expects this full and inalienable fellowship of the Christians "with Christ," and thereby with God, this "deliverance from the bondage of perishability into the glorious liberty of the children of God" (Rom. 8:21), of the day of Christ's appearing, when "the future glory is to be revealed unto us" (Rom. 8:18; cf. Col. 3:4). Of course for Paul it is certain that "flesh and blood cannot inherit the kingdom of God, nor can what is perishable inherit imperishability" (I Cor. 15:50). Hence for him "leaving the body and coming home to the Lord" (II Cor. 5:8) means the "liberation of our body" (Rom. 8:23), an actual new creation: When the Lord comes, "those who have died will be raised incorruptible and we shall be changed" (I Cor. 15:52). Thus Paul anticipates a *resurrection* of the Christians who have fallen asleep before the Parousia, at which the resurrected ones are to receive in place of their "psychical body" that was buried a "spiritual body," or, in a different figure, are to "put on our dwelling from heaven," while the Christians who are still living at the Parousia are to experience a corresponding transformation (I Cor. 15:44, 52; II Cor. 5:3). In addition, Paul also gives expression to the hope that the Christ who will appear from heaven "will transform our lowly body, so that it is made like his glorious body" (Phil. 3:21; cf. also Rom. 8:29: God has predestined the elect "that they should be conformed to the likeness of his dear Son") and that God "who raised Jesus from the dead will also make alive your mortal bodies through his Spirit that dwells in you" (Rom. 8:11). Yet there is no basis for the assumption that with these somewhat divergent formulations Paul intended to say anything other than in the previously mentioned texts, namely that at the Parousia the Christian is to receive a "spiritual body" which is made like the body of the risen Christ and takes the place of the fleshly body.

Of course in the context of Paul's anticipation of the end two other much discussed questions arise: did Paul expect the reception of final bliss and therewith also of a "spiritual body" by the Christians exclusively for the time of the future appearing of Christ in glory, or is there not also disclosed in his later epistles the hope of attaining final bliss at the death of the Christian? And did Paul promise participation in the consummation of salvation only to Christians or did he not also proclaim the hope of God's intention of salvation for all men? These two questions have urged themselves upon the readers of Paul's epistles and also upon scholarship because some of Paul's statements in fact appear to lead in these directions.

Expectation of the end-time and consummation of salvation after death

Paul expected, as we have seen, that at the appearing of Christ in glory, hoped for in the near future, the departed Christians would rise with a "'spiritual body" and the Christians still living then would be changed, in order forever to be "with Christ." But now in II Cor. 5:1 ff. Paul expresses the yearning to put on the "house from heaven," in order not to be found naked, and with these words he appears to give expression to the wish immediately after death to receive the heavenly body, and thus to die before the Parousia. Although this interpretation of II Cor. 5:1 ff. is disputed, yet in Phil. 1:23-24 Paul incontestably expresses this wish: "I am hard pressed between the two. My desire is to depart and be with Christ, for that is far better. But to remain in the flesh is more necessary on your account" (RSV). Here Paul connects the being "with Christ" with the death which may come to him, as its immediate consequence, but nothing is said of resurrection or transformation at Christ's future appearing. On the basis of these two texts, the assumption has been held in various forms that Paul's eschatological expectation has changed: while he at first (in I Thessalonians and I Corinthians) firmly counted on remaining alive until Christ's appearing, he subsequently saw himself compelled to reckon on the possibility of his dying before the Parousia, and he accordingly replaced the hope of "being with Christ" at the Parousia or combined it with the expectation of being "with Christ" immediately after death.

Of course there are serious objections to this assumption. It must be said first of all that we have only partial knowledge of the sequence in time of Paul's epistles, that above all the place and hence the time of composition of the Philippian epistle are not known for certain. Many students think that Philippians comes from an imprisonment of Paul in Ephesus (cf. the introductions to the New Testament); if this supposition is correct, which to be sure is only inferred, Philippians in any case would be earlier than II Corinthians and could then in no case be a witness for a later form of the Pauline hope of salvation. Similarly, on the basis of this presupposition the Roman epistle would be written later than Philippians, but in any case Romans is later than II Corinthians. Now in Romans Paul very plainly and unequivocally sets forth the hope of the imminent consummation of salvation for Christians at the "revelation of the sons of God" (Rom. 8:19, 23; 13:11). Thus Paul would have to have changed his hope again, if Philippians were the witness for such a change and were composed between I Corinthians and Romans, and the same also applies to II Corinthians in relation to Romans. Thus one would have to assume a second change in Paul's hope, and therefore in no case can II Corinthians and Philippians serve as witnesses for a later form of the Pauline hope of salvation. In addition, it must be said that these two epistles, in which some think they find a changed hope of salvation on the part of Paul, contain unequivocal testimonies to Paul's hope of the consummation of salvation at the appearing of Christ in glory which is hoped for in the near future: "We know that he who raised Jesus will also raise us with Jesus and present us [before himself] together with you" (II Cor. 4:14); I have righteousness from God on the basis of faith [and wait] "if I might attain the resurrection from the dead" (Phil. 3:11); from heaven "we await the Lord Jesus Christ, who will transform our lowly body, so that it is made like his glorious body, by the power with which he is able to subject all things to himself" (Phil. 3:20-21; cf. 1:6, 10; 4:5).

Hence the two passages named, II Cor. 5:1 ff. and Phil. 1:23, must be understood against the background of this expectation, which always dominates Paul, of the consummation of salvation at Christ's appearing. In this connection it is helpful to note that already in his earliest extant epistle Paul takes for granted that the Christians who have died before the Parousia are not separated from Christ, even though their being finally united with the Lord openly is not to take place until the Parousia of Christ: "The dead in Christ will rise first, then we, the living who remain, shall also be caught away into the air with them to meet the Lord, and so we shall ever be with the Lord" (I Thess. 4:16b, 17). Quite in keeping with this, a little later Paul says that "in Christ shall all be made alive," and by this undoubtedly means the resurrection of men "who belong to Christ," at the Parousia (I Cor. 15:22-23). As Paul takes for granted in these two early epistles that the deceased Christians are not separated from Christ, so in I Corinthians he already is clearly reckoning with the possibility of having to die before the Parousia, although he continues to hope to experience the Parousia as one living on the earth: "Why do we stand in peril every hour? I die daily . . . . If I have fought with wild beasts in Ephesus, humanly speaking, what does it profit me?" (I Cor. 15:30-32; cf. 15:52). The almost inescapable danger of death, experienced before II Corinthians was written (II Cor. 1:8-9) therefore cannot have had for Paul the significance that in it he became aware for the first time of the possibility of his dying before the Parousia.

So then even in II Cor. 5:1-4 Paul in no way gives expression, as some have thought, to the wish to die as soon as possible: "We know that if our earthly tabernacle is dissolved, we have a building from God, a house not made with hands, eternal in heaven. Indeed, we also groan because we desire to put on further our dwelling from heaven, insofar [only] that by putting it on we shall not be found naked. For while we are in the tabernacle, we groan, being oppressed, because we do not wish to be unclothed, but to be further clothed, so that what is mortal may be swallowed up by life." In this text also Paul hopes to be permitted at the coming of the Lord in glory to exchange the earthly body for the heavenly one, because this means "going home to the Lord" (II Cor. 5:8). To be sure in II Cor. 5:3 Paul added by way of supplement that only if he were further clothed with the heavenly house (i.e., body) which he desires could he hope not "to be found naked." The meaning of these words has long been disputed: some have tried to find an indication in them that Paul wanted to deny the possibility of standing before God apart from divine righteousness; or some have assumed that he is rejecting the hope of his opponents in Corinth of a disembodied immortality; some have even thought that Paul intends only dialectically to banish a rising doubt of the promise of final salvation, by using this auxiliary idea. But even though we can hardly attain utter certainty about the correct understanding of these words, the fewest difficulties are presented by the interpretation which sees Paul as using the figure of nakedness as a paraphrase for the state which awaits the Christian if through death he goes home to the Lord without at once receiving "the house from heaven." This says that Paul is reckoning with the possibility, which he does not hope for, that Christians, himself included, can die before the Parousia and yet not be able immediately to "put on immortality," which is thought of as connected with the Lord's appearing (I Cor. 15:53; here also, as in II Cor. 5, the figure of "putting on"!). Thus it can hardly be denied that in this passage in II Corinthians Paul is speaking of what will happen if Christians must die before the Lord's appearing; but with the figure of "nakedness" he is scarcely thinking of a disembodied existence, which for him is inconceivable (cf. I Cor. 15:35 ff.), but he is thinking of a temporary waiting for Christ's appearing, which brings with it at last the manifestation of salvation: "When Christ, who is our life, appears, then will you also be manifest with him in glory" (Col. 3:4).

This understanding of the difficult text now finds its confirmation from two sides, and with this confirmation also the deeper meaning of this expectation of salvation on Paul's part first comes to light.

We have already seen (above, p. 169) that, according to Paul's experience and proclamation, through the gift of the Spirit the Christian has quite personally received the down-payment and guarantee of participation in the promised final bliss (see II Cor. 1:22; 5:5; Rom. 8:23), and that God has "transferred him into the kingdom of his dear Son" (Col. 1:13). Thus, through the gift of the

Spirit bestowed on him personally, the Christian already has a share in the consummation of salvation that is begun by Christ's death and resurrection. Indeed, Paul can say that God has already glorified the Christians who are called and justified (Rom. 8:30); cf. II Cor. 4:17: the present affliction "is working for us in increasing abundance an eternal fullness [literally, "weight"] of glory." Correspondingly, Paul describes the present reality of being a Christian as a "being changed from glory to glory, as [it proceeds] from the Lord of the Spirit" (II Cor. 3:18; see above, pp. 222-23). Thus Paul is convinced that in spite of all earthly affliction ("Even though our outward man is perishing . . . ," II Cor. 4:16a), already in his present life in the evil eon that is passing away, through the divine Spirit and the participation in the body of Christ the Christian has concretely received and ever again receives a share in the coming end-time: "our inward man is being renewed day by day" (II Cor. 4:16b; cf. Rom. 12:2). Therefore, Paul cannot at all doubt "that neither death nor life . . . can separate us from the love of God in Christ Jesus our Lord" (Rom. 8:38-39). Hence not even death before the Parousia can tear the Christian from his relationship of belonging to the risen Lord.

Corresponding to this now is Paul's reckoning in Phil. 1:23 on his coming through death to the "being with Christ." This assurance undoubtedly is only the obvious consequence of the conviction that nothing, not even death, can separate the Christians, whose "life is hid with Christ in God" (Col. 3:3), from Christ, because they were called by God "to fellowship with his Son Jesus Christ our Lord" (I Cor. 1:9). Hence it is not surprising in Phil. 1:23 that Paul expects through death immediately to be "with Christ"; it is surprising only that Paul wishes for this death, which he does not do in II Cor. 5, in spite of the same assurance of salvation. But now this wish of Paul in Philippians is not explained by a change in Paul's expectation of salvation, since in fact the Philippian epistle, as we have seen (above, p. 238), clearly maintains the expectation of the early coming of the Lord in glory and the hope of the future resurrection or transformation of the Christians at this coming (besides, we do not in fact know at all certainly whether Philippians was written before or after II Corinthians). Paul's wish "to depart and be with Christ" (Phil. 1:23) instead is very likely explained by the peculiar situation in which Paul found himself at the time of the composition of Philippians: the imprisoned Paul does not know whether the forthcoming trial will end in life or death (1:20), and hence he is uncertain whether he should wish for the death that will bring him to Christ, or for continuing life which will enable him to render service to the community (1:22-23), and this latter wish gains the upper hand (1:25-26; 2:23). Thus in this epistle nothing has changed in Paul's hope of salvation, though in Philippians, as in II Corinthians and more strongly than in the earlier epistles, Paul does also reckon with the possibility that he will not live to experience in the earthly body the appearing of Christ, though he does not at all doubt the early coming of the Lord. As we have seen, the conjecture has often been expressed that the particularly grave peril to his life to which Paul alludes in II Cor. 1:8-9 is responsible for the fact that Paul now (in II Corinthians and Philippians) more seriously contemplates this possibility of dying before the Parousia. This is possible, but by no means certain, and more important than this biographical conjecture is the observation that in the context of this possibility of dying before the Parousia, that has become more pressing for him, Paul gives expression to the certainty which obviously has always been dominant for him, that such a death can only bring the Christian to Christ. That is, in Philippians (as in somewhat different fashion in II Corinthians) *one* side of Paul's expectation of salvation comes more strongly to the fore, which shows that Paul combines the two expectations, that death will bring the Christian to Christ, even though this should signify a "being naked," and that then at Christ's appearing in glory the resurrection or transformation of the Christians will take place, which will make manifest to all the world the final bliss of "being forever with the Lord."

This combination of the hope of "being with Christ" after death and of the ultimate salvation at Christ's appearing in glory, which Paul obviously did not sense as a problem, very probably is to be explained historically in terms of the conceptions of Palestinian Judaism which Paul knew and appropriated: there too the idea of the dwellings of the righteous in heaven and of retribution after death is combined with the expectation of the resurrection and of the future judgment (a similar juxtaposition is also found in the Gospel of Luke: cf. 16:22 ff.; 23:43 along with 11:31-32; 20:35). But more important than this historical question is the observation that Paul neither shows any interest in the description of existence after death or the resurrection nor in any way strives to reconcile the two forms of the expectation of salvation; Paul obviously is interested only in the fact that the Christian always remains in fellowship with his heavenly Lord, but that likewise "the last enemy to be destroyed is death" (I Cor. 15:26) and "we shall live with him [i.e., Christ] by the power of God" which is already bestowed upon you (II Cor. 13:4). Thus because for Paul the only essential thing is that "whether we live or whether we die, we belong to the Lord" (Rom. 14:8), he can hold side by side the eschatological expectations which are familiar to him but for us are not at once reconcilable, and from the expectation of death as well as from the hope of final salvation can draw the same conclusion: "Therefore whether we are at home or away [i.e., whether we live in the earthly body or have died], let us also be zealously concerned to be well-pleasing to him" (II Cor. 5:9).

Salvation for all mankind?

But here the second question mentioned above (see p. 237) arises: did Paul hold out the promise of participation in the consummation of salvation only to Christians, or did he not also proclaim salvation for all mankind? We have seen that Paul spoke of God's plan (see above, p. 233) to lead those who are called in Christ to ultimate deliverance, while nothing is said of God's plan for the men who were not called or who did not accept the call. But now did not Paul speak on the one hand quite generally of men who "are lost" (I Cor. 1:18; 15:18; II Cor. 2:15; 4:3; II Thess. 2:10; Phil. 1:28), and of the divine wrath on the day of judgment against those who obey unrighteousness (Rom. 2:8; cf. 2:5; I Thess. 1:10), and on the other hand of God's mercy upon all men: "As in Adam all die, even so in Christ shall all be made alive" (I Cor. 15:22); "hardening has come upon Israel in part, until the full number of the Gentiles has come in, and so all Israel will be saved" (Rom. 11:25-26); "God has shut up all men under disobedience, in order to have mercy upon all" (Rom. 11:32)? The first half of this question clearly is to be answered thus: Paul indeed reckons with the fact that there are men who are condemned by God and lost, and he warns even the Christians not to take God's wrath and condemnation lightly (Rom. 2:5; 11:22). But Paul did not say that God has destined these men for condemnation, any more than he anywhere expressed himself more precisely about the fate of those condemned. Important to him is only that God will condemn those who refuse or do not take seriously his offer of deliverance in Jesus Christ. The second half of the question, on the other hand, is very difficult to answer and therefore has always been disputed. It is true that one can say with great confidence that in I Cor. 15:22 Paul does not intend to say that "in Christ" all men will be resurrected, but that in this verse in fact he rather has in mind only the resurrection of Christians. However, Rom. 11:25-26, 32 undoubtedly says, according to its wording, that God ultimately will include all men, Jews as well as Gentiles, in his saving mercy. Thus it has repeatedly been inferred from these texts that Paul held the doctrine of the "restoration of all men." But if one observes the total context of Rom. 9–11, to which these verses belong, one will hardly be able to deny that Paul could scarcely have had in view God's having mercy on all men without exception without contradicting Rom. 9:32 and 11:22. This holds true all the more when one takes into account also the just-named texts from Paul which speak of being lost and of God's wrath. Hence one may not say that in Rom. 11:25-26, 32 Paul taught that in the end God will have mercy on all men without exception. To be sure, in Rom. 11:33 Paul adds his praise of the unsearchable ways of God, whose mind no one has known, and thus one also will be unable to assert that Paul could not venture to cherish such a hope in God's all-encompassing grace. This exegetical uncertainty shows only this much: if we meant to attempt to create for ourselves by means of exegetical observation or even by means of inferences from exegetical observation an insight into God's plans, we should undoubtedly be overstepping the bounds of what is possible for us men to know and also of what Paul intended to teach us. It is not without reason that he concludes chaps. 9-11 of Romans, toward the end of which stand the vss. 11:25-26, 32, which we have just discussed, with the cry: "For from him [i.e., God] and through him and to him are all things; to him be glory forever! Amen" (Rom. 11:36). Paul's preaching of salvation ends with this worshipful note of praise and not with a rationally sensible answer.

7. *Paul and Jesus*

At the beginning of our century the question of "Paul and Jesus" most strongly concerned theological discussion, and *W. Wrede's* thesis of Paul as the "second founder of Christianity" who first "made Christianity into a religion of redemption" (1904) only expresses in intensified form the basic outlook which at that time was dominant, particularly among the liberal theologians, namely that the theologian Paul had corrupted the simple religion of Jesus. The opposition to this historical overestimation and theological depreciation of Paul, which arose immediately at that time, was easily able to show that in this evaluation of Paul the crucial role of the primitive community in the emergence of the belief in

Christ had been underrated, but above all one could point to the fact, which *A. Schweitzer* in particular singled out, that through their both being dominated by the anticipation of the imminent final salvation, Jesus and Paul belong significantly closer together than the liberal theologians had seen. Of course this does not yet explain why in spite of this commonality the epistles of Paul make such a different impression on the reader of the Bible and have a significantly more alien effect than the preaching of Jesus in the first three gospels. This question, which at that time remained open, has drawn new attention since the First World War by means of the form-critical investigation of the gospels and the higher estimation of Pauline theology in the newly revived biblical studies. Yet it is only since the Second World War that the question has had the attention which it undoubtedly deserves. Contributing to this, for one thing, is the fact that Jewish scholars like *M. Buber,* using the historical-critical method, now applied themselves not only to Jesus but also to Paul, and, in so doing, consistently represented Jesus in the framework of Judaism with evident sympathy; but set Paul off from Jesus as one who had forsaken Judaism, and more or less clearly rejected him. On the other side, a contribution was made to the serious consideration of the problem by the fact that Paul was accused anew of having placed himself between Jesus and Christianity and had rejudaized Christianity (E. Stauffer), but above all by the fact that the lively discussion over the propriety and the possibility of the question of the historical Jesus in the last decade and a half (see above, pp. 22 ff.) rendered unavoidable the questions of the historical and substantive relationship of Paul's theology to the person and preaching of the earthly Jesus. A clear answer to these questions is in fact of fundamental importance, because the significance of Paul's theology indeed lies in the fact that Paul was the first Christian theologian out of whose utterances the theologically reflected-upon message of earliest Christianity addresses us with the call to faith. The Christian who believes this testimony or who would like to clarify his faith by listening to Paul's theological reflection is vitally interested in whether there is or is not an agreement between this Pauline message of Jesus Christ and the historical Jesus to whom this message refers (see above, p. 25) .

a. THE HISTORICAL CONNECTION

It is appropriate, in answering this question, to begin with the problem of the historical connection between the theology of Paul and the tradition of Jesus' activity and preaching. We have already indicated that Paul mentions hardly anything from the life of Jesus and cites only isolated sayings of "the Lord" (see above, pp. 165-66), In spite of this, we can recognize that the man Jesus is of crucial importance for Paul's preaching of salvation and that the words of Jesus, where they can be cited, form the final authority for Paul. Nevertheless it remains strange that references to Jesus' activity and preaching play so slight a role in the epistles of Paul. But this state of affairs can be explained neither by saying that in Paul's time the gospel tradition was as yet hardly known anywhere in Christendom nor by suggesting that a lack of interest in the Jesus tradition or a reluctance to profane it on Paul's part caused him so rarely to refer to this tradition. All such attempts at an explanation of the curious state of affairs overlook the fact that Paul's epistles do not afford us a complete picture of his missionary preaching, because they are addressed exclusively to Christians and only go into the questions which were in dispute or which in Paul's opinion required special emphasis. Moreover, Paul's reserve, strange to us, in referring to events of Jesus' life and words does not alter the fact that Paul uses the name of the man Jesus in precisely the same way for the earthly Jesus as for the resurrected One: it is God "who raised Jesus from the dead" (Rom. 8:11) and "Christ has risen from the dead" (Rom. 6:9) ; Paul has not "preached another Jesus" (II Cor. 11:4), and "we preach Christ crucified" (I Cor. 1:23). Hence when Paul speaks of "God's Son, Christ Jesus, who was preached among you by us" (II Cor. 1:19), he means by this the man Jesus, who for him is identical with the risen Lord. Thus there can be no doubt that Paul was convinced that his message referred to the historical Jesus and included Jesus' work and message. But was Paul correct in this conviction? What was the substantive relationship of Paul's message to the work and message of Jesus?

b. THE SUBSTANTIVE RELATIONSHIP

The different historical and salvation-historical situation

It is obvious that the preaching of Jesus and the theology of Paul significantly differ in form, and this is readily explained by a twofold historical state of affairs.

Paul was a rabbinically trained theologian, while Jesus, in spite of his knowledge of rabbinical arguments, did not have any rabbinical schooling, as the gospels know specifically (Mark 6:2; John 7:15). Paul knows both Palestinian and Hellenistic Judaism and to a limited extent also Hellenistic paganism (see above, p. 140), and he draws his language and his arguments from all these spheres, while Jesus knows only the Judaism of Palestine and its language and thought world. Yet these formal differences, striking as they are, are not so profound that they could have been the essential cause for the substantive differences between Paul and Jesus.

But in a very important respect the proclamation of Paul is necessarily distinguished from the preaching of Jesus, namely because according to their basic understanding Jesus and Paul found themselves in different situations in the history of salvation. We have seen that Jesus and Paul in the same way anticipated the consummation of salvation in the near future and that both were convinced that the hoped-for final salvation had already dawned in their time. If this combination, completely new as compared with Judaism, of the actual presence of final salvation and an assured hope of the imminent appearing of the consummation of salvation, signifies a very important commonality between Jesus and Paul, still with a more exact understanding of this present an equally important difference between the two is disclosed. Jesus had seen the kingdom of God exclusively as having dawned in his words and deeds, in his person and its effect upon men. But the first Christian community had experienced that through the resurrection of Jesus from the dead and his exaltation to the presence of God, the anticipated bearer of salvation, who as man had worked upon earth and had died a criminal's death, had already been installed in his heavenly kingdom, and therefore they believed that the final salvation had already dawned in Christ's rule from heaven. The Christian community likewise had the experience that the risen and exalted Lord, by sending the eschatological Spirit of God, had already created the people of God of the end-time, whose outward signs were baptism and the Lord's Supper. Now when Paul became a Christian, through the vision of the risen Christ, and joined the Christian community, he found this developed faith already present, and therefore he could not do otherwise than to recognize the presence of the end-time in the resurrection of Jesus and the founding of the Christian community as well as in the life of the earthly Jesus, and to appropriate baptism and the Lord's Supper as the decisive forms of expression of this self-understanding of the primitive church. Even if, as can only be made probable (see above, pp. 85 ff.) , Jesus affirmed his imminent death as a transition to the presence of God, for him death and resurrection lay in the future, and Jesus did not speak at all of the founding of the church through the resurrection of Jesus and the gift of the eschatological Spirit. But for Paul all this was actuality, and because Paul thus stood in a new reality of God's salvation-history, he was obliged to think from the perspective of this salvation-historical situation. And unless one wishes to contest the rightfulness of the faith of the primitive community and of Paul in God's new saving acts in the cross, in Jesus' resurrection, and in the founding of the church, one must concede that Paul was bound to interpret the present reality of his being a Christian from the perspective of this salvation-historical situation, which is different from that of Jesus. In their basic understanding of God's eschatological saving acts, therefore, Jesus and Paul are in agreement, if one adequately takes into consideration the changed situation of Paul in the course of salvation-history.

The understanding of salvation in detail

But now against this background arises the crucial question whether in the more detailed statement of this understanding of salvation, Paul does not follow paths which bring him into a genuine substantive conflict with Jesus.

The idea of God

This is not true with respect to the idea of God. Jesus and Paul proclaimed God's gracious, unconditional forgiveness toward the sinner and conceived of the deliverance from divine condemnation as not dependent on human achievement. But in addition, Jesus and Paul spoke of God's judgment, of reward, and of God's wrath, and reckoned on man's being judged by God according to his deeds. In both cases this apparent contradiction is explained by the fact that the subject is the actions of the man to whom God's forgiveness *has* come and who acts by the power of the love of God which he has experienced, who therefore is not responsible for his own achievement, but for the working of God in him.

The law

The same may be said concerning the law. Jesus acknowledged the Jewish law in its traditional exposition as the expression of God's will, but at the same time declared the era of the law to have ended and made the claim that he was proclaiming an exposition of the law which actually corresponded to God's intention in the law. Paul likewise affirmed the law as God's demand even for Christians, but declared the time of the law as a way of salvation to have ended and affirmed that only the Christians, who possess the Spirit, can actually understand the law in its divine meaning. In one respect, however, Paul goes beyond Jesus, when he describes it as the task of the law to lead man deeper into sin, and sees God's will being worked out in this function of the law (see above, p. 183). This connection between law and sin asserted by Paul certainly is foreign to Jesus in its explicitness; but Jesus' critique about the agreement of certain commandments of the law with God's intention (Mark 10:5-6 par.; 7:10 ff. par.; Matt 5:33 ff.) does also lead to the conclusion that the strict fulfillment of such commandments becomes a transgression of the actual will of God. Jesus also declared that boasting of the correct fulfillment of the law makes man deaf for the actual hearing of God's commandment (Mark 10:17 ff. par.). Thus Paul only drew the consequence from the understanding, which he held in common with Jesus, of the significance of the law for the relationship of man to God, without thereby bringing to light any basic difference between Paul's view and that of Jesus.

The preaching of salvation

The state of affairs is more complicated with respect to the preaching of salvation. Jesus promised and brought God's forgiveness to the repentant sinner and therein saw the realization of God's promise of salvation in the end-time already in the present. Thus he by no means simply renewed the Old Testament-Jewish certainty that God is ready to forgive the sinner when he repents, but his message of forgiveness was a specific promise in word and deed, which became a reality only for the man who acknowledged the authority and the divine right of this preacher and opened himself to his claim. Of course Paul did not see God's forgiveness as grounded in Jesus' call to repentance, nor in Jesus' fellowship with tax-gatherers and sinners, but in Jesus' death and resurrection: God's righteousness is to be reckoned to those "who believe on him [God] who raised from the dead our Lord Jesus, who was delivered up for our transgressions and was raised for our justification" (Rom. 4:24-25). This tying of God's forgiveness to the event of Jesus' death and resurrection is unknown to Jesus. But we must also note that in this Paul is following the primitive community— even in Rom. 4:24-25 a tradition of the primitive church presumably has been assimilated—and on this point it can be seen that here too the altered situation with respect to the salvation-history is operative: for the primitive church God's eschatological saving purpose can be seen most clearly in the event of Christ's cross and resurrection; but since for Paul the crucified and resurrected Jesus is identical with the man Jesus who "pleased not himself but, as it is written, 'The reproaches of those who reproached you fell on me' " (Rom. 15:3), in the changed situation of the primitive church Paul says the same thing as does Jesus, namely that "when the fullness of time had come, God sent his Son, born of a woman, placed under the law, that he might redeem those under the law, that we might receive the adoption as sons of God" (Gal. 4:4).

But now Paul indeed not only recognized God's eschatological saving activity in Jesus above all as manifest in the cross and in Jesus' resurrection, but he speaks of Jesus' death as a means of expiation for the forgiveness of sins and of Christ as the sacrificed Passover lamb (Rom. 3:25; 5:8-9; I Cor. 5:7). But according to all that we can see (above, pp. 89-90), Jesus indeed took upon himself his death as the consummation of his mission as the heavenly "Man" and perhaps even expected that his death would bring in God's eschatological covenant; but it cannot be inferred from the earliest Jesus tradition as Jesus' own opinion that his death was to have a special connection with God's forgiveness of sins. On the other hand, this undoubtedly is Paul's opinion: by means of Jesus' death God has cleansed mankind of the guilt of sin and precisely therein has caused his loving righteousness to become reality. Thus according to Paul's understanding God has wrought his forgiveness by the fact that "Christ died for us" (Rom. 5:8), and it also is not to be doubted that here, in his employment of a formula of the primitive church, Paul is accepting the ancient conception that sacrificed blood cleanses of the guilt of sin (Rom. 3:25; cf. Heb. 9:22!). But Paul does not say that God could remove mankind's sinful guilt only by this shedding of blood, nor does he give any explanation of how Jesus' death could cause this saving intention of God to become a reality. Paul only proclaims that God has chosen this way and that through his death on the cross "Christ has redeemed us from the curse of the law, by becoming a curse for us" (Gal. 3:13).

But now there are two further points to be noted. This event of Christ's death for us for the expiation and forgiveness of the sins of mankind is a reality only for the believer (Rom. 3:25a; II Cor. 5:19-20); one must have believed and maintained that "Christ died for our sins in accordance with the Scripture" if one is to be saved thereby (I Cor. 15:2-3). Thus Paul is not proclaiming a generally evident truth, but testifies to his faith that "in Christ God reconciled the world to himself," that is, with concepts taken over from Jewish religion this interpretation of Jesus' death expresses for the believer and only for him the conviction that in Jesus

Christ, who died on the cross and was raised, God has wrought his eschatological salvation. This interpretation of Jesus' death adopts the ancient idea that blood shed vicariously can wash away guilt, a conception which sounds strange to us and which we can comprehend only with difficulty. It is easy to see, however, that this conception was by no means indispensable for Paul; it appears in his writings only now and then, and Paul can also express the same idea without making use of this conception: God "spared not his own Son, but delivered him up for us all" (Rom. 8:32) ; "Insofar as I now live in the flesh, I live in faith in the Son of God who loved me and gave himself for me" (Gal. 2:20). That is to say, the idea of Christ's atoning death, which undoubtedly appears in Paul, is *one* form of expression of his faith that God has done the utmost to save men from perdition. Hence the belief in God's saving act in the death of Christ is not at all obliged to subscribe to this form of expression or else cease to be actual belief in this saving act of God in the death of Jesus. But in any case there is no basic difference between Jesus and Paul on this point in the understanding of the divine saving action, if one properly takes into account the changed situation for Paul.

Christology

A certain difference does exist between Jesus and Paul, however, in Christology. It is true that we can form only a very tentative judgment about Jesus' personal claims, but a cautious testing of the tradition has yielded the great probability that Jesus regarded himself as destined to be the heavenly Son of Man and was convinced that this future dignity was already, in his earthly present, being shown in hidden fashion, so that one can recognize it if one has eyes to see and does not stumble at Jesus. Other titles expressing eminence cannot be verified on the lips of Jesus, but on the other hand it is plain to see that Jesus claimed to be acting and judging with divine authority. But Paul saw in Jesus Christ the Son of God, through whom all things were created and who was in the form of God when he humbled himself to become man; Paul addressed the One whom God had raised from the dead as the exalted "Lord," called him the "image of God," and awaited his appearing from heaven as the "last man" in order to make our lowly body like his glorious body. We have seen that in this connection Paul appropriated various Jewish and pagan mythical conceptual forms, in order with their help to give expression to the conviction that God himself achieves his eschatological salvation in Jesus Christ.

That is to say, in their ultimate intention these mythical conceptual forms adopted by Paul express the same belief, that God has wrought eschatological salvation in Jesus, as did Jesus' claim that God's eschatological kingdom became reality in Jesus' teaching and working. But above all we must remember here that in fact Paul, in agreement with the Christian community, sees the person of Jesus from the perspective of belief in God's raising and exaltation of the crucified One, and therefore his christological concepts and views were bound to be different from those of Jesus, even if there were not the additional consideration that Paul had to proclaim the message of God's eschatological saving action in Jesus Christ to pagan and not to Palestinian Jewish hearers in their conceptual forms. Hence in spite of the great formal differences, there is no essential substantive difference between the personal claim of Jesus and Paul's proclamation of Christ.

Baptism and the Lord's Supper

While Pauline Christology in spite of all the differences stands in clear substantive connection with the personal claim of Jesus, yet the Pauline doctrine of baptism and the Lord's Supper has no direct connection in Jesus' activity. For Jesus did not baptize at all and furthermore gave no directions for baptism; and Jesus' charge to the disciples to continue to observe the common meal until the coming of the kingdom of God and thereby to maintain the fellowship with him and with the new covenant through his blood has hardly any connection with the Lord's Supper as Paul understands it. Of course Paul took over these two community customs from the Hellenistic Christian community, and the conceptions of baptism as dying with Christ and of the Lord's Supper as participation in the body of Christ presumably were also already Hellenistic-Christian. These interpretations of baptism and the Lord's Supper, however, have no direct connection with Jesus. But what, in Paul's mind, is the actual significance of the two customs of the community? We have seen that Paul does not understand baptism and the Lord's Supper in the sense of actions that have their effect in an elemental way; instead, in his opinion in these practices are accomplished the incorporation and the renewed participation of the Christian with reference to the divine salvation wrought through Jesus' life, death, and resurrection. Thus baptism and the Lord's Supper bring the believer personally and concretely into connection with the salvation event initiated by Jesus. Paul certainly expresses this understanding of the two practices of the community in a way that is subject to misunderstanding and therefore was misunderstood already quite early; yet a precise interpretation in the context of the whole of Pauline theology clearly shows that for Paul, baptism and the Lord's Supper allow one to gain a share in God's historical saving action as do faith and justification. Therefore the Pauline interpretation of these practices does not stand in opposition to Jesus' preaching of salvation.

The church

In the Pauline doctrine of the church also there is no direct connection with Jesus. This is true not only in the sense already mentioned, that Jesus did not speak of a church, but Paul found the church already at hand (see above, p. 248); it is true above all for the Pauline understanding of the church as the "body of Christ" and of Christ as "head" of the body. Here not only does the personal character of Christ appear to be replaced by the conception of Christ the "universal man," but here also membership in the body of Christ appears not to stand in any clear connection with the historical figure of Jesus or with the anticipated consummation of salvation through the appearing of the resurrected Christ in glory. It cannot be disputed that the conception of the body of Christ affords occasion for such a nonhistorical interpretation. We have seen, however (above, pp. 215 ff.), that, according to Paul, incorporation into the body of Christ through baptism effects participation in God's eschatological saving work that is begun in Christ; and belonging to the one man, the last man Christ, enables the Christians to be heirs of the promise of salvation (Gal. 3:28b, 29; I Cor. 15:48-49). The conception of the Christian's belonging to the church as the body of Christ therefore also in Paul's mind describes the participation in the final salvation which began with the resurrection of Jesus Christ and waits for the appearing of Christ in glory. Hence on this point also there exists no actual conflict between the preaching of Jesus and the theology of Paul.

The world and men

Undeniably Paul sees the world and men as farther removed from God than does Jesus. It is true that Jesus too assumes that men are sinners and need forgiveness, and he knows of the rule of the demons and their threat to men (Matt. 6:12 par.; 12:43-45 par.). But what Paul says of Satan as the "god of this eon," of the universality of sin in mankind, and of the inescapable helplessness of fleshly man (II Cor. 4:4; Rom. 3:19, 23; 7:24) has no parallel in Jesus' words. This difference is without doubt explained primarily by the fact that upon his becoming a Christian Paul experienced a break which taught him to regard his pious Jewish past as "refuse," and that from that time on, Paul sees the possibility of standing in the presence of God exclusively in one's turning to God's saving work in Christ. Along with this, we may also think that Paul is more strongly influenced by the image of man held by apocalyptic Judaism than is Jesus, although this must remain mere conjecture. Thus if at this point an important difference between Paul and Jesus cannot be disputed, still this affects only the *presuppositions* of the message of salvation, and therefore only the periphery, not the core, of the message of Jesus and of Paul.

C. THE LORD AND THE MESSENGER

On *one* point, however, there exists an evident difference between Jesus and Paul which runs deep and does not allow any leveling-up: Jesus is not only the preacher but also the bearer of the kingdom of God through whom God is already causing his eschatological salvation to be actualized and through whom God intends to complete his salvation. Paul, however, is only the messenger and the slave of this his Lord; he only announces the eschatological salvation and is under obligation to obey the Lord who is proclaimed (Gal. 1:1; I Cor. 1:17; Rom. 1:1; II Cor. 4:5). This basic distinction, together with Paul's changed situation with respect to the salvation-history, brings with it the fact that with Paul Christology, instead of the kingdom of God, stands at the center, and with it at the same time the salvation wrought by the Lord in his community and the hope of the consummation of salvation at the Lord's appearing in glory. Therein, however, God's final salvation which was begun in Jesus' preaching and works is demonstrated to be the foundation of Pauline theology, and, as one cannot play off Jesus against Paul, because the two proclaim the same salvation from God in different situations, so also one cannot make a choice between Jesus and Paul: "To anyone to whom Paul is offensive and sinister, Jesus must be equally offensive and sinister" (R. Bultmann). Jesus and Paul are witnesses to the same historical truth, but Paul only points backward and forward to the salvation brought by Jesus and expected from Jesus. We shall have to come back to this context when at the end of this volume we ask about the unity of the message of Jesus, of Paul, and of John. But first we must turn our attention to the theology of the Johannine writings.

CHAPTER IV

THE JOHANNINE MESSAGE OF CHRIST
IN THE FOURTH GOSPEL AND IN THE EPISTLES

1. *The historical position of Johannine theology*

a. THE LITERARY PROBLEM

The New Testament contains five writings which since the end
of the second century have been identified by the church's tradition
as works of the same author, namely the apostle John, the son of
Zebedee: the fourth gospel, three epistles, and the book of Revelation. Only Revelation identifies itself as the work of a certain
John, the slave of Jesus Christ (Rev. 1:1, 4), while the other four
writings give no indication of any sort of their author which could
make possible an unequivocal identification. It is one of the most
certain results of New Testament scholarship, however, that Revelation cannot come from the same author as the four other writings
handed down under the name of John (cf. the introductions to
the New Testament). If Revelation must therefore be left completely out of consideration when we consider the Johannine theology, still the question whether the fourth gospel and the three Johannine epistles come from the same author continues to be disputed to the present day. The assumption held by many students
that these four writings come from the same author is not based
simply on a maintenance of the church's tradition, but on the
observation that the language and the thought world of these four
writings are in agreement to an extraordinary degree. When in
spite of this, numerous other students are of the conviction that the
author of I John—and then also of the other two epistles—cannot
be the same as the author of the fourth gospel, the reasons cited
for this, in addition to certain linguistic differences, are primarily
two facts: that in a number of theological conceptions I John
diverges from the fourth gospel, and that the polemic of the two
writings is aimed at different adversaries. Of course the different
polemical front is no convincing argument against the same author

for both writings, since indeed the situation could have changed in the period between the composition of the two writings; the divergences in individual linguistic phenomena and theological conceptions, however, can be explained at least in part by the different literary form and the respective aims of the two writings. Thus there is quite a lot to argue that the fourth gospel and I John have the same author. But even if this should not be the case—the question cannot be answered in a compelling way—still in any case the author of I John belongs to the evangelist's closest circle of associates or is directly dependent on this circle, and hence it is entirely appropriate in the presentation of the Johannine theology to cite I John and in so doing to mention occasional divergences. Whether II and III John come from the same author as I John is likewise an open question; here, too, there is a great deal to argue that the same author is speaking here, yet it is not essential to decide this question in the context of a presentation of Johannine theology, since the shorter epistles make hardly any theological utterances. In any case, it follows from what has been stated that only the fourth gospel is normative for the answer to the question as to the historical position of Johannine theology.

But a glance at the fourth gospel immediately shows the real theological difficulty. The fourth gospel indeed tells in a way similar to that of the Synoptics of Jesus' works and preaching, beginning with the appearance of John the Baptist and ending with the death and resurrection of Jesus. And because the Gospel of John and the Synoptics thus resembled each other in that they gave testimony to Jesus Christ in the form of an account of Jesus' deeds and words, until well into the nineteenth century it was regarded as self-evident that the fourth gospel, as well as the first three, intended to present the historical picture of Jesus, and the attempt has often been made, and is still repeatedly made today, to show that important features of the historical Jesus are more reliably handed down in the Gospel of John than in the three synoptic gospels. To be sure this assumption has become questionable since D. F. Strauss in his *Leben Jesu* ("Life of Jesus," 1835/36) proved that the Gospel of John cannot serve together with the Synoptics as a source for knowledge of the historical Jesus, because it is constructed from the perspective of a faith image of Jesus which can be understood only as the end product of the development of the New Testament doctrine of Christ. Since Strauss called attention to this state of affairs, it can no longer be disputed that the Gospel of John in no case can be employed in the same measure as the

Synoptics as a source for knowledge of the historical Jesus. This statement holds true although we know today that even the synoptic gospels are not historical accounts, but missionary and preaching documents; for in the synoptic gospels, oral tradition is incorporated in more or less considerable framing and even reshaping, and in any case this tradition in part goes back to the earliest period of the Christian community and can be detached in considerable measure from the narrative framework (see above, p..25). But in spite of the same literary form of a "gospel" the Johannine account displays an entirely different literary character and is also distinguished from the synoptic gospels in theological content, and we must therefore first explain the historical situation before we can recognize its theological character.

The Gospel of John displays a not inconsiderable number of *contradictions* in the geographical, chronological, and narrative sequence, and even the continuity of thought is frequently contradictory. Hence since the early church the conjecture has been expressed in the most diverse fashion that the text of the Gospel of John that has come down to us has become confused through intentional or accidental rearrangements, or that it was never finally arranged by its author at all, and accordingly numerous attempts have been undertaken to restore the original order. Of course all these attempts are not very convincing; yet the problem of the original order of the account is of no essential significance for the understanding of Johannine theology, so we do not need to go into this problem further here. More important is the question whether the substantive contradictions to be observed in the Gospel of John may be explained by the theory that an ecclesiastical editor or or even a reviser of the original text has inserted alien material, because these secondary component parts of the traditional text then indeed would have to be regarded as alien elements in the original gospel and accordingly in I John. Now the twenty-first chapter of the gospel is in all probability to be regarded as an appendix by another hand, which to be sure must already have been added in the second century, because the earliest manuscript tradition already displays this chapter (cf. the commentaries on John 21). The story in John 7:53–8:11 of the adulteress is, on the basis of the manuscript tradition, certainly to be regarded as a secondary insertion. Thus though the text of the Gospel of John was undoubtedly very early expanded, still it is hardly necessary to postulate other insertions in the gospel; yet as a rule this question can be decided only on the basis of criteria related to contents, and we must return to it from time to time in the appropriate context.

Thus if one can with good reason assume that, apart from 7:53–8:11 and chap. 21, the Gospel of John is preserved in essence as its author left it, still the question is posed all the more insistently: On the basis of *which traditions or sources* and with what intellectual tools did the author write his gospel? Arguing against the numerous theories that are propounded, that the author appropriated one or several written sources, is not only the fact that the uniformity in language of the entire gospel hardly allows one to ascertain any sources. But above all, arguing against these theories is the fact that actually convincing arguments for the connected literary character of the traditions employed by the evangelist have not been brought forward. But it is incontestable that the Gospel of John concurs with the synoptic gospels in a relatively small number of accounts and sayings of Jesus; yet the opinions as to how this fact is to be explained are widely divergent. For the state of affairs is also surprisingly contradictory: the geographical and chronological framework of Jesus' activity in the Gospel of John diverges sharply from the indications in the Synoptics; while the Synoptics are composed of individual reports and individual sayings or groups of sayings and only the passion narrative affords a continuous account, the Gospel of John consists of long composite, in part dialogical discourses placed one after another, and here too only the passion narrative offers a continuous account. In these composite discourses, however, Jesus speaks a language considerably different from that in the Synoptics, and the few narratives which John has in common with the Synoptics apart from the passion narrative, such as the healing in Capernaum (4:46 ff.) and the feeding of the five thousand with the related walking on the sea (6:1 ff.), are also formulated otherwise than in the Synoptics. On the other hand, John occasionally alludes to accounts of the Synoptics which he himself has not related (for example, Jesus' baptism in 1:32; the circle of the twelve in 6:67; the Gethsemane story in 12:27), and in his composition he scatters sayings of Jesus which strongly resemble sayings of Jesus in the Synoptics (cf. John 2:19 with Mark 14:58 par., and John 4:44 with Mark 6:4 par.). In some passages there occur peculiar verbatim and substantive connections between John and the Synoptics (cf. John 6:7 with Mark 6:37; John 12:3 ff. with Luke 7:36 ff.). While some scholars conclude from these agreements that John must have been familiar at least with the Gospels of Mark and Luke, others wish to explain these connections by suggesting that John had an independent knowledge of the tradition which was accessible to the Synoptic authors also. The attempt is repeatedly made to discover in the Gospel of John isolated sayings of the historical Jesus which belong to the earliest tradition but remained unknown to the Synoptic authors or at any rate were passed over by them. Now to be sure, if linguistic similarities, above all, suggest that John knew the Gospels of Mark and Luke, still there is no compelling proof of such knowledge; and if, as is likely, John knew these synoptic gospels, in any case he was extremely free in his use of them. But this corresponds to the free fashion with which John employed the Old Testament quotations which he appropriated, and even from this use it becomes clear that it obviously was not the intention of the author of the Gospel of John to reproduce as carefully as possible the tradition which he had at hand or the sources which he used. Instead, John unquestionably recoined the material which he appropriated into his language. Therefore for a proper historical understanding of Johannine theology two questions must be clarified: What is the source of the language and the conceptual world which John employs, and what is his aim in his reproduction or reshaping of the tradition in this language and conceptual world?

b. THE CIRCUMSTANCES OF COMPOSITION

Yet for the historical classification of Johannine theology, it is also important to consider the question, in what time and by whom the gospel and, probably, the first epistle of John were written. We have already seen that since the end of the second century, the Gospel of John, together with the three Johannine epistles and the book of Revelation, has been regarded as the work of the apostle John, the son of Zebedee. While the author of Revelation in fact is called John, it is impossible for us to discern from the other four writings attributed to the apostle John the name of their author, since they give no name at all. Now it is true that John 21:24, in connection with 21:20, gives the indication that "the disciple whom Jesus loved" is the author of the gospel. But if the twenty-first chapter is an appendix to the gospel by another hand, then in the indication in John 21:24 we are dealing only with a tradition from the circle of the evangelist's pupils and not with the claim of the evangelist himself. Besides, it is not possible to ascertain the identity of the man whom we meet in John 13:23; 19:26; and 20:2 under the designation of "the disciple whom Jesus loved," so that even the identification of the author with the "favorite disciple," if it should be a matter of a reliable report, would not help us. But the Gospel of John does not contain any other indications of its author. Should II and III John come from the same author as the gospel, which is after all possible, we could infer from the openings of these epistles that the author can identify himself as "the elder" [presbyter] and therewith apparently at once establish his identity. But even this indication does not help us, because it is true that bishop Papias of Hierapolis (around 140) mentions a "John the elder," but neither do we know anything else about this man nor is it at all certain that the self-designation, "the elder," in the shorter epistles of John is meant to denote this "John the elder." Thus the tradition which we encounter at the end of the second century, that the author of the Johannine writings was the apostle John, the son of Zebedee, cannot be confirmed from the gospel and the epistles, and for two reasons this tradition is unusable. First, this tradition cannot be traced further back; earlier is only the report that church fathers in the middle of the second century were connected with a "disciple of the Lord" named John. But neither do we know anything else about this "disciple of the Lord" John, nor is there a clear tradition that he was the author of the four Johannine writings or even of one of them. Second, the Gospel of John cannot have been written by one of Jesus' closest disciples at all, as is shown by the religious conceptual world of the gospel as well as by the church's resistance to the inclusion of this writing among the recognized works for reading in public. Finally, the dependence of the Gospel of John upon the Gospel of Mark also argues against Jesus' closest disciple as the author of the fourth gospel, because even according to the church's tradition the Gospel of Mark did not come from a personal disciple of Jesus. Hence we must resign ourselves to the fact that we do not know the author of the fourth gospel and the epistles of John, if they come from the same author, and the designation of the author of this gospel as "John" and of the writings as "the Gospel of John" and "the Epistles of John" is used in the following only as traditional identification, with no intention of rendering a historical judgment thereby.

Since the historical value and the theological character of the Gospel of John are determined by the material and its presentation and not by the author, the question of the identity of this author is not so important even for the historical understanding of his theology as is the question of the *dating* of this writing. Today we can say with certainty that the Gospel of John must have been in existence at the beginning of the second century, because according to the judgment of experts, a small papyrus fragment with some verses from John 18 stems from the early second century, and accordingly the gospel must already have been known in Egypt at this time (a fragment of an apocryphal gospel, from the same time, confirms this conclusion). Therefore while the Gospel of John must have been written before the beginning of the second century, it is considerably more difficult to say how long before this date it was written. If the assumption is correct, as it most probably is, that the author of the fourth gospel knew the Gospel of Luke, then the Gospel of John cannot have been written before about A.D. 80-90. If this assumption is not correct, still even the development of the gospel tradition that is to be discerned in the Gospel of John hardly allows us to place the composition of this gospel at an earlier date. Hence there is widespread agreement today that the Gospel of John must have been written approximately in the last decade of the first century. If I John should have the same author as the gospel, it was written at about the same time, perhaps somewhat later, and this assumption presumably holds true even if we should not be dealing with the same author for the two works. Thus in any case, Johannine theology is a late form of the primitive Christian witness to Christ, and hence it is important to get a clear idea of the historical and substantive relation of this theology to the preaching of Jesus according to the synoptic tradition and to the theology of Paul. The Gospel of John and the first epistle of John betray nothing at all directly about the *geographical area* from which the two writings come. From the end of the second century on, the church's tradition has named Asia Minor as the home of both writings, but there likewise is nothing to argue for this. On the other hand, as we shall see, the intellectual world of the Gospel of John exhibits a kinship with religious phenomena of the Palestinian-Syrian area, and thus there is something to argue that the Gospel of John was written in Syria (and the same would hold true for the epistles). Yet in our context the settling of this question is of little significance.

2. The essential character of the Johannine message of Christ

a. THE GOSPEL OF JOHN AS THE PERFECT WITNESS TO CHRIST

While the account of Jesus in each of the first three gospels was developed by arranging the individual traditions in the context of a particular theological orientation, John used the traditions available to him to construct longer compositions in the context of which there are extensive discourses of Jesus, and to a large extent the narratives serve only as introductions to such composite discourses. Even from this it follows that the Gospel of John can in no way be primarily interested in the narrative, but must pursue didactic aims or aims of proclamation. This goal then also clearly follows from the conclusion of the gospel. "Jesus did many other signs in the presence of the disciples which are not written in this book. But these [signs] have been written that you may believe that Jesus is the Christ, the Son of God, and believing may have life in his name" (20:30-31). Thus it is not John's intention to offer a complete report, but to strengthen belief in Jesus' sonship to God and thereby to mediate [eternal] life. This aim of proclamation, however, is carried out not by means of sermon or teaching, but in the setting of a "gospel," and this is the thing that is remarkable. For indeed John undoubtedly found the literary form of the "gospel" already at hand, and he quite clearly takes for granted for his readers that they are acquainted with certain reports of the Synoptics or at least with the synoptic tradition, to which therefore he only alludes, as for example the baptism of Jesus (1:32-33), the arrest of John the Baptist (3:24), the existence of the circle of the twelve (6:67), and so forth. But why did John give to his proclamation the form of a "gospel"? As early as the end of the second century, Clement of Alexandria asserts that John intended to supplement and at the same time surpass the Synoptics: John produced a "spiritual gospel," while the Synoptics had set forth the "corporeal things." The assumption that John intended to supplement or correct the Synoptics then has been repeatedly held. However, it is extremely unlikely, because John nowhere indicates that he intends to add anything new to what was already known, and because on the contrary he plainly declares that he does not aim at completeness (20:30). Thus indeed also a large part of the synoptic material is lacking in John, and occasionally one cannot escape the impression that an account has been deliberately omitted, as for example the institution of the Lord's Supper or Jesus' agonizing in prayer in Gethsemane; it is evident that John is acquainted with both stories (cf. 12:27-29 and 13:1 ff.; 6:51b ff.). Thus John's intention is neither to supplement the Synoptics nor to supplant them; but his gospel is meant to sketch the picture of Jesus which will strengthen faith and thereby produce "life." That is to say, presupposing acquaintance with the synoptic tradition, John intends to draw the complete picture of Jesus as faith sees him, and *to this extent* his presentation makes the claim to offer the perfect testimony to Christ.

b. THE LANGUAGE OF THE JOHANNINE WITNESS TO CHRIST

Now the most striking feature of this perfect witness to Christ is the form of expression which John has given to this witness. By this we mean not only the language which Jesus himself uses in the Gospel of John, but the language of the entire gospel. It is in fact an often observed peculiarity of this gospel that the language of the Johannine discourses of Jesus is likewise the language of John the Baptist, of the Jews, and of all other persons who speak in the gospel, but also that of the evangelist himself: cf. 1:7, "He came as a witness, to bear witness to the light, that all might believe through him" (= the evangelist); 1:34, "And I have seen and have testified that this one is God's chosen one" (= John the Baptist); 8:13, "You bear witness to yourself, your witness is not true" (= the Pharisees); 5:31-32, "If I bear witness concerning myself, my witness is not true; it is another who bears witness concerning me, and I know that the witness that he bears concerning me is true" (= Jesus; cf. also 1:9 with 3:19 and 3:34 with 5:36, etc.). Thus John apparently coined this language for his whole gospel, including the sayings of Jesus, as is shown especially clearly in the re-shaping in the Gospel of John of synoptic sayings of Jesus: cf. John 3:5, "Truly, truly, I say to you, if a man is not born of water and of spirit, he cannot enter into the kingdom of God," with Matt. 18:3, "Truly, I say to you, unless you are converted and become as little children, you will not enter into the kingdom of heaven"; cf. also John 12:25 with Mark 8:35 and John 5:23 with Luke 10: 16. Now this Johannine language is primarily characterized by numerous pairs of opposites: light and darkness, falsehood and truth, above and below, spirit and flesh, freedom and bondage; and further by the identification of God and Jesus as "the Father" and "the Son" or as "the Father who sent me" and "him whom thou hast sent"; then also by concepts related to salvation such as water of life, bread of life, and light of the world; and finally by the statement that the Son has descended from heaven and again as-cended into heaven. This conceptual world of the Gospel of John and hence also this language of the Johannine Jesus has only very slight parallels in the synoptic sayings of Jesus (apart from the saying, hardly an early one, in Matt. 11:27 par.; see above, pp. 75-76). If Jesus had spoken as does the Johannine Jesus, he would have had to use side by side two significantly different forms of language, which is hardly conceivable, although it is repeatedly asserted.

However, it is after all very difficult to determine precisely what religio-historical sphere is the native home of the language form that is characteristic of John, since neither the Old Testament nor Palestinian-rabbinical Judaism can explain more than individual expressions or concepts. But no more help is actually offered here by Hellenistic Judaism or Hellenistic paganism, because, while it is true that in these spheres stronger linguistic echoes are found, on the other hand there is no point of contact here for the idea, characteristic of Johannine Christology, of the sending of the Son of God from above and of his return to heaven. The thought world of the separate Jewish group of Qumran, with which many scholars would like to connect the Johannine thought world, also affords no adequate explanation. It is true that the ethical dualism and especially the contrast between light and darkness in the Qumran writings present actual parallels to the Johannine theology; yet in Qumran these conceptions occur in the context of a radical cultic legalism and of the demand for adherence to the group of "unity," which detaches itself from the rest of Judaism, while in Qumran also the message of the sending of the Son from above, especially characteristic of John, has no analogy of any sort.

For a long time, however, it has been observed that strikingly strong parallels both to Johannine dualism and to the idea of the sending of the redeemer from above are found in hymns of a heretical Christianity from the second century, the so-called "Odes of Solomon," and in the considerably later writings of a religious group still existing in remnants today on the Euphrates, the Mandaeans. Both sources are undoubtedly more recent than the Gospel of John, so that a direct influencing of the Gospel of John by the Christian or pagan source is impossible. But, as recent studies have made very probable, the Mandaean religion goes back to a baptist group which existed in Palestine or Syria already in the first century; and the Odes of Solomon are an early example of a kind of piety which arose at the latest at the same time as Christianity, but probably somewhat earlier, and then penetrated Christianity and there, already in Paul's time, became a dangerous adversary, the so-called *"Gnosis"* (i.e., knowledge). This religion saw salvation in the knowledge of the true origin of man in the celestial world of light and combined this basic idea with the most diverse speculations, even about heavenly redeemer figures. Such gnostic religion was also combined with the Jewish belief about creation, and we have sure evidence from the second century of such a Jewish Gnosis, yet the connection between a heterodox Judaism and a gnostic doctrine of redemption undoubtedly was already present in the Palestinian-Syrian area in the first century—the Samaritan Simon, mentioned in Acts 8:9 ff., belongs to this context. Hence a Jewish Gnosis, which had also appropriated the mythical idea of the descending redeemer, is most probably to be assumed as presupposition for the religious language of the Gospel of John. Though this may remain hypothetical, in any case the language which the Johannine Jesus speaks is not the language of Palestinian Judaism which the Jesus of the synoptic tradition uses, and even this fact alone shows that the full Christian witness to Christ of the Gospel of John cannot be interested in repeating Jesus' preaching in his language.

Thus John composed the stories about Jesus as well as Jesus' discourses in a form which was better suited for his testimony, but this is only the most striking indication that John not only portrays *the figure and the preaching of Jesus* as a believer, but *consciously forms this picture from the faith of the community.* One can further discern this in the fact that in a comparison of the gospel with I John, it can frequently be seen that in the gospel, the community's utterances of faith have become Jesus' own statements: I John 3:14, "We know that we have passed from death to life," is turned, in John 5:24, into "Truly, truly, I say to you: Whoever hears my word . . . has passed from death to life"; or I John 3:11, "This is the message which you have heard from the beginning, that we should love one another," becomes, in John 13:34, "I give a new commandment to you, that you should love one another." Finally, that John consciously pictures the figure and history of Jesus from the perspective of the faith of the community is also shown in the fact that in the Gospel of John the testimony of the community not only is expressly stated ("The word became flesh, and we beheld his glory," 1:14; "At first his disciples did not understand this, but when Jesus was glorified, then they remembered that this was written concerning him, and they had done this to him," 12:16), but also occasionally breaks through unexpectedly in a saying of Jesus: "Truly, truly, I say to you, we speak what we know and we testify what we have seen, and you do not accept our testimony" (3:11; Jesus is speaking to Nicodemus). John undoubtedly intends to report actual events, and therefore he emphasizes the reality of a miracle that occurred (4:53; 9:20-21; 11:39) or the reliability of a report (on the occasion of the miraculous flow of blood and water from the wound in Jesus' side, 19:35). Nevertheless, the picture of the historical Jesus as the tradition afforded it is not the object of John's presentation, but the picture of Jesus as the faith of the community saw it, because only in this way could John bear witness that "Jesus is the anointed one, the Son of God" (20:31).

If therefore in the Gospel of John "Christ lets himself be heard, but through the medium of Johannine language" (E. Mussner), still John does not derive the right of such projecting of faith back into history from his personal authority or from poetic inspiration, but from the conviction that the resurrected One has given to his community the Spirit as its helper, who "will guide you into the whole truth" (16:13), and that the believers who *abide* in Jesus' words "will come to know the truth" (8:31-32). "Because John already knows the whole truth, thanks to the Spirit, he can have the earthly Jesus already preaching the full truth" (E. Haenchen). Therefore the theological problem which the Johannine theology poses for us is not the question—in itself of course justifiable—to what extent the reports about Jesus and the sayings of Jesus in the Gospel of John offer trustworthy historical accounts in detail; the crucial theological question with respect to the Gospel of John is rather whether this faith image of Jesus can be understood as an appropriate exposition of the divine action in the person of Jesus from the perspective of the believing community in the late period of primitive Christianity.

3. The Johannine image of Christ

a. THE ANOINTED ONE

Since John wrote his gospel "that you may believe that Jesus is the anointed one, the Son of God" (20:31), it is evident that for him these two titles adequately and unexceptionably interpret the significance of Jesus, and therefore it is proper to take these titles as our point of departure. When this is done, it is seen immediately that the title "the anointed one" (Christ) does not occur in John with any great frequency, but it is heavily stressed. Already in 1:41 Andrew directs his brother Peter to Jesus with the words, "We have found the Messiah," and the evangelist adds for the benefit of his readers, "which translated means 'the anointed one'" [Christ]. To the Samaritan woman, who refers to the traditional expectation of the Messiah, Jesus says, "I who speak to you am he" (4:25-26).

Martha, who has an intimation of Jesus' significance, confesses, "I have believed that you are the anointed one, the Son of God, who is coming into the world" (11:27). And according to I John 5:1, one "who believes that Jesus is the anointed one" is born of God. Correspondingly, the unbelieving Jews dispute the possibility that Jesus could be the Christ, because people know that this man Jesus in fact comes from Galilee (John 7:26-27, 41-42), and anyone who "denies that Jesus is the anointed one" is the antichrist, that is, the satanic adversary of Christ (I John 2:22). In all these passages "the anointed one" has a confessional meaning, though of course along with this, the word "Christ" also occurs, as already in Paul, in the sense of a proper name in the combination "Jesus Christ" (John 1:17; 17:3; and frequently in I and II John). In the fact that John, in the texts mentioned, makes the confession of Jesus, the anointed one, the crucial demand of faith, and twice, on the lips of Peter and of Jesus himself, even uses the Aramaic word "Messiah" (1:41; 4:25-26), he clearly shows the intention to identify Jesus as the bearer of salvation who is promised to the Jews, and accordingly, Nathanael is directed by Philip to Jesus with the words, "We have found the one of whom Moses wrote in the law and [of whom] the prophets [wrote], Jesus, the son of Joseph, of Nazareth" (1:45; cf. 5:39), and thereupon Nathanael confesses, "You are the king of Israel" (1:49c; cf. 12:13). But John's heavy stress in all these expressions on the confession of Jesus as the Messiah, that is, the anointed one, and his intention thereby to identify Jesus as the anticipated Jewish bearer of salvation (not, of course, in the political sense; cf. 6:15) are combined with a lack of ultimate importance for him of the title "the anointed one."

This is shown not only in the fact that John 6:68 reshapes Peter's confession of Jesus as the anointed one in the Synoptics (Mark 8:29 par.) into the confession, "You are the *holy one of God*" (6:69), and thus presumably takes up an unusual Jewish designation for the expected bearer of salvation just as is done in 1:34, where John the Baptist says of Jesus: "I have borne witness that he is *the chosen one* of God." It is shown above all in the fact that in the crucial passages, still another title is added to the confession of "the anointed one" ("the Son of God, the king of Israel," 1:49; "the anointed one, the Son of God who is coming into the world," 11:27; similarly 20:31), or that "the anointed one" simply alternates with "the Son of Man" (12:34). Only in I John 2:22 and 5:1 do we meet the blunt demand to confess Jesus as "the anointed one," but there it is a matter of parrying false teachings. Thus John's firm maintenance of the confession of Jesus as the anointed one in whom God's promises in the Old Testament have been fulfilled is combined with a lack of independent content for this concept, and therefore this title of honor can teach us no more about the Johannine image of Christ than that John too saw in Jesus the anticipated eschatological bearer of salvation.

b. THE SON

It is quite a different matter, however, with the second title of honor mentioned in John 20:31, namely *"the Son of God."* Of course the title in this form likewise does not appear very frequently, but it is used very emphatically. Already in 1:49 Nathanael declares, in view of Jesus' supernatural knowledge, "Rabbi, you are the Son of God, you are the king of Israel." Fully in harmony with this, at the end of Jesus' trial before Pilate, the Jews who are accusing Jesus declare: "We have a law, and according to the law he must die, because he has made himself the Son of God," and when Pilate hesitates to condemn Jesus, they add: "If you release this man, you are no friend of Caesar; for anyone who makes himself king speaks against Caesar" (19:7, 12). Jesus' sonship to God and his position as "anointed one," i.e., as king of Israel, are thus equated in the two passages. Now Jesus' sonship to God is grounded in the fact that "God sanctified him and sent him into the world" (10:36; cf. 11:27), and as the Son of God Jesus is the coming judge of the world (5:25). Consequently the confession of Jesus as the Son of God is the crucial demand: "Whoever confesses that Jesus is the Son of God, God abides in him and he in God" (I John 4:15; cf. 5:5, 10). These few passages (cf. further John 11:4; I John 3:8) show clearly that the Son of God as the one sent by the Father represents God's acting in the present and future. Yet these few passages do not allow any more exact definition of the meaning, and this more precise meaning can only be discerned when we hold in view the statements about "the Son" which are actually characteristic of John.

The frequent designation *"the Son"* naturally first of all describes the relationship between Father and Son: "God sent his Son into the world . . . , that the world might be saved through him" (John 3:17; cf. I John 4:14); "The Father loves the Son and has given all things into his hand" (John 3:35; cf. 5:20); "The Father has given all judgment to the Son" (5:22). Consequently, according to John "the Son can do nothing of himself, but only what he sees the Father doing" (5:19); but it is also true that

"As the Father raises the dead and gives them life, so also the Son gives life to whom he will" (5:21 RSV), and "if the Son makes you free, you will be free indeed" (8:36 RSV). Therefore men are bound to the Son who is sent by the Father and does the Father's works: "Whoever believes on the Son has eternal life, but whoever does not obey the Son will not see life" (3:36; cf. 6:40; I John 5:15); the Father has given all judgment to the Son, "that all may honor the Son as they honor the Father; whoever does not honor the Son does not honor the Father who sent him" (John 5:23; cf. I John 2:22-24).

Thus the *relationship of Father and Son* appears to be that of complete equality, so that the Son stands beside God as a divine being and cannot actually be distinguished from God. This impression is strengthened further when we see that John can also identify the one sent by God directly as "God" (without the article), even though this is rare: "The Word was with God, and the Word was God" (John 1:1); "No one has seen God; the only God, who is in the bosom of the Father, has told of him" (1:18); "Thomas answered and said to him, 'My Lord and my God'" (20:28). Is the Son, as John describes him, thus in reality "God descending into the human sphere and there becoming manifest," so that the theme would be the "veiling of a divine being in lowliness" (E. Käsemann)? Opposing such an interpretation of the "Son" in John's understanding, however, are other passages which show the Son in dependence upon the Father. The Jesus of the Gospel of John says expressly, "The Father is greater than I" (14:28), and speaks of the Father as the "only true God" (17:3); yet all that the Son has he has received from the Father (3:35): "It is the Father who glorifies me" (8:54); the Father has "consecrated" the Son "and sent him into the world" (10:36). Corresponding to this is the fact that "the Father loves the Son and shows him all that he himself is doing" (5:20), so that "what he does, the Son does likewise" (5:19). Therefore the Johannine Christ emphasizes: "I have not spoken of my own accord, but the Father who sent me has himself given me commandment what to say and to speak" (12:49; cf. 3:31-32; 15:15), and "The Son can do nothing of himself, but only what he sees the Father doing" (5:19). Thus the Son does not speak and act independently of the Father, and the whole issue turns on how this participation of the Son in the Father's speaking and acting is understood.

Now John describes the relationship of the Father and the Son in a twofold fashion. In the present time of the earthly Jesus the

Father and the Son stand in a relationship of giving and receiving: "The Father loves the Son and shows him all that he himself is doing, and will show him still greater works, that you may marvel" (5:20). In harmony with this, "whatever he does, the Son does likewise" (5:19*b*), and "He who is of God hears the words of God" (8:47 RSV). The intention is not to use this love on the Father's part and this acting and speaking on the part of the Son who sees the Father acting and hears him speaking to describe a relationship which is to be understood as analogous to a human father's affection or to a prophet's obedience. This is shown in the fact that the Son's present seeing and hearing has its ground in *the Son's pre-existent being with the Father.* "I say what I have heard with the Father" (8:38*a*) can only mean that the earthly Jesus speaks of what he as pre-existent has heard with the Father (cf. also 1:18); and thus, also, "Not that any one has seen the Father except him who is from God; he has seen the Father" (6:46 RSV). And in 3:31-32 it is explicitly said: "He who comes from heaven bears witness to what he has seen and heard, and no one receives his testimony." But the eternally existing election of the Son by the Father underlies, as the root of the present testimony of the man Jesus, this vision and this hearing of the pre-existent one: "I [am] in them and thou [art] in me, that they may be perfected in one, that the world may know that thou hast sent me and loved them. Father, for all that thou hast given me, I desire that they may be with me where I am, that they may see my glory which thou hast given me, because thou hast loved me before the foundation of the world" (17:23-24). Even if elsewhere the theme is the present love of the Father for the Son (3:35; 5:20; 10:17), 17:23-24 plainly says that the revelation of the Father to men by the Son is based upon the Son's belonging to the divine world and upon his being sent from the divine world by the Father.

That raises the question once more of how, more precisely, John conceives of this belonging to the Father on the Son's part and at the same time the relationship of the man Jesus to the "Son" who is sent from the Father. John indeed not only speaks occasionally of the pre-existent Son as "God" (see above, p. 269), but also portrays the earthly Jesus with features like those employed by Hellenistic piety to characterize men who were believed to be endowed with divine power: Jesus has access to supernatural knowledge about men (1:47-48; 4:24-25; 13:18-19); he knows about distant and future events (13:11, 24-26); he can, with a simple word of command, turn water into wine (2:7 ff.). But what is still more striking in comparison with the synoptic presentation of Jesus is this: the Johannine Jesus actually is not able to pray, because he already knows that he is heard even before he has prayed (11:41-42), and Jesus' fear before death, which the synoptic scene in Gethsemane allows us to detect, is thrust aside by the Johannine Jesus in favor of the prayer for the glorifying of the divine name (12:27-28). But as much as all these features appear to indicate that in the Gospel of John the subject is a divine being and not a man, to just the same extent this impression is misleading. John repeatedly emphasizes *the human features of Jesus:* Jesus hungers and thirsts (4:7, 31), he is weary, he weeps and becomes angry (4:6; 11:35, 33), loves Lazarus and his sisters (11:5), even changes his plans (7:8, 10). Corresponding to this is John's strong emphasis at the very beginning of his gospel on the reality of Jesus' humanness: "The Word became flesh" (1:14); for to John also, "flesh" is the mark of the earthly, mortal man: "That which is born of the flesh is flesh" (3:6). Hence Jesus can say of himself: "You seek to kill me, a man who has spoken to you the truth which I have heard from God," and for just this reason the Jews seek to kill Jesus (8:40). They accuse Jesus: "We do not seek to kill you because of any good work, but because of blasphemy, because you, though a man, make yourself God" (10:33; similarly 5:18; 19:7). Against Jesus' claim the Jews cite the fact that his parents and brothers and sisters are known, and that he comes only from Nazareth (1:45; 2:1, 12; 6:42; 7:3, 5, 27). For John Jesus is an earthly man without any subtractions. John has no knowledge of the idea, which appears in Matthew and Luke, of Jesus' birth without a human father, and he could not even accept it (the reading in 1:13, whose attestation is quite scattered—"who was not born . . . of the will of man, but of God"—is without doubt a later emendation of the text).

Although John accordingly takes entirely seriously Jesus' humanness, he emphasizes the *unity of the earthly Son with the Father* ("I and the Father are one," 10:30) just as he does the unity of the Son who returns to the Father with the Father: "I am no longer in the world . . . , and I come to thee. Holy Father, keep those in thy name whom thou hast given to me, that they may be one as we are one" (17:11; cf. 17:22). He expresses this unity by means of the reciprocal formula which is found in all forms of mysticism: "That you may know that the Father [is] in me and I [am] in the Father" (10:38); "Do you not believe that I [am] in the Father and the Father is in me?" (14:10; cf. 14:11, 20; 17:21, 23). Thus the Johannine Jesus can say of himself: "He who has seen me has seen the Father" (14:9). But precisely this formulation shows that the unity of the earthly Jesus with the Father is not meant by John in the sense of a speculation about the human and divine "natures" of Jesus Christ, regardless of how much these and similar formulations were later the occasion for such speculations. For the saying about seeing the Father in Jesus has a characteristically divergent parallel in 12:45: "He who sees me sees the one who sent me," and this saying about the Father's sending the Son is undoubtedly John's most common formulation for the relationship of the Father and the Son and discloses to us most clearly in what sense John wishes to have the unity of the Father and the Son to be understood.

Not only is it quite generally said that "God sent the Son into the world" (3:17; I John 4:9; "We have seen and bear witness that the Father has sent the Son as savior of the world," I John 4:14), but the Johannine Jesus very frequently identifies God as the "Father who has sent me" (5:37; 6:44; 12:49, etc.) or "the one who sent me" (4:34; 7:16, etc.), and calls himself "him whom the Father has sent" or something similar (10:36; 3:34; 6:29, etc.). But these formulations are not only meant to say that the Son is to reveal the Father ("He whom God has sent speaks the words of God," 3:34; cf. 8:16; 12:49; 17:18) and that therefore the hearing of the words of Jesus has as its presupposition the belief in the sending of the revealer: "I have given to them the words which thou hast given me, and they have received them and truly acknowledged that I have come from thee, and they have believed that thou hast sent me" (17:8). But this *sending of the Son* also means, as is shown by the passage just cited, that the Son has come forth from the Father and is sent from the Father into the world: "I proceeded and have come from God; for I have not come from myself, but he has sent me" (8:42); "I proceeded from the Father and have come into the world" (16:28a); "I have descended from heaven, that I . . . might do the will of the one who sent me" (6:38; cf. 7:28-29). This sending of the Son into the world from heaven is paralleled by the return to the Father: "Now I go to the one who sent me" (16:5); "Again I leave the world and go to the Father" (16:28b; cf. 7:33). Thus the Father who sends and the Son who is sent belong inseparably together: "I am not alone, but I and he who sent me" (8:16); and therefore the disciples are to "know thee, the only true God, and Jesus Christ, whom thou hast sent" (17:3). "Whoever believes on me does not believe on me but on him who

sent me, and whoever sees me sees the one who sent me" (12:44-45).
Hence the content of the revelation and therefore the object of
faith is that the Father has sent the Son from heaven and the Son
has returned to the Father. We saw earlier that John very probably
appropriated this mythical discourse of the heavenly emissary, together with a large part of his religious language, from a gnostically
influenced form of heterodox Judaism; indeed, the myth of the
descending redeemer was already earlier adopted by Hellenistic
Christianity before Paul and had been used by Paul (see above,
pp. 264, 120, 152-53). But only with John did the language about the
mission of the Son and about the emissary really acquire central
significance and become the actual conceptual form which comprehensively describes the relationship of Father and Son.

In this connection two further points must be noted. For John
the full manhood of the Son who was sent by the Father into the
world is, as we have seen, beyond doubt. In fact, it is precisely this
humanity of the emissary that offends the unbelieving Jews, because the devil, not God, is their "father" (8:40-44a); and in the
first epistle it is precisely the disputing by false teachers of the identity of the man Jesus with Christ that John describes as a denial of
the Father and of the Son and hence as a work of the antichrist
(I John 2:22-23; 4:2-3).

Further, in John's opinion this man Jesus not only came at a
quite definite time, namely in the time of the procurator Pilate
(John 18:19 ff.), but also at the end of this world epoch. For John
not only quite generally counts on the "return" of Christ and the
coming judgment of the world (14:3; 5:28-29) and the future
resurrection (6:54), but he also describes the approaching persecution of the Christians as the age of the premessianic woes (16:1-4),
and thus he is conscious of living just before the end. Corresponding to this also is the assertion of I John 2:18: "Little children, it is
the last hour, and, as you have heard that [the] antichrist comes,
so even now many antichrists have appeared; from this we know
that it is the last hour." The language of the Gnostic myth of the
sending of the Son and, expressed therein, the extensive assimilation
of the man Jesus to God, thus is meant to give expression to the
belief that God has quite personally and eschatologically disclosed
himself in the man Jesus and has spoken and acted through this
man. Thus for John Jesus as "the Son" is the *full-fledged presence
of God,* because he shares in the working of the Father, and God
personally meets men exclusively through the man Jesus: "No one
comes to the Father but through me" (14:6). Herewith John has

moved the man Jesus so close to God that down to the present the opinion has repeatedly been held, not without some justification, that the Johannine "Christology of glory" no longer takes seriously the humanity of Jesus. But even though there may be the danger of such a misinterpretation, such an understanding contradicts the evangelist's clearly recognizable intention. Precisely because he wishes to give expression to the belief that God has spoken perfectly and finally in the man Jesus, John does not shy away from the danger that in his presentation of Jesus, the humanity of Jesus will be eclipsed and obscured by the glory of the Son of God. But this does not change the fact that John too intends to bear witness to God's eschatological saving action in the man Jesus, and we shall have to ask whether the other christological predicates of honor used by John confirm this understanding of the Johannine Christology or not.

C. THE SAVIOR OF THE WORLD

In addition to the predicates of "anointed one" and "Son of God," which the author himself identifies in 20:31 as fundamental, John uses a large number of designations of honor for Jesus Christ, several of which however appear only occasionally and without particular emphasis. Thus Jesus' conversation with the Samaritan woman about the Messiah leads to *"the savior of the world"* (4:42), and this confession is described as the Samaritans' confession won by means of the encounter with Jesus himself. The title occurs elsewhere in the New Testament only in I John 4:14: "We have seen and testify that the Father has sent the Son as savior of the world." The designation "savior" is indeed used in the angel's saying in the Lukan birth narrative ("Unto you is born this day the savior, who is the anointed one, the Lord," Luke 2:11) and once by Paul ("we await from heaven the Lord Jesus Christ as savior," Phil. 3:20), in both cases in the Jewish sense of the anticipated eschatological bearer of salvation. In the late writings of the New Testament, on the other hand, "savior" as a title for Christ occurs in keeping with the language of Hellenism, which used this title to identify a wide range of deities, but also men, and above all, the emperor. Fully Hellenistic, however, is the title "savior of the world," adopted only by John, and in it John clearly is employing a designation which is immediately understandable to the Hellenistic reader. Yet from the mere mention of this title by John no more can be inferred than that Jesus brings salvation for all men, in connection with which in I John 4:14 the Father is expressly identified as the initiator of this salvation through the Son.

Even the designation *"the prophet"* (John 6:14; 7:40), who in 7:41 is clearly distinguished from "the anointed one," cannot be more exactly defined in this special sense. And it is curious that the identification of Jesus as *"the Lord"* (*Kyrios*), so important for Paul and also common in later primitive Christianity, does not occur in the Gospel of John (with the exception of 11:2) for the earthly Jesus (for John the form of address *"kyrie"* is a mere formula of courtesy, as 12:21 shows), while the resurrected One frequently is spoken of as "the Lord" (20:2, 13, 18, 25), and Thomas addresses the resurrected One as "my Lord and my God" (20:28). Up till now, no convincing explanation has been found for John's avoiding the designation "Lord" for the earthly Jesus ("Mary, who had anointed the Lord," in 11:2 is the exception; is it to be charged to a moment of absentmindedness, particularly since the anointing is not mentioned until 12:1 ff., or do we have an insertion here?), and the title is also lacking in the Johannine epistles. Thus we can hardly say more than that John can also identify and address the resurrected Jesus as "Lord." But these three designations of honor which occur only in scattered places do not offer any further help.

d. THE SON OF MAN

On the other hand, the title "the Son of Man" is important for John also. We have seen that in the synoptic gospels this title occurs only on the lips of Jesus, and in the rest of the New Testament, apart from the Gospel of John, is used only in Acts 7:56 by the dying Stephen (see above, pp. 76 ff., 106-7). Since in the Gospel of John also this title appears only in sayings of Jesus—in the apparent exception in 12:34 the crowd only picks up Jesus' expression in 12:23, 32—it obviously does not characterize the evangelist's own language; the concept also does not occur in the epistles of John. Hence it can hardly be doubted that John employs the title "the Son of Man" in association with the gospel tradition known to him. It is true that John has given the concept a different turn, since there is no more said about the eschatological manifestation of the Son of Man than about his earthly lowliness. The Johannine use of the concept rather is marked by a twofold connection of ideas.

First, the concept "Son of Man" in the Gospel of John is bound up with the idea, already familiar from our consideration of the concept "Son of God," of the heavenly origin and the return thither. "No one has ascended into heaven except he who came down from heaven, the Son of Man. And as Moses lifted up the serpent in the wilderness, so must the Son of Man be lifted up" (3:13-14). In this text, both the future exaltation (likewise in 8:28; 12:34; "ascend" in 6:62; "be glorified" in 12:23; 13:32) and the already accomplished state of having ascended (similarly 13:31: "Now is the Son of Man glorified") stand over against the descent of the Son of Man from heaven. This shows that John can, from the standpoint of the earthly Jesus, describe the ascension, exaltation, and glorification of the Son of Man as yet to come, as well as describe, from the standpoint of the believing community, this return of the Son of Man to heaven as having already taken place. Accordingly, the concept of the Son of Man in essence serves for John to make comprehensible the person of the earthly Jesus from the perspective of the community's belief in his resurrection and exaltation.

Correspondingly, the Johannine Jesus says that the Son of Man even now bestows full salvation: "Labor . . . for the food which abides unto eternal life, which the Son of Man gives you; for him God has sealed" (i.e., confirmed; 6:27; cf. 6:53). Likewise, the man born blind, who has been healed and has come to believe in the Son of Man, can fall down before Jesus and worship him, with the words: "Sir, I believe" (9:35, 38). But the Johannine Jesus also claims that the coming judgment is committed to his hands, "because he is the Son of Man" (5:26-27). Thus here, too, the present Son of Man is described as the bearer of salvation in the present, without disregarding the future consummation of salvation by the Son of Man. In John's connecting the figure of the Son of Man as transmitted to him in the tradition with the myth of the descending and ascending redeemer, the title "Son of Man" serves him above all to describe the present glory of Jesus Christ.

In this connection, of course, one must also place the saying in 1:51, which is isolated from all the other Son-of-Man sayings in the Gospel of John: "Truly, truly, I say to you: you will see heaven opened and the angels of God ascending and descending upon the Son of Man." Nowhere else in the Gospel of John is anything said of a communication of Jesus with God mediated by angels, nor is anything related of the vision of the open heaven promised here to the disciples. Hence it is to be presumed that John has taken over this Son-of-Man saying in order to give expression to the fact that even the earthly Son of Man already has the angels at his disposal, and thus shares in the divine rule. Thus this saying too emphasizes that God's activity is fully present in the man Jesus. For the present Son of Man also has received his power from God (5:26-27), and his glory is only for the believer to recognize (1:50-51; 9:35-38) and is first perfected by the death of the man Jesus (12:23-24). This title also serves to describe the historical Jesus as the perfect revealer of God.

It is true that some doubt about this judgment could be raised by the fact that in the context of the Son-of-Man words in 8:28 it is said: "When you have lifted up the Son of man, then you will know that I am he, and that I do nothing on my own authority but speak thus as the Father taught me" (RSV). This grammatically strange *"I am he"* without any further addition is clearly meant by John as a title, as 8:24 proves: "If you do not believe that I am he, you will die in your sins" (similarly 13:19). This curious identification is found elsewhere only in the Old Testament and in apocalyptic Judaism as a self-designation of the one creator-God: "You seek the God of gods and the Creator in the thoughts of your heart; I am he" (Apocalypse of Abraham 8.4). But it also appears to have been used as a "messianic" self-predication, as is shown by the polemic in Mark 13:6 par. against false bearers of salvation: "Many will come in my name and say, 'I am he,' and will lead many astray." When the Johannine Jesus relates this Old Testament-Jewish designation for God to himself, this can only have the meaning that he means to put himself in the place of God. But even here the humanness of Jesus is not actually eliminated. For on the one hand, precisely in 8:28 (see above), in fact, stress is placed upon the utter dependence upon the Father of the exalted Son of Man who can say of himself, "I am he," and on the other hand, in 13:19-20, bound up with the belief in the "I am he" is the declaration, "Whoever receives me receives the one who sent me." When, with the introduction of this Old Testament-Jewish predicate of God for Jesus, John makes the claim that God himself appears in the man Jesus, still even in this context he has not forgotten that God is making himself perfectly visible in the man Jesus, and therefore even here he has not simply equated Jesus with God or presented him as a divine being.

e. THE WORD (THE LOGOS)

But does not the prologue of the Gospel of John utterly refute this view, by not only calling the man Jesus "God" but, to identify him, introducing the concept "the Logos" (i.e., the Word)? From

277

the fact that John begins his gospel with this concept, without then making further use of it, it has often been concluded that "all other christological titles in John in essence serve only as exposition of this one basic title" (H. Conzelmann), and therefore this concept has been made the key to the exposition of the Johannine picture of Christ. Now of course this is very precarious in view of the fact that the Greek word "logos" occurs very frequently in the rest of the gospel outside the prologue (1:1-18), but exclusively to denote the discourse of Jesus or of other men (e.g.. 5:24; 4:39), without any specific meaning. Even in I John, which begins with the sentence: "That which was from the beginning, which we have heard, which we have seen with our eyes, which we have beheld and our hands have handled, of the word of life . . . , that we declare unto you" (1:1, 3), "the Logos" elsewhere likewise only denotes divine and human discourse. Hence what John intends to express with the concept "the Logos" which introduces the gospel and (somewhat altered) the first epistle does not arise out of the usage of the entire gospel, but also not from the few expressions of the prologue, but only from the gospel as a whole, and it is undoubtedly correct that "the gospel must not be interpreted by the term Logos, rather we must understand this term with its varied history in the light of the Gospel as a whole" (W. F. Howard). Nevertheless it must not be overlooked that John introduces his gospel with this concept and therefore intends with it to say something important, which the reader of the gospel is to keep in mind when he reads what follows.

But what is the reader to keep in mind? The answers to this question are widely divergent because a sure understanding of the prologue in detail is possible only when beforehand three problems are solved, whose solution up until the present has been only approximated.

It is true that, over against what follows, John 1:1-18 forms a clear unity, in that the concrete narrative begins only with 1:19. But while vss. 1-5, 9-13, 16-18 make general statements whose connection with the earthly-historical event is indicated only by means of the proper name of Jesus Christ in 1:17, vss. 6-8 and 15 speak of the appearing of the historical person of John the Baptist, of course without more precisely identifying him or relating anything concrete about him; and vs. 14, with the statement about the incarnation of the Word, obviously also points to a historical occurrence, yet again without describing it concretely. If the prologue consequently gives the impression of being a composite piece, the same impression arises from a consideration of the style of the individual statements, which is partly of a hymnic-confessional sort, and partly matter-of-fact. On the basis of these observations, numerous attempts have been made to reconstruct a hymn which the author of the gospel might have incorporated into his prologue and expanded, while other students prefer to interpret the entire prologue as formulated by the author of the gospel. But since we have at our disposal no sure methodological arguments for the reconstruction of a possibly underlying text, none of these hypotheses has been able actually to offer convincing proof, and thus the question must remain provisionally open, whether in the Johannine prologue an already existing text has been reworked, which would account for the breaks in the train of thought and in style. and in any case the exposition of the prologue must attempt to understand the text in the scope in which it comes to us in the sense of the author of the gospel.

But if one seeks to understand the text in its traditional wording and scope, two questions above all arise. It has always been unclear what figure is the subject in the first half of the prologue, since it is only in 1:14 ("The Word became flesh") that clear reference is first made to the man Jesus. But if one attempts for this reason to understand the text down to 1:14 of the "Word" before the incarnation, then the statement about John the Baptist in vss. 6-8 appears as a disrupting insertion. That is to say, the questions as to who is actually the subject in John 1:1-13 and why the Baptist is. abruptly mentioned in 1:6-8 belong together and can only be answered together. Now the way in which the Baptist is introduced in 1:6 ("There appeared a man who was sent from God; his name was John") shows that the author of the gospel can assume that the reader knows at once of whom he is speaking, and correspondingly, the author evidently takes it for granted that the reader knows from the outset who is meant by the designation "the Word." That is to say, the reader undoubtedly, from the moment in which reference is made to an event in the world, is to think of the "Word" which became flesh and was named Jesus Christ (1:14, 17), and this is the case in the statement: "And the light shines in the darkness, and the darkness has not received it" (1:5). But if from 1:5 onward the theme is the event of which 1:14-18 speaks clearly, then the reference in 1:6-8 to the appearance of John the Baptist remains indeed stylistically harsh, but substantively understandable. Yet even this answer to the two related questions of who is the subject in 1:1-13 and why the Baptist is abruptly mentioned in 1:6-8 is only a plausible hypothesis, and consequently the exposition of the entire text 1:1-18 remains uncertain.

Finally, this uncertainty has its basis in the fact that we do not know for sure what intellectual sphere is the source of the concept adopted by John, "the Logos" or "the Word," and what ideas the readers connected or were meant to connect with this concept that was familiar to them. We have seen that in the rest of the gospel outside the prologue John does not use the concept "the Logos" as a personal designation. and that this concept thus is not his usual form of expression of his testimony to Christ. On the other hand, in the prologue he employs the concept with emphasis and takes it for granted that the readers understand it without explanation. Now the concept "the Logos" first of all reminds those familiar with ancient civilization of Greek philosophy and the Hellenistic piety connected with it, in which the Logos frequently appears as a designation for the world reason, of course without assuming a personal character. But in Hellenistic Judaism the concept approaches a personal character ("Thine almighty Word sprang from heaven into the midst of the earth," Wisdom of Solomon 18.15) , and therefore it frequently has been attempted to find the origin of the Johannine concept of the Logos in this sphere. But an argument against this is the fact that the mythical statement, "[the Word] came to his own possession, and his own people did not receive him [or: it]" (1:11), is not explained by this assumption. The belief, basic to rabbinic-Palestinian Judaism, in the law as the mediator of creation and giver of life and light also offers a certain parallel to the Johannine statements about the Logos. But the law was never personified in Palestinian Judaism, and moreover, the mythical statement of the prologue also is not explained from this perspective. Now on the other hand, striking parallels undoubtedly exist between the statements of the Johannine prologue about the Word and the speculations of Palestinian and Hellenistic Judaism about "Wisdom." It was told of Wisdom that God had formed her before the creation of the world and that she had had a part in the creation of the world; that God sent her into the world to be the light of men; that men however rejected Wisdom, and that Wisdom therefore returned to God (cf., e.g., Prov. 8:22, 27; Ecclus. 24:3, 8; Eth. Enoch 42) . In this Jewish Wisdom speculation the mythological conceptions which we find in the prologue are preserved here and there, though it is true that they are not connected with "the Word." But since the Wisdom myth obviously was a form, adapted to Jewish thought, of the myth, native to Gnostic piety, of the descending redeemer, one can conjecture that in the circles of Jewish Gnosticism by which the Johannine conceptual world was generally influenced (see above, pp. 264-65) the myth of the descending redeemer also had been used in connection with "the Word." But this remains a conjecture, and thus on this point also we do not have assured information as to what conceptions John could presuppose as present among his readers.

But in spite of these uncertainties, the *train of thought of the prologue* can be paraphrased on the whole as follows: when the world was created, there was already "the Word," and this Word "was with God"; indeed, John can even say: "The Word was God," without thereby meaning to make a complete identification of the two. The creation in its entire scope was formed with the help of this Word, with nothing excepted: "of all that came to be, nothing came to be without the Word" (1:3; cf. 1:10). Hence men also have their life and their salvation as well from the Word: "The life was the light of men" (1:4). This general statement now becomes specific with the declaration that this light became manifest in the world, but found no acceptance (1:5). This hardly refers to the fall, but to the lack of understanding which the light that had become visible in Jesus (present tense: "The light is shining in the darkness!") encountered (1:10). When now following this, in 1:6-8 the subject is the appearing and testimony of John (the Baptist), the indication of aim which appears in this connection ("that all might believe through him," 1:7) shows that one cannot believe on this light without a witness, and it also appears from the caution, "He was not the light" (1:8), that the parenthetical comment about the Baptist in this passage also has a polemical aim: what is intended is a parrying of the estimation of John the Baptist as the bearer of salvation, an estimation held by the Baptist's followers at the time of the writing of the Gospel of John (cf. also John 1:15, 20-23; 3:28; 5:35-36). After this anticipation of the actual narrative, 1:9-11 returns to the declaration that the Word came into the world as world creator and thus appeared to the people who belonged to him and was not acknowledged. Thus men have not seen in the person of Jesus the light, except those who have come to believe and thereby were born anew and became God's children (1:12-13).

A parallel statement in 1:14 that serves further to define what was said in 1:5-13 now says unmistakably: the Word became a mortal man and took its dwelling among men. When it is added: "and we beheld his glory, a glory which [belongs] to the only

281

[Son] from the Father, full of grace and truth," this cannot mean that everyone could see this glory; otherwise no one would have been able to resist it; this glory could be seen only by those "who believed on his name" (1:12c). Then in 1:16 it is explicitly said of these believers that in Jesus Christ they have encountered grace and truth as an event whereby at the same time the law of Moses was superseded. When, before this statement, reference is once more made in 1:15 to the witness of the Baptist, the latter's declaration, "This was the one of whom I said, 'The one coming after me was above me, because he was before me,'" is meant to emphasize that the Word become flesh was as the eternal Word prior in time and hence substantively superior to the appearing of the Baptist. The entire series of statements is concluded with the lapidary sentence: "No one has ever seen God; the only God, who is in the bosom of the Father, he has brought knowledge [of him]" (1:18). Of Jesus Christ, who had been named immediately before this, it thus is said that he could proclaim what no other man could ever proclaim, because no man has ever seen God: God himself. For this Jesus Christ was the only one of whom one can say that he is "God" and is always in the Father's immediate presence; even as man he was "in the bosom of the Father."

There can be no doubt that here John is speaking of Jesus Christ in the language of myth: "the Word" is an eternal, divine person, of whom a human, historical activity is predicated (see above, p. 171). The relationship of "the Word" to God is described in such a way that the equating of the Word with God is avoided, but the Word is nevertheless set immediately next to God. This mythical language therefore has again and again created the impression of nonhistorical speculation and has provided an abundance of material for the christological speculation of the early church. But however much John uses mythical language here, yet what is involved here is not at all speculation. For all that is said about the eternal "Word" indeed serves to make visible the man Jesus in his unique and ultimately indescribable relationship to God, but it does not serve the purpose of portraying this human life itself: "As surprisingly as the author sees the exalted and the earthly redeemer intermingled, so that the glorified one also already glorifies the earthly one, just so carefully does he avoid applying the Logos-designation to Christ after 1:14" (F. Gaugler). If one understands the prologue in the sense of the evangelist, then what is said about the "Word" in no way imperils the humanness of Jesus, because it presupposes this humanness and seeks to understand the man Jesus Christ in terms of this presupposition. It is also quite evident why John at the beginning of his gospel adopts the traditional concept of "the Word": he wishes to testify with the utmost clarity that the man Jesus, of whose glory the gospel will bear witness, embodies God's own action. The creator himself has appeared in Jesus Christ, speaking and acting in him: this is said by the prologue of the gospel ("The Word came to his own . . . . The Word became flesh, and we beheld his glory," 1:11, 14) as well as by the "beginning of the epistle" of I John: "That which was from the beginning . . . , which we have seen and our hands have handled, of the word of life . . . , that we declare to you" (I John 1:1, 3). The New Testament also says elsewhere that in Jesus Christ God's perfect word was and is being uttered: "God's Son Jesus Christ . . . was not Yes *and* No, but in him was [only] Yes; for all the promises of God [have become] Yes in him" (II Cor. 1:19 ff.); "After God had spoken to the fathers through the prophets in many ways and many forms, now at the end of time he has spoken to us through the Son" (Heb. 1:1-2); "And I saw the heavens open, and behold, a white horse, and the one who sat upon it is called Faithful and True . . . , and his name is The Word of God" (Rev. 19:11, 13). But the prologue of the Gospel of John, and in somewhat different fashion the opening part of I John, go beyond this, by calling the man Jesus the self-revealing God himself, meaning the person of Jesus, not merely his words. This is certainly an ultimate statement, which cannot be explained, but can only be believed. But it is a statement which takes the humanness of Jesus fully and quite seriously; "We do not get a teaching about God, but are confronted by God himself, and that indeed in the world" (H. Conzelmann). Hence already in the prologue, alongside the predicates which characterize Jesus in his relation to God—the Son, the Son of Man, the Word—John places a number of concepts which disclose Jesus' significance for salvation—life, light, truth—and which in the rest of the gospel are joined by still other similar concepts.

f. THE BEARER OF SALVATION

The Johannine Jesus lays claim to all these concepts just named with the formula "*I am,*" supplemented by abstractly used metaphors: the bread of life (6:35); the light of the world (8:12); the door (10:7); the shepherd (10:11); the resurrection and the life (11:25); the way, the truth, and the life (14:6); the vine (15:1). With Oriental deities and Hellenistic redeemer figures, but also with the God of the Old Testament (Deut. 32:39) and with the Jewish Wisdom (Ecclus. 24:18), self-presentations and self-commendations frequently occur in the form of "I am" statements. Of course the Johannine addition of abstract images is entirely unusual and has a parallel only in Gnostic texts. But without parallel even in such related texts are the qualifying adjectives appearing in this connection in John: "I am the *real* shepherd" (10:11); "I am the *true* vine" (15:1); cf. also: "the *true* light came into the world" (1:9). These adjectives set Jesus apart from other figures who wrongly are also claimed as bearers of salvation. Likewise without parallels in the context of such self-commendations are the conclusions frequently attached in John, which make further specific reference to the saving significance of Jesus: "He who follows me will not walk in darkness . . . " (8:12b); "He who enters in through me will be saved" (10:9b; similarly 6:35b; 11: 25b, 26; 14:6b; 15:5b). That is to say, in John, with the help of the "I am" formula, Jesus makes the exclusive claim that final salvation is mediated only through him.

Occurring most frequently in the context of the "I am" formula is the predicate of salvation *"life"*: "I am the bread of life" (6:35, 48, 51a); "I am the resurrection and the life" (11:25); "I am the way, the truth, and the life" (14:6). But already in the prologue it is said of the Word: "In him was life, and the life was the light of men" (1:4), and in related images it is said that Jesus is able to give "living water" (4:10-11, 14) and has "words of eternal life" (6:68). So then also in I John it is said: "He [Jesus Christ] is the true God and eternal life" (5:20). It is the conviction of many ancient religions, and of Judaism as well, that the deity is in possession of life and is able to bestow divine life, and therefore the Johannine statements which attribute life to Christ of course first of all only confess that Jesus Christ belongs to the world of God and can impart God's life. But now John expressly emphasizes that the Son has received this life from the Father: "As the Father has life in himself, so also has he given to the Son to have life in himself" (5:26); "The life was made manifest, and we have seen and bear witness and declare to you the eternal life which was with the Father and has been revealed unto us" (I John 1:2). In addition, in John 11:25 ("I am the resurrection and the life") the resurrection is set beside the life, and therewith it is made evident that the earthly Jesus has and can give life only as the one who through death and resurrection has been exalted to the Father's presence, that is, as the man whom the Father loves because "I lay down my life in order to receive it again" (10:17).

Closely connected with the predicate of salvation "life" is *the light,*" as is already shown in the prologue: "The life was the light of men. And the light shines in the darkness . . . . The true light which lights every man came into the world" (1:4, 5, 9). Thus Jesus calls himself the light for the world: "I am the light of the world" (8:12); "So long as I am in the world, I am the light of the world" (9:5); "I have come as light into the world" (12:46); "Light has come into the world" (3:19; cf. 12:35-36). These state- ments first of all intend to indicate that Jesus Christ belongs to the realm of the divine. This is already evident in the fact that in I John 1:5 God himself also is described as light: "God is light, and in him is no darkness at all." But here also the crucial statement is that the divine light has been sent into the world in the person of Jesus and that by means of the encounter with Jesus as the light one can escape the darkness: "He who sees me sees him who sent me. I have come as light into the world, that everyone who believes in me should not abide in the darkness" (John 12:45-46). That is to say, the appearance of the divine light in the world is bound to the history of the man Jesus in its temporal limited character: "The true light is already shining" (I John 2:8b); (the crowd asks:) " 'Who is this Son of Man?' Jesus then said to them: 'Yet a short time the light is among you' " (John 12:34b, 35a). If a man desires to encounter the divine light, he must hold to this time of God's saving revelation: "So long as you have the light, believe on the light, that you may become children of the light" (12:36a).

The third predicate of Christ pertaining to salvation that appears in the prologue is *"the truth":* "We have seen his glory, . . . full of grace and truth" (1:14b, c). The Johannine Jesus directly claims this predicate also for his person: "I am the way, the truth, and the life" (14:6), and John also seeks to use this concept to describe the revelation event: "The law was given through Moses, but grace and truth came through Jesus Christ" (1:17). From these state- ments it is evident that for John Jesus is not only the proclaimer of divine truth, though of course for John Jesus is that *too* (cf. 18:37: "For this purpose I was born, and for this purpose I came into the world, to bear witness to the truth"; cf. 8:40); for John Jesus is rather the truth itself. This statement is understandable only when one realizes that with "truth," John does not denote, in the Greek sense, the known reality behind things, but neither does he simply mean, in the Old Testament sense, that which is firm, valid. Instead, he means God's reality: "I have spoken to you the truth which I have heard from God" (8:40; cf. 18:37; see above). Hence in Jesus' prayer to the Father it is said: "Sanctify them through the truth; thy word is truth" (17:17). Therefore the statement that Jesus is "the truth" also means, to begin with, that he belongs to God. But then it says above all that in Jesus God has become quite personally audible and that through the encounter with this truth that has appeared personally, salvation is to be imparted to men: "If you abide in my word, you are truly my disciples, and you will know the truth, and the truth will make you free" (8:32).

In addition to these predicates for the bearer of salvation which appear already in the prologue, the body of the gospel offers still further designations. In the discourse about the shepherd in John 10, Jesus first says of himself: "I am *the door* of the sheep" (10:7); cf. 10:9: "I am the door; anyone who enters in through me will be saved." Like the related figure of the *way* ("I am the way, the truth, and the life," 14:6a), the rarely encountered figure of the door as the entrance to the sphere of salvation says that Jesus alone provides access to salvation, to the Father ("No one comes to the Father but through me," 14:6b), to life (cf. 10:10b). Thus it emphasizes that Jesus is the exclusive mediator of salvation. Immediately adjoining this, in John 10:11, stands the figure of the *shepherd:* "I am the real shepherd" (10:11, 14), which is used in many religions and in the Old Testament also as a description of the protecting function of deity. The Johannine use of the figure for Jesus, however, displays two peculiarities: first, the shepherd's readiness to lay down his life for the sheep is stressed (10:11b, 15b), and second, the relation between shepherd and sheep is characterized by their mutual knowledge: "I know my own [sheep] and my own know me, just as the Father knows me and I know the Father" (10:14b, 15a). Thus Jesus is the good shepherd because he goes to death for his flock, because by laying down his life (10:18) he protects the disciples from ruin (10:12). Jesus is also the good shepherd because he and the disciples have a sure knowledge of each other, as the shepherd and his flock know each other (this is the way the figure puts it in 10:3b, 4). This mutual knowledge of Jesus and the disciples, however, has its basis in the close reciprocal relation between Jesus and the Father. That is, Jesus' fellowship with the Father establishes the fellowship of the disciples with Jesus, and Jesus is the good shepherd because in accordance with the Father's will he lays down his life for those who are his: "Therefore the Father loves me, because I lay down my life in order to take it up again. No one has taken it from me, but I lay it down of my own accord. I have the power to lay it down, and I have the power to take it up again. This commandment I have received from my Father" (10:17-18).

As the figure of the shepherd thus expresses the disciples' fellowship with Jesus, so also does the figure of the *vine* in a slightly different expression: "I am the true vine . . . . I am the vine, you are the branches. He who abides in me and I in him, that one will bear much fruit, for without me you can do nothing" (15:1*a*, 5). The portrayal of how the vineyard keeper deals with the vine (15:1-2, 6) is reminiscent of the Old Testament and early Jewish figure of Israel and of wisdom as God's fruitful or unfruitful vine; yet the bearer of salvation is described as a vine only in late Gnostic texts. In John, in a contradistinction to false bearers of salvation which is not further developed, Jesus is portrayed as the bearer of salvation from whom alone the disciples receive their strength. But as the true vine Jesus works through his word: "You are already clean through the word which I have spoken to you" (15:3), "If you abide in me and my words abide in you, you shall ask what you will and it shall be given to you" (15:7). That is to say, the figure of the vine is not so much a description of Jesus' relation to the Father—15:1*b* does this by an allusion—but rather of Jesus as the revealer who communicates the Father's will to the disciples: "I have called you friends, because I have told you all that I have heard from my Father" (15:15). Because this figure portrays Jesus primarily as the revealer, the disciples' abiding in the vine is accomplished primarily in obedient hearing: "You are my friends if you do what I command you" (15:14).

Thus in this figure it becomes especially clear that John is not primarily interested in statements about Jesus' nature, but wishes to describe God's saving activity through Jesus. This also becomes evident in the use of a whole series of verbs to describe *Jesus as the revealer:* "The only God, who is in the bosom of the Father, has declared it" (1:8); "I have spoken to you the truth which I have heard from God" (8:40*a*); "The words which I have said to you are spirit and life" (6:63); "I have revealed thy name to the men whom thou hast given me out of the world" (17:6); "I am the one bearing witness to myself, and the Father who sent me bears witness to me" (8:18); "I have a testimony which is greater than the testimony of John [the Baptist]; for the works which the Father has given me to do, these works which I am doing testify for me that the Father has sent me" (5:36). In all this it has become evident that John sees God's salvation being actualized in the person as well as in the word of the man Jesus, and therefore we can only come fully to understand Jesus as the bearer of salvation as John sees him when we also inquire into what John says about the salvation which has become reality in Jesus Christ.

4. Salvation and the way of salvation

a. THE LOST CONDITION

The Johannine proclamation of the salvation that is made possible in Christ also takes for granted that men are to be saved from a lost condition and that for this reason salvation is offered to them. This lost condition is most comprehensively characterized for John by the concept of *"the world"* (*kosmos*). John can use this concept, which appears in his work very frequently, in the neutral sense of "that which has been created" ("before the foundation of the world," 17:24; ". . . joy, that a man has been born into the world," 16:21; cf. 1:9, etc.), and in the majority of these cases "world" is used to denote mankind without implying any special valuation: "The world has gone after him" (12:19); "that the world may know that I love the Father" (14:31, *et passim*). Now John gives the label *"this* world" to the world in which men find themselves, and this designation too can be used in a more or less neutral sense: "If any one walks in the day, he does not stumble, because he sees the light of this world" (11:9 RSV); "Jesus knew that his hour had come to depart out of this world to the Father" (13:1 RSV). But in most cases the concept "this world" has a negative connotation: men belong to this world, but Jesus does not belong to it: "You are of this world, I am not of this world" (8:23 RSV); "For judgment I came into this world" (9:39 RSV); "My kingdom is not of this world" (18:36). For this world has the devil as its ruler: "Now is the judgment of this world, now shall the ruler of this world be cast out" (12:31 RSV); " . . . the ruler of this world is judged" (16:11 RSV; cf. 14:30). Hence to be determined by this world leads to perdition: "He who loves his life will lose it; and he who hates his life in this world will preserve it for eternal life" (12:25).

Now John describes this *contrast of the world with God* more precisely, without therein speaking expressly of this world: The works of the men who belong to the world are evil ("[the world]

hates me because I testify concerning it that its works are evil,"
7:7; "All that is in the world, the lust of the flesh, and the lust of
the eyes, and boasting of possessions, is not of the Father but is of
the world," I John 2:16; cf. John 17:15b), because "the whole
world is subject to the evil one" (I John 5:19b). Correspondingly,
the world also is incapable of believing in the risen Christ; the
"Helper" "will convict the world of sin . . . , because they do not
believe on me" (John 16:8-9; cf. 14:19; I John 3:1); and it is unable to understand the divine Spirit: "The Spirit of truth, whom
the world cannot receive, because it does not know and does not
understand [him]" (14:17). Instead, the world hates Christ as well
as the Christians: "If the world hates you, know that it hated me
first . . . . Because you are not of the world, . . . therefore the
world hates you" (15:18-19; cf. 16:33; 17:14; I John 3:13).

This world, which is opposed to God and Christ and is ruled by
the devil, is also occasionally described by John, as by Paul, as
perishable: "The world is passing away, and its lusts with it"
(I John 2:17a), and thus it stands as temporary in contrast to
eternal life: "He who hates his life in this world will preserve it
for eternal life" (John 12:25b; cf. I John 2:17b). But much more
frequently, "this world" stands in opposition to the "world above"
or something similar: "You are from below, I am from above;
you are of this world, I am not of this world" (John 8:23 RSV);
"When Jesus knew that his hour had come to depart out of this
world to the Father" (13:1 RSV); "Now is the judgment of this
world . . . . When I am lifted up from the earth, I will draw all
to me" (12:31-32; cf. 3:31-32; 18:36; I John 4:4-6). Hence it is a
likely assumption that John understands the world in the gnostic
sense as the world of matter, so that men must be saved by being
liberated from the corporeal world and returning to the celestial
world. But even though the concept of the world in the Gospel
of John presumably does not simply arise out of earlier Christianity,
but owes its origin to the gnostic conceptual world which is characteristic of John, still John uses the concept in a way which is
thoroughly in opposition to the ideas of Gnosticism. This is already shown in the fact that the Christ who is taking leave of the
world does not pray for the liberation of his people from the
world: "I do not pray that thou wilt take them out of the world,
but that thou wilt preserve them from the evil one" (17:15). Thus
it is not being in the world that is evil, but being "of the world,"
that is, being determined by the world: "If you were of the world,
the world would love its own; but because you are not of the world,

but I chose you out of the world, therefore the world hates you" (15:19 RSV).

While this distinction in itself alone proves that John does not understand "world" in the gnostic sense as "a foreign country," this becomes all the more evident when we inquire in what way the "being of the world" is made manifest at all. We have already seen that doing evil is a characteristic mark of those men who are "of the world" (I John 2:16; John 7:7; 17:15b; cf. above, pp. 288-89). But the crucial point is first reached in the opposition in which the world stands to the salvation event: the world "did not know him [the Logos]" (1:10); the "helper" will judge the world "because they do not believe on me" (16:9); the world "hated me before it hated you" (15:18b). That is, "it is in its negative, rejecting attitude toward the Christ event that the cosmos first takes on its distinctive, obdurately negative accent" (J. Blank). Hence the world is, in the last analysis, at enmity with God, because the men who are "of the world" "do not know him who sent me" (15:21b with 15:19).

The lost condition of the world, which gains its crucial sharpness in the resistance to the coming of Christ, becomes concrete in death and sin. Of course for John also the universality of *death* is the presupposition of his interpretation of the human fate of mortality: "He who does not love remains in death" (I John 3:14b; John 5:24; 8:51; 11:25); but we do not find in John any statements about the beginning or the cause of this universal mortality. Death is endless: "If anyone keeps my word, he will never see death in eternity" (8:51), and man cannot set himself free from his state of mortality (I John 3:14b; see above). Even the Jewish certainty of the future resurrection ("I know that he will rise at the resurrection on the last day," 11:24) is thrust aside: "If you do not believe that I am he, you will die in your sins" (8:24b). Thus eternal death is the inevitable and inescapable end of man in the world; but such necessity of dying is not, however, a mysterious fate, but is grounded in *sin:* "I have told you that you would die in your sins" (8:24a). Thus for John also death is the consequence of sin, and thus it is also self-evident for John that all men are sinners. It is true that this is not explicitly formulated, but it follows from the fact that Jesus is described as "the lamb that takes away the sin of the world" (1:29). But this universality of sin is to be seen above all in the fact that the devil, the ruler of the world, stands behind sin: "You are of your father, the devil, and it is your will to do the lusts of your father" (8:44a); "Whoever commits sin is of the devil; for the devil sins from the very beginning" (I John 3:8). The sinfulness of men, and their being therefore subject to death, of course are also manifest to John in their sinful acts. Yet the plural, "sins," seldom appears in John (John 8:24; 9:34; more frequently in I John: 1:9; 2:2, 12; 3:5; 4:10, mostly in formula-like expressions), and he does not often say anything even of committing sin ("Everyone who commits sin is a slave," John 8:34; I John 3:4, 8-9). What is crucial is rather that men are subject to sin: "Whoever commits sin is of the devil" (I John 3:8; cf. John 8:34, 44a). This subjection leads to the rejection of Christ and hence to unbelief and the refusal of the divine revelation: "If I had not come and spoken to them, they would have no sin; but now they have no excuse for their sin" (15:22; cf. 15:23-24); "If you were blind, you would have no sin; but now you say, 'We see,' and [so] your sin remains" (9:41; cf. 8:24; 16:9). That is to say, just as the world shows itself to be the world precisely in the fact that it does not believe in Christ, so men are decisively under the power of sin and are perishing because they do not believe: "You will die in your sins; for if you do not believe that I am he, you will die in your sins" (8:24). However, from all this it is evident that the Johannine conception of man's lost condition in the world and hence under death and sin does not arise out of a pessimistic evaluation of the world as "a foreign country" nor from a hopeless judgment about man's mortality and wickedness, but from the belief that in Jesus Christ God has put an end to this lost condition: "Who is he that overcomes the world but he who believes that Jesus is the Son of God?" (I John 5:5). It is not on the basis of his own insight that John sees himself and mankind as lost; instead, it was only as a believer that he came to see in what lostness men live and to what doom they are traveling.

b. LIBERATION FROM THE WORLD AND FROM DEATH

Therefore it is the crucial message of John that God in Christ overcomes this lost condition: Christ liberates man from domination by the world. John can say this in a quite general way by referring to the love or the saving intention of God: "For God so loved the world that he gave his only Son, that anyone who believes on him should not perish but have eternal life" (John 3:16); "God sent the Son into the world . . . , that through him the world might be saved" (3:17; cf. 4:42; 12:47; I John 4:14). John can also emphasize that Jesus Christ has already overcome the world and thereby has made possible the victory over the world for those who believe in him: "In the world you are oppressed, but be of good cheer; I have overcome the world" (John 16:33); "Whatever is begotten of God overcomes the world; and this is the victory that overcomes the world, our faith. But who is it who overcomes the world except he who believes that Jesus is the Son of God?" (I John 5:4-5). Accordingly, it is also said that through Christ the disciples are delivered from the world: "Because you are not of the world, but I have chosen you out of the world, therefore the world hates you" (John 15:19); "You are not of the world, as I am not of the world" (17:16; cf. 17:6). It is also evident that the liberation from the world does not mean flight from the world, but liberation from the compelling power of the world: "I do not pray that thou wilt take them out of the world, but that thou wilt preserve them from evil" (17:15). That is to say, the liberation from domination by the world is not an exodus from the world; instead, it signifies a change in lordships. These general statements about the liberation from the world remain general and do not give a concrete description of salvation, however; this shows that John has no speculative interest in the salvation that is wrought by Christ, but intends to speak of a concrete reality. Hence it is only the Johannine statements about liberation from death and from sin that make concretely discernible the salvation that is accomplished in Christ.

As men's lost condition in the world is most clearly discernible for John in their mortality, so also salvation is to be seen above all in the *gift of life*. For John, Christ is "the life," because he bestows life: "The bread of God is he who descends from heaven and gives life to the world" (6:33); "My sheep . . . follow me, and I give to them eternal life, and they shall never perish" (10:27-28; cf. 17:2). Christ has "words of eternal life" (6:68) and by means of his gift creates eternal life: "Whoever drinks of the water which I shall give him will never thirst again; but the water which I shall give him will become in him a spring of water welling up to eternal life" (4:14). In this connection, "life" and "eternal life" are used alternately with the same meaning: "Whoever believes in the Son has eternal life; but anyone who does not obey the Son shall not see life" (3:36); "Whoever hears my word . . . , has eternal life and does not come into judgment, but has passed from death to life" (5:24; cf. 5:39, 40; 6:63, 68, etc.). Now it is all the more striking that in the passages just quoted, and in numerous other passages as well, John speaks of the believer's having eternal life already in the present: "Whoever eats my flesh and drinks my blood has eternal life" (6:54) ; "This is the testimony, that God has given us eternal life" (I John 5:11; cf. John 3:15-16; 5:40; 6:40, 47, 53; 10:28; I John 3:14; 5:13). Accordingly, because for John "eternal life" is a present possession, the assumption has often arisen that with this term John is describing a mental attitude, a religious consciousness, or a frame of mind, and some of John's formulations seem to make this assumption even more probable: "The Son of Man must be lifted up, that everyone who believes on him may have eternal life" (3:14b, 15) ; "I have come that they may have life, and have it abundantly" (10:10) ; "This is eternal life, to know thee, the only true God, and Jesus Christ, whom thou hast sent" (17:3) ; "Whoever follows me shall not walk in darkness but shall have the light of life" (8:12b; cf. 6:53c). Here the primitive Christian hope of a future consummation of salvation appears to be abandoned in favor of the belief in the consummation of salvation in the present, which is realized in knowledge and sight.

But surprisingly, John places unequivocal *promises of the future* alongside these statements about the present. This is true first of all for the statements about eternal life: "He who eats me will live because of me . . . . He who eats this bread will live forever" (6:57-58) ; "Whoever . . . hates his life in this world will preserve it for eternal life" (12:25) ; "This is what he has promised us, eternal life" (I John 2:25 RSV; cf. John 8:12). Further, the resurrection at the last day is placed alongside the possession of eternal life: "He who eats my flesh and drinks my blood has eternal life, and I will raise him up at the last day" (6:54; cf. 6:39, 40, 44) ; John also speaks of the "resurrection to life" (5:29a). But these are not the only eschatological-futurist sayings. He also speaks of the future entrance into the kingdom of God. "If a man is not born of water and spirit, he cannot enter into the kingdom of God" (3:5; cf. 3:3), of future deliverance and exaltation (10:9; 12:32), and of future judgment: "The word which I have spoken to you will judge him at the last day" (12:48; cf. 5:28-29; 12:31b; I John 4:17). Thus the departing Christ also promises his return: "When I have gone and prepared a place for you, I shall come again and receive you unto myself" (14:3; cf. 14:28) ; "And now, little children, abide in him, that, when he will be revealed, we may have boldness and not be ashamed of him at his coming" (I John 2:28). I John speaks still more plainly of the last hour: "Little children, it is the last hour" (I John 2:18), and of the future consummation of salvation: "Beloved, now are we children of God, and it has not yet been revealed what we shall be. We know that when he is revealed,

we shall be like him, for we shall see him as he is" (I John 3:2).
But these promises in I John differ only in plainness of statement,
not in substance, from the Gospel of John, which in the traditional
text also clearly reckons on the judgment and the consummation of
salvation at the last day, the coming of the resurrected One in
glory and the dawning of the kingdom of God.

Now there can be no doubt that this juxtaposition of statements
which confess full salvation in the present and promises of the end-
time appears contradictory, especially since such contradictory statements frequently appear in immediate conjunction: the assurance
that the believer will not come into judgment stands beside the
prediction of the hour when all those who have fallen asleep will
hear the voice of the Son of Man and will come forth [from their
graves] to the resurrection unto life or the resurrection unto judgment (John 5:24, 28-29); and the promise, "I will come again
and receive you unto myself" (14:3, 28), conflicts with the promise
that the resurrected One will always remain with his own: "If
anyone loves me, he will keep my word, and my Father will love
him, and we shall come to him and abide with him" (14:23; cf.
also 6:40a alongside 6:40b; 6:54a alongside 6:54b; 12:31a alongside
12:31b). It has often been assumed that the relatively few futurist
statements are additions of a redactor for purposes of adaptation
to the general Christian belief, or at least are not to be understood
in the sense of an eschatological expectation of the future. But in
favor of the assumption of interpolations there is no other basis
than the reference to the rational contradictions, and the futurist-
eschatological sense of the texts cited can be disputed only by forcing them.

Instead, it is by no means accidental, but *substantively necessary
that* even in the Johannine theology *the expectation of the future
consummation of salvation not be lacking.* This is necessary because John knows that the exalted Christ has indeed "overcome
the world," but that this world nevertheless continues to exist and
the Christians therefore have "tribulation in the world" (16:33);
and John likewise knows that "the ruler of this world is judged"
(16:11), and yet he is not destroyed, and from this there follows
the paradoxical statement: "Now is the judgment of this world;
now will the ruler of this world be cast out" (12:31). Already in
the present the believers have seen the glory of the incarnate and
exalted Son of God (1:14; 16:20b), but this glory has remained
hidden from the world (16:20a; 1:10b). John also, like Jesus and
Paul before him, therefore waits for the ruler of this world finally

to be stripped of his power and for Christ's glory to become manifest to the eyes of the world. Therefore, by John's placing the references to the future consummation of salvation alongside the heavily stressed statements about the present, he shows that for him also the present reality of being a Christian is determined by the divine saving act which began in Jesus Christ and therefore is present reality, but also waits for its promised completion.

Consequently the liberation from death and the gift of life are for John a reality which occurs in the present in the life of the Christian. As long as this world still stands, it oppresses the Christians: "In the world you have tribulation" (16:33a); "Now you have sorrow" (16:22a); "the world hates you" (15:19c), and the Christians are in danger of letting themselves be overwhelmed by it: "Marvel not, brethren, if the world hates you" (I John 3:13); "Let not your heart be troubled, neither let it despair" (John 14:27c). But such despair only shows, according to John, that the disciples have not yet grasped the reality of the gift of life. For Christ gives to his disciples *peace:* "Peace I leave with you, my peace I give to you" (14:27a); "I have said this to you, that you may have peace in me" (16:33a). This does not mean a state of mind, but the certainty that Christ has overcome the world (16:33c) and that therewith the Christian who has peace "in Christ" (16:33a) is likewise delivered from the compelling power of the world: "Little children, you are of God, and have overcome them [the heretics, who are of the world, vs. 5a]; for the one who is in you is greater than the one in the world" (I John 4:4). Therefore the Christian lives in the *joy* that in Christ's resurrection God has conquered death: "I shall see you again, and your heart will rejoice, and no one will take your joy from you" (16:22b; the promise is to be related to the Easter experiences). Thus the Christians have an abiding joy, because this joy is based upon God's saving act in Christ: "If you loved me, you would rejoice that I am going to the Father, for the Father is greater than I" (14:28b); "I have said this to you that my joy may be in you and your joy may be made full" (15:11; cf. 17:13; I John 1:4). But this joy can be made full only if the Christian abides in love and in faith: "If you keep my commandments, you will abide in my love" (John 15:10a); "If you loved me, you would rejoice that I am going to the Father . . . ; and now I have told you before it happens, that when it happens you may believe" (14:28-29).

With this there emerges the question of the Johannine understanding of the way of salvation, which however we can answer only when we have seen in what sense, according to John's message, Christ sets men free from the dominion of the world by saving them from sin.

C. LIBERATION FROM SIN

As we have seen (above, p. 290), for John, men in the world have become subject to sin and therefore are guilty, which is shown above all in their unbelief. For John also it is the *death of Christ* that keeps sinful men from being lost, even though this idea is not so central for John as in the primitive community or with Paul. It is true that in John there is frequent talk of Jesus' dying for the world or for those who are his: "I risk my life for the sheep" (10:15; cf. 10:11, 17-18); [the high priest] "prophesied that Jesus should die for the nation, and not for the nation alone, but also in order to bring together the scattered children of God" (11:51-52); "Caiaphas was the one who had advised the Jews that it would be expedient that *one* man should die for the people" (18:14); "Herein we know love, that he laid down his life for us" (I John 3:16). But these statements are so broadly formulated that it cannot be determined from them alone just how, in John's opinion, the death of Jesus benefits the world or his people. But now John also describes Jesus' death as a "going away": Jesus knew "that he had come from God and was going to the Father" (John 13:3); "Now I am going to the one who sent me" (16:5; cf. 8:14, 21-22; 13:33; 14:4, 28; 16:17), or as an "ascending" ("Now when you see the Son of Man ascending to where he was before," 6:62), which means the return to the divine glory: "Now glorify me, Father, in thy presence with the glory which I had with thee before the world was" (17:5; cf. 7:39; 8:54; 12:16, 23, 28; 13:31-32; 17:1). Though in this connection the Jesus who is returning to the Father explicitly declares: "It is expedient for you that I go away. For if I do not go away, the 'Helper' will not come to you; but if I go away, I will send him to you" (16:7; cf. also 14:3*a*), yet John undoubtedly also saw the import of Jesus' death for his people in the fact that for Jesus his death was the transition into divine glory, so that now he who has died and returned to the Father can give his people a share in his glory: "If I am lifted up from the earth, I will draw all men to me" (12:32; cf. 17:24).

But still more important, according to John, is another effect of Jesus' return to the heavenly glory through death: in Jesus' death and exaltation God's victory over the world and its ruler is accomplished: "Now is the ruler of this world cast out" (12:31*b*;

cf. 12:32-33) ; "The ruler of this world is coming, and he has no power over me" (14:30) , i.e., no claim to lordship; "I have overcome the world" (16:33c) . But at the cross, along with the ruler of this world, sin also is robbed of its power, and thus John can say in various ways that through the Son the Christians have been set free from the compelling power of sin: "Everyone who commits sin is a slave to sin. Now if the Son has set you free, you shall be free indeed" (8:36) ; "I sanctify myself for them, that they too may be sanctified through the truth" (17:19) . I John goes a step further and declares that the man who is newly created by Christ no longer sins: "No one who is begotten of God commits sin, for his seed remains in him, and he cannot sin, because he is begotten of God" (I John 3:9; cf. 3:6; 5:18) . It is true that for the author of I John this assertion of the impossibility of the Christian's committing sin holds true only with the condition that the Christian "abides in him [i.e., Christ]": "No one who abides in him sins" (3:6a) . Therefore, in spite of its statements about the impossibility of the Christian's sinning, the epistle does reckon with the reality of their committing sin (2:1; 3:20; 5:16) . Thus the conviction that, through Christ's death and exaltation, the power of sin is broken, is more pronounced in I John than in the gospel, but even the gospel discloses this belief (John 17:19 [see above] undoubtedly has in mind the imminent death of Jesus) .

Of course one will have to ask whether this statement that refers to Jesus' death, "I sanctify myself for them" (17:19) , does not also include the idea that the dying Christ sanctifies himself as a sacrifice for his people, and in that case this saying would not only be about the liberation from the power of sin through the death and exaltation of Christ, but also about the *eradication of the guilt of sin*. But the saying of John the Baptist unquestionably expresses this idea: "Behold the Lamb of God, that takes away the sin of the world" (1:29) . It is true that it can no longer be determined with certainty to which conception the figure of the Lamb alludes—most likely the idea is that of the daily sacrifice of a lamb in the temple at Jerusalem—but there can hardly be any doubt that here Jesus is compared with a sacrificial lamb which removes the guilt of sin. Therewith the common Christian conception that Jesus' death took place "for our sins," and that is to say, to remove man's guilt for sin, clearly is taken up, even though we are unable to say anything more specific about how John conceived of this removal of sinful guilt. Thus John clearly is acquainted with the conception of

Jesus' dying for our sins; therefore in the statement, "God so loved the world that he gave his only Son, that whosoever believes on him should not perish, but have eternal life" (3:16), one may not limit the "giving" of the Son by the Father to the sending of the Son. Instead, the "giving up" of the Son to death must also be heard in these words, particularly since just before this (3:14-15), the lifting-up of the Son of Man on the cross and into heaven is identified as the precondition for the reception of eternal life. Finally, in the saying in the discourse on bread, "But the bread which I shall give is my flesh for the life of the world" (6:51c), there is certainly the idea that Jesus surrenders his body in order to secure life for the world. In this, the allusion to the saying about the bread in the Lord's Supper tradition (I Cor. 11:24; Luke 22:19b) is not to be overlooked; it shows that the removal of the guilt of sin must be included by John.

Thus John did not pass over the idea, important in the primitive community and with Paul, of the removal of sinful guilt by Jesus' death; yet this idea does not play a central role in the Gospel of John. In I John, on the other hand, not only do we hear of Christ's taking away sins and of the giving up of Christ's life for us (3:5; 3:16), but also of the cleansing effect of Christ's blood: "The blood of Jesus, his Son, cleanses us from all sin" (1:7), and here Jesus is called "expiation for our sins, and not for ours only, but also for the whole world" (2:2; 4:10). That is to say, I John more strongly emphasizes the idea of the expiation for sins through Jesus' death, and even though this is not in conflict with the more cautious statements of the gospel, still in any case there is a shift in the accenting of the idea. Presumably the gnosticizing language of the Gospel of John is responsible for the fact that in the gospel the reflection upon the saving significance of Jesus' death recedes into the background, yet for this recession of the idea, the decisive thing above all may very well be the fact that John sees the essential salvation event in the sending of the Son into the world and in his return to the Father, so that the death of Jesus is regarded only as an important stage in the exaltation of the Son of Man (John 3:13-14). And in this recession of the idea of the expiation for sin through Jesus' death, with John in the gospel, it is clearly shown that this evaluation of Jesus' death can be altogether pushed into the background without thereby endangering the statement of belief that Jesus has come in order to set men free from their state of subjection to sin.

d. FAITH AND LOVE

Hence we can turn now to the question which has posed itself for us repeatedly: How do men gain a share in the liberation from the world's domination that now has become a reality through the sending, death, and exaltation of Jesus Christ? But when we pose this question, it immediately becomes evident that, from the beginning to the end of his gospel, John emphatically points to *faith* as the way to the reception of salvation: "To those who receive him [i.e., the Logos], he gave power to become children of God, [those] who believe on his name" (1:12); "these things are written that you may believe that Jesus is the Christ, the Son of God, and that believing you may have life in his name" (20:31). In harmony with this, the verb "to believe" occurs with extraordinary frequency in the Gospel of John and in I John, while the substantive "faith" is employed only once, in I John: "This is the victory that overcomes the world, even our faith" (I John 5:4). This usage itself shows that, for John, faith means an attitude and, in any case primarily, not intellectual agreement with a content of belief. Therefore he often speaks of "believing" in an absolute way, without any indication of the object of faith: "The Son of Man must be lifted up, that whosoever believes in him may have eternal life" (3:14-15); "You do not believe, because you do not belong to my sheep" (10:26 RSV; cf. 6:47; 11:40; *et passim*). Yet even in these texts it is plain to see that faith means a decision with respect to Jesus: "that whosoever believes may have in him eternal life" (3:15), alongside "that everyone who believes on him . . . may have eternal life" (3:16). But still much more frequently, the verb "to believe" appears connected with a dative object or a "that"-clause, and among these cases, in fact, there are isolated instances where the author speaks of believing in God (14:1; I John 5:10), in the Scripture (John 2:22; 5:46-47), in the light (12:36), in the works of Jesus (10:38), in the word or the words of Jesus (4:50; 5:47)—I John only speaks in addition of believing in the love of God and in the testimony of God (4:16; 5:10). But closer examination discloses that in all these cases also, in reality it is believing in Christ that is meant: "Believe in God, believe also in me" (14:1); "If you believed Moses, you would believe me; . . . if you do not believe his writings, how will you believe my words?" (5:46-47 RSV); "So long as you have the light [i.e., the Son of Man; see vss. 34-35], believe in the light" (12:36, etc.). And so then in the great majority of cases he speaks directly of believing in Christ: "If I speak the truth, why do you not believe me?" (8:46b) ; "He who believes in me will never thirst again" (6:35c) ; "I believe that you are the Christ, the Son of God, he who is coming into the world" (11:27 RSV). While occasionally in these we hear of belief in Jesus' messiahship or in his being the Son of God (11:27; 20:31), yet as a rule the accent falls on the point that God has sent the Son or that the Son has come from God: "For the sake of the people standing by, I have said this, so that they may believe that thou hast sent me" (11:42b) ; "that the world may believe that thou hast sent me" (17:21b) ; "The Father loves you because you have loved me and have believed that I have come forth from God" (16:27) ; "They know in truth that I have come from thee, and have believed that thou hast sent me" (17:8b) . Thus belief in Christ is belief that God has acted in Christ: "Whoever believes in me does not believe in me but in the one who sent me" (12:44) .

This says, on the one hand, that for John *belief in God and belief in Christ coincide,* because in Christ one encounters God: "He who has seen me has seen the Father" (14:9; cf. 14:1; 17:3) and because "no one comes to the Father but by me" (14:6b) . But on the other hand, with this it is also said that faith is not oriented to a set of facts or a doctrine, but that it grasps the divine action in Jesus Christ: "My Father is still steadily at work, and thus I too am working . . . . That is to say, whatever he does, this the Son does in the same way . . . . Whoever hears my word and believes the one who sent me has eternal life" (5:17, 19c, 24a) . Therefore, according to John, faith can quite well be kindled also by Jesus' miracles. Of course one can also take note of these miracles only as facts, but thereby in no way come to faith: the chief priests and Pharisees say, "What shall we do? For this man is performing many signs" (11:47) ; Nicodemus says, "Rabbi, we know that you are a teacher come from God, for no one can do the signs which you do unless God is with him" (3:2) ; "His [Jesus'] brothers now said to him: . . . 'Go to Judea, that your disciples also may see your works which you are doing.' . . . His brothers in fact did not believe in him" (7:3-5; cf. 10:25-26) . Consequently, according to John, a belief that is awakened by miracles is only a first step and therefore an uncertain belief, which indeed has recognized the miracle-worker, but has not seen the Father in Jesus and can only lead on to real faith: "If I am not doing the works of my Father, do not believe me; but if I am doing them, then even if you do not believe me, believe the works, that you may ever better understand that the

Father is in me and I am in the Father" (10:37-38) ; "Believe me that I am in the Father and the Father is in me; or believe in me because of the works themselves" (14:11; cf. 4:48; 5:36; 6:26, 36) .

Hence the crucial step for man toward his salvation is a faith which requires no seeing: Jesus says to Thomas: "Because you have seen me, you believe; blessed [are those] who have not seen and [yet] believe" (20:29) . Such faith is awakened by the word of Jesus or his witnesses: "The man [the father of the dying son] believed the word which Jesus had said to him and went away" (4:50) ; "Believe me that I am in the Father and the Father in me" (14:11a) ; "I pray for all those who will believe in me through their word" (17:20) . Because faith thus represents a turning to Jesus himself, John can also describe the "believing in his name" as "receiving" Jesus (1:12; cf. 5:43; 13:20) , or his words (12:48; 17:8) or can speak of "coming to Jesus" (6:35; 7:37) , of "following Jesus" (8:12) , or of "keeping Jesus' words" (8:51-52) .

But now it is very important not to overlook two sets of facts in this connection.

John takes it for granted that the Christ in himself will find no acceptance and hence also no belief among men: "The one who came down from heaven bears witness to what he has seen and heard, and no one accepts his testimony" (3:31b, 32) ; "The true light . . . was in the world, and the world knew him not. He came to his own possession, and his own people did not receive him" (1:10-11) ; "The world cannot hate you, but it hates me" (7:7) . If many people nevertheless believe (cf. 3:33: "he who receives his testimony sets his seal to this, that God is true" [RSV]; similarly 1:12) , this shows that *faith is God's work in man*: "This is the work of God, that you believe in him whom he has sent" (6:29) . In other words, no one can believe of his own accord: "I said to you that you have seen and yet you do not believe" (6:36) ; instead only he whom God draws comes to faith: "All that the Father gives to me will come to me" (6:37) ; "No one can come to me unless the Father who sent me draws him" (6:44 RSV; cf. 6:65) ; "If I speak the truth to you, why do you not believe me? Whoever is of God hears the words of God; the reason why you do not hear is that you are not of God" (8:47) ; "You do not believe, because you do not belong to my sheep" (10:26 RSV; cf. 17:6, 9-10, 24) . Thus if a man comes to believe, it is God who has taken the first step, but this does not mean that the man himself does not have to take the second step: "Labor . . . for the food which abides unto eternal life, which the Son of Man gives you" (6:27) . It is quite true that John says that only he whom God "draws" comes to believe, that the only ones who have kept God's word are those whom the Father has given the Son out of the world (6:44; 17:6) ; but this does not imply that God had made a definitive decision as to who belongs to Jesus' sheep and therefore hears Jesus' voice (10:27). Instead, the urging to let oneself be given the everlasting food by the Son of Man (6:27; see above) corresponds to the statement that "every one who has heard and learned from the Father comes to me [Jesus]" (6:45). At first the man born blind does not know at all who this Jesus is who has healed him (9:17b, 25, 36), but when Jesus has confessed himself to be the Son of Man, he falls down before Jesus with the cry, "Lord, I believe!" (9:38). Hence the main thing is that one not only hear, but also obey: "Every one who is of the truth hears my voice" (18:37c) ; "I have other sheep . . . . ; these too I must bring, and they shall hear my voice, and there shall be *one* fold and *one* shepherd" (10:16-17; cf. 5:24). This is in harmony not only with the call to faith ("Believe me, that I am in the Father and the Father is in me; or believe me because of the works themselves," 14:11; cf. 10:38; 12:36; 14:1), but also with the assurance that certain events will awaken faith ("And now I have told you [that I am going to the Father] before it happens, so that when it happens, you may believe," 14:29; cf. 11:15, 42; 13:19; 17:21; 19:35). Accordingly, the refusal of belief is to be blamed on those men who seek their own standing and are not willing to acknowledge their blindness: "How can you believe, you who receive glory from one another and do not seek the glory of the only God?" (5:44) ; "If you do not believe that I am he, you will die in your sins" (8:24; cf. 9:39-41; 12:37-43). John too, like Paul (see above, pp. 232 ff.) , knows accordingly that faith rests solely on God's working, but he knows likewise that God allows us the freedom to let his work occur through us or to reject it. John also refrained from attempting to bend the two truths to each other, because only the two together allow both God's saving action and the responsibility of man to stand.

Because faith is God's work through us, real faith, as a turning to Christ, embraces *the whole life* of the believer: "Whoever believes in me, as the Scripture says, out of his body will flow streams of living water" (7:38). Thus the believer is a person who can pass along divine life, because by his being joined to Christ the divine life has come to be dominant in him. Hence the truth of the witness to Christ can be recognized only by the man who has let himself be taken into the service of this truth: "My teaching is not mine, but [the teaching] of the one who sent me. If anyone will do his will, he will know whether the teaching is from God, or whether I am speaking on my own authority" (7:16-17). Thus to believe means to follow Jesus' words: "If anyone hears my words and does not keep them, I do not judge him" (12:47); "If anyone loves me, he will keep my word" (14:23a); and the disciples are Jesus' friends only if they keep his commandments: "You are my friends if you do what I command you" (15:14).

Thus the keeping of the commandments is necessarily a part of believing; therefore John occasionally sets faith and love side by side: "This is his commandment, that we believe on the name of his Son Jesus Christ and that we love one another, as he has commanded us" (I John 3:23; cf. also the connection of John 14:20 and 14:21), but he frequently calls for *love*. In these passages he often speaks of love for God or for Christ: "If God were your Father, you would love me; for I have come forth from God and am [now] here" (8:42; cf. 14:28). But in almost all these cases either love for God or love for Christ is combined with love for one's brother: "We have this commandment from him, that he who loves God is to love his brother also" (I John 4:21; cf. 4:20; 5:1-2). Or it is said that love for God or for Christ is actualized in the keeping of the commandments: "If you love me, you will keep my commandments" (John 14:15; cf. 14:21a, 23a); "By this we know that we love the children of God, if we love God and keep his commandments; for this is the love of God, that we keep his commandments" (I John 5:2, 3a). But the crucial commandment of God and of Christ is love for one's brother: "A new commandment I give to you, that you love one another; as I have loved you, you also are to love one another. By this all shall know that you are my disciples, if you have love for one another" (John 13: 34-35); "This is my commandment, that you love one another, as I have loved you" (15:12); "This is his commandment, that we should believe in the name of his Son Jesus Christ and should love one another, according to the commandment which he has given us" (I John 3:23; cf. John 13:14-15; 15:17; I John 2:10; 3:11, 14; 4:19). Faith in Jesus Christ and love for one's brother belong for John so closely together that for him faith is real faith at all only when the one who believes has become one who loves.

John now calls the *commandment of brotherly love a new commandment* (John 13:34). By this he does not mean to say that such a commandment had never before been expressed; for

John can even declare, paradoxically: "Beloved, it is not a new commandment that I am writing to you, but an old one, which you have had from the beginning. . . . Again I am writing a new commandment to you, which is true in him and in you, because the darkness is passing away and the true light is already shining" (I John 2:7a, 8). By this John means to say, first, that the readers already have heard this commandment, when they became Christians ("The old commandment is the word which you have heard," I John 2:7b), without thereby ruling out the origin of the commandment in the Old Testament-primitive Christian tradition. But the commandment is new because "the true light is already shining" (I John 2:8b) and because Jesus *has* loved the disciples (John 13:34b). Because God "so loved the world that he gave his only Son, that whoever believes in him should not perish but have eternal life" (3:16), Jesus' commandment to love one another is new; for faith indeed allows the believer to participate in God's saving action which is accomplished by the exalted Christ, and now on the basis of this divine action the Christian has life and can transmit it to others: "Whoever believes in me, as the Scripture says, out of his body shall flow streams of living water. This he said of the Spirit which those who believed in him should receive. For the Spirit was not yet, because Jesus was not yet glorified" (7:38-39).

Now to be sure, arguing against this understanding of faith in John, according to which faith is a state of being seized by God's action in Christ and therefore embraces the whole of one's life, there appears to be the fact that John sees *faith and perception* or knowledge in close connection. John simply names "believing" and "perceiving" side by side: "We have believed and perceived that you are the Holy One of God" (6:69); "The words which thou hast given to me I have given to them, and they have received them and perceived in truth that I have come from thee, and have believed that thou hast sent me" (17:8); "And we have perceived and believed the love which God has toward us" (I John 4:16). When moreover believing is described as the result of perceiving ("Now we know that you know all things and do not need that anyone question you; it is for this reason that we believe that you have come from God," 16:30), but likewise that perceiving is identified as the result of believing ("If you do not believe me, believe the works, that you may come more and more to perceive that the Father is in me and I am in the Father," 10:38), then, so it seems, there can be no question that for John believing and perceiving or knowing denote the selfsame human attitude, and that faith therefore must be described as the intellectual acknowledgment of a state of affairs. And this impression is further strengthened when one sees that John frequently talks of the believing and the perceiving of one and the same object: "that they may believe that thou hast sent me" (11:42) along with "that they may know thee . . . and [him] whom thou hast sent" (17:3) ; "If you do not believe that I am he" (8:24) along with "then you will perceive that I am he" (8:28) ; "Do you not believe that I am in the Father and the Father is in me?" (14:10) along with "On that day you will know that I am in my Father and you are in me and I am in you" (14: 20) ; moreover, he frequently speaks of perceiving or knowing God or Christ (7:28; 8:19; 14:7, 9; 16:3; 17:23, 25; I John 2:3; 4:6).

But even though these texts plainly show that to a great extent John can say the same thing about believing and knowing, still it is not true that for John the two are simply identical, so that faith in its essence could be described as knowing. This already appears from the fact that nothing is said of Jesus Christ's believing God, but of his knowing God, which corresponds to the disciples' knowing God: "Righteous Father, the world has not known thee, but I have known thee, and these [the disciples] have known that thou hast sent me" (17:25; cf. 7:29; 8:55; 10:15). But that for John faith cannot simply be described as "knowing" is evident above all from the statement that for John faith can be identified as knowing only when it is an enduring faith: "He said to the Jews who had believed in him: 'If you abide in my words, you are truly my disciples, and you shall know the truth [i.e., the divine reality; see above, pp. 285-86], and the truth shall make you free' " (8:31-32). But this is not meant to say that faith leads to the knowledge of the truth only when it temporally endures; "abide" here rather denotes the fact that the entire person is affected by the liberating truth: "Truly, truly, I say to you that every one who commits sin is a slave to sin . . . . Now if the Son makes you free, you shall be free indeed" (8:34, 36). That is to say, however, that faith is enduring and likewise can be described as knowledge of the truth when it leads to a turning away from sin and to obedience to the words of Christ. This corresponds to John's use of "abide" elsewhere to denote the believer's activity which is inseparable from faith: "Whoever abides in me and I in him, he will bear much fruit" (15:5) ; "I have chosen you and appointed you that you should go and bear fruit and that your fruit should endure . . . . This I command you, that you love one another" (15:16-17) ; "Whoever says that he

abides in him must also walk as he walked" (I John 2:6). Hence
to a large extent John can say the selfsame thing about believing
and knowing; faith is not simply knowledge, however, but it describes the fact that the whole person is affected by the historical
saving act of God in Christ, an effect which has its point of departure in the recognition of the sending of the Son by the Father.
"Faith is not the acceptance of a dogma . . . , but faith is everything.
Knowing cannot be detached from believing and hover above it;
but faith is also a perceiving faith . . . . Knowing is a structural element of faith" (R. Bultmann).

e. THE BIRTH FROM GOD AND THE SACRAMENTS

Now to be sure in the context of the Johannine statements about
believing we frequently encounter the idea of "being in Christ"
and of "being in God" and of birth from God, and these ideas have
often led to the view that John represents a Hellenistic mysticism
which "is based upon the attainment of immortality through the
condition of being in the bearer of immortality" (A. Schweitzer).
In that case faith would be, in the last analysis, a timeless absorption
into the divine being, and the understanding of believing as a
state of being seized by God's historical saving action in Jesus
Christ, which had previously emerged for our view, would have to
be set aside as erroneous. But is this interpretation of the ideas of
"being in God" and "in Christ" and of regeneration as forms of
expression of nonhistorical mysticism correct?

Being in God and in Christ

It is beyond doubt that John talks of the Christians' being in
Christ as Christ is in the Father: "On that day [after Jesus'
resurrection] you will know that I [am] in my Father and you
[are] in me, as I [am] in you" (John 14:20); " . . . that all may
be one, as thou, Father, [art] in me and I [am] in thee, that they
also may be in us" (17:21; cf. 17:23). And John speaks likewise
of the Christians' *abiding in Christ* as Christ abides in them:
"Whoever eats my flesh and drinks my blood abides in me and
I [abide] in him" (6:56); "If you abide in me and my words
abide in you, you shall ask what you will and it will be granted
to you" (15:7); "Whoever keeps his commandments abides in him,
and he in him" (I John 3:24; cf. 2:5b, 27c). Moreover, the Gospel
of John speaks by allusion, and I John unequivocally, of the
Christians' *abiding in God*: "If anyone loves me, he will keep my
word, and my Father will love him, and we will come to him and

make our dwelling with him" (John 14:23; cf. 17:21; see above);
"God is love, and whoever abides in love abides in God, and God
abides in him" (I John 4:16b; cf. 2:6, 24; 4:12-13, 15). But even
though this talk of being in Christ and in God undoubtedly is the
language of mysticism and appears to describe the being of the
Christians in analogy to the eternal communion of the Father and
the Son ("Believe me, that I [am] in the Father and the Father
[is] in me," 14:11a; cf. 14:20; 17:21; see above), still with these
statements John by no means intends to speak of the believers'
becoming equal to the Father and the Son in essence, which is the
ultimate aim of all mysticism.

This is already evident in the fact that John not only speaks of
the Christians' being or abiding in Christ and in God—or of
Christ's and God's being or abiding in the Christians—but can
make statements of the same sort about the Christians' relation to
the Word, to love, etc.: "that the love with which thou hast loved
me may be in them and I [may be] in them" (17:26b; cf. 5:42);
"If one closes his heart against him [the brother in need], how
does the love of God abide in him?" (I John 3:17b; cf. 4:12);
"Abide in my love" (John 15:9b; cf. 15:10; I John 4: 16b) —"If
you abide in me and my words abide in you . . . " (John 15:7; cf.
5:38; I John 2:14, 24); "If you abide in my word . . . " (John 8:31)
—"I have said this to you in order that in me you may have peace"
(16:33a) —"whoever loves his brother abides in the light" (I John
2:10). It is immediately evident that in all these cases John is using
the phrases with the preposition "in" not in the sense of a location
but as a description of a relation or even of a state of subordination
(quite similar to Paul's usage; see above, pp. 218 ff.), and that it
therefore would be incorrect to interpret the Johannine expressions
of "in Christ," etc., otherwise.

The view that the idea in all these statements in actuality is the
relation between Christ and the believers is confirmed then by a
look at the *parable of the vine* and its branches (John 15:1 ff.).
Here the same preposition "in" first clearly denotes the connection
of the branches with Christ the vine: "Every branch *on* me" (15:2;
similarly 15:4), and one can even translate 15:3: "Stay on me, as I
[stay] on you." But then the discourse gradually loses its vivid
imagery, and even in 15:5 one can hardly translate any way but:
"Whoever abides *in* me, as I [abide] in him, brings forth much
fruit; for without me you can do nothing," and in what follows this
translation is the only one possible (cf. 15:7): "If you abide in me
and my words abide in you . . . . " But now the continuation of this

parable also shows quite clearly that abiding in Christ denotes holding fast to faith and love, thus not a mystical communion with Christ, but the believer's being determined through the message of the saving event that has occurred in Christ: "If you abide in me and my words abide in you, you shall ask what you will and it will be granted to you. In this my Father is glorified, in your bearing much fruit and becoming my disciples. As the Father has loved me, so have I loved you; abide in my love. If you keep my commandments, you will abide in my love . . . . You are my friends if you do what I command you" (15:7-10a, 14).

Finally, this state of affairs, namely that what is said about "being in Christ" describes the believer's being totally seized by the divine action in Christ, also indicates that according to John, the winning of more people to faith and thus to "being in" God and in Christ is a perceivable occurrence which must lead still others to believe: "I pray also for those who will believe in me through their word, that all may be one, as thou, Father, [art] in me and I [am] in thee, that they also may be in us, that the world may believe that thou hast sent me" (17:20-21; cf. 17:23).

Birth from God

But the idea of birth from God also, in John's mind, is not meant to denote a redemption of a natural kind. To be sure there are only two passages in the Gospel of John that speak of the *birth from God*. In the prologue it is said of men who received the Logos: "To them he gave power to become children of God, to those who believe on his name, who were born not of blood, nor of the will of the flesh, nor of the will of man, but of God" (1:12-13). In the conversation with Nicodemus, Jesus says: "Truly, truly, I say to you, if a person is not born from above, he cannot see the kingdom of God." To Nicodemus' countering question, whether a man can be born a second time from his mother's body, there follows the explanation: "Truly, truly, I say to you, unless one is born of water and spirit, he cannot enter into the kingdom of God. What is born of flesh is flesh, and what is born of spirit is spirit" (3:3-6). I John, on the other hand, speaks more frequently of being *begotten of God* and the state of being a child of God attained thereby: "Anyone who is begotten of God does not commit sin, for his seed remains in him. And he cannot sin, for he is begotten of God" (I John 3:9); "Behold what love the Father has given to us, that we are called children of God, and such we are . . . . Beloved, now we are children of God, and it has not yet appeared what we shall be"

(3:1a, 2a; cf. 2:29; 3:10; 4:7; 5:1-2, 4a, 18). The idea of rebirth or of being begotten of God which thus clearly appears in John has its roots in Hellenism or at least in strongly hellenized Judaism, and only later primitive Christianity adopted the idea of rebirth above all as a description of the effect of baptism (I Peter 1:3, 23; 2:2; Titus 3:5; probably also James 1:18). Now in John on the one hand it is very strongly emphasized that God is the originator of this begetting and birth and thereby has wrought the possibility of our becoming children of God (John 1:12-13; I John 3:1), that is, man can only accept the birth from God as a gift. On the other hand, the context in which the statements about the birth from God are found clearly shows that the acceptance of the proclamation and hence faith bring about the birth from God: according to John 1: 12-13, those who believe in the name of the Logos were born of God, and according to 3:5, 11 ff., that one is born of water and spirit who has accepted the testimony of the community and believed it. According to I John, it is the mark of the children born of God that they practice righteousness, love the brethren, and fulfill God's commandments (2:29; 3:9-10; 5:1, 3), and in 5:4 our faith is identified as the victory over the world by the one who is born of God (cf. 4:7-8). Thus birth or begetting from God takes place for the man who in believing and knowing grasps the message of God's saving action in Christ (cf. the context of I John 4:4-15) and thereby is led to brotherly love, so that "God abides in us and his love is made perfect in us" (4:12b). The idea, taken from nature, of the birth from God and the status of being children of God that is bestowed thereby thus serves John only to express in vivid terms the personal reality of the transforming experience of being grasped by God's saving act in Christ.

Finally, this is also shown in the fact that this status of being children of God, that is bestowed by God, is characterized as provisional, because the assimilation of the Christian begotten of God to the divine existence of Christ is hoped for only for the time of Christ's appearing in glory: "Beloved, now we are God's children, and it is not yet manifest what we shall be. We know that when he is revealed, we shall be like him, because we shall see him as he is. And everyone who has this hope toward him sanctifies himself, just as he is holy" (I John 3:2-3). Thus in spite of the terminology employed by John, we cannot speak of a Johannine mysticism, since all these mystical-sounding ideas only describe the historical participation of the believer in the salvation that is wrought through the sending of Jesus Christ and that waits for the perfection of the believer.

Baptism and the Lord's Supper

Even less is this statement called in question by the Johannine interpretation of the sacraments. For, in view of the curiously few references to baptism and the Lord's Supper in the Johannine writings, the assertion that in John "a strong interest . . . in the sacraments is present" (O. Cullmann) certainly is not apposite. Baptism is clearly mentioned only in John 3:5: "If a person is not born of water and spirit, he cannot enter into the kingdom of God"; and the command to eat Jesus' flesh and to drink his blood, which appears in 6:51b-58 abruptly, in the context of the saying about the bread, can only be understood as a reference to the words of institution of the account of Jesus' last supper. In addition to these two allusive but clear references to baptism and the Lord's Supper, we find in John only two enigmatic statements about water and blood: After a Roman soldier had pierced the breast of the dead Jesus with his lance, "at once blood and water flowed out" (19:34) ; and to strengthen the belief "that *Jesus* is the Son of God," I John declares: "This is the one who came by water and blood, Jesus Christ; not in water only, but in water and blood; and the Spirit is the one bearing witness, for the Spirit is the truth" (I John 5:6-7) . Since after mentioning the flowing of blood and water from the wound in Jesus' breast, in the gospel John places extraordinarily heavy emphasis on the point that the testimony for this set of facts in trustworthy (John 19:35) , he can hardly intend with the mention of this flow of blood and water only to portray a miraculous occurrence, and the assumption is obvious that with the mention of blood and water he wanted to indicate that Jesus' death was just as real as his baptism. It has often been conjectured that this account is also meant as a reference to the Lord's Supper and Christian baptism, but this is in no way obvious.

This exposition is confirmed by I John 5:6, where in parrying a Gnostic heresy, water and blood are explicitly identified as signs of Jesus' coming, and hence the reference can only be to the reality of Jesus' baptism and death as events of the past ("This is the one who *came* . . . ") . But then the epistle continues with a statement in the present tense: "For there are three that bear witness, the Spirit and the water and the blood, and the three agree. If we do not accept the testimony of men, [yet] the testimony of God is greater, for this is the testimony of God, that he has testified concerning his

Son" (5:7-9). Here seems to be placed, beside the testimony of the divine Spirit who attests to the believer the sending of the Son (4:13-15), the testimony of baptism and the Lord's Supper, which in the community again and again point to the actuality of the sending of God's Son and therewith also to Jesus' baptism and death. If this interpretation of the difficult text should be correct—it cannot be fully assured—then here reference is made to the fact that baptism and the Lord's Supper are for the community just as much a testimony to Jesus' coming and dying as God's saving act, as is the preaching. That seems to show at the same time that here John attributes to the two sacraments no significance for the gaining of salvation that goes beyond the significance of believing.

Since this interpretation of I John 5:7-8 nevertheless stays uncertain, there remain as rather firm references to baptism and the Lord's Supper in the Johannine literature only the two texts, John 3:5 and 6:51b ff. Since these references to baptism and the Lord's Supper stand in a somewhat isolated position in their respective contexts and no other references to these sacraments are found in John, it has often been assumed that the words "water and" in 3:5 and the entire passage 6:51b-58 were first inserted into the Gospel of John by an ecclesiastical redactor, in order to make good the lack of any mention of the sacraments. But neither the indication of certain peculiarities of language in 6:51b-58, which to be sure stand in contrast with typically Johannine features, nor the fact that the references to baptism and the Lord's Supper in the two texts appear unexpectedly, will suffice as reason for asserting that they are interpolations. But even if these two texts belonged to the original Gospel of John, it cannot be denied that baptism and the Lord's Supper are mentioned here only incidentally. While in 3:5 it is presupposed as self-evident that man can enter into the kingdom of God only if he is born [anew] from God through receiving baptism and the endowment with the divine Spirit, in what follows it speaks only of being born of the Spirit: "What is born of flesh is flesh, and what is born of spirit is spirit . . . . So it is with everyone who is born of the Spirit" (3:6, 8). The continuation clearly shows that it is faith which receives the birth from God: "Truly, truly, I say to you, we speak of what we know and we testify of what we have seen . . . . And as Moses lifted up the serpent in the wilderness, so must the Son of Man be lifted up, that everyone believing in him may have eternal life" (3:11a, 14-15). Thus baptism is only the vehicle of the divine new creation by the Spirit, which faith receives (cf. also 15:3: "You are pure because of the word which I have spoken to you").

The reference to the Lord's Supper in 6:51b ff. is quite in harmony with this. For this text, it is true, clearly is speaking of participation in the Lord's Supper: "If you do not eat the flesh of the Son of Man and drink his blood, you have no life in you . . . . Whoever eats my flesh and drinks my blood abides in me, and I [abide] in him" (6:53b, 56). But on the one hand, at the end of this section reference is made back to 6:32 ff.; compare "This is the bread which has come down from heaven . . . . Whoever eats this bread will live forever" (6:58) with "I am the living bread that has come down from heaven; if one eats of this bread, he will live forever" (6:51a). In the discourse about the bread in 6:32 ff., the theme clearly is believing on the bread that has come from heaven, the believing that attains eternal life: "Everyone who has heard and learned from the Father comes to me . . . . Truly, truly, I say to you, the one who believes has eternal life" (6:45b, 47). On the other hand, in the continuation of the discourse in 6:60 ff. in explanation of the statements about eating the flesh and drinking the blood we read: "It is the spirit that makes alive, the flesh profits nothing; the words which I have said to you are spirit and life" (6:63). It is evident from both these facts that eating the Lord's Supper mediates the same salvation as does faith, because the believer receives the divine Spirit even in the Lord's Supper. As to why John does not tell anything of the institution of the Lord's Supper by Jesus at the last meal—the narrative of the footwashing at the last meal with the disciples, in 13:1 ff., can be interpreted as a reference to the institution of the Lord's Supper only by forcing it—one can only venture a guess, and so there remains for us only the statement that even the sacraments in John do not call in question the fact that, for John, participation in the divine saving action which has occurred in Christ becomes a reality exclusively through the believing acceptance, one that embraces the whole life, of the message of this divine saving action. "Only the words given by the Spirit . . . save, because they say to us that all our salvation hinges on Jesus' having given his flesh for the life of the world, and because we accept them, believing, by coming to the Lord's Supper" (E. Schweizer).

f. THE HOLY SPIRIT AND THE COMMUNITY
The Spirit of God

In the Johannine statements about the sacraments we repeatedly encounter the reference to the activity of the divine Spirit, and so, in conclusion, we must inquire as to the role which, for John, the Spirit of God plays in the life of the Christian. Like Paul, John presupposes, as self-evident, that in baptism the Christian has received the Spirit of God, and he interprets this gift of the Spirit as birth from God and as the gift of the divine life: "If one is not born of water and spirit, he cannot enter into the kingdom of God" (John 3:5; cf. 3:8); "The Spirit makes alive, the flesh profits nothing" (6:63a); "Whoever believes in me, as the Scripture says, out of his body streams of living water will flow. This he said of the Spirit whom they who believed in him should receive" (7:38, 39a). That the Spirit has such a crucial significance for the reality of being a Christian is based in the fact that "God is Spirit"; consequently, "those who worship [God] must worship in spirit and in truth," and for the Christian as one endowed with the divine Spirit it is true that "the hour is coming and now is [here], in which the true worshiper will worship the Father in spirit and in truth" (4:24, 23). But the Spirit also brings about the confession of Jesus Christ: "By this you will know the Spirit of God: every spirit that confesses Jesus Christ as having come in the flesh is of God" (I John 4:2; cf. 4:13).

If the gift of the divine Spirit thus brings it about that Christ "abides in us" (I John 3:24), must we not then presume that John understood the Spirit as something almost physically bestowed on man and received by him as possession? This assumption could seem all the more justified since John relates of the resurrected One who appeared to the disciples, "He [Jesus] breathed on them and said to them, 'Receive the Holy Spirit; to those whose sins you remit, they shall be remitted; to those whose sins you retain, they shall be retained'" (20:22-23). It cannot be disputed that here the endowment with the divine Spirit by Jesus is portrayed as if it were a "thing," possibly in association with God's quickening breath in the creation narrative (Gen. 2:7). But the effect of the bestowal of the Spirit thus portrayed is not supernatural abilities, but the authorization of the disciples to pronounce or to refuse forgiveness of sins, and thus a purely spiritual gift, and John—in contrast to Paul—says nothing at all of the divine Spirit's enabling one to perform miraculous deeds. In John, apart from the exception in 20:22-23, it is rather the message of Jesus that awakens faith and thereby mediates the Spirit: "It is the Spirit that gives life . . . ; the words that I have spoken to you are spirit and life" (6:63); "This he said of the Spirit whom those who believed on him should receive" (7:39a). Because the Spirit bears testimony to the reality

313

of the sending of Jesus Christ, the faith that is awakened by the Spirit can overcome the world: "Who is he who overcomes the world but he who believes that Jesus is the Son of God? He, Jesus Christ, is the one who has come through water and blood . . . . And the Spirit is the one that bears witness, for the Spirit is truth" (I John 5:5-6; cf. also 4:6).

But still more important than the observation that for John the Spirit is not a power that is physically added, as it were, to the believer, but the source of the testimony to the Son of God who became man and was crucified, is the observation that for John the gift of the Spirit is strictly bound up with the salvation event. Indeed, according to John the earthly Jesus also possesses the divine Spirit, and John expressly emphasizes that he was in constant possession of the Spirit: "I [John the Baptist] saw the Spirit descending upon him as a dove from heaven, and it remained on him" (1:32); "The one whom God has sent speaks the words of God; for he [God] does not give the Spirit by measure" (3:34); "The words which I have spoken to you are spirit and life" (6:63*b*). But this conception of the earthly Jesus' endowment with the Spirit plays no essential role for John, and according to John the earthly Jesus does not bestow the Spirit at all. And correspondingly, John explains that Jesus has bestowed the Spirit on the believers only since his resurrection: "Whoever believes in me, as the Scripture says, out of his body streams of living water will flow. This he said of the Spirit which those who believed in him should receive. For the Spirit was not yet, because Jesus was not yet glorified" (7:38-39). Thus just as for Paul, so also for John it is only the resurrected One who is the giver of the Spirit, and this means that for John too the Spirit is the characteristic mark of the end-time which has begun in an anticipatory way with Jesus' resurrection. Therefore anyone who receives the Spirit obtains a share in the eschatological salvation that has been introduced through Jesus' resurrection.

The Paraclete

The observation that with John the divine Spirit is bound up with the salvation event in Jesus Christ now receives its confirmation through the Johannine sayings about the Paraclete. That is to say, in the "farewell discourses" of the Gospel of John (John 14—16) there occur five sayings which treat of the "Paraclete" (14:16-17, 26; 15:26; 16:7-11, 12-15), though earlier in the gospel there is no reference whatsoever to this figure, and this figure is equated in 14:17 and 15:26 with the "Spirit of Truth," and in 14:26 with the

"Holy Spirit." Thus there can be no doubt that John intends with "Paraclete" to denote the same reality as with "Spirit" (he speaks of the "Holy Spirit" also in 1:33 and 7:39; "Spirit of Truth" occurs in I John 4:6; in John 4:23-24 and in I John 5:6, Spirit and truth are combined). Yet the effects of the Spirit and of the Paraclete are not altogether described as the same; cf., on the one hand, "to be born of water and Spirit" and the Spirit as the source of life in the believer, and on the other hand, teaching, recalling, testifying, and convicting as functions of the Paraclete (John 3:5; 7:39; 14:26; 15:26; 16:8). The concept "Paraclete" occurs elsewhere in the New Testament only in I John 2:1: "If a person sins, we have a Paraclete with the Father, Jesus Christ, the righteous; and he is the expiation for our sins"; here Christ is clearly characterized as "intercessor," a meaning of the word which does not fit in the Gospel of John. For in the gospel two things are said of the Spirit as Paraclete. On the one hand, the Spirit is to work in the Christian community when Christ has "gone away": then Christ will "pray the Father, and he will give you another Paraclete, that he may be with you forever . . . . You know him, for he abides with you and will be in you" (14:16, 17a); "The Paraclete, the Spirit of Truth, whom the Father will send in my name, will teach you all things and will remind you of all that I have said to you" (14:26); "When the Paraclete comes, whom I shall send from the Father, the Spirit of Truth, who proceeds from the Father, he will bear witness of me" (15:26); "If I do not go away, the Paraclete will not come to you; but if I go, I will send him to you . . . . I have yet much to say to you, but you cannot bear it now; but when that one, the Spirit of Truth, comes, he will guide you into all truth. He will not speak of his own accord, but will speak what he hears; and he will proclaim to you what is to come. That one will glorify me, for he will receive from what is mine and announce it to you" (16:7, 12-14). On the other hand, the Paraclete will work beyond the bounds of the community: "the Spirit of Truth, whom the world cannot receive, because it does not see him and does not understand him" (14:17a); "the Spirit of Truth . . . will bear witness to me" (15:26b); "When that one comes, he will convict the world of sin and of righteousness and of judgment" (16:8).

From all these utterances it clearly emerges, first, that the Paraclete too is to be at work only after Jesus' exaltation. It is equally evident that the Paraclete continues the work of Jesus with the disciples and in relation to the world, after Jesus has gone to the Father, and this means, "Since the Paraclete can come only when

Jesus departs, the Paraclete is the presence of Jesus when Jesus is absent" (R. E. Brown). This further means not only that Jesus himself occasionally can be identified as the first Paraclete in contrast to the Holy Spirit as the second Paraclete (the Father "will give you another Paraclete, that he may be with you forever," 14:16; cf. also I John 2:1), but also that, "Whatever is said about the Paraclete is said elsewhere in the Gospel about Jesus" (R. E. Brown): Jesus and the Paraclete are sent by the Father, both proceed from the Father (John 8:42; 14:26; 15:26); both bear witness to Jesus (8:14; 15:26); Jesus accuses the world just as does the Paraclete (7:7; 16:8), etc. Thus the Paraclete continues the work of God in Jesus, he is the representative of the exalted Christ until promise becomes fulfillment: "I will come again and receive you unto myself, that you also may be where I am" (14:3).

Now this continuation of Jesus' work by the Paraclete or the Holy Spirit consists, as the texts cited show, primarily in the continuation of the testimony to Christ, in relation to the world as well as to the community. For on the one hand the Paraclete calls to remembrance Jesus' own words and bears further witness to Jesus; indeed, the Paraclete "will not speak of his own accord, but will speak what he hears" (16:13; cf. 15:26), entirely in harmony with what is said of Jesus himself in relation to the Father (8:26b; 15:15). On the other hand, the Paraclete will guide the disciples "into all truth" and "will teach you all things" (16:13; 14:26), and this corresponds to John's conviction that only after the resurrection did the disciples fully understand the words and events of the life of Jesus (2:22; 12:16; 20:9), because only the encounter with the resurrected One allowed the disciples fully to discern the divine origin of Jesus: "On that day you will know that I [am] in the Father and you [are] in me and I [am] in you" (14:20). Just as the testimony of Jesus and hence the knowledge of Jesus thus is continued by the Paraclete in the community, so also Jesus' accusation against the world. For the world "cannot receive [the Spirit of Truth], because it does not see him, nor does it know him," and therefore the Paraclete will convict the world of sin, "because they do not believe in me" (14:17; 16:9). This in fact means that with the departure of the earthly Jesus from this world the witness to Christ is not at an end, but that the response to this ongoing witness to Christ is just as decisive for the ultimate destiny of those who hear it as the relation to the message of Jesus was for the contemporaries of Jesus. For God the creator speaks to us just as directly in the Paraclete's witness as in the word of Jesus himself.

But why does John talk at all of the "Paraclete," and what is specifically meant by this talk of the Paraclete?

The Greek word "*paráklētos*," which occurs in the New Testament only in the Paraclete sayings of the "farewell discourses" and in I John 2:1, literally means "the one called alongside," and accordingly the early Christians already very soon translated this Greek word with the Latin "*advocatus*," which is identical with it as far as the meaning of the word is concerned. This specifically juristic interpretation of the word Paraclete in the sense of a legal counsel, which fits only in I John 2:1, is not attested in the Greek language of John's time and furthermore does not correspond to the use of the word in the Gospel of John; the same is even more true of the translation "comforter," which was adopted by Luther and the King James Version from similarly ancient Latin tradition. The common Greek usage knows only the meaning of "proxy" or "helper," and this meaning fits in completely with the functions of the Paraclete in the Gospel of John, although these functions are not adequately described thereby; it lacks the idea of testimony as well as that of accusation. If one wishes to translate the Greek word at all, one therefore will preferably choose "helper." Yet it is evident that even in the early church many Christians had the feeling that the word could not be reproduced by a concept in another language, and hence they contented themselves with the appropriation of the word Paraclete as a foreign word in the Latin and Syriac languages. Even today the adoption of the term as a foreign word may well be least subject to misunderstanding, if one then clearly paraphrases the function of this concept.

John himself undoubtedly did not create this conception, but took it over from Judaism. For even though it has not yet been possible to prove a fully corresponding conception in Judaism, still there are good reasons for assuming that the two conceptions, occurring in the Judaism of that time, of a prophet and his successor and of the Spirit of God as witness and accuser, and the designation "helper" had already merged in Judaism. But John could all the more easily appropriate this idea of the Spirit as "helper" and continuator to portray the activity of the divine Spirit after Christ's exaltation since the earlier Christian tradition had already described Christ as well as the Spirit as "helper," though without using the title of "Paraclete" for this idea: "Everyone who confesses me before men, him will I confess before my Father in heaven" (Matt. 10:32 par.) ; "When they bring you to trial and deliver you up, do not be anxious beforehand what you are to say; but say whatever is given you in that hour, for it is not you who speak, but the Holy Spirit" (Mark 13:11 par.; cf. also Rom. 8:26). But now it surely is no accident that before the farewell discourses John speaks only of the "Spirit" and then only of the Paraclete who is equated with the Spirit (the curious exception in John 20:22 only confirms the rule; cf. above, p. 313). For the Paraclete indeed represents the continuing impact of Jesus after his death and exaltation, and the strictly futurist statements of the farewell discourses about the Paraclete prepare the disciples and then the Christian community for this new situation in the salvation-history. This not only means that the divine Spirit continues God's historical action in the person and history of Jesus and therefore has a share in this historical reality of the salvation event, but it also shows that this activity of the Spirit is accomplished in the concrete reality of the Christian community.

For what the Paraclete does is the teaching and reminding, the testifying and accusing, the leading into all truth and the glorifying of Christ (14:26; 15:26; 16:8, 13-14), and indeed all this does not take place through the intervention of supernatural beings, or through inward experiences, but through the disciples' preaching. This is evident first from 15:26-27: "When the Paraclete comes . . . he will bear witness to me. And you bear witness, because you are with me from the beginning." Here it is clearly stated that the disciples, who can tell of Jesus because they have joined themselves to him, disseminate the Paraclete's witness to Jesus in that the Paraclete is speaking through them. Hence in John's view the working of the Paraclete is achieved precisely in the fact that "the Paraclete will teach you all things and bring to your remembrance all that I have said to you" (14:26). But this means that where the Paraclete is at work, there the words of Jesus are repeated and interpreted, and the author of the Gospel of John understands his own gospel as part of such teaching of the Paraclete. Where the message of Jesus Christ is believingly reported, proclaimed, and made alive as the life-giving word, there Jesus Christ himself is at work through the Paraclete (cf. 20:31).

The community

Hence the Johannine message of the work of the Holy Spirit as the Paraclete presupposes the reality of the community of Jesus Christ. To be sure, it has often been doubted that John is at all interested in the community or church, the existence of which of course he knows. For the word "church" or community occurs in the Johannine writings only in III John 6, 9, 10, and there only as designation of the local congregation; and moreover, only in III John is anything said of the holder of a function of leadership in the community of the recipient of the epistle ("Diotrephes, who likes to have the chief role," III John 9). And alongside this statement about terminology has been placed the still more important observation that "the Fourth Gospel is one of the most strongly individualistic of all the New Testament writings, and that the 'realized eschatology' which is so familiar a feature of this Gospel is the result rather of this individualism" (C. F. D. Moule). Now of course in view of the literary character of the Gospel of John as a "gospel," the fact that here the designation "church" is lacking does not say much—the same also applies to Mark and Luke —because indeed the church could after all be spoken of in the Gospel of John only by means of a backward projection. It is true, however, that I John also does not speak of the "church"; nevertheless it clearly presupposes the opposition of the church to the heretics who are separated from her: the antichrists "went out from us, but they were not of us; for if they had been of us, they would have remained with us, but it was in order that it might become manifest that they all were not of us" (2:19). The epistle likewise sets the Christian community over against the world: Christ "is the expiation for our sins, but not for ours alone, but also for the whole world" (2:2); "Do not marvel, brethren, if the world hates you; we know that we have passed from death to life because we love the brethren" (3:13-14). It is certainly correct that the Johannine proclamation with its call for faith and its confession of the eternal life that is received is oriented primarily to the individual (cf., e.g., John 3:18; 5:24). But here too the contrast with the world shows that John conceives of Jesus' disciples as a unity: "When the hour had come that he [Jesus] should depart from this world to the Father, having loved his own who were in the world, he showed them his love in perfect fashion" (13:1; cf. 15:18-19). Thus John's lack of interest in the outward form of the Christian community is balanced by his strong emphasis on the significance of the church for the salvation event.

This is shown above all by the two *figures of the flock and of the vine*. The flock is "given" to the true shepherd, is protected by him, and from him receives eternal life: "My sheep follow me, and I give to them eternal life, and they shall never perish, and no one will snatch them out of my hand" (10:27-28; cf. 10:9-10). Only the branches that abide in Christ the vine bear fruit and do not wither: "I am the true vine . . . . As the branch cannot bear fruit by itself, if it does not stay on the vine, so also you, if you do not abide with me . . . . Without me you can do nothing" (15:1, 4, 5b). This flock and these branches, which belong to the shepherd and the vine, are then also called "my disciples" who love one another (15:8; cf. 8:31; 13:35), or Jesus' "friends," who "go and bear fruit" (15:15-16), or "his own" (13:1). The Father has given these men to the Son, the Son who is approaching death prays to the Father for them, not for the world (17:6a, 9); for them he prays "that they may be one just as we [are one]" (17: 11c). Hence John knows of being a Christian only in connection with the Christian community, as branches of Christ the vine.

It is important to see that for John too the existence of the Christian community is strictly bound to God's historical saving action in Jesus Christ. Even though the lines to the past are not drawn with heavy strokes, still John repeatedly emphasizes that according to the testimony of Scripture there were many witnesses to Christ in Israel: "Moses wrote concerning me" (5:46); "Abraham your father rejoiced that he was to see my day, and he saw it and rejoiced" (8:56); "Isaiah said this [Isa. 6: 9-10] because he saw his [Christ's] glory, and he spoke of him [Christ]" (12:41). As "salvation is of the Jews" (4:22b), i.e., as the "savior of the world" (4:42) was a Jew, so also the savior has first gathered "his own" out of Israel: Nathanael, who will confess Jesus as Messiah, is "truly an Israelite in whom there is no guile" (1:47), and the sheep "of this fold" (10:16), who stay with the true shepherd, are Jesus' Jewish disciples. But even though this connection of the Christian community with God's history in the Jewish people is not heavily emphasized, still John lays all the more emphasis on the point that the community is founded by Jesus' death and resurrection and that the effect of this death and this resurrection reaches beyond the bounds of Israel to all peoples: "The real shepherd lays down his life for the sheep . . . . I am the real shepherd, and I know my own, and my own know me. . . . And I have still other sheep who are not of this fold; them too I must lead, and they will hear my voice, and there shall be one flock and one shepherd" (10: 11b, 14, 16); Caiaphas "prophesied that Jesus should die for the nation, and not for the nation only, but to gather into one the children of God who are scattered abroad" (11:51b, 52 RSV); "If I am lifted up from the earth, I will draw all men to me" (12: 32). Now this connection shows that for John the working of the Holy Spirit as the Paraclete in fact presupposes the existence and activity of the Christian community: the testimony of the community wrought by the Paraclete effects the extension of the message of Jesus Christ and hence the spread of the community: "When the Paraclete comes . . . , he will bear witness of me; and you bear witness, for you are with me from the beginning" (15: 26-27) ; "I do not pray for these alone [i.e., the Jewish disciples of the earthly Jesus], but also for those who shall believe on me through their word, that all may be one, as thou, Father, [art] in me and I [am] in thee, that they also may be in us, that the world may believe that thou hast sent me" (17:21-22). Thus for John the working of the Holy Spirit as well as the reality of the church is tied to God's historical revelation in Jesus Christ, and "between the hour of the farewell discourses and the last day the time of the church unfolds, in which Jesus . . . is present in his word, which is handed on from generation to generation" (H. van den Bussche) .

Thus it has been shown again and again that the Johannine message sees and presents the activity and the preaching of Jesus Christ deliberately and consistently from the perspective of the belief of the community of the late period of primitive Christianity in the sending and the exaltation of Jesus by God. But it has also been shown that the superelevation of the human reality of Jesus from the perspective of this belief certainly occasionally has brought with it the danger of doing away with this human reality. John very plainly met this danger by repeatedly turning the gaze back to the humanity of Jesus. It has likewise been shown that in spite of his Hellenistic language and conceptual world, and in spite of the receding of the expectation of the future, John strictly joins not only the person of Jesus but also the salvation wrought by Jesus to God's historical saving action in Jesus Christ, and thereby proclaims Jesus and this salvation as the eschatological salvation event. If therefore with the presentation of the Johannine message of Christ as the "consummation of the New Testament witness to Christ" the circle of a "Theology of the New Testament According to Its Major Witnesses" is properly completed, still it remains as the last task of this presentation to pose the question of what the message of these major witnesses has in common.

CONCLUSION

JESUS—PAUL—JOHN:
THE HEART OF THE NEW TESTAMENT

a. THE "HEART OF THE NEW TESTAMENT"

The presentation offered in this volume of the preaching of Jesus, of the theology of Paul against the background of the primitive community, and of the message of Christ of the Johannine writings has confirmed the presupposition (see above, p. 16) that the individual writings or groups of writings of the New Testament must first speak for themselves, because in them different voices are speaking, voices which cannot be heard in unison at the outset. When we now ask in conclusion whether in spite of the diversity of these voices a commonality can be discerned, this question is indispensable because we have started out from the assumption that the three forms of the proclamation set forth here in detail afford an adequate picture of the central proclamation of the New Testament (see above, p. 18). But the primary reason this question is indispensable is that as Christians we do not come to the New Testament as to just any historical document of the past, but in the more or less clear conviction that in the writings of the New Testament we encounter the knowledge of God's revelation in Jesus Christ, and that therefore the question as to the message of the New Testament, of the unity in the multiplicity, must be crucial for us. For if it is not to be disputed—the presentation in this book has repeatedly demonstrated this—that even the major witnesses of the New Testament are not to be found from the outset in agreement with one another, still one could not speak of a message of the New Testament at all if these witnesses did not have the same message on essential points, if the Christian could not, in spite of all the diversity, hear the one essential message sounding forth from the multiplicity of witnesses. The question, to be posed here in conclusion, of the common message of the major New Testament witnesses thus does not thrust itself upon us from the involvement with the proclamation of these witnesses themselves, who stand in no direct connection with one another, but from the awareness of their common membership in the canon of the New Testament.

The New Testament is in fact a collection, developed in the early church through the elimination of writings and through delimitation ecclesiastically pronounced, of Christian writings from the time of the apostles, for which the church made and makes the claim that in it are contained all the writings which can assuredly bear witness to what God has wrought through the life and work, the death and resurrection of Jesus Christ, and through the founding of the church by his Spirit. That all these writings proclaim in essence the same thing was assumed as self-evident until, first, Martin Luther and then, since the middle of the eighteenth century, theology working historically gained the insight that the writings of the New Testament do not always say the same thing, but in part very clearly are contradictory (see above, p. 14). If the New Testament thus is not a unity, but if its writings nevertheless are normative for the belief of the Christian, then the compelling question is posed as to where the "heart of the New Testament" is to be found, by which the individual writings or even the individual teachings of the New Testament can be measured. As is well known, in his prefaces to the translation of the New Testament into the German language of 1522, Luther named the "true touchstone for testing all books, when one sees whether they urge Christ or not," and he identified it as "the office of a true apostle to preach of Christ's sufferings and resurrection and office." Even though we should ever anew take our bearings from this discovery by Luther of the "gospel" in the New Testament, still research in the last two hundred years has provided for us a significantly clearer insight than Luther could have into the historical development of the writings of the New Testament and of the collection of these writings into the New Testament canon, and therefore we can better judge concerning the order in time of the individual writings and the historical circumstances affecting each individual writing. Therefore the question of the "heart of the New Testament" can rightly be answered by ourselves only through reflection upon the development and the nature of the New Testament canon.

It was undoubtedly the intention in the delimitation of the New Testament canon to protect from later expansions and forgeries the testimony of the men of the apostolic age to God's historical saving act in Jesus Christ and to the founding of his community by the Holy Spirit. The multiform witness of the writings of the New Testament has its normative significance in the fact that it stands in a more or less close relationship temporally and substantively to the historical revelation in Christ. We can expect to encounter this witness in its purest version in those forms of primitive Christian proclamation which stand closest in point of time to the historical Christ event, that is, (1) in the message and figure of Jesus as these become perceptible to us in the earliest tradition of the synoptic gospels; then (2) in the proclamation of the primitive community which interpreted Jesus' death and resurrection and attested the founding of the community by the Holy Spirit; and finally (3) in the first theological reflection on this proclamation by Paul. The survey of these three forms of the proclamation in fact lets us see, in spite of all the differences, a common message which can be labeled as foundational and by which the message of the rest of the New Testament can be measured.

But it would be a mistake to assume that the unadulterated witness to Christ of the apostolic age could have been deposited exclusively in the earliest writings of the New Testament. Yet it is significantly more difficult to say which further writings are to be questioned next as to whether in their central proclamation they are in agreement with the message that is common to Jesus, the primitive community, and Paul. When in the present volume the message about Christ in the fourth gospel and the Johannine epistles has been adduced with this intention, of course one reason has been the large scope of this group of writings in the context of the rest of the writings of the New Testament. But above all, the Johannine writings have been included in the investigation because in the fourth gospel we have the attempt consistently to present the person and preaching of Jesus from the perspective of the faith of the primitive community after Easter and Pentecost and because, in the light of this presentation, the question arises to what extent therewith the original message about Christ has been appropriately developed or seriously adulterated (see above, p. 266). Hence it is just as much in harmony with the development of the primitive Christian proclamation as with the theological meaning of the New Testament canon when in what follows we inquire about the substantive unity in Jesus' message, the theology of Paul, and the proclamation of Christ in the Johannine writings, and in this way at the same time draw attention to the problem of the "heart of the New Testament." It will be self-evident that in this summarizing

backward look the examples that have been cited cannot be repeated.

b. THE FUTURE AND THE PRESENCE OF SALVATION

Jesus

Jesus appeared with the message of the imminent coming of the
kingdom of God, and he meant this announcement very concretely,
as is shown by his expectation that the kingdom of God would
appear even before his generation had died out. But in contrast
to all Jewish conceptions, Jesus connected the promise of the imminent coming of the kingdom of God with the bold assertion that
the kingdom of God had already become a present reality in his
own work and preaching. However, the contradictory and, for his
contemporaries, undoubtedly puzzling combination of these two
statements can be understood as coherent when one recognizes that
the two statements precisely when taken together are saying something about God and about Jesus.

For Jesus, God is the challenging Lord and summoning judge,
and the certainty of the imminent coming of the kingdom of God
intensifies the urgency of the divine demand and the threatening
character of the divine judgment. Because Jesus expounds the will
of God in definitive fashion and by personal address, God's demand
and the awareness of God's judgment come anew and directly into
the hearers' presence. But above all, God is for Jesus the Father who
will receive his children into his coming kingdom and will forgive
them if they heed the call to conversion. But this Father who will
act in the future is already intervening in the present, in that Jesus
is overcoming the demons and is causing God's forgiveness to become a present reality for despised and sinful men, by accepting
them into the fellowship of his life and promising them God's forgiveness. Thus when Jesus speaks of the presently accomplished
action of the God of the future, still this present-ness of the end-time
is clearly tied to the person of Jesus.

In spite of the difficulty with respect to the sources, it may be
said with great probability that Jesus not only announced the
imminent coming of the "Son of Man" in glory, but also by allusion
gave it to be understood that he himself would appear as the Son
of Man and then would pass judgment upon the present attitude
of men toward himself. Jesus also expected the coming of the Son
of Man, like the coming of the kingdom of God, in the near future,
and the life of men therefore should be determined by the aware-

ness of this imminent coming. That is to say, Jesus answered the question posed to him about the significance of his person in the context of the announced event of the end-time, on the one hand, by referring to the future judging to be done by the Son of Man. On the other hand—once again in total contradiction to all Jewish expectation of the end-time—he spoke of himself as the present Son of Man and regarded the promised end-time as having dawned in his deeds and words.

All this shows that Jesus did not only announce to his contemporaries the imminence of the end of the world and of the time of salvation—apocalyptic groups also did this. Jesus spoke also of the present beginning of the coming kingdom of God and of the presence of the eschatological salvation. Even if in early Judaism some should occasionally have spoken of the final salvation that is already present, still with Jesus the presence of the eschatological salvation is so strictly and exclusively tied to the person of Jesus that thereby something completely new is said: association with Jesus allows man to participate in the final salvation that has begun with Jesus, the consummation of which Jesus promises for the immediate future. Thus it is a quite definite divine eschatological history which Jesus sets before his hearers, and he challenges them to participate in it.

The primitive community and Paul

With the execution of Jesus on the cross, this preaching of Jesus appeared to be proved illusory. But the vision of the resurrected Jesus caused the disciples who had fled in despair to gather themselves together again, and the belief in the resurrection of the crucified Jesus from the dead signified for them that this Jesus had been installed by God as heavenly Lord. At the same time the disciples, gathered together in this belief, had the experience that the Spirit of God promised for the end-time was already at work in their midst, and the *community of the end-time* created thereby prayed to the heavenly Lord that he might soon appear in glory and that therewith God's rule over all the world might dawn. Thus according to the belief of these earliest Christians also, in the community led by the Spirit the end-time had already dawned, although they too still waited for the early coming of the Kingdom.

This experience of salvation in the primitive community is the presupposition for the theology of *Paul*. Paul too lives in the expectation of the early appearing of the resurrected Christ in glory; he even hopes for the dawning of the final salvation in his own lifetime. This expectation is determinative for the insistent urgency of his missionary activity as well as for his reserve with respect to changing existing circumstances and his admonition to constant readiness. But Paul is just as firmly convinced that the time of salvation has become present through the sending of God's Son and that the Christians have already received the Spirit of God as a down-payment toward the future salvation; thus he speaks in paradoxical fashion of the "present evil eon" as well as of the present "day of salvation," but likewise also of the Lord's being "at hand." According to Paul, the coming of the Son of God into this perishing world, his cross and resurrection on the one hand, and the expectation of his imminent appearing from heaven on the other hand, bring it about that the present is the time of salvation before the end, and the existence of the believers is determined by this reality of salvation: even now the believer is taken up out of the present evil eon and "transferred into the kingdom of his dear Son," but he still lives in the flesh, and hence "by faith, not by sight," and awaits "the liberation of our body," when the Lord shall appear from heaven who will "refashion our body, so that it will be made like the body of his glory."

Paul also thus sees the present as the combination of the time of salvation and the hope of the consummation of salvation, both bound to the concrete Christ event and hence provisional and oriented to the consummation. Yet with Paul, in agreement with the primitive community but going beyond Jesus, the presence of salvation has become more clearly discernible by virtue of the fact that the risen Christ is present in his community and through his Spirit and thus rules the life of the Christians. That is to say, Paul interprets the reality of his present time afresh from the perspective of the experienced reality of the divine action at Easter and Pentecost and in keeping with the altered situation in the history of salvation, but in spite of this, still in basic agreement with Jesus' preaching. His thanksgiving to God, "who gives us the victory through our Lord Jesus Christ" (I Cor. 15:57), only leads him all the more to confess that as a Christian he "stretches forward" and "pursues the goal, the prize of victory, [which consists in] the upward calling of God in Christ Jesus" (Phil. 3:14).

The Johannine writings

Central to the Gospel of John is its message of the sending of the Son by the Father into the world and of the Son's belonging eternally with the Father. Nevertheless John does not mean to speak of an eternal, timeless reality. For on the one hand he places great worth on the historical reality of the man Jesus, and on the other hand he emphasizes that this man Jesus has been sent into the world by God at the end of time as fulfillment of Old Testament expectations. This Jesus points to his coming again from the Father, to the coming resurrection and the final judgment and the eschatological revelation of the children of God in glory. John too interpreted Jesus' appearing as an eschatological salvation event and counted on the future consummation of salvation at the appearing of the exalted Christ in glory. But as indisputable as that is, John just as clearly, indeed even more clearly, stressed the present-ness of salvation: the believer has eternal life, and in comparison with this, earthly death is insignificant; the exalted Christ has given to his own the Spirit as Paraclete, who will guide them into all truth. But as clearly and heavily as John emphasizes the present-ness of salvation, he just as clearly also knows that the presence of salvation is tied to faith, which must endure in order actually to free the believer from the world, and that only those branches that abide in the vine bear fruit. Hence John too promises the vision of the glory of the Son as the future consummation of salvation.

Thus John without doubt more heavily emphasized the presence of the time of salvation than did Paul, and only rarely do we find in him any mention of the future eschatological salvation. But for John too the present is the time of salvation only because in the past God sent the man Jesus as "savior of the world" and because through the Spirit the exalted Christ causes those who are his to participate in this salvation. And for John too, salvation in the present is incomplete, for him too therefore the believer awaits the final casting out of the ruler of this world. Because salvation is tied to the man Jesus and thus to the divine action in history, with John too the believer knows himself to be set in the interim between Jesus' resurrection and the eschatological advent of the exalted Lord and in such faith has a share in the final salvation that was begun in Jesus Christ and that awaits the consummation.

Now it is true that the Johannine message of Christ is not, in all its important features, directly influenced by the preaching of Jesus, and just as little does it represent a continuation of the Pauline theology. Nevertheless, in an important respect these three major forms of the New Testament proclamation of Christ stand in sequence in a line of development, namely, in the belief in

God's eschatological saving action in Jesus. Jesus, Paul, and John do not simply proclaim that the present is the time of salvation, but they justify this belief by the fact that the eschatological bearer of salvation has or had already appeared on earth and is achieving or has achieved salvation, and that this bearer of salvation, Jesus, would appear in the future in his full dignity. That is, these three major witnesses know in the same way about the (early) advent of the time of final salvation and about the presence of this eschatological future in the man Jesus or else in the resurrected One. But this belief has shifted when we move from Jesus to Paul: while for Jesus this presence of salvation was a reality only in his person, Paul—following the experience of the primitive community —sees the presence of the final salvation also in the existence of the community as the body of Christ and in the bestowal of the Spirit on the individual Christians; and John gives the present character of eternal life significantly more emphasis than does Paul, and therewith describes primarily the existence of the individual Christian, without forgetting the community. In keeping with this greater prominence of the belief in the presence of salvation, the expectation of the future final salvation recedes: Paul still counts on the coming of the heavenly Lord in his lifetime, but regards a separation from the Lord even by death before the Parousia as not possible, so that in Philippians he can be undecided whether he should wish for death or for witnessing the Parousia in his lifetime. And in the Gospel of John nothing more is clearly said of the *imminence* of the end-time—I John 2:18, "It is the last hour," nevertheless points to this recollection—although the expectation of the coming final salvation is not abandoned.

The fact that in these major witnesses of New Testament theology the emphasis upon salvation as present reality is more and more strengthened, and the expectation of the imminent end recedes, shows that the apostolic witnesses have already sensed the problem of the *imminent* expectation. Nevertheless we cannot overlook that for these witnesses of New Testament theology the combination of the belief in the presence of divine salvation through the sending of Jesus and the expectation of the consummation of salvation through the coming of Jesus Christ in glory is constitutive. For with all these witnesses the experience of the present as the time of salvation is determined by the belief in God's eschatological action in Jesus Christ and therefore is just as much bound to the historical appearing of Jesus as to the hope of the consummation of salvation. And because the awareness that salvation is a present reality is determined by the belief in God's eschatological action in Jesus Christ, this awareness cannot be separated from the hope of the consummation of salvation by the eschatological bearer of salvation.

C. THE DIVINE CONDESCENSION

To be sure this is only half the truth. For the faith that is common to the major witnesses to the New Testament proclamation, that God's time of salvation has dawned in Jesus Christ, and will be brought to consummation by Jesus Christ, would be empty speculation if it were not accompanied by a clear statement about the salvation which occurs in this eschatological divine action. But closer examination easily shows that the belief in the presence of the anticipated future of salvation is the setting for the message of God's condescension in Jesus Christ.

Jesus not only preaches the coming kingdom of God and not only promises sinful men God's forgiveness, but brings God's kingdom to realization by conquering demons and helping sick people, but most of all by accepting despised and sinful people into his fellowship and, through the pronouncing of God's forgiveness, by causing God's eschatological saving intention to become present reality for sinful people. Thus in Jesus the love of God the Father comes to men, though not because a loving man encounters them and awakens their love in response, or their gratitude. Instead, in Jesus, according to his claim expressed in veiled form, the expected "Man" of the end-time comes to his Jewish contemporaries, though not in splendor, but as a man who in spite of the authority given to him submits to God's will and obediently goes to his death, and thereby completes his mission. In Jesus' being delivered into the hands of sinners God's love reaches its consummation; then there becomes finally effective the dawning of the kingdom of the God who as the Father seeks his children, precisely when they appear lost. That is to say, in Jesus the coming kingdom of God becomes present, because in Jesus as the "Man" of the end-time God stoops and himself achieves the deliverance.

On the basis of the belief in the resurrection of the crucified One, and on the basis of the experience of the gift of the Spirit, the primitive community extended this claim of Jesus to say that the promised bearer of salvation of the end-time already now as the heavenly Lord rules his eschatological community; in it are assembled those who, in faith in the Lord who is even now presently at work, are already experiencing together the reality of the final salvation that is promised to them. But now out of the experience of the resurrection of the crucified One and the confession of Jesus as God's Son which arose out of that experience, there also results in the primitive community a new understanding of Jesus' death: Jesus died "for our sins," through Jesus' death God has canceled the sin of mankind. Therewith Jesus' death is understood as the culmination of God's condescension, of the divine offer of the forgiveness of sins, and precisely for this reason as a crucial part of the eschatological salvation event; in this it becomes evident that, in the last analysis, the primitive community's confession of the final salvation that has begun in Jesus Christ is meant to bear witness to God's love which we encounter in Jesus, the love which draws the believer into this divine loving activity.

This understanding in the primitive community of Jesus' death is the presupposition of the theological thinking of *Paul*. When Paul understands the present time as the conjunction of the time of salvation and hope of the consummation of salvation and connects both expressions of faith with God's saving action in the historical person of Jesus Christ, he describes this saving action as liberation of the believers from the powers of this world, but above all as liberation from sin and guilt through God's justifying and reconciling action in Christ. By Christ's "humbling" himself and God's "giving up his Son for us all," the believers have been acquitted of the guilt, God has reconciled himself with us and made us a "new creation," even though all this still awaits its eschatological consummation. Here too it is God's stooping to man who is lost in the world and sinful that produces the present and future salvation, and in this connection Paul lays special emphasis upon Jesus' death as the atoning event wrought by God and as the giving up of God's Son for sin. Yet one must not overemphasize the idea of Jesus' atoning death in Paul, since Paul also can speak in a different way of the fact that in Jesus Christ God has gone to the limit in stooping in order to save us men (see above, pp. 250-51). But it is clear that for Paul too the message of the present and future character of the eschatological salvation is the setting for the glad tidings of God's descending to lost man in Jesus Christ and hence of the divine love addressed to men, which is intended to re-create us into loving men.

While Paul's proclamation of salvation thus presents itself as a direct continuation of the message of Jesus and the primitive community, the case is somewhat different with the *Johannine message of Christ*. John consistently portrays the figure and message of

Jesus from the perspective of the faith of the community of a later time, and his interpretation of Jesus Christ as the eternal Son of God who has become man carries Paul's preaching of Christ further, to the point where the unity of Jesus' person and word with God's saving will is expressed in unsurpassable fashion, but also when the limit is reached beyond which one cannot go without endangering the humanity of Jesus. If then the belief in the realization of God's eschatological saving intention in the person of the man Jesus finds in John its ultimate expression, still in John the significance of Jesus' death for the salvation event recedes, without being abandoned (see above, pp. 297-98). Yet with John also the condescension of God is a central theme. For the liberation of the believers from domination by the world and the promise of being with God and Christ is the consequence of the love of God, who so loved the world that he gave his only Son for it and has given to the believers the power to become his children. Thus while in John the idea of removal of the guilt of sin through Jesus' death does not play so emphatic a role as in Paul, and in this respect John's proclamation of salvation does not present a straight-line continuation of Pauline theology, yet for John also the essential message is that in the eschatological Christ event God comes to men who are lost in the world, in order to free them from the world and to take them into his love and thus to make them into loving men.

d. THE MESSAGE OF THE MAJOR WITNESSES

Thus in spite of the development of thought exhibited in them, the three major witnesses of the theology of the New Testament are in agreement in the twofold message, that God has caused his salvation promised for the end of the world to begin in Jesus Christ, and that in this Christ event God has encountered us and intends to encounter us as the Father who seeks to rescue us from imprisonment in the world and to make us free for active love. That this "heart of the New Testament" is divine truth which is of unconditional concern to us, and not human fantasy which we can even disregard—this, of course, the historian cannot determine. But anyone who believes that in Jesus Christ God comes to us in a saving encounter will learn a twofold lesson from the survey of the major witnesses of the New Testament.

In spite of our inability to cling to the expectation of the imminent consummation of salvation as Jesus and Paul shared it, our faith certainly can actually grasp the New Testament's message of salvation only when we take seriously the coming of Jesus as God's eschatological action, so that our present is just as much determined by the unique past of this saving action of God as by the hopeful look toward the future consummation of this action.

Even though the major witnesses of the New Testament do not entirely agree in their interpretation of the person and the death of Jesus, still there sounds forth from them the one message in common, that in Jesus God, the Lord of the world, has come to us. But this coming of God can become a personal reality for us only if we so allow ourselves to be grasped by God's love that has come to us in Jesus Christ that we become new persons, who let our "light so shine before men that they may see your good works and glorify your Father who is in heaven" (Matt. 5:16). Thus the "Epistle to the Hebrews" (13:8) has classically summed up the basic outlook that is common to the major witnesses of the theology of the New Testament: "Jesus Christ [is] the same yesterday, today, and forever."

INDEX

INDEX OF NEW TESTAMENT PASSAGES

Index of Topics